Communist China, 1949–1969
A Twenty-Year Appraisal

COMMUNIST CHINA, 1949-1969
A TWENTY-YEAR APPRAISAL

EDITED BY

Frank N. Trager and William Henderson

1970

PUBLISHED FOR THE AMERICAN-ASIAN EDUCATIONAL
EXCHANGE BY THE NEW YORK UNIVERSITY PRESS

The American-Asian Educational Exchange was founded in October 1957, having as its major purpose ". . . the exchange of information, literature and personnel for the purpose of creating a broader understanding between the peoples of the United States and the independent nations of Asia."

Since that time, the Exchange has maintained an effective international educational program with two basic categories: publication, circulation and translation of printed material on the subject of concern in the United States and Asia; the maintenance of liaison and cooperation between the Exchange and similar organizations and academic groups in Asia and the United States.

The analyses and interpretations presented in this volume are those of the several authors, and do not necessarily reflect the views of the American-Asian Educational Exchange. As a matter of policy, the Exchange does not express opinions on political and economic questions.

SECOND PRINTING, 1972
COPYRIGHT © 1970 BY NEW YORK UNIVERSITY
LIBRARY OF CONGRESS CATALOG CARD NUMBER 78-114765
ISBN: 0-8147-0485-9
PRINTED IN THE UNITED STATES OF AMERICA

To B.T. and C.F.H.
With Great Respect

Preface

The Chinese Communist Party, organized in 1921, won control over the mainland after almost three decades of unremitting struggle. Its triumph was formally marked by proclamation of the People's Republic of China on October 1, 1949. Certainly this event must be regarded as one of the most significant in the long history of that extraordinary country. To unify China and govern it effectively, to provide the material resources necessary to sustain its hard-working, hard-pressed, and enormous population, to vindicate its millenial claim as the center of world civilization—these have been the major aspirations of the many regimes that have come and gone on the mainland. Now it was the opportunity of the Communists to achieve them if they could.

It is said by some that the Communist regime should properly be interpreted as the continuation of the Chinese revolution begun with the overthrow of the Manchus in 1911, and that the main thrust of its policy has been to repair the debility brought on by the decay of the Ch'ing dynasty and by the inroads of Western imperialism during the nineteenth and twentieth centuries. In this context, the Maoist regime is seen—despite its excesses, its monumental errors of political and economic policy, and its Communist ideological baggage—as preeminently inward-looking, preoccupied with the immensity of China's problems, instinctively cautious in its external relations: in brief, as essentially "Chinese," whatever that word means.

Others hold that the People's Republic represents a fundamental break with the earlier republican revolution; that, however much it undoubtedly strives to repair the ravages of the past, it is even more concerned to establish the primacy of its variant of Communist theory and practice, not only at home but throughout the world at large. In this perspective, the Maoist regime suffers—in both senses of the word—domestic hardship and privation so as to achieve for itself, in its own Communist image and at whatever cost, a dominant and controlling place in Asia and the world.

Any analysis of any period in Chinese history is peculiarly difficult precisely because China is so huge, the fabric of its civilization so complex, its memories so long. Interpretation of the Communist regime, now in power for two decades, is perhaps more than usually difficult because the free inspection of its institutions and policies has been denied to foreign scholars. The contributors to this book, like all others who study the multiple phenomena of the People's Republic, do have access, however, to a veritable mountain of materials put out by the regime and its external supporters, as well as to a comparable avalanche of data monitored and translated by the various institutions, government agencies, and individuals who are collectively the professional "China-watchers." From these rich and varied sources, it is possible to form valid judgements on the trend of events.

The several contributors include:

Theodore Hsi-en Chen — Director, East Asian Studies Center, and Professor of Education and Asian Studies, University of Southern California.

Jürgen Domes — Director, Research Unit on Chinese and East Asian Politics, and Senior Associate Professor, Free University of Berlin.

William Henderson — President, William Henderson Consultants, Inc., and Research Professor of Asian Studies, Seton Hall University.

C. T. Hsia — Professor of Chinese, Columbia University.

Frank A. Kierman, Jr. — Director of Research, Chinese Linguistics Project, Princeton University.

E. Stuart Kirby — Professor of Economics, University of Aston in Birmingham.

Father L. LaDany — Publisher and Editor, *China News Analysis*.

Franz Michael — Director, Institute for Sino-Soviet Studies, and Professor of International Affairs, George Washington University.

Robert A. Rupen — Professor of Political Science, University of North Carolina.

Vincent Y. C. Shih — Professor of Chinese Philosophy and Literature, University of Washington.

Richard C. Thornton — Member, Institute for Sino-Soviet Studies, and Assistant Professor of History, George Washington University.

Frank N. Trager — Director of Studies, National Strategy Information Center, and Professor of International Affairs, New York University.

Richard L. Walker — Director, Institute of International Studies, and James F. Byrnes Professor of International Relations, University of South Carolina.

Colonel William W. Whitson — Member, Policy Planning Staff, Office of Assistant Secretary of Defense for International Security Affairs.

Yuan-li Wu — Professor of Economics, University of San Francisco, at present on leave for service with the United States government.

These contributors are independent scholars, and they offer their own distinctive analyses and interpretations of the Chinese Communist scene over the past twenty years. While the editors gladly take responsibility for inviting them to participate in this cooperative volume, they alone are responsible for their chapters; and the editors have made no effort to impose an artificial consistency of interpretation.

Twenty years is a brief moment of time in the vast panorama of Chinese history. Some will say that the time span is too short to permit worthwhile interpretation. But if we are ever to see peace in Asia, or at least the peaceful co-existence of competitive political systems, then it is necessary that we have some understanding of the Maoist period in China. The editors undertook this volume for the American-Asian Educational Exchange in order to promote such understanding. The authors speak for themselves. If the future is not doomed to repeat all the errors of the past, perhaps their labors will have made a contribution.

Frank N. Trager
William Henderson

Contents

		Page
Preface		vii
Chapter 1.	Communist China in the Light of Chinese History *Frank A. Kierman, Jr.*	1
Chapter 2.	Ideology and the Cult of Mao *Franz Michael*	27
Chapter 3.	Problems of Administration and Control *L. LaDany*	45
Chapter 4.	Party Politics and the Cultural Revolution *Jürgen Domes*	63
Chapter 5.	The Military: Their Role in the Policy Process *William W. Whitson*	95
Chapter 6.	The Economy After Twenty Years *Yuan-li Wu*	123
Chapter 7.	Agrarian Problems and the Peasantry *E. Stuart Kirby*	153
Chapter 8.	Education in Communist China *Theodore Hsi-en Chen*	175
Chapter 9.	Literature and Art Under Mao Tse-tung *C. T. Hsia*	199
Chapter 10.	The State of the Intellectuals *Vincent Y. C. Shih*	221
Chapter 11.	Peking and the National Minorities *Robert A. Rupen*	243
Chapter 12.	China and the Communist World *Richard C. Thornton*	259

Chapter 13.   Peking's Approach to the Outside World
                Richard L. Walker   281

Chapter 14.   The United States and Communist China
                Frank N. Trager and William Henderson   301

Brief Chronology: 1949-1969   321

Selected Bibliography   329

Index   341

Chapter One

Communist China in the Light of Chinese History

Frank A. Kierman, Jr.

A people conditions its government as rigorously as soil and climate condition crops. To the Chinese people, their millennia of history and pre-history are always vividly present, and felt as valid—indeed, inescapable—models for daily action. It is perhaps a main characteristic of any viable civilization to have an awareness of its roots. Yet China's people, including the humble, illiterate masses, know their heritage with a breadth, intensity, and detail that is unique.

Their lively awareness of history has inculcated in all Chinese a deep and wary understanding of government and has trained them in sophisticated techniques for enduring life under any government. For generations, they have been giving the prevailing regime a well-judged necessary minimum of compliance, while preserving intact the individual and social values they perceive as essential to personal and group survival. For the common man, the notion that government might be something with which he might ac-tively identify himself simply did not arise, though emotional attachments to individual rulers of course existed from time to time.

For the Chinese Communists, the decisive question is whether or not they have succeeded, during their tumultuous first twenty years of rule, in radically altering such fundamental psychological sets and social patterns, which enabled Chinese to live essentially unaffected by the exactions of former regimes. The time calculus raises doubts: a mere twenty years of conditioning against something like two hundred times that much habitua-tion through history. These odds would not be good in most contests.

Societies can surely change, but they cannot be totally transformed. There is an inertia, whether of stasis or of development, which sets limits upon both the degree and the pace of national evolution, regardless of how much it may be forced. Drastic change, especially when combined with overcrowding, may indeed produce a dynamic neuroticism that leads on more or less necessarily to further change; yet nations have endured ex-treme trauma, profound revolution, deeply dislocating and rapid develop-ment, and they have yet remained essentially, recognizably the same.

1

Consider Japan, Turkey, Russia, Great Britain. Is China alone exempt from this law?

There is a deeper question still. Can China "make it?" Here it is vital that China aspires to succeed in two important but probably incompatible ways: she wishes to remain China, "all below Heaven," "all within the four seas," the sole sovereignty of the world, dispensing her beneficences over the barbarian minorities of her empire and shedding the radiance of her example upon the outer barbarians; and she must also somehow come to terms with the necessity of living within the modern world of nation states, with modern technology and up-to-date scientific and social achievement. This second area of striving is as demanding and as alien for China as it is for any other of the "less developed" nations of the world, since it is an area created and defined by European ideals of social progress and international intercourse. China, like many much newer nations, finds these ideas and demands ill-fitting and costly in many ways, indeed perhaps beyond her economic and psychological means.

In purely socio-economic terms, China is a unique and unprecedented construct, the largest human organism of all time. The approaches and habits of mind that are appropriate to other polities, including those that have worked in earlier phases of Chinese development, or that have shown results in other settings, may not work for China today and tomorrow. Social initiatives taken millennia ago still condition her deeply, most vitally in the areas of her large population and intensive agriculture. Many of her essential enterprises run on the same lines as they have for centuries past. China is confronted with a task she has never liked and has never tackled wholeheartedly: to make the shift from a culturally defined entity to a modern nation state among nation states. It would not be an easy task even if China approached it with the ruthless energy which the Meiji revolutionaries manifested in nineteenth-century Japan.

The Pattern of Chinese Society

In one respect, at least, China has agreed with the West completely. Western observers have uniformly viewed her as something special, a different type of society from those known in the West. Marco Polo, Matteo Ricci, Karl Marx (and other classical economists), most modern Sinologists, all would agree that China is a distinct and separate kind of social entity, in both structure and development. And the Chinese concur in their own simple, direct, and sweeping assertion that China is indeed unique, the Central Kingdom, the sole sovereignty on earth. The Chinese even refused to take part in the 1961 Moscow International Congress of Orientalists on the ground that China was not an appropriate subject for study by foreigners.

The most symmetrical, stimulating, and satisfactory single theoretical model of Oriental society yet produced by modern social science is the one described most succinctly in the early writings of Karl August Wittfogel.[1] The following description is largely based upon his work.

Chinese society is deeply conditioned by the requirement that water be controlled, both for irrigation and for flood control. Wittfogel has suggested the term "hydraulic society" for societies in which this is true (Egypt, Mesopotamia, and the Pueblo Indians, for example) and also for "marginal hydraulic societies," which display most of the authoritarian traits of true hydraulic society but which lack the direct connection with massive flood control and irrigation problems (here, post–Mongol Russia is his favorite example). The agricultural practices that undergird Chinese society developed in the tributary valleys feeding the middle reaches of the Yellow River, in what is now Shensi and Shansi provinces. In those narrow valleys, the flood-defensive aspect of water control was relatively minimal, and the light soils of the region made cultivation easy, even with the most primitive tools. The region is semi-arid, with undependable and usually inadequate rainfall, which meant that intensive agriculture was possible only through irrigation. But intensive agriculture is people-intensive, and thus large populations based upon good-sized families soon occupied all that was easily arable of those valleys. The early Chinese were thus able to support considerable manpower and to derive the grain resources and wealth to employ that manpower in subduing and Sinicizing nearby tribes. In consequence, expanding Chinese pushed out to the valley of the Yellow River itself and to the great plain of North China, with its vast expanse of arable land and its tremendous problem of flood control, necessary to protect the fructifying peasantry against the consequences of natural disasters and human shortsightedness.

Individual Chinese, however, are no more highminded or magnanimous than other peasants the world over, and they could not be depended upon to drop their own pressing concerns and engage voluntarily in great water control projects. Even if public spirit did somehow actuate them, small farmers, with their intensely restricted view of things, could hardly have the objectivity or broad perspective needed to perceive larger tribal needs, and could not be relied upon to turn up at the right place and in appropriate numbers to perform the arduous and sometimes desperate labors necessary to yoke great rivers. They had to work on order. As a logical development of such imperatives, Chinese society acquired an implacable control mechanism, a theoretically absolute authoritarianism founded upon the proposition that the individual could not be expected to do what was essential for society and thus for himself, but must be coerced, or at least induced, to do so.

[1]See especially "Die Theorie der orientalischen Gesellschaft," *Zeitschrift für Sozialforschung*, Vol. 7 (1938), pp. 90–122.

Once the administrative machinery for accomplishing such mobilization of the society's energies was created, it could be used to accomplish tasks far removed from those that called it forth, such as military defense or adventure, great public works (grand canals to insure expeditious arrival of grain, great walls to deter barbarians or other opponents), or other enterprises designed to reinforce the central power, to sanction or symbolize it, or to gratify its whims. Some quantitative idea of how these burdens weighed upon the people may be derived from one scholar's estimate of a peasant's service obligations under the Han dynasty (roughly 200 B.C. to A.D. 200). The citizen had to provide one month per year of labor on government tasks from ages twenty to fifty, and he also had to serve two years of army duty, possibly with occasional garrison service in addition.[2]

Chinese society fell quite simply into two classes, the few rulers and the mass of the ruled. The former comprised the royal house plus its administrative extension, which Wittfogel calls "the monopoly bureaucracy;" the latter, in the simplified agricultural model, was the peasantry. The ruling class can be viewed in more detail as divided into the royal family and its immediate favorites (retainers, bodyguards, eunuchs, and so on), plus the gentry class, from which the government bureaucracy came and which worked locally with the mandarins as the necessary muting and negotiating medium between the demands of officialdom and the raw needs of the people.

Another element existed early and continued throughout Chinese history: the commercial class. But this class was denigrated and victimized, and otherwise largely ignored in traditional China; and even though (from the early nineteenth century on) the atmosphere and the safe haven of the treaty ports offered commerce unusual opportunities, merchants remained throughout Chinese history practically an eccentric entity with no real power position and no lasting distinctness.[3] For the aspiration of those who became wealthy was to enter the gentry class, and commercial enterprise often gave energetic peasants a roundabout road to the official status that Chinese sought almost instinctively. Numerically, of course, the fortunate few who found the commercial or other paths upward made no impact upon the statistical fact that the peasantry constituted the overwhelming

---

[2]See Michael Loewe, *Everyday Life in Early Imperial China* (London: Batsford, 1968), p. 75.

[3]Although this is a fair generalization, it is worth noting that (a) two of the most prominent ministers of third-century B.C. China were wealthy merchants; and (b) from Sung times onward, and especially in the last few centuries of the imperial era, growing links between gentry and merchants in the burgeoning urban centers, what one might style "a diversification of interests" for both groups, considerably blurred the distinctions between them and require modification of the simplistic view that the merchant class was always despised and victimized. The merchant impulse to seek gentry status was also realistically motivated, in that there existed no security for wealth in imperial China except through owning land and having official connections.

mass of the population. Even today, few scholars estimate China's peasantry as less than eighty percent of the population.

This vision of Chinese government as an engine of dour and unrelenting oppression is the "oriental despotism" of Wittfogel's later works.[4] His view undoubtedly has some validity; but in fact, the system did not usually operate in quite so impersonally terrifying a fashion. Mention has already been made of the gentry's Janus-like role as negotiators, middlemen, and shock absorbers in the rural areas of China. It was part of the genius of the Chinese, developed no doubt through the hard experience of living within this system, that they always sought to avoid naked and direct confrontation on tough or potentially embarrassing issues. This is why the go-between is such an essential element in Chinese society. He is the person who canvasses any general situation to see whether the principals involved can confront one another without fear of disastrous unpleasantness.

Inevitably, in a polity so potentially appalling, there were many other factors which tended to divert or soften its impact. Perhaps the most important was that the central government's direct control did not go very far down into traditional society. In a *hsien* (generally translated as "county," "prefecture," or "district"), which in the later imperial millennia usually contained a population of some hundreds of thousands and might exceed a million, the nerve end of central authority was the *hsien* or district magistrate. The government was, to be sure, not devoid of influence or control below that level. From quite early times, family and group responsibility had been sanctioned by philosophers and widely employed by rulers, and this developed in various ways, such as the *pao-chia* system of imperial and Kuomintang China,[5] or the practice of guild responsibility and the institution of sponsorship within the bureaucracy. This *pao-chia* sort of organization operated in a considerable variety of spheres: tax collection, census, population control, police, and even indoctrination. But it was essentially in the hands of local people, led by the local gentry.

Yet there was a clear discontinuity at this precise level. The local gentry

---

[4]The classic statement of Wittfogel's theoretical and polemical position is *Oriental Despotism* (New Haven: Yale University Press, 1957).

[5]The *pao-chia* system was a system of mutual responsibility, which implied surveillance and sometimes the provision of military manpower, and under which an entire family or group of families was punishable for the offense of any member. The concept may have originated in military practice under which, as early as the sixth century B.C., members of small units were not supposed to survive one another. As an arrangement applied to the control of civilian populations, it is ascribed to the Ch'in dynasty, which ruled ever broader areas of China from 230 to 207 B.C., establishing the first empire in 221 B.C. The *pao-chia* system was revived and adapted repeatedly in later ages, into republican times; and it operates effectively—though, of course, not under the same name—in Communist China today. For its working during the nineteenth century, see Hsiao Kung-ch'uan, *Rural China* (Seattle: University of Washington Press, 1960), Ch. 3.

might be indistinguishable from the magistrate in speech, education, class interest, and habit of mind, but they were from that area and he was not. He was a transient in the community; they and their kin had to live there long after he had departed. If the government gave orders that were unrealistic or unduly harsh in view of the situation in that place, the magistrate might well accept and try to enforce them; the gentry in such a case could only refuse to assist him, seek to dissuade him, or resist. And since the local gentry usually had connections in the government hierarchy separate from the *hsien* magistrate and often above him, they could act as a real check upon his power and conduct.

The function of the gentry in cushioning and diffusing the stresses of society was not only crucial but very delicate, offering the fullest scope for display of the Confucian virtues and for all the resourcefulness and sincerity a man could bring to bear. Both formally and informally, the scholar-gentry class, which was the main vehicle of Chinese culture, constituted also a check upon it, through remonstrance, both individual and group, both private and official; through noncompliance, refusal to participate, or retirement; even through leadership in dissident movements. As one great Chinese political scientist says: "Autocracies such as imperial China presuppose a sharp distinction between rulers and subjects and a consequent divergence of interests between them."[6] The gentry, living between these opposed elements, were at once the ultimate instruments of central authority and the leading elements in another great level of society, to which the great bulk of people belonged and which was organized on a quite different principle.

Within this great lower stratum, Chinese society is cellular. The family is the agricultural work and ownership unit; and in prosperous times, this becomes the large, extended family all living under one roof. Villages are sometimes composed of a single clan or a few clans linked by marriage, but in any case, government within such an entity is logically an extension of the family, having paternal authority as its basis but with paternal kindness and responsibility mitigating that dominance. Life within such a social unit requires of all the members much the same constant cooperation, mutual assistance, and forebearance as are demanded in the extended family. Villages are in considerable measure self-sufficient, capable of withdrawing upon themselves and surviving in harsh or turbulent times.

Although the scholar-gentry is conventionally regarded as the major vehicle of Chinese culture, the other main element in the population, the peasantry, is also a powerful conservative force. The peasant's life is full and highly ordered by folkways, habits, beliefs, and techniques as subtle and satisfactory in their way as the elaborate literary, administrative, and personal structures within which the *literati* live. The directness and inten-

[6]*Ibid,* p. 3.

sity with which the peasant must face the brute forces of his small sphere (the inexorable cycle of the agricultural year, often complicated by flood, drought, or pests; official demands for taxes, labor, or military service; expensive periodic climacterics such as weddings and funerals) breed in him a canny and realistic flexibility in the face of such problems. Ignorance, habit, and the fact that radical change is beyond his conception reconcile him to his environment, except when it is simply unbearable. He may not seem the beneficiary of his society, but he is not constantly alienated from it. His psychological autonomy within the system is an important factor in mitigating the impact of that system upon him. In his humble way, he is the most essential element of his society; and he is, therefore, indestructible.

The state's intolerance of overt organizations to perform various intermediate functions led naturally and perhaps inevitably to the emergence of secret societies, usually with a strong philanthropic, ethical, and localistic bias. Significant extralegal bodies, often with an ideology rooted in Taoism or Buddhism, have existed for at least two thousand years; and these are doubly important in that they can accomplish socially vital tasks (such as group selection and management for conscription or forced labor, mutual self-help or insurance in disaster), and also furnish alternative foci of power within the state, much interwoven with its normal functioning, but also potentially and often actually inimical to it—which is, of course, the reason for the regime's hostility to them. In times of trouble, they are an inevitable matrix of dissidence and outright armed revolt. The dedication and tenacity of their members also furnish standing proof that, when real grievances and ideology combine, the Chinese are capable of an extreme fanaticism quite different from at least one Western stereotype of them: the "quiet positivist" that one scholar has described.[7]

One final mitigating factor is the notion of cyclical change, perhaps the most basic and ancient element of Chinese ideology, being derived from the seasons and the heavens. Dynasties are founded, flourish, age, weaken, and die, as humans pass and families prosper and wither. The Chinese have a profound consciousness of how conditional and temporary most situations are; in consequence, they hesitate to push their good luck very far, and they are fatalistic under ill fortune. Perhaps in part precisely because of this basic view that change is circular, returning upon itself, society in China has in fact seemed to change less rapidly and less radically than societies have in the West, especially since the Industrial Revolution. If one expects life to be as faithfully repetitious as the phases of the moon, it is easy to discourage, or overlook, or reinterpret out of existence whatever changes do actually occur.

[7]Peter Boodberg, *The Art of War in Ancient China* (doctoral dissertation) (Berkeley: University of California, 1930), p. xiii.

Chinese Ideology

The nostalgia for an idealized past, which is a highly romantic sentiment, is deeply ingrained in Chinese thought and in the Chinese treatment of their history. Confucius (sixth century B.C.) criticized the undoubtedly violent world of his day by setting against it a vision of an earlier golden age characterized by virtuous kings, instinctively compliant subjects, and universal harmony.

Long before Confucius' day, indeed, by the time we first find connected written history, China seems to have had a religion. This may well have been closer to a primitive Taoism than to anything Confucius or his later adapters taught. The great historian Ssu-ma T'an (second century B.C.) seems to imply that such a Taoism was antecedent to all the other schools of Chinese thought, and that it was the common fund of belief from which they variously drew fragmentary and partial insights.

We can descry only generally what the characteristics of this ancient Chinese religious philosophy may have been, yet certain reasonable inferences are possible. It was dualistic and cyclical, enlarging on the analogy of summer and winter, male and female, day and night, sowing and harvest—the elemental verities of the agricultural milieu. It was firmly based upon personal relationships, including those obtaining within the family and others derived by extension from the familial connection. These were later codified into the "five relationships": lord and subject, father and son, husband and wife, elder and younger brother, friend and friend. A deep congruence was felt between society and family, so that improper action, even at the personal level, struck at the entire order of the universe. This was especially so if the action were that of a ruler, while proper action by the ruler brought proper action throughout the realm as surely and as rightly as night follows day. If night failed to follow day in normal fashion (because of an eclipse, for example), this was immediate evidence of obliquity in the human sphere. Ancestors were regarded as intermediaries with the ruling forces of the cosmos, and they were reverenced accordingly. Mourning for parents was thus a crucially important rite, which even in later and less religious ages required absolute retirement from the world for extended periods. Paternalism was built into the system.

These elements interacted in a highly sophisticated and flexible fashion. While a son owed his father absolute filial piety, it was the father's obligation not only to nurture the boy in filial thinking, but also to offer in his own daily conduct an example which would naturally inspire reverence. The son was duty-bound to remonstrate with the father if he detected any laxity; but he was also obliged to conceal parental defects from all others. Thus, too, the subject owed loyalty (and remonstrance) to his lord, and the lord appreciation and nourishment (and rectification) to the subject.

Although what information we have of him is frustratingly fragmentary and at least as indirect as what we know of Jesus Christ, Confucius seems to have codified and idealized this generalized set of beliefs and pragmatically applied it to the circumstances of his own age, which was certainly an era in need of correction. He was so meticulous in his concern for proper conduct that a nineteenth-century Protestant missionary found him rather stuffy. Hardly more successful in his life than Jesus, Confucius nevertheless set a compelling example for later generations of Chinese by convincing them that the key to right action was in knowing the models of the past. Only thus could one avoid putting a foot wrong; only thus could one avoid shame; only thus could man be at ease in society, and society secure about man. Confucianism can be described as a system of humane and willing mutual obligation.

It is basically to his disciples that Confucius owes his survival; and like disciples everywhere, they undoubtedly bowdlerized the master's teaching. Certainly the two most eminent early interpreters of Confucian thought diverge markedly enough to make us wonder whether they are talking about the same man. Mencius (c. 372 to 289 B.C.) asserted that men are by nature good, basing this inference upon observed generous impulses, such as the normal tendency to help a child in danger. Hsun Tzu (c. 300 to 237 B.C.) plucked another strand out of Confucius, considering men basically evil but capable of correction by intensive education and training. The crucial event in the survival of Confucianism, however, was its institutionalization as a state religion under the Han dynasty, and this exacted a greater tax of distortion than Mencius or Hsun Tzu could have dreamed of. Confucianism became a false face for the structurally appalling social engine of despotism.

The doctrines appropriate to that engine were those of Legalism, a body of thought which starts from the concept that man is "fond of gain and of sensual gratification," and that society's task is simply to contain him for its welfare and his own. This required a polity of clear laws and harsh punishments; and since officials are also human and not exempt from the general obliquity of their fellow subjects, it also required strict and effective techniques of administrative control to see that officers performed efficaciously and without potentially dangerous self-aggrandizement. The two aspects of this philosophy have been associated with different schools of thought within Legalism. Confucians in later ages have almost unanimously execrated the harshness of the Legalists; but they have generally accepted and used the technical methods of government and made them their own.

Within the capacious philosophical tradition of China—the epithet of the "Hundred Schools" may divide the spectrum too daintily, but it is justifiable even today, despite our only partial knowledge of early China—there are many approaches to governmental problems. One early Han dynasty premier, a practicing Taoist, stayed drunk as a matter of policy while in office; and he also required that his advisers marinate their enthusiasms in wine. Buddhism, too, had profound influence upon government for longer or shorter periods, although it is an individualistic and socially centrifugal faith, an odd ideology for a centralized despotism. In the long run, however, the dominant approach of Chinese government was a marriage of convenience between Legalism, its structural principle, and Confucianism, the model of its outward form.

Other influences had significant impact upon the shape and the phasing of China's development. Perhaps the most pervasive were the omnipresent barbarians. In the first formative years of the North China *chung-kuo* or "central states" (the name by which Chinese still designate China), this heartland was surrounded by barbarians on all sides. Scholars debate about such questions as whether or not the early Chinese had a generalized concept of the barbarians, even a general word to categorize them as being definitively different from the sons of Han, and—perhaps most important —whether barbarians were regarded with fear, scorn, or loathing. At any rate, the various kinds of barbarians were a constant challenge to the close-packed and relatively sedentary populations of the *chung-kuo;* and although as a problem they soon became localized in the north and north-western border regions, the barbarians remained a constant preoccupation of Chinese security forces. For centuries, non-Han regimes held sway in large areas of China, two of them (the Mongol Yuan dynasty and the Manchu Ch'ing dynasty) conquering the entire nation. If one adds the piquant and widely held view that at least two of the earliest and most revered dynasties of China's prehistory (Shang and Chou) may have seized the throne as barbarians, it is clear that the barbarian impact on Chinese history (not to mention trade, technology, art, and even dress) has been tremendous. Certainly the presence of these tough horsemen demanded authoritarian measures to keep them beyond the Great Wall; and just as clearly their contribution when they could not be fended off and seized power over "all below Heaven" was hardly a softening one.

With all its potential for structural brutality, the Chinese polity was still a rather roomy edifice. Its ideology sanctioned a wide variety of conduct. Some modern Chinese, forced to explain themselves to foreigners, have said that a Chinese "is a Confucian in office and a Taoist out of office." A peasant might increase his holdings through a combination of luck and hard work, become well off, gather his family about him in the country seat, increase his wealth by commercial enterprise and well-judged bribery, and even aspire to having his son become a scholar-official; or he might lose his land, become a hired laborer, sell or abandon his wife and children, and become a beggar or a mendicant monk or a brigand. Unquestionably the upward curve was preferred, but the downward one was accorded a place, and the two seemed to fit together as a whole. In fact, on the old analogy of the sun and the moon, the downward, passive, recuperative, fallow phase was felt to be necessary in generating the irresistible upward drive by which founders of dynasties arose from among mendicant monks or humble officers, or great advisers of emperors were lured from the enticements of the wine cup and bamboo grove. The range of permissive behavior often varied from place to place and from time to time; but in general, traditional Chinese society was so all-encompassing that a prospective deviant was unlikely to find any retreat that was actually outside the shell of the old mansion.

The Phases of Chinese History

Karl Marx readily agreed that Oriental societies seemed to develop along different lines from his tribal-slave-feudal-bourgeois-Socialist ladder. Only later Communist theoreticians, authoritarian in all things, require that the development of China be somehow squared with the Marxian phasing, at whatever cost in wrenching, cropping, or fictionalizing the data. The inherent difficulty is that China passed beyond tribalism probably before the dawn of connected history, manifested only a brief and rather marginal slave period, and never developed anything like self-conscious, urban middle class society until modern times. This means an embarrassingly lengthy period of "feudalism;" and—the simple fact is—that much-abraded term simply has to mean something quite different in China from what it signified in medieval Europe. Thus Communist theologians such as Kuo Mo-jo (who wrote the first Marxist history of Chinese antiquity in the 1920s and who also served as President of the Chinese Communist Academy of Sciences in the 1950s and 1960s) have been engaged in a laborious but essentially sterile endeavor.

On the other hand, nobody else has come up with any widely satisfactory analysis of the stages of Chinese history. The traditional Chinese method of counting by dynasties obscures rather than illuminates developments; and it is cumbersome in the extreme, especially in several long periods of division or uncertain sovereignty. Rather than attempting to devise any general schema, it seems best to note certain points in Chinese history that seem to have been watershed moments.

The earliest such moment after connected history began seems to have been the period 685 to 642 B.C. in the state of Ch'i (modern Shantung Province, roughly), the era of Duke Huan and his advisor, Kuan Chung. Before this, Chinese society had evolved from tribal to "feudal" form; but during this period of Ch'i hegemony, there emerged the outline of an administrative pattern which would develop over subsequent centuries and become the framework of China's imperial unification. Systematic codes of law were drawn up, so that society no longer relied entirely upon the old proprieties of conduct. Patriotism was promoted and focused upon the person of the ruler. A new type of functionary arose, relying upon his own skill and personal merit and owing his place to the sovereign's recognition of those qualities, rather than to noble familial connections. The territory of the state was divided into local areas called *hsiang,* allowing the central power to assign clear responsibility for local government and to supervise how it was carried out. An inspectorate was instituted outside the normal chain of command. A militia system based upon the *hsiang* became the foundation of the Ch'i army. Commerce was encouraged but taxed; and government monopolies of salt and iron strengthened the state's economic and military grip. Control was less effective than it later became, due mainly to poor communications; and the power of Ch'i waned after the passing of Duke Huan and Kuan Chung. But other sovereigns and chief ministers followed and developed their model until, four centuries later, the first emperor of the Ch'in dynasty and his minister Li Ssu used clearly related techniques on a national scale.

Although the Ch'in dynasty (230 to 206 B.C.) is generally execrated by Chinese scholars for its harshness, its efforts to destroy the ancient Chinese culture, and its persecution of the *literati,* the dynasty's accomplishments and contributions to Chinese culture were tremendous. The Ch'in united China by conquest, and administratively reorganized the country on a single plan; cemented that unification by a network of post roads; broke up the remnants of the feudal order and, by destroying arms and transporting noble families, made a reversion to feudalism or to any lasting regionalism much more difficult; standardized the form of the written language; systematized the currency, the laws, weights and measures; and—precisely by having a hand in the destruction of many ancient books—gave future employment to generations of Chinese scholars seeking to reconstitute the lost past. All of these were probably crucial to the preservation of Chinese culture. The remarkable thing is that they were performed so rapidly. The Ch'in made their first conquest of an entire state in 230; the conventional date for the unification of the whole of China is 221; and after the first emperor died in 210, the dynasty fell into an abrupt decline that permitted little positive work during its last three years of nominal existence. Thus the work of the dynasty was performed within the space of two decades, almost half of which was also devoted to major military campaigns. Such purposeful and rapid progress would have been unimaginable under the aegis of the humane and permissive Mencian tradition; it was made by a state which was semibarbarian, regarded as beyond the pale, and which functioned within a Legalist doctrine devoted to rooting out Confucianism and completely changing the old ways. It was not to be the last time that happened in China.

The fact that China was thus unified and established under this peculiar and partial system of thought is especially significant if we remind ourselves of the main outline of Chinese society as Wittfogel portrays it: a merciless despotism designed to coerce its people beyond any possibility of resistance. It is ironic that Karl Marx considered Oriental despotism a system of the most inhuman and ruthless oppression; and that Lenin, the arch-engineer of coercion, was lamely defensive against Plekhanov's charge that the Bolshevik program would "Asiaticize" Russia.

It has been argued that Legalism is merely Confucianism naked, that even Mencian Confucianism contains in its suppressed premises the justification for Oriental despotism. Others have pointed out that Li Ssu was a student of Hsun Tzu and went straight from that master into the employ of Ch'in. They do not generally add that Li Ssu's action so distressed Hsun Tzu that the latter abruptly retired from teaching. Confucianism was not cynical, however far modern dialecticians may push its premises in making it seem so.[8] A Confucian ruler was in a real sense the servant of the people, and he held office only conditionally and as long as he did in fact serve the people. Under the Legalists, to stress the essential contrast, the state became a self-perpetuating end in itself, with no check upon its power.

After unification, one important step remained before the structure of Chinese empire was complete. It had to have an ideology less harsh than Legalism in order to blur the stark outline, to soften the impact of the brutal machinery and make it respectable. This took place under the Han dynasty (roughly 200 B.C. to A.D. 200), and specifically during the reign of the Emperor Wu (140 to 86 B.C.). The Han took over essentially intact the centralization of political, economic, military, and administrative power which the Ch'in had created; but they eventually established state Confucianism—an amalgam of optimistic Mencian humanism, Hsun Tzu's greater administrative realism, and some non-Confucian elements such as soothsayers' superstitions and naive pseudo-historical sanctions—as the official ideology. Sacrifices designed to stress the emperor's status as Son of Heaven were instituted. Of the old "five relationships," the obligation of a subject to his sovereign came to be most important by far, at least for the state ideology. The intrafamilial relationships were still vital as a way of ordering the sphere that lay beyond the regime's direct control; but except for this administrative convenience, they were a quasi-religious "opium of the people."

After this development, the basic power arrangements of Chinese society changed slowly, inconspicuously, and not very much. The bureaucratic *literati* acquired a vested interest in maintaining both the essentially Legalist techniques by which they ran the government and the Confucian ethical values by which they ordered their personal lives and gave sanction to the

---

[8]For a discussion of this, see Hellmut Wilhelm, "The Reappraisal of New Confucianism," in Albert Feuerwerker (ed.), *History in Communist China* (Cambridge: M.I.T. Press, 1968).

system. The mass of peasants were far below and quite uncomprehending of the implacable machine which pressed down upon them, and which they supported by the sweat of their labor. Between the conservatism of the scholar-gentry and that of the peasants, Chinese society maintained its unique stability for nearly two millennia.

The crucial factors in the freezing of Chinese society were probably two: first, the steady production, throughout the Warring States period, of a class of dispossessed nobles who tended to group themselves as attendants around a powerful ruler or subruler; and second, the Ch'in unification of the script. When China was unified, there thus existed a ready-made class to staff the bureaucracy and the essential administrative tool—the written language—for them to use.

Two further climacterics have been suggested in later Chinese history. One may be defined as commencing with the Sui dynasty and ending in the middle of the T'ang dynasty (that is, the end of the sixth to the eighth century A.D.). Like the Ch'in, the Sui was a very brief, energetic, showy, tyrannous dynasty which accomplished great things (digging the Grand Canal, refurbishing the Great Wall, building capitals, conducting grandiose campaigns along the borders), and did them all in the most expansive style; but the Sui fell of overextension after little more than two decades. The T'ang dynasty, culturally the most glorious and one of the most virile of Chinese history, was brutally interrupted by rebellion halfway through. Thereafter Chinese history, by this view, gradually became characterized by a withdrawal of China inward upon itself, systematizing and rigidifying its own institutions, becoming less open than before to foreign or barbarian contacts and influences, and underscoring civilian hegemony in government while downgrading the military both as an internal power factor and as an instrumentality for projecting state power abroad.

The final breaking point was the impact of the West, barbarians who came from an entirely new quarter and whom the Chinese found impossible to contain or ignore by the second quarter of the nineteenth century. Although the Sino-Soviet split may seem to have restored something of a *status quo ante,* with the most dangerous barbarians restored to their proper place in the northwest, contemporary China must probably be considered still in the phase produced by the arrival of Western troops and traders, concomitant with the decline of the Ch'ing dynasty into what might otherwise have been a normal time of interdynastic troubles.

The cultural importance of the "Chinese language" can hardly be overestimated. The quotation marks serve to underline the fact that, in comparative terms, no such entity as the Chinese language really exists. There are a minimum of five or six Chinese dialects or dialect-families, and these vary among one another as much as the Romance languages of Europe do. In all probability, a comparable measure of regional linguistic diversity has existed in China since the dawn of history. There are, in addition, two great divisions within the central body of the written language: the highly composed literary language and the more diffuse writing based upon speech. Each of these, in turn, has various distinguishable subdivisions, both historically and now. The most important form of the language in modern times is the so-called national language *(kuo-yu)*, which is based upon the way people speak. Earlier forms of this have been used in novels and drama for centuries; but *kuo-yu* was standardized by a government commission in the 1920s and early 1930s on the basis of combining a slightly modified Peiping pronunciation with a stock of vocabulary selected from all of North China down to the Yangtze Valley. This language has again been diverging into two stems as it is variously used and taught on the mainland and abroad.

The unifying and dominant factor in the "Chinese language" is its ideographic, or logographic, script. This allows all the tongues of China—plus others still more variant such as Japanese and Korean—to be written in a *scriptum francum* which serves most needs more or less well. The Chinese writing system has been criticized as an instrument of oppression, a way of recording language so inherently difficult that it inevitably becomes the property of a limited elite. Yet the scholar-gentry whom this theory would accuse of such arcane conspiracy were, in fact, the most self-conscious preservers of the Chinese tradition, and the writing system is unquestionably the vehicle that has conveyed Chinese culture in all its diversity down through the centuries. China has, indeed, been a culture rather than a nation.

Yet China was moving, haltingly and not very effectively, but with increasing impetus, toward modern nationhood as early as the nineteenth century. The first half of the twentieth century can be conceived as a typical phase of Chinese rebellion, characterized by great activist energy, warlordism, and vulgarized heterodox ideologies. Two of the ideologies—a loose democracy and Marxism-Leninism—were Western and implied an array of social and personal values new to China and hard to square with her Great Tradition, a fact which accounts for much of the confusion, irresoluteness, and random behavior that have characterized a good deal of Chinese history in this century. The task of making this progress more rapid and purposeful was perhaps the main challenge the Communists inherited, though it is not obvious how clear they themselves were on this point.

It may reasonably be asked whether the victory of communism in China was somehow inevitable, either in the special light of Chinese history or in the context of the challenges China faced in entering and existing in the world of nation states. Certainly it is not surprising that communism has had a profound effect in China. It has virtually preempted the world of discourse, not only in Asia, but in many other areas and in many fields. It has conditioned politics throughout the world, almost as much in nations that are non-Communist or anti-Communist as in states that cleave to one or another brand of communism. And its pretensions to scientific correctness have had an understandably strong appeal to new, underprivileged nations yearning for some sort of spiritual surety and for shortcuts to economic development. Yet China resisted communism stoutly.

It is obviously impossible to prove what might have been if history had not developed the way it did. Nevertheless, it does seem clear that the Communists would have succeeded in China only much later than they did, if indeed they succeeded at all, had it not been for the pervasive influence of Japanese imperialism and World War II. The Japanese menace gave the Communists a national issue with which to capture the imagination of students and intellectuals. It was an issue that appealed most forcefully to the Young Marshal, Chang Hsueh-liang,[9] whose Manchurian homeland the Japanese had seized; and thus it set the stage for the Sian Incident and the plunge into full-scale war.[10] The Japanese seizure of the main communication lines and industrial areas of East and Central China not only deprived the Kuomintang of its economic base but, more importantly, severed the liberal elements of the party from their political homeland, insulated the Communist areas from KMT power, established a war situation in which Communist guerrilla doctrine was more relevant than anything peculiar to the KMT, and thus allowed communism to grow in strength at the same time that passivity, negativism, and corruption debilitated the KMT.

It is peculiarly appropriate that this profound cataclysm in Chinese history—the victory of communism—should thus have been so radically conditioned by a foreign power coming from across the sea. For of all the

[9]Chang Hsueh-liang (1898–   ), called the "Young Marshal" to distinguish him from his father, succeeded "Old Marshal" Chang Tso-lin as ruler of Manchuria in 1928. His strong feelings of personal failure (a drug addict and womanizer, he was blamed for losing Manchuria to the Japanese), of Manchurian patriotism, and of hatred for the Japanese (who engineered the assassination of his father), led to his involvement as the key figure in the Sian Incident (see note 10, below).

[10]In 1936, Chang Hsueh-liang was commanding Kuomintang forces loyal to himself but assigned to contain and fight the Communists north of Sian. Motivated partly by reverses in the field and partly by detestation of the Japanese, he concluded a cooperative truce with the Communists, who were then pushing for an anti-Japanese united front. When Chiang Kai-shek came to Sian to initiate new moves against the Communists, the Young Marshal seized him; and a series of negotiating sessions was held among the Nationalists, rebels, and Communists. The Generalissimo was released on Christmas Day after almost two weeks in custody. He accepted most of the rebel demands; but Chang Hsueh-liang was court-martialed and has been under detention ever since, having been taken along when the Nationalists retired to Taiwan. The Generalissimo's agreement to take a strong stand against Japanese incursions made the outbreak of all-out war inevitable; and this occurred little more than six months later, in July 1937.

great movements of Chinese history, the clearest and most aberrational was the seaborne impact of Western power and Western ideas. China has always boasted of absorbing her conquerors. The conquest of China by an originally Western ideology has set the stage for a new test of the Middle Kingdom's absorptive power.

What of the Communists?

The Chinese Communists came to their task of ruling, and radically re-moulding, China with many things going for them and at least as many factors impeding them. They had as clear a mandate as could be imagined. They had the positive allegiance of almost the entire intellectual class, especially the young, and the passive acquiescence of the people. Simply by ceasing to function disruptively themselves, they could give China dramatic surcease from all sorts of economic and political ills and could take total credit for the state of peace, unprecedented for over two or three or four decades, depending upon how one chooses to count. They owed nobody any political debts. They were endowed with a healthy reputation for toughness, virtue, and dedication which led people to hope and to fear much from them—both useful items for a political arsenal. They had, above all, the advantage of displacing a regime that had progressively lost its nationalist *élan* and, during and after the last phases of World War II, its standing both at home and abroad.

On the other hand, the very factors that favored them implied handicaps. They were their own men, indeed, owing little to the Soviets or anybody else—except, of course, the Japanese; but the leaders were by the same token an extraordinarily ingrown and insular group, few of whom had any significant experience of the world, and those few generally incapable of exerting a power position. They were ideologically tied to the Soviet Union ("lean to one side"), but this was the USSR of Stalin, whose approaches to Chinese questions had been uniformly unrealistic, who must have resented the unexpected victory of the Maoist forces (though he may also have felt in some sense vindicated in his conviction of the late 1920s that China could be communized), and who was in any case soon dead, and soon thereafter worse than dead. The sheer numbers of the Chinese people, not to mention their intense energy and capacity to make their way in many contexts, made them a dreadful element to control or shape. Above all, there was the fact that the Communists had come to rule a nation with several millennia of deeply known and deeply felt history.

How, then, have they performed? It is a pet conceit of some American journalists[11] that the Communists are bound to follow the course of other energetic and draconian dynasties in Chinese history, especially the Ch'in

---

[11]Most notably Joseph Alsop, who has used this similitude repeatedly.

and the Sui. They will strive and soon fall, giving place to something "more Chinese" and more acceptable to the world at large. Yet this calculus ignores a vital difference. The Communists were not seeking to be merely another Chinese dynasty, to exert control in the old ways. They wanted to change Chinese habits of mind.

In the mid-1950s, a distinguished East European visited China, where he was done great honor and given access to leading cadres. One evening, he was with P'eng Teh-huai, then at the height of his power.[12] There arose the question of deep plowing in Manchuria, where the regime had carried Soviet deep-plowing techniques to great, and disastrous, extremes. Why engage in this ridiculous adventure, asked the European, when anybody with any common sense, indeed any farmer, could predict catastrophe? P'eng answered with a lengthy disquisition on *shun-ming* and the necessity to abolish it as a habit of mind. *Shun-ming* means "to follow one's fate," to accept the world as it is, to agree that nothing much can be done to change things. The Communists, P'eng insisted, must eradicate this attitude or it would destroy them. The deep-plowing idea had been suggested by a humble peasant; and the fact that such a man would advance so striking a concept—regardless of whether it was sensible or not—was a great step forward. Furthermore, if it proved counterproductive, the altered situation might offer yet other new perspectives, and one of them might prove as realistically glowing as the deep-plowing had seemed to the peasant adviser. At all events, it was vital to smash the idea that nothing much could be done, that the world had to be accepted as it was.

In a deep sense, this has been the controlling factor in the attitude of the Chinese Communists toward their history and their use of it. They have, understandably, been ambivalent, divided, and vacillating, though always insisting that they were decisive, unified, and consistent. Neither a nation nor an individual can afford to denigrate its provenance. Without respect for its past, a state has no respect for its present or hope for its future. Yet the past of China is so massive, so homogenized by centuries of myth-making, so oppressive at every point for anyone who would budge the myth for his own purposes, that one need hardly be surprised at some pulling and hauling on the part of the Communists.

Paradoxically, for example, the Communists have made great contribu-

[12]P'eng Teh-huai (1896- ?), a Communist Party member since 1927, was one of the most experienced Red Army commanders. He led the Chinese "volunteers" who entered the Korean War in 1950. He was Minister of Defense, with several collateral party posts, until he was purged in 1959, apparently for having challenged Mao Tse-tung over the disastrous Great Leap Forward and the impact that adventure would have upon Chinese relations with the USSR. (The best account of this may be found in David A. Charles, "The Dismissal of Marshal P'eng Teh-huai," reprinted from the *China Quarterly* in Roderick MacFarquhar (ed.), *China Under Mao* [Cambridge: M.I.T. Press, 1966] pp. 20-33.) P'eng was still alive to be execrated during the Great Proletarian Cultural Revolution.

tions to the study of China's remote past. In large measure, these archaeological initiatives have been inspired by the hope that new discoveries would contribute to new and ideologically useful perspectives on China's history. But some discoveries, at least, have been incidental to great public works, or have been so represented. One gets hints of Communist engineers breaking through the walls of a Shang dynasty tomb, and then gruffly agreeing to postpone their excavations for a few weeks so that scholars might come in and catalogue the bones of the past. Here the ambivalence is almost tangible. The land is shaped, the people are shaped, their world view is shaped, by that past. The Great Wall or the Grand Canal is an enormity, wrung from the common people by a despotic and despicable regime; but it is also a product of those people. It belongs to China, it is a testament to the frequently expressed idea that the people, with proper organization, can do anything. If they can accomplish something so stunning under the aegis of a Sung or Ming dynasty, what can be impossible for them under a shiny new Communist one?

Everything from China's past is similarly equivocal, at once a treasure and a burden, now to be praised, now to be execrated. In the sphere of written history, the Communists have followed every other dynasty, seeking to bend the Chinese tradition to their purposes. Yet their basic recasting of that tradition has been more extreme than usual, making heroes into villains and drafting new heroes from quite unexpected quarters, until the historians themselves abruptly fell silent out of personal fear and simple bewilderment over what would be the next acceptable, safe line to take. Even before the Great Proletarian Cultural Revolution halted intellectual activity, historical studies in China were interpretively sterile, though rich in new materials and objectives. The Marxist-Maoist canon simply has not provided usable theoretical tools, and no other tools are acceptable.

One of the most omnipresent and most frequently denigrated elements of the national heritage has been the language, an entity so central to the Chinese tradition that it—or perhaps the script more clearly than the language—has been described as holding China together. In this area, the Communists have done a lot. A mere catalogue of the regime's major linguistic achievements speaks for itself:

(a) They have effectively pushed *p'u-t'ung-hua* ("ordinary speech") in schools throughout China, so that this *lingua franca* can now be found and understood virtually everywhere, at least among the young, even in areas where non-Mandarin "dialects" still hold sway.

(b) They have standardized that language in terms of vocabulary, grammar, usage, and so forth.

(c) They have standardized the applied language, especially modern technical terms, and published normative word lists.

(d) They have promulgated a new official romanization, *pin-yin*.

(e)   Within the script, they have created a few hundred simplified characters in order to simplify the eradication of illiteracy.

One may object to this list of achievements, or deprecate it in various ways. True, most of them are based upon earlier conceptualization and research, for which the Communists can take little credit. True, much of the work has been done in ways that some linguists find intellectually shoddy. True, one cannot really say what the ultimate effect will be. True, these happen to be tasks peculiarly suited to Communist approaches. Yet they were tremendously difficult things to do; and the Communists have had the grip, the will, and the drive to do them.

Since the Communists have perceived the nationalistic dimension of the Chinese language, it is not surprising that they have also taken effective action to control and contain the ethnic minorities within the borders of China. Here the policy has been clear: pay lip service to the minority culture, but do everything possible to see that it Sinicizes itself out of existence. Although there has been dark talk of genocide, the most effective tactic has been simple racial drowning. Chinese immigration into Inner Mongolia, Sinkiang, and Tibet has made the indigenous people true minorities even in their own areas. It is a complex calculus, since at many points the ethno-linguistic dimension underlies thorny problems of borders and foreign relations.

In general, China's borders are almost as far-flung as they have ever been in history. Taiwan is not really an exception, since both Communists and Nationalists regard it as part of China. It may, of course, be in the process of becoming an exception. The most significant point about China's modern frontiers is that they are more firmly drawn than ever before. In every quarter, whether still disputed or effectively settled, the boundaries of China are far more clearly defined than they have been historically. This is not to say that they are ethnically neat; they are not. But the presence of self-conscious, established, modern polities, such as North Korea and North Viet-Nam, India and Pakistan, has greatly diminished the elasticity of China's boundaries. Even in such cases as the Burma-Thailand-Laos border area, where minority tribesmen speaking both T'ai and other languages span the border, the Chinese threat seems more one of causing trouble than of seriously seeking expansion—although one can easily imagine a condition of irresistible weakness in northern Burma, for example, that might revive Chinese territorial aspirations. And on China's longest border, the overwhelming military preponderance of the Soviet Union has thus far effectively foreclosed Chinese irredentism in Soviet Asia and Outer Mongolia.

In foreign policy, China still is not living in a world of nation states, let alone of United Nations, nor is she effectively competing on the world stage either economically or politically. Looking at twenty years of Communist foreign policy, we see the rather open and relaxed Bandung spirit of 1955 as an aberration. China has managed to encircle herself with enemies, largely nations she has forced or declared into enmity. Tiny, remote Albania is the only tolerated consort for this perpetually and shrilly irascible giant. With the Great Proletarian Cultural Revolution, China virtually terminated her capacity to make or support foreign policy initiatives, by stripping her already hermetic overseas missions of two-thirds of their personnel. This was perhaps the ultimate comment upon Chinese foreign relations: the Chinese did not care enough to maintain them (although, since the Ninth Party Congress, some ambassadors have again been assigned to embassies abroad). For over two years, China in effect had no foreign dealings at all, except of course for the periodic outbreaks of violence against foreign missions within China or in those countries which theoretically maintained some sort of diplomatic connection with Peking. But those were simply outward manifestations of the Cultural Revolution and apparently as shapelessly impulsive as that great convulsion itself.[13]

The Chinese were right. What really matters is what goes on in China. What has? Does there indeed exist that oft-mentioned entity, a New China? All in all, are there more new strands than old in the fabric of the nation today? One must doubt it.

It is significant that the Great Proletarian Cultural Revolution has its roots in controversy with a clear historical dimension. Wu Han and others of his stripe[14] were actively using their own particular vulgarized version of what China's history is and means, applying it to modern developments —"lauding ancient times to stigmatize today." The fact that Wu Han turned so instinctively and effectively to historical similitudes suggests that maybe there has been less change than Mao Tse-tung wishes and claims to believe. Wu Han not only invoked the past as a device; he did so in a way common to Confucius and Mencius, indeed to the great persuaders of China from the beginning of history.

Despite such exercises in rooting out *shun-ming* as the Great Leap Forward and the Cultural Revolution, the Communist regime does not seem to have recast Chinese government in any basic structural way. Rather, it

---

[13]The fact that the Chinese commenced to reassign ambassadors abroad in mid-1969, and even reopened talks with the United States in January 1970, merely underlines the anomaly of the nearly three years during which China pretty much suspended the conduct of foreign relations.

[14]Wu Han, a historian specializing in the Ming dynasty, was also a leading party cadre and Deputy Mayor of Peking. He was the target of Yao Wen-yuan's November 1965 article in the Shanghai *Wen-hui Pao,* which is often counted as the first overt signal of the Cultural Revolution. Another prominent historian and party member, Teng T'o, was the next victim; and almost every other leading historian—Chien Po-tsan, Hou Wai-lu, and Liu Ta-nien, to mention only a few of the bigger names—endured severe criticism.

has simply substituted new and often quite comparable elements for what existed before.

China is still a profoundly ideological society; the ideology has been changed, but it is still profoundly Chinese. If Marx stood Hegel on his head by stressing economic factors in societal development, Mao has in turn stood Marx on his head with his assertion that "politics takes command." And Lin Piao has capped the trick with the idea (in Geoffrey Hudson's summary phrasing) that ". . . the coming world revolution would be extended from the predominantly agrarian regions of the world to the more urbanized and industrialized areas."[15]

China is still a rigorous society run by a small elite set off against a largely peasant mass of the ruled. Entry into the elite is no easier today than it was under the empire, though the qualifications now have become a proletarian background and a simplistic Maoist fanaticism, rather than control of the Confucian tradition and the knack of writing eight-legged essays. The most basic new departure is that, aided by modern communications and Leninist organization, the government has reached down farther into society and farther out into the hinterland than any imperial government could. The individual no longer has the safe havens of retirement, nonparticipation, and silence.

It is impossible to document, yet one must question whether the gulf between rulers and ruled has been bridged, whether the masses are really in step with the Maoist line. Until recently, there were many indications that the regime had not succeeded in abolishing the old folkways and family-based practices of the people at large. In fact, there has been no basic legal step designed to reform society radically, except for the marriage law of 1953, though of course administrative moves such as the on-again off-again push for more complete forms of communization have undoubtedly shaken old patterns. One must doubt that the realistic, flexible, tough-minded peasant can have retained any illusion that there exists a shapely Communist plan for the recasting of society, after the brute facts of repeated campaigns, repeated failures, and repeated changes of line. There were some indications that, for at least some of the common people, Red Guard excesses were the last straw that released their desperate and—by the old definition—righteous rage.

Economically, there seems to have been no radical restructuring. China is still basically an agricultural society. Indeed, recent initiatives to deport urbanites and students to rural areas seem intended to diminish, rather than increase, the proportion of the trained, skilled urban population as against those who till the soil and need experience rather than skill. And China has not succeeded in finding a successful Socialist answer to the

---

[15]G. F. Hudson, *Fifty Years of Communism* (New York: Basic Books, 1968), p. 218.

problem of agricultural productivity, any more than any other Communist nation.

Although the historical tension between civilian and military seems to have been resolved with the total victory of Lin Piao and the People's Liberation Army, this is not necessarily or simply true. What has happened may rather have been a civilianizing of the military, involving them in agitational and administrative tasks for which they are as ill-suited as soldiers anywhere, and withdrawing them from concern with preserving and enhancing a genuine Chinese military capability. In fact, China is now—with the proliferation of modern guerrilla-type weapons and Mao's doctrine—an enemy formidable in defense but pathetically vulnerable in any large-scale offensive effort.

One fine old Chinese tradition the Communist regime has honored is that of killing off the most trusted comrades of the drive to power. The facade of party solidarity was preserved for so long that it seemed the regime was never going to lose its virginity. China-watchers greeted the purge of Kao Kang and Jao Shu-shih in the early 1950s with an almost audible sigh of relief, but were then let down and bemused by its failure to become a full-scale purge. The holocaust ushered in by the Great Proletarian Cultural Revolution has at last been almost as ruthless and certainly as sweeping as any purge in Chinese history. The fact that families are involved as well as principals also provides a little nostalgia for students of China's past.

After a first decade of quite remarkable energy, unity, and morale (especially among the elite), China appears now to have slipped back to the point where she must run very hard to stay in the same place. The ancient Chinese penchant for role-playing, for complying with what one cannot avoid, would be a natural, even an inevitable, reaction to the ceaseless exigency of the Communists, even if the people of China had not practiced these arts for centuries.

Coda

China's problems, in no small measure rooted in historical choices, are colossal. Above all looms that of the greatest population-mass any nation has ever had—intelligent, industrious, tough, adaptive, shrewd, magnificent material for citizens, but undoubtedly too little altered by Communist efforts at remolding, and certainly far too numerous. Mao Tse-tung is not the first of China's modern leaders to rationalize this tremendous population as being an advantage. Sun Yat-sen did the same, as did imperial leaders. But in the superhuman effort to heave forward in real industrial progress, this sheer bulk of people, set against a physical landscape which was by no means lush to start with and which has been harshly used for generations without end — this proportion of population to resources is a crushing, perhaps an unmanageable, burden.

The isolation that China has imposed upon herself is a mixed blessing. At the start, the "lean-to-one-side" policy was an understandable retreat toward purity, keeping China's opportunistic millions cut off from the corrupt attractions of the capitalist West. It was a small cycle: Mao's China as anti-Western as the Empress Dowager's, and for much the same reasons. But with the loss of the Soviet partnership, isolation became too much of a good thing. In the modern world, if you want to compete you must mix. The academic hiatus of the Cultural Revolution may seem necessary to Mao, in the interests of ideological regirding. But it has meant a degree of isolation truly unique in the world, and this to a nation which lacks many things: shipping, for example; technologists, for another.

The commitment of the People's Liberation Army, first to the Cultural Revolution and then to the administration of the country, must appear as a move of dire desperation. Military officers in societies where diversification of function has occurred lack the skills which bureaucrats need; and if they must man a bureaucracy, they no longer have the time to keep modern military skills sharp. Certain theorists of the modernization process regard the recourse to the military as a predictable and normal phase in that development, and one which is benign, since military men tend to be relatively pragmatic and efficient in pursuing national goals (although such theorists also regard the military as usually lacking progressive internal programs or the psychic mobility to implement them.)[16] In terms of purely military potential, however, it must spell incapacity, especially if the sergeant level, that essential repository of the techniques that make an army function, comes to be skilled chiefly in mass organization and propaganda.

Some historians, looking at the broad sweep of Russian history, believe that the Communist revolution of 1917 interrupted a process of modernization and of adaptation to the world which had been going on at least since 1861, and that purposeful progress was reinstituted only expensively and fitfully by the five year plans.[17] If this is so, consider the Chinese case. Her revolution, coming at the end of a century of troubles, has been going on for decades and cannot yet be counted as safely over. Although Chinese thinkers and rulers had turned toward the extremely difficult tasks of modernization during the nineteenth century, their progress was reluctant and

---

[16]See John J. Johnson (ed.), *The Role of the Military in Underdeveloped Countries* (Princeton: Princeton University Press, 1962), especially the first two chapters by Edward Shils and Lucian W. Pye. For the conceptual framework, see also C. E. Black, *The Dynamics of Modernization* (New York: Harper, 1966), pp. 62–67 and 119-123.

[17]See, for example, C. E. Black, *op. cit.,* pp. 73, 80, 146, and 160; and his *The Transformation of Russian Society: Aspects of Social Change since 1861* (Cambridge: Harvard University Press, 1960), especially pp. 664–668 and 677–678.

halting. The colossal and ever-increasing population, the largest in the history of the world, hobbles advance. Isolation and Maoist doctrine conspire to reduce Chinese freedom of movement. Of all underdeveloped countries, China alone—since 1960—receives no significant amount of aid from any quarter. Her program of five-year plans has been derailed. It is a desperate case.

From their beginnings, the Chinese have found their history to be an abundant spring of socially useful ideas. They have lived by it, argued by it, governed by it, made revolutions by it. If China can find a role in the new world, it may well be through yet another reconsideration and reworking of her own tradition. It is noteworthy that, in a time when few historians are advancing interpretations, the Communists have been industriously producing large and useful collections of meticulously edited historical documents. Maybe in time they will produce the man brave enough to interpret them.

Chapter Two

Ideology and the Cult of Mao

Franz Michael

Seldom in modern times has ideology played such an all-pervasive part as in the cult of Mao Tse-tung in Communist China. The Maoist cult has evolved out of the role that every Communist leader must assume, that of Marxist theoretician who can apply the tenets of the doctrine to the political realities of time and place. But it has grown far beyond this concept into the image of personal infallibility, akin to that created by other recent leaders of totalitarianism in Nazi Germany and Fascist Italy. Since the beginning of the Great Proletarian Cultural Revolution in 1966, the role of Mao has transcended and replaced that of the Communist Party; the Thought of Mao Tse-tung has become the measure of all things and the guide of all action; and the homage paid to Mao's person has assumed the characteristics of quasi-religious veneration.

Every success in every field of endeavor in Communist China is now ascribed to Mao's thought. Discoveries in physics and chemistry, and any other scientific advance accomplished by Chinese scholars, are the result of the Thought of Mao Tse-tung. In medicine, numerous lives have been saved, and miraculous operations performed when doctors, despairing of the hopelessness of their case, were suddenly struck by the Thought of Mao and saved the life of the patient. The growth and sale of watermelons, victory in international Ping-Pong matches, all have been ensured by the application of Mao's thought, and it is in effect the constant study and application of Mao's thought that is to lead China to the Communist millennium.

The creator of this thought, Mao Tse-tung, is himself portrayed as a superman, with extraordinary physical and mental qualities. In July 1966, when rumor had explained his prolonged disappearance as illness and decline, Mao asserted his vigor in an extraordinary feat, the alleged swim in the Yangtze River. Mao not only broke all speed and endurance records, but carried on a theoretical discussion with a fellow swimmer while doing so. The ultimate aspect of the Mao cult has been the deification of the leader. In factories, communes, and homes, the picture of Mao has become an object of worship. Each worker, peasant, or family member supposedly performs a ceremony morning and evening in which he reads from

the red book of Mao's quotations, sings the three songs ("The East is Red,"
"Sailing the Seas Depends on the Helmsman," and "Father and Mother are
Dear but Mao Tse-tung is Dearer"), and asks advice from the Chairman on
the problems of the day or reports to him in the evening. Mao has thus
become a superhuman figure, and his thought is proclaimed as the highest
expression of Marxism-Leninism in the present epoch and the guide for all
action in China and the world.

The Thought of Mao Tse-tung

What, then, is the substance of the Thought of Mao Tse-tung? In fact,
Mao has made few, if any, contributions to Communist theory. His writings,
in contrast to those of Marx, Lenin, or even Stalin, do not provide a comprehensive system of Communist doctrine in terms of philosophy, political
theory, and political economy. Mao's writings have served, in the main, to
popularize Communist tenets, or to direct policy in any given situation;
few of them have dealt with theoretical themes. They are mainly the product
of the war years in Yenan. This was the time when Mao finally gained
control of the Chinese Communist Party. The Second United Front, at
the end of 1936, gave him a reprieve from the daily worries of guerrilla
warfare and surcease from the government campaigns of the civil war
period before the Long March.

During the war with Japan, when the Communists expanded their power
from their base at Yenan, Mao read the Communist classics and produced
most of his well-known writings. His best-known theoretical pieces are *On
Contradiction* and *On Practice,* allegedly composed in 1937. The history
of these essays demonstrates Mao's limitations as a theoretician. *On
Contradiction,* treating the concept of opposing elements in the dialectical
process, is the more important of the two, and in content and history more
revealing of the man. There has been some argument as to the dating of
this piece. When Mao's *Selected Works* were published starting in 1951,
On Contradiction was first included in the second volume and only later
transferred to the first volume, where it chronologically belonged.[1] This
raised the question of an attempt to antedate the essay, in order to demonstrate that at the time of his assumption of power Mao had the theoretical
qualifications for his leadership role. This claim appeared more question-

[1]The first volume was published by the People's Publishing House of the New China Bookstore. The first edition was published in October 1951 without the item "On Contradiction."
This item first appeared in the second volume, published by the same publisher, with the
explanation that the publication of "On Contradiction" had been delayed because of the
necessity of editing the document, and the promise that in later editions it would be transferred to Vol. 1. A standard English translation is Mao Tse-tung, *The Selected Works of Mao
Tse-tung* (Peking: Foreign Languages Press, 1961-65), four vols. (Hereafter cited as *Selected
Works.*)

able in view of the suppression of another work written by Mao during the Yenan period, a piece on dialectic materialism which was to a large degree copied from an article in a Soviet encyclopedia. Only recently, a Japanese historian has uncovered evidence that *On Contradiction* also closely paraphrases Soviet textbooks of the prewar period. In a close check on this and other texts, the same historian comes to the conclusion that Mao had little grasp of Marx or Engels, whom he seems never to have read in the original, and from whom he has quoted only a few well-known statements.[2] To a lesser degree, the same holds true for Mao's familiarity with Lenin's writings. Mao appears to have relied mainly on Stalin as a source of inspiration. What Mao himself contributed to the concept of the dialectic are mainly homilies meant to popularize the idea of the interplay of opposed elements, as when he used the similes of day and night to demonstrate opposites in nature, or the image of the chicken and the egg as a parallel to dialectical development. Mao's real contribution was his ability to expound Communist strategy as it applied to China and to formulate operational directives. Indeed, Mao's most important writings are his many general statements on, and specific prescriptions for, revolutionary action. Mao's *On New Democracy,* written in the winter of 1939–40, was a reiteration of Lenin's concept of national liberation movements, as subsequently expanded by Stalin. The combined revolution of the four classes — the workers, peasants, petit-bourgeoisie, and national bourgeoisie — in a preindustrial country formed, in Lenin's concept, an anti-imperialist movement which the Communists would support and exploit. This revolution would lead to a pre-Socialist united front seizure of power, a "new democracy" or "people's republic," as a prelude to eventual Communist takeover. Communism could thus be established through a combined revolution and without the necessity of the full development of capitalism and an industrial proletariat as in the industrialized countries of the West.

This strategy of national liberation movements has a long history of discussion in the Socialist movement in Europe, and predates the Bolshevik revolution. In contrast to those who believed that the liberation of the colonial peoples would come through the victory of the proletariat in the industrial countries, the Eastern school of Socialist thought, to which Lenin belonged, always held that the struggle against the imperialist powers was to be fought by the people in the colonial countries. It was to be, in reality, a fight against monopoly capitalism and, therefore, a part of the Communist world revolution, and was to be given full support.

After their victory in 1917, when the great hopes of the Bolshevik leaders for an immediate proletarian revolution in industrial\Europe were dashed, Lenin turned East to promote the national liberation movements through a

---

[2]Mineo Nakajima, *Gendai Chugo-koron* (China Today) (Tokyo: 1966), pp. 44–53.

strategy outlined by him and his successor, Stalin. The two social classes intended for major roles in this strategy were the national bourgeoisie and the peasantry of the colonial countries. The Communists would participate in this anti-imperialist revolution, which they would eventually take over from within. Two aspects of this strategy became especially important for China. One was the emphasis placed by Lenin on the role of the peasant. In his invitations to representatives of the peoples of the East to the conference at Baku, Lenin graded the countries of Asia according to their development, by appealing either to the peasants and workers, or simply to the peasants alone. Stressing the nonproletarian element in the anticipated revolutions, Lenin and his colleagues emphasized a shift in semantics from the "proletariat" to the "toilers of the East." The broader scope of an appeal to all the working people who formed the "revolutionary masses" was thus introduced, to be reflected later in Mao's direct appeals to the masses. This strategy of national liberation movements became the basis of Mao's revolutionary experience, and the field in which he developed his expertise as a revolutionary leader.

What Mao, as the ideological leader of Communist China, derived from the period before the conquest of power in 1949, affected his thinking in two ways. For one, the revolutionary strategy of national liberation movements implied a direct path to socialism and communism without the necessity of a full capitalist development beforehand. In Soviet theory, and in the textbook *Fundamentals of Marxism-Leninism*,[3] this different path to communism was accepted as a staged economic advance; in Mao's interpretation, it became a shortcut to communism. In the utopian radicalism of Mao's thought, instant communism could be achieved through revolutionary organization and sheer will power.

Second, the strategy of wars of national liberation gave the revolution in China its military character. In the words of Stalin, the difference between the revolutions in the West and in China was that while in the West ". . . revolutions usually began with the uprising of the people for the most part unarmed or poorly armed, who came into collision with the army of the old regime, which they tried to demoralize or at least to win in part to their own side. . . . In China, the armed revolution is fighting the armed counter-revolution. . . . And therein lies the special significance of the revolutionary army in China."[4] In contrast to the proletarian revolution in the West (based on workers' organizations, the general strike, and the political strategy of the Communist Party), the revolution in China was to be accomplished by the victory of a revolutionary army in a specially

---

[3]*Fundamentals of Marxism-Leninism*, second revised edition (Moscow: Foreign Language Publishing House, 1963).

[4]J. V. Stalin, *Works* (Moscow: 1954), Vol. 8, p. 379.

developed type of warfare. Wars of national liberation were based on the exploitation of nationalism and agrarian discontent in the colonial countries of Asia.

These were the features of the Chinese revolution as outlined by Moscow and implemented under the leadership of Mao Tse-tung. It was for this revolutionary warfare that Mao prescribed his practical directives, which comprise the major part of the Thought of Mao Tse-tung and for which he is most renowned. These directives can be subdivided into directives on political and on military strategy. The political directives dealt mainly with united front strategy in the various stages of political development, with or without the cooperation of the Kuomintang.[5] The directives on military strategy dealt with the role of the military as the source of all power, a concept derived from that of the revolutionary army and finally formulated in Mao's dictum that "political power grows out of the barrel of a gun." The directives also clarified and prescribed the political structure of the army, and the concept that "the party controls the gun."[6]

The use of the Chinese Red Army was meant to accomplish the conquest of power. Once the victory was won, Chinese communism would follow the ideological lead of Moscow and apply the concepts of the phased development of Communist transformation prescribed by Marxist-Leninist theories and Stalinist practice in the Soviet Union. The people's republics in Eastern Europe, as well as in China, were to reach socialism through the development of heavy industry and the collectivization of agriculture, and were to follow the Soviet pattern toward the final goal of the Communist self-regulating collective. However, the military heritage

[5]Directives of that time on political strategy include: "The Role of the Chinese Communist Army in National War," October 1938, *Selected Works,* Vol. 2 (in which Mao justified the policy of collaboration with the Kuomintang); "The Present Situation and Our Tasks," December 25, 1947, *Selected Works,* Vol. 4 (in which Mao announces an all-out offensive on all fronts); and "On People's Democratic Dictatorship," June 30, 1949, *Selected Works,* Vol. 4, which together with "On New Democracy," January 1940, *Selected Works,* Vol. 2, laid the groundwork for the political structure of the People's Republic.

[6]Directives on military strategy include: "Why Is It That Red Political Power Can Exist in China?" October 5, 1928, *Selected Works,* Vol. 1; "The Struggle in the Chingkang Mountains," November 25, 1928, *Selected Works,* Vol. 1; "On Correcting Mistaken Ideas in the Party," October 1929, *Selected Works,* Vol. 1; "Problems of Strategy in China's Revolutionary War," December 1936, *Selected Works,* Vol. 1; "On Protracted War," May 1938, *Selected Works,* Vol. 2; "Problems of War and Strategy," November 6, 1938, *Selected Works,* Vol. 2; and "Concentrate a Superior Force to Destroy the Enemy Forces One by One," *Selected Works,* Vol. 4.

of the strategy of wars of liberation was eventually to reassert itself in the Great Proletarian Cultural Revolution.

What Mao had accomplished by the time of the Communist takeover in China was a position of leadership under which he was recognized as the ideological and institutional head of the Communist regime set up in 1949. Mao's writings, together with those of Stalin and the second ranking theoretician of the Chinese Communist Party, Liu Shao-ch'i, had been quoted in the rectification campaign during 1942 and 1943 as a theoretical basis for Mao's authority to purge deviationists from the right as well as from the left. The Communist Party constitution of 1945 referred to "the theories of Marxism-Leninism and the combined principles derived from the practical experience of the Chinese revolution—the ideas of Mao Tse-tung—as the guiding principles of all its work." There was no claim in this or other statements of the time that Mao had done more than inter- pret the tenets of the faith as they applied to conditions in China, which was a minimum position to establish Mao's claim to Chinese Communist leadership. Even in this respect, moreover, Mao closely followed the con- cepts of Lenin and Stalin. It was Lenin who had turned to the "eight hun- dred million people of Asia" to start the "fire of the world revolution," and who believed that "the way to Europe is through Asia—China and India— and Peking is the gate to Paris."[7] And it was Stalin who—contrary to a widely held opinion—called for the shift in China from a united front to that of rural-based guerrilla warfare. But it was Mao who carried out the policy, and it was Mao who gained the reputation for inventing concepts of which he was but the translator.

The claim of Mao's originality was first made by the American Com- munist, Anna Louise Strong, in 1947. In her version, "Mao Tse-tung's great accomplishment has been to change Marxism from a European to an Asiatic form. Marx and Lenin were Europeans; they wrote in European languages about European histories and problems, seldom discussing Asia or China. The basic principles of Marxism are undoubtedly adaptable to all countries, but to apply their general truth to concrete revolutionary practice in China is a difficult task. Mao Tse-tung is Chinese; he analyzes Chinese problems and guides the Chinese people in their struggle to victory. He uses Marxist-Leninist principles to explain Chinese history and the practical problems of China. He is the first that has succeeded in doing so. . . . He has created a Chinese or Asiatic form of Marxism."[8]

This claim was vastly exaggerated. It ignored the whole Comintern

[7]The Baku Declaration, drafted by Lenin, in *Stenographic Record of the Congress of Baku of the Peoples of the East* (Moscow: 1928); see also Wang Chien-min, *Chung-kuo kung- ch'an-tang shih-kao* (History of the Chinese Communist Party) (Taipei: 1965), Vol. 1, p. 6.

[8]Anna Louise Strong, "The Thought of Mao Tse-tung," *Amerasia,* Vol. 2, No. 6 (June 1947), p. 161.

literature on China and Lenin's role in conceiving the strategy applied by Mao. It also contributed to the misunderstanding of the importance of Stalin, whose direction of Comintern strategy in China, first misinterpreted by his Trotskyite opposition, has never been fully appreciated in the West. The myth of a Maoist communism, even of a Maoist "heresy," found here its first expression.

Mao himself was satisfied with his place as a regular Communist leader in China, a loyal follower of Stalin, to whom he dedicated paeans of praise, as did most other Communist leaders of the time. Nevertheless, to bolster his ideological leadership after the seizure of power in 1949, Mao had his writings compiled and published in what eventually became the several volumes of the *Selected Works of Mao Tse-tung*. Although these writings do not present a theoretical system, they do restate most of the main Communist doctrinal concepts for Chinese readers, and they comprise the general Marxist-Lenin framework from which Mao could not divorce himself, even in his recent heresy of the Great Proletarian Cultural Revolution. This edition of Mao's writings was selected and published in order to establish the claim that Mao was correct at all times, and that from the beginning he was the true leader of the Chinese Communist movement. His chosen role was as the recognized doctrinal leader of his party, within the framework of the Moscow line.

Mao *versus* the Party

It is debatable whether Mao felt comfortable with his position after the regular Communist system had been established in the Chinese People's Republic. Following a transitional period of military occupation, the political structure of Communist China provided for an enlarged bureaucracy to manage the phased economic development of the country, based on five-year plans and Soviet economic aid. The need for economic expertise and administrative detail may have given Mao, the revolutionary leader, a feeling that his authority was being restricted. His retrospective attack, at the time of the Cultural Revolution, against the eighteen years of mismanagement by Liu Shao-ch'i and other party leaders, the "capitalist roaders and revisionists," and his bitter, detailed charges against their actions, may indicate that he was inwardly always unhappy about the change of tempo from revolution to practical government. But if so, very little of this disagreement became evident, and the myth of the Chinese monolith and the unique unity of Chinese leadership was maintained by many outside observers long after the fissures in the edifice had appeared.

What triggered the division between Mao and the regular party leadership (typified by Liu Shao-ch'i) was Khrushchev's de-Stalinization policy, which was initiated at the Soviet Twentieth Party Congress in 1956. It affected the position of Mao, who had obviously not been forewarned, and who as a Stalinist was vulnerable. He was perhaps not directly threatened, as were other Stalinist leaders in European parties, but he found his authority challenged. At the Chinese Communist Party Congress of 1956, a new party constitution was adopted, eliminating the reference to the ideas of Mao from the preamble and asserting collective leadership.

The years from 1956 to 1958 are the watershed of the shift in Mao's ideological role. First, Mao attempted to follow the new Soviet line, and at the same time to gain ideological stature by explaining these dramatic events in theoretical terms. The Soviet "thaw" was matched by the Chinese Hundred Flowers movement. The historical slogans, "Let the hundred flowers bloom" and "Let the hundred schools of thought contend," were to introduce a period of tolerance in criticism and free expression. But while the Soviet thaw was a protest movement, initiated by Soviet writers against the restraints and suppressions of Stalinist orthodoxy, the Hundred Flowers movement was a government-sponsored invitation to constructive criticism of the regime. Mao supported it in a speech on February 27, 1957, which was published in June of that year under the title *On the Correct Handling of Contradictions Among the People.*[9] In its published form, which called for restrictions not part of the original, oral version, the permission to criticize was severely circumscribed. By this time, a devastating outpouring of criticism against the Communist system had surprised and shocked the leadership. The lid was quickly placed on again, and was followed by vigorous prosecution of the "anti-rightists," the "poisonous weeds" that had been trapped into coming out in the open. Mao, in his theoretical treatment of this situation, drew a distinction between what he called "antagonistic" and "non-antagonistic" contradictions. The distinction, which had a precedent in Soviet literature, defined contradictions with the enemy as antagonistic; these had to be solved by force. The non-antagonistic contradictions were those with the people; they were honest misconceptions that could be reformed by persuasion and education. Mao admitted that the Communists had made mistakes. They were not attributable, however, to the leadership—he could not de-Mao himself—but rather to the party cadres who had misapplied directives. Indeed, Mao spoke of the possibility of contradictions between the party and the people. Blaming the cadres for past mistakes and for undermining the position of the party as the ultimate source of truth, Mao laid the foundation for his own role as arbiter of affairs. In this way, he began to assert his own brand of communism.

[9]For the text, see G. F. Hudson (ed.), *Let A Hundred Flowers Bloom* (which is the complete text of "On the Correct Handling of Contradictions Among the People"), with notes and an introduction by the editor (New York: A Tamiment Institute Publication Service Pamphlet, no date).

It was on this basis that Mao went to Moscow at the time of the 1957 interparty congress in order to gain acceptance as Khrushchev's partner in determining the world Communist political line. Mao's purpose was to demand not only more economic aid, as many commentators have speculated, but also to obtain the assurance of "real, not formal, consultation" in the determination of policy. He also came to propagate a hard line toward the West, which he felt was justified by the technical advance of the Soviet Union and the general strengthening of the Communist camp. As a senior Communist world leader, Mao expected after the death of Stalin to be offered a partnership which would have protected him against the risk of surprise policy decisions emanating from Moscow. But Khrushchev refused the partnership, and Mao returned to Peking determined to challenge Moscow's hegemony.

In order to prepare for this challenge, Mao applied the concept of instant communism, which grew out of his past revolutionary experience. Moscow's leadership was no longer founded on an institutional base, as at the time of the Comintern and the Cominform. All parties were proclaimed equal and independent, although Soviet leadership was accepted on the basis of the advanced state of Soviet development on the path to communism. Since this was the same path for all, the Soviets were leading in a way that could not be institutionally challenged. A challenge could come from China only if she could compete with the Soviet Union in economic and social development.

This is what Mao attempted with his revolutionary methods in the Great Leap Forward and the introduction of the commune system in 1958. The economic difficulties in China at that time, resulting from agricultural collectivization, and Mao's discontent with the slow pace of revolutionary progress, might have induced him to such a radical course in any event. But it was the Soviet slight and the goal of "bypassing the Soviet Union on the way to communism" which led him to a fanatical effort to multiply Chinese production through sheer organization and will power. The eighteen-hour work day, backyard steel furnaces, the militarization of economic production, and similar steps were to create the needed affluence to introduce the communal living of a Communist society. Mao's grandiose, utopian schemes, derived from an oversimplification of the concept of a combined anti-feudal and anti-capitalist revolution, were meant to transform China within a few years into a Communist society and to make her the model for Communist revolution in Asia and the world.

The new Maoist line was introduced in a lengthy article published on July 16, 1958, in *Hung-ch'i* (Red Flag) (Peking), with the title "Under the Banner of Comrade Mao Tse-tung."[10] The article, written by Ch'en Po-ta,

[10]For the text, see *Survey of China Mainland Press,* No. 138 (August 11, 1958), pp. 5-17.

Mao's secretary and ghost writer, was a eulogy to Mao Tse-tung, under whose leadership the party had gained its victories. The party was "armed with . . . Marxist-Leninist thinking," but "each country must independently think" out its own problems, and for China this was to be done by Comrade Mao. The "thinking" in China was especially difficult, as had previously been pointed out by Lenin, who told the Chinese comrades:

> You are confronted with a task never before encountered by the Communists of the world, that is, you must, in the light of special conditions unknown to the European countries, apply the general Communist theory and Communist measures and realize that peasants are the principal masses and that it is not the capital but the survivals of the Middle Ages that is to be opposed . . . this is a difficult and special task, as well as an extraordinary and noble task . . . .

Ignoring the entire body of revolutionary literature written by Lenin and Stalin, Ch'en proclaimed that it was Comrade Mao alone who "achieved this extremely momentous task courageously and magnificently in the Chinese revolution." Mao had done this by integrating his work:

> . . . with the creativeness of the masses. He puts faith in the masses, relies on the masses and respects the intelligence of the ordinary masses, thereby to increase the invincible power of Marxist-Leninist theory under new conditions and in new surroundings.

For the first time, Ch'en Po-ta proclaimed that "the banner of Mao Tse-tung's thought" provided the answer to China's problems. Allegedly, Mao invented rural guerrilla warfare, new forms of transition to Socialist ownership, and discovered the necessity of continued class struggle after a Communist takeover. Mao had found the way to "resolve the contradictions . . . between the cadres and the masses." Mao's thought replaced the party, because "Once Comrade Mao Tse-tung's thought has a grip on the masses or, conversely, once it is grasped by the masses, it becomes a weapon of the masses. . . ." But in order to become effective, Mao's thought must be studied by the masses in order to affect their thinking.

In spite of grandiose claims, the Great Leap proved to be a massive failure, resulting in serious economic setback and famine. Mao's ideological slogans were never officially abandoned, but the policy was quietly discarded. Moreover, Mao was demoted. At a Central Committee meeting in December 1958, where the first retreat from the Great Leap was resolved, Mao gave up his position as Chairman of the republic. His successor, Liu Shao-ch'i, thereafter dismantled Mao's ambitious program step by step during the following years and brought China back to Communist normalcy.

Mao did not accept defeat, however. Instead, he attempted a return to power in a new way, outside the framework of the party whose support he had lost. The Thought of Mao Tse-tung, as propagated by Ch'en Po-ta, was not enough to establish Mao's leadership over the "masses" in defiance of the party. Mao needed an instrument of power; and for this he turned back to the strategy of the civil war and to the use of the People's Liberation Army as a "revolutionary army," this time not against a nationalist enemy but against his own Communist Party. In August 1959, following the purge of P'eng Teh-huai, who had criticized Mao's Great Leap, Lin Piao became Minister of Defense. Under his command, the People's Liberation Army became a new instrument of power and also the vehicle to spread the Thought of Mao Tse-tung to the masses. The army was to be the organizational basis of a leader cult that would place Mao outside the restrictions of party control. It was from this position that Mao moved against the party and state in what has been called by him the Great Proletarian Cultural Revolution.

Immediately after his appointment, Lin Piao began to initiate a policy in close support of Mao's bid for power. In September 1959, he issued a statement stressing the importance of Mao's military thought for the army.[11] In this statement, all credit for Communist military victories during World War II, the civil war, and the years that followed the seizure of power, were credited to Mao's military guidance. Lin quoted from Mao's article on "Problems of War and Strategy," where Mao underlined the political importance of the army. It was to be a revolutionary army in which "members of the Communist Party will not fight for their own personal power over the troops but . . . for the power of the party over the troops, and the power of the people over the troops." Lin repeated Mao's dictum that the party must direct the gun, meaning clearly that it was the party in the army which was to control the gun. In the revolutionary army, all officers and noncommissioned officers and one third of the privates were members of the Chinese Communist Party. In Lin Piao's words: "The broad masses of cadres of our armed forces have continuously enhanced their party character," and thus "the party has been able to exercise its leadership over the troops." To strengthen this political role in the army, Lin Piao advocated conscientious study of the theories of Marxism-Leninism and the Thought of Mao Tse-tung.

In October 1960, the Maoization of the armed forces was organized under a resolution of the Military Affairs Committee.[12] "Living ideology" was emphasized for the political indoctrination of the troops. The Thought

[11]See Lin Piao, "Hold High the Red Banner of the Party's General Line and Chairman Mao Tse-tung's Thought and Advance in Big Strides," reprinted in *Current Background,* No. 596 (October 7, 1959), pp. 1–13.

[12]See J. Chester Cheng (ed.), *The Politics of the Chinese Red Army* (Stanford: Stanford University Press, 1966), pp. 67–68.

of Mao Tse-tung was to be thoroughly studied, and "all those teaching materials which are not in conformity with Mao Tse-tung's thought must be eliminated." The indoctrination was now expanded to nonparty members of the army as well as to the military party cadres. In fact, private soldiers, party members or not, were mobilized to check on the loyalty of officers, who might be inclined to side with the civil party leadership against Mao and Lin Piao. There was an element of revolution from below in this indoctrination campaign, in which private soldiers were given additional political authority in so-called "revolutionary army men's councils." This trend culminated, five years later, in the abolition of all insignia of rank and the removal of all status distinctions between officers and men.

The Great Proletarian Cultural Revolution

One last attempt was made by Mao to regain doctrinal authority within the party through the "Socialist education" movement between 1963 and 1965, which was defined as a class struggle between socialism and capitalism and an attack against "the capitalist roaders." But the effectiveness of this effort within the party apparatus remained doubtful. In the meantime, army officers, by now revolutionary paragons steeped in the Thought of Mao Tse-tung, were sent into party and government organizations, as well as industrial plants and the collectives, to propagate the Thought of Mao and, coincidentally, assert political control.

The results of these measures remained inconclusive. A new, more intensified indoctrination drive within the People's Liberation Army, and eventually among all sections of the population, got under way in 1964. As preparation for this move, Lin Piao published a selection of Mao's sayings in May 1964 under the title *Quotations from Chairman Mao Tse-tung,* and issued a revised edition to the army on August 1, 1965, the anniversary of its founding.[13] This was the little red book which spread over China and the world in numerous editions in all major languages, exceeding 350 million copies during the first three years of publication. It was given to every Chinese soldier as a "weapon" designed to speed the revolutionization and modernization of the military. It was the Thought of Mao—no longer the party—that commanded the gun. The *Quotations* contained simple excerpts from Mao's writings, homilies intelligible to the semi-literate, easily memorized slogans full of appeals to self-sacrifice and service. The study of these selected sayings was an exercise in memorization rather than intellectual analysis; and could, therefore, easily be directed to all age and educational levels of the population. The little red book became the main instrument of the cult of Mao, eventually spilling out from China to the rest of the world.

[13]See "Preface" of *Mao Chu-hsi yu-lu* (Quotations from Chairman Mao), edited and published by the General Political Department of the People's Liberation Army, August 1, 1965.

While the propagation of Mao's thought and the Maoist cult was being intensified through the army, the party countered with indirect attacks against Mao in the news media. By implication and insinuation, Mao was ridiculed, his infallibility questioned, and his attempt to place himself above the party challenged. In an historical play written at this time, the author chose the dismissal of a loyal Ming official to criticize Mao's dismissal of Marshal P'eng Teh-huai. A group of writers used satire in a series of essays to ridicule Mao's claims of omniscience, and Mao's attempt at image-building was undercut in many allusions drawn by more sophisticated writers.[14] Mao retaliated; and the first phase of the Great Proletarian Cultural Revolution was joined at a Central Committee meeting in September 1965.

The cultural component of this revolution consisted of a contest for control of the communications media that had dared to challenge Mao's ideological image-building through satire and criticism: in particular, for control of the Ministry of Propaganda, editorial positions on the newspapers, and over the publication of literature. The Communist Party Central Committee accepted the concept of a cultural revolution as proposed by Mao but attempted to deflect it, apparently willing to halt the attacks against Mao but not to sacrifice the critics. P'eng Chen, a leading member of the Politburo and Chairman of the powerful Peking Municipal Party Committee, who was appointed as chairman of a committee on the Cultural Revolution, drew up a report in February 1966 belittling the conflict between Mao and the news media as a theoretical debate.[15] Mao countered with his famous circular of May 16, 1966, celebrated by all Maoists as the directive signalling the start of the Great Proletarian Cultural Revolution.[16] To Mao, this was not a theoretical debate, but a fight against bourgeois scholar-tyrants in the party, "the various monsters and freaks who for many years have abounded in our press, radio, magazines, books, textbooks, platforms, works of literature, cinema, drama, ballads and stories, the fine arts, music, the dance, etc.;" the diatribe set the tone for the Cultural Revolution.

The fall of P'eng Chen, brought about with the assistance of the People's

---

[14]Wu Han's *Three-Family Village* (a series of essays written by an anti-Maoist intellectual group under the pen name Wu Nan-hsiang, an acronym of the names of three people, Wu Han, Ma Nan-tsung, and Fan Hsiang).

[15]"Wu-ch'an-chieh chi wen-hua ta-ke-ming wan-sui" (Long Live the Great Proletarian Cultural Revolution), editorial, *Hung-ch'i*, No. 8 (1966), pp. 4-11; K'ung Teh-liang, "Erh-yueh t'i-kang yu wu-yueh t'eng-chih" (The February Outline Report and May Circular), *Fei-ch'ing yueh-pao* (Chinese Communist Affairs Monthly) (Taipei), Vol. 10, No. 5 (July 1967), pp. 39-40; Jen Li-hsin, "February Outline Report is a Sinister Program for Bourgeosie Dictatorship," *Survey of China Mainland Press*, No. 3961 (June 16, 1967), pp. 3-7.

[16]"CCP Central Committee Circular," *Hung-ch'i*, No. 7 (1967), pp. 1-6; "A Great Historical Document," *ibid.*, pp. 7-11; *Selections from China Mainland Magazines*, No. 578 (June 5, 1967), pp. 6-9.

Liberation Army, initiated a contest for control of the news media that ran parallel to the political fight waged between Mao and the party leadership throughout the summer of 1966. The importance of victory on this "newspaper battleground" was emphasized by the Maoist press following the successful seizure of decisive positions in the news media by the Maoists. Under the new leadership, the press immediately began to propagate the Thought of Mao Tse-tung with unparalleled energy. According to an editorial in *Jen-min Jih-pao* (People's Daily),[17] Mao's thought was:

> . . . the sole correct guiding principle in the different stages of the Chinese revolution and a powerful ideological weapon of revolution in the hands of the oppressed people and oppressed nations against imperialism, modern revisionism and all reactionaries.

> Mao Tse-tung's thought is Marxism-Leninism inherited and developed with genius, creatively and in an all-round way in the era in which imperialism is approaching complete collapse and socialism is advancing to victory over all the world; it is the acme of Marxism-Leninism in the present era; it is living Marxism-Leninism at its highest. Comrade Mao Tse-tung is the greatest Marxist-Leninist of the present era.

This victory in the fight for control of the news media was thus quickly used by Mao to establish throughout the country, and without any chance of opposition, the image of himself as the source of all wisdom. Mao understood the importance of image-building and image destruction. In his words, "To overthrow a political power, it is always necessary first of all, to create public opinion, to do work in the ideological sphere." This was the task for the press, which henceforth carried on its mastheads the sayings of Mao and constantly ran his picture.

Mao was now ready for the political phase of the Cultural Revolution, which was initiated at a Central Committee meeting in August 1966 through the acceptance of his sixteen-point resolution on the Great Proletarian Cultural Revolution.[18] This session could not be considered a regular meeting of the Central Committee. Fewer than half the members were present, while the meeting was packed by Maoist supporters from outside the committee and pressured by Lin Piao's military forces. The sixteen-point resolution was to be the guiding directive of the Cultural Revolution, which was described as a class struggle against "the handful of ultra-reactionary bourgeois rightists and counter-revolutionary revisionists" who had opposed the Thought of Mao Tse-tung. It was a re-

[17]*Jen-min Jih-pao* (Peking), July 1, 1966, reprinted in *Peking Review,* Vol. 9, No. 27, of the same day, p. 5.

[18]For text, see "Declaration of the CCP Central Committee concerning the Great Proletarian Cultural Revolution," adopted on August 8, 1966, *Peking Review,* Vol. 9, No. 33 (August 12, 1966), pp. 6-11.

volution by "the masses," not within the party, and the masses were to maintain final control. Mao's thought was to be the guide for action by the masses; the party cadres must become "pupils" and "learn from the masses." The works of Mao selected for this educational process consisted mainly of procedural guidelines stated in broad terms, and contained little theoretical substance.

The sixteen-point declaration was the first in a series of directives that were to determine the course of the Cultural Revolution over the coming years. These directives were not specific; in fact, the more flexible and vague their terms, the easier it was to shift position, to retreat where necessary, or to advance against the party structure. It was also easier to impress the young, who were to be the shock troops of the revolution, with vague, high-sounding appeals and flattery, and easier to blame them when things went wrong. It was very simple to justify action in the name of Mao; it was equally simple to condemn it. The political turmoil of the Cultural Revolution, in which everyone claimed to be for Mao and accused everyone else of being against him, was magnified by this ambiguity. Mao called for support of the "left," but did not define the left. The "far left" was accused of being a concealed "right." Infighting between revolutionaries who accused each other of false Maoism was condemned as "factionalism," but those chosen by the Maoist center were supported in their factional attack against others. Party cadres were the targets of attack, but those willing to defect to Maoism were accepted because their expertise was needed. They were termed "revolutionary cadres," to be helped and emancipated; but if these cadres appeared to obtain too much influence, they were in turn attacked as the "evil wind of restoration." Mao's authority must triumph, but with this authority one had to accept Mao's concept of revolution.

The first group to be brought under Mao's ideological spell were the high school and college students, who as Red Guards were to be the shock troops of the revolution. The hard core of the Red Guards came from among the discontented and the misfits in the schools: ill-prepared and poorly qualified children from families of impoverished social background, accepted for their social origin rather than their ability. Many of them had had difficulties with their studies and examinations; they hated their teachers and were grimly jealous of their more gifted classmates. In June 1966, Mao unleashed the students by his directive temporarily suspending admission to higher schools and promising further proletarianization of education. In the fall of 1966, the universities remained closed, and the students were told that as the "small generals of the revolution," they were to attack the old order and usher in the revolutionary future. In big-character wall posters and great debates in the schools, they first attacked academic authority, physically abused many of their teachers and administrators, and brought about their purge. They "immediately organized, lifted high the picture of Chairman Mao and the sayings of Chairman Mao, beat drums and sang revolutionary songs." The pro-Mao Red Guards were gathered mainly from families of the five "proper" social backgrounds: the workers, peasants, revolutionary cadres, the army, and revolutionary martyrs. They bitterly opposed students from other social backgrounds, especially from the families of the Communist elite; but even these social pariahs might expiate themselves if they "tore out their guts," repudiated their family background, and revolutionized themselves.

These Red Guards, as they were by now officially called, were sent on a rampage in the cities to change street signs, break into middle class houses, loot, smash furniture, and attack passers-by in the streets who in dress and demeanor attracted their hostility. Then they were sent out to the provinces to assault the "small clique of capitalist roaders in power" in the party. In preparation, they were gathered together for a series of mass rallies in Peking between August and November 1966. Some eleven million Red Guards saw their leader, Mao Tse-tung, listened to speeches by Lin Piao, Chou En-lai, and others, and were provoked into the hysteria which was to propel them on their work of revolution throughout the country.

From the outset, the Red Guards appeared as a front for the army, which organized their units and rallies, arranged their marching orders, and transported them to the provinces, where they attacked and tore down the party and government structure under Mao's directives. These youngsters were not qualified, however, to replace the authorities they had assaulted; and the phase of the Red Guards, which lasted from August 1966 to the end of the year, was followed by the "seizure of power" beginning in January 1967. For this, the Maoist left was expanded into the "revolutionary rebel" organizations, incorporating some Red Guards. The revolutionary rebels were basically recruited, with the help of the military, from dissatisfied elements in the lower and middle levels of government offices, the communes, factories, and other agencies who responded to Mao's appeal to seize power and introduce a radical course for the future. This was "the revolutionary left" of Mao's utopian concept. They were, in fact, a mixed group of revolutionary opportunists, an extra-party force, who were now supposed to form a new political structure to fill the void created by the collapse of the two hierarchies of the party and government systems.

The Maoist concept of direct rule by the masses was based on the model of the Paris Commune of 1871. This model was mentioned in Maoist literature in early 1966, and was proclaimed as the basis of the future Chinese system in the sixteen-point declaration of August 1966. A few attempts were made in January and February 1967 to introduce such communes, staffed by Mao's revolutionary rebels, in Shanghai, Manchuria, Peking, and several other places. These communes were meant to represent rule by the "masses," the Maoist masses, to whom the rebel leaders could refer. The masses theoretically retained control and the right of recall over their representatives in the communes. This utopian Maoist scheme proved highly impractical for the actual management of affairs, and was obviously unacceptable to the military, on whose support Mao depended. Instead, an attempt was made through the so-called "three-in-one combination" to combine the revolutionary rebels, the revolutionary cadres (who provided necessary expertise), and the People's Liberation Army, the real source of power, into a new political structure, the so-called "revolutionary committees." The revolutionary committees, established in lieu of the Paris communes, were actually a compromise of Mao's original concept and handed real power to the military in the new political system emerging from Mao's Cultural Revolution.

But the Maoist element, the revolutionary rebels, continued to cause difficulties. The many competing Maoist groups, all claiming to be the revolutionary left, organized against each other with quasi-military forces and carried on small-scale warfare in the provinces, backed frequently by regular army units. An attempt to overcome this internecine warfare by forcing the rival groups into "great alliances" failed. In July 1968, Mao had to abandon his support of the rebels and permit the formation of a new force by the army, called "the workers and peasants Mao Thought propaganda teams." These teams, consisting of the least educated, largely illiterate elements of the population, were now sent into the schools with army backing to "teach the teachers," and into the factories, communes, and offices to reorganize and exercise control. They were claimed to be the new proletarian force of Chairman Mao. In fact, they were the crudest tool of direct, military power.

What of the Future?

The system that emerged was Maoist in leadership, military in structure. The Communist Party, which had disintegrated under the impact of the Cultural Revolution, was to be revamped into a Maoist party, based on loyalty to the leader cult of Mao. Anyone for Mao was a proletarian; anyone against him was a capitalist roader and revisionist. The draft of a new party constitution, published in October 1968 and subsequently adopted at the Ninth Party Congress in April 1969,[19] enshrined the preeminent role of Mao Tse-tung and of Lin Piao as Mao's constitutionally recognized successor. Mao's utopian, revolutionary program was reaffirmed; a new leap was in the making.

[19]For the text of the constitution, see "The Constitution of the Communist Party of China," *Peking Review,* Vol. 12, No. 18 (April 30, 1969), pp. 36–39.

What Mao has been striving for is to combine into one system the two opposite forms of totalitarianism, Marxist-Leninist communism and the leader cult. To what degree the present military rule of China represents this concept is debatable. Even more doubtful is the future. Lin Piao has been Mao's loyal paladin, his "closest comrade in arms," and he has been promised the inheritance of the charismatic mantle. To date, however, no leader cult has survived its founder. It is hard to believe that the cult of Mao, with its ruthless and grotesque manipulation of the minds of men, can long prevail.[20] What then? A military leadership under Mao's heir apparent, Lin Piao, may have enough force to continue in power for a brief span of years. But even that appears doubtful. There are other military leaders conceivably strong enough to step forward, but under what standard? They may have enough force at their command to make a break with the Maoist past and follow what other concepts they may believe in. A return to Marxism-Leninism, a revival of a true indigenous nationalism, a synthesis of new beliefs—none is precluded. But will the military remain united? A regional decentralization has already taken place. Will there be disintegration, civil war? Will any force be strong enough to keep together a nation shaken by such vast and bitter internal conflict? All we know is that large groups of people have been banished and alienated, that millions have been moved from the cities to the countryside, and that a revolutionary situation exists. Who knows what ideas and values are waiting below the frozen concepts of Maoist doctrine in a country with as rich an intellectual past as China?

[20]Since the summer of 1969, the Mao cult appears to have declined. There is no more mention in the Chinese Communist press of the daily quasi-religious ceremonies before the picture of the leader. There are no more directives by Mao; directives are issued in the name of the Central Committee of the party rather than in the name of the leader. While the Thought of Mao is still claimed to be the source of all truth, Mao himself is no longer referred to as frequently as in the heyday of the Cultural Revolution.

Chapter Three

Problems of Administration and Control

L. LaDany

The Problem

In what follows, we shall deal with the history of administration (that is, the ways and means of governing) in the Chinese People's Republic less as a sequence of events than as a series of problems posed by the task of administering so vast a country.

What are the elements that keep a country together? How much spontaneous cooperation from the governed must be presupposed? These are fundamental questions of political science. In China, as in all Asian countries, such questions are immensely complicated by the drastic break in tradition that these countries have experienced. This break was caused by the irruption of modern Western ideas of government. The shock of the encounter with that strange foreign world and its ideas has not yet been fully absorbed anywhere, not even in Japan. There is, however, a great difference between the Chinese and Japanese reactions. Historically, Japan has shown the ability to absorb foreign elements eclectically, whereas the Chinese temperament demands a complete, total, comprehensive solution; it demands, in short, a system.

Such a system persisted throughout the long history of imperial China. As dynasty followed dynasty, each formulated its own legal code; and they were admirable legal codes that gave clarity and stability to political and social life. Yet every new code was but a further development, an improvement, of a traditional system. This stability of rule was supported by the body of consciously or subconsciously adopted forms of behaviour that is commonly called the Confucianist system of government. It was this system that was shattered by the irruption of Western political ideas. China regarded the armed interference of Western countries as a humiliation, not so much because it was foreign as because it appeared to be directed by a superior civilization. China had lived for centuries under foreign rulers without showing much resentment. The rulers might be foreigners, but they were foreigners to whom the Chinese felt superior.

45

The Chinese system was not challenged by them. But the coming of the West was different.

The shock was great. Ever since the T'ai-p'ing rebellion in the middle of the nineteenth century, China has been looking for a new system, adequate to the demands of modern times. Early in this century, the imperial system was overthrown and political development turned away from the ancient social ethics. Western constitutions and legal codes were copied and changed in rapid succession. Not until after years of turmoil did a new government emerge, the Nationalist government with its seat in Nanking.

The establishment of this government was itself the result of a deep ideological clash, a non-pragmatic process typical of the Chinese temperament. The Bolshevik revolution in Russia had exercised its fascination on the Chinese elite, and the Nationalists invited Russian advisers to help in the modernization of the country's political institutions. Later, however, they turned against their tutors to assert their own essential Chineseness. The doctrine adopted as the foundation upon which to build a new state was laid down in the writings of Sun Yat-sen, who was considered the father of the republic. There followed ten years of prosperity, years rich with the promise of stability. But from the beginning, this advance was harassed by the Communists from their armed rural bases; and it was interrupted in 1937 by the Sino-Japanese War. After the war, the Nationalist government was visibly suffering from battle fatigue. Communism emerged as a force with fresh energy and with men ostensibly dedicated to dealing with the vast problems confronting the country. The Communists were not unwelcome, but the bulk of the people received them with indifference.

For centuries, the people of China took little interest in government. No doubt the imperial system had its overall prominence in the scheme of things, but the *yamen* (or government office) and all that it represented was considered an inevitable, necessary evil. The ordinary Chinese had recourse to it, or brought a case to court, only as a last resort. This indifference to politics has now changed. The beginning of the century witnessed an effervescence of new political ideas; and, later, the Japanese War inspired a wave of patriotism. The Communists came to power supported by young soldiers recruited during that war. After 1949, there was not much room left for youthful enthusiasm. But when, during the Great Proletarian Cultural Revolution, the iron discipline cracked, mass organizations of young people took shape spontaneously, and the authorities in Peking found them hard to control. In Soviet Russia, changes in leadership take place without the participation, without even the knowledge, of the ordinary man. Not so in China today. There is here a new element, an important new factor that points toward the future.

Contemporary China is a troubled country that has not yet found her new identity. This is the lesson we learn from the history of the last twenty years. The Communists took a system of political rule from a foreign country and tried to make it Chinese. But in the effort China found herself struggling with her own national characteristics, accepting some new concepts, rejecting others; she has combined extraordinary fickleness and mutability with astonishing forces making for stability. This tendency to stability is not, however, based on a tacit consensus of the people, not even on a lasting consensus among the leaders. The new doctrine, the new system of government, has not yet been found.

Foreign Elements

Marxism offered itself as an answer to the subconscious Chinese aspiration for a system. The most ardent discussions of Marxism took place in the 1920s, more than twenty years before the entry of the People's Liberation Army into Peking. Before 1949, the Communist Party already ruled vast areas of China. It had its own local governments, had adopted the necessary administrative legislation, and introduced reforms. Nevertheless, when the moment came to take over the whole country, the Communists had to rely heavily on the assistance of foreigners, the Soviet Union. Soon the Russian presence was felt everywhere. There were teams of Russians in the ministries. The economy and even the legal system were adjusted to the Soviet model. Mao said that China was leaning to one side, the side of the Soviet Union.

Two elements of the system imported from Russia are worthy of special consideration. One is the mechanism for the control of people—something that may be called a police system, though there was more to it than mere police work. The other is the legislative edifice, beginning with the constitution of the state.

STALINIST CONTROL. It was not easy to establish control over so vast a population, but it was accomplished with great skill. Let us look at this from a particular angle, namely, what it meant in the life of the ordinary citizen.

When the troops of the People's Liberation Army marched into the cities in 1949, the population watched them in a wait-and-see mood. At first, the Communist troops were civil and restrained. They established order and gave an impression of impeccable honesty. The new regime had many points of appeal. Gradually, however, the new order began to show another face. It turned out to be a system that penetrated into every corner of human life. This was the exact opposite of the millenary Confucianist rule, which had rested on broad principles of government and an all-pervading ethical doctrine, but had not sought to interfere in the life of the individual—with his family and family clans, business life and normal social activities. Confucianism was not a police system. Marxism in its Russian Stalinist form was.

It took the Chinese population some years to realize fully what had happened. Moreover, the attention of the new rulers was directed not only to acts, but to thoughts and feelings as well. Every individual was involved and became a potential victim of a system to which no private activity was a matter of indifference. Gradually a whole spider's web was woven around the individual person; there was no way out.

The most obvious form of this was the presence of the police. They were everywhere. In the cities, there was a police station every few blocks. The police paid visits to private homes in order to "help," so they said. (This use of the word "help" was not invented in China; it was a gift from Russia. The word is dreaded throughout the Communist world, and today not least in China.) When the public authorities came to "help" you in your private affairs, they might be polite in the beginning—traditional Chinese courtesy made that inevitable—but there was no knowing how the matter would end. You might be asked why you were corresponding with someone abroad, or whether you really needed to subscribe to a newspaper from another region of China, and what your real motives were for doing so. The point they were always driving at was, were you pleased with the present regime, or were you not? If you were not pleased, you might be an opponent; and if you were an opponent, you might be what they called a counter-revolutionary. In the end, you might find yourself confronted with what were termed the weapons of dictatorship. And the principal weapon of dictatorship, odd as it may sound, was called the law.

The word law, like so many words in the Chinese People's Republic, has received a meaning entirely different from what it had in pre-Communist days. Very few Chinese, in the first years of the new regime, read Mao's booklet *On the People's Democratic Dictatorship,* published in 1949, which exposed with remarkable clarity what law now meant.[1] As the newspapers kept repeating, law and the courts were the weapons of dictatorship.

If you found yourself in court accused of some illegal action or thought, the only thing expected was a plea of guilty. In this system of legal thought, once you were accused your crime had already been proved, and denial was no more than a sign of contumacy.

If you landed in prison, you naturally wanted to get out. You were told that if you had "merits," your sentence might be shortened or you might even be released. To acquire merits meant accusing others, not only people outside but those in prison as well. People with prison experience have described brutal scenes: not brutalities committed by the wardens, but in the cell block where prisoners often manhandled their cellmates in order

[1]*Selected Works,* Vol. 4.

to force them to confess in the naive belief that by this means they might earn "merits" and a way out of prison. Prisoners were rarely treated with physical brutality by those in authority. Indeed, they were told that prison and hard labor would create a new man and reform his thoughts as well. This was the Soviet system of conditioned reflex training applied with surpassing skill. The Western world has termed it "brain-washing."

Confrontation with the law contained a strong element of uncertainty. A victim might have been sentenced to forced labor and sent to a factory or a farm managed by the security forces. At the end of his term, the state had discretionary power to "retain" the former convict in the same factory or farm, although he was now technically a free man. He would find that his *ch'eng-fen* had not changed. The term *ch'eng-fen* designates the political category a man belongs to in society. It is marked down in his police dossier. The basic point is what kind of family he comes from: proletarian, bourgeois, capitalist, or landlord. His past record appears there, too— especially whether he has ever written or said anything, even privately, which reflects disbelief or doubt in the regime.

As an example, there is the story of a university student in Chungshan University, Canton. At a meeting for scrutinizing student thoughts, another student reported that this young man had once said that Mao Tse-tung was an ordinary mortal human being. This was in 1964. He was thereupon subjected to what is called an accusation meeting, at which all are called upon to condemn the accused. Ultimately the student was expelled from the university. This went down in his dossier, and he will never get into another university. He was lucky to fare no worse.

As can be seen, the difference between the control of one's life in prison or a labor camp, and the control exercised over an individual's life on the outside, is only a matter of degree. Fundamentally, the status of the individual is the same in both situations. Everybody took part in Stalinist "criticism and self-criticism," public meetings at which all must expose not only their own faults, but also the faults of their friends and colleagues, and often of members of their own family as well. This kind of criticism, known in China as *cheng-feng* campaigns, differed hardly at all from criticism and self-criticism as practiced in Soviet Russia in the Stalin period. Nothing of this is laid down in the legislation of the Chinese People's Republic, nor is it visible to the foreign visitor. But it is the system that controls life in China today.

Pre-Cultural Revolution China was not a police state in the sense that the police controlled the behavior of people. The whole system was elaborated in such a way that everyone seemed to control everyone else. As a child, you were a young pioneer. A few years later, you were a member of the youth corps, the Chinese version of the Komsomol. In the factory, there was the trade union, which had nothing in common with trade unions in other parts of the world except the name. Your wife was on the neighborhood street committee which, under the guidance of the local police station, had wide discretionary powers and kept an eye on the whole life of your family, even the mail you received and the guests who visited you. There was (and still is) a food rationing system, introduced in 1953, which required an identity card; this, in turn, determined your place of residence. And so on. All this created in the individual a feeling of utter dependence.

This sophisticated system of control was borrowed from the Soviet experience. The system still stands; but since the Cultural Revolution, the controlling bodies are no longer the same. The police have been taken over by the army; trade unions are no more; the street committees still exist; and a beginning has been made in the re-establishment of the youth corps, which was wiped out by the Cultural Revolution.

THE LEGAL SYSTEM. A few years after its establishment, the Communist regime introduced a facsimile of the Russian legal system: the Stalinist constitution, introduced in 1954, the regulations on the organization of courts, and so on. This was welcomed by the middle classes, since it at least meant settled legal norms of some kind and a fixed mode of procedure. It seemed that the first punitive campaigns were over at last, and that a more orderly pattern of life would now follow. The first People's Congress convened in 1954. Elections followed the Russian model, and the whole procedure was kept under the strict control of the Chinese Communist Party. The only deviation from Soviet practice was that some small non-Communist political parties were allowed to linger on; these acted not as an opposition, but as a kind of window dressing for the regime.

This legal system had a short, precarious existence. A "revolt" of the intellectuals in 1957 against the excesses of Communist rule was followed by a repression manifested in the establishment of a new type of forced labor, by the introduction of the communes and the adverse reaction to them among the people and within the party leadership itself. From 1957 on, constitutional niceties were forgotten. The Communist Party took the administration directly into its own hands, and the trend towards legality, even Stalinist legality, came to an end. Direct rule by the party lasted until 1966, when the party machine itself perished; thereafter, in the spring of 1967, the dominant role was taken over by the army.

The Great Proletarian Cultural Revolution made clear how deeply the institutions of the Stalinist police system had penetrated. Forced labor camps became one of the central issues of the Cultural Revolution. Many of those under forced labor seized their opportunity in the general confusion and joined the Maoist "rebels." The police and security organs that had formerly guarded them disintegrated. Ultimately, Peking issued orders to the army to restore order: those under forced labor were not to be al-

lowed to cause trouble. At the end of 1968, new *ad hoc* organs were set up
to keep these social outcasts under control; and many former members of
the Communist Party were also condemned. How deeply rooted the idea of
forced labor had become was shown by the fact that between 1967 and
1968, rival mass organizations organized their own labor camps for their
enemies. These organizations were composed of young people who had
grown up under the Communist regime.

WESTERN POLITICAL IDEAS. Of the two elements of political life borrowed from Soviet Russia, one, police methods, persisted, and the other,
legality, vanished. The past few years, however, have revealed that another
tradition of foreign ideas was still alive—the Western political tradition of
freedom and democracy. Our knowledge of the power and range of this
tradition is incomplete, but what we know is highly significant. After
twenty years of the Communist regime and ten years of direct party rule,
in the very midst of the turbulence of the Cultural Revolution, groups of
young people issued manifestos and published political programs demanding a new political system for China. In 1967, certain groups called for the
introduction of universal suffrage. In the second half of 1968, provincial
news broadcasts revealed that illegal organizations were proclaiming that
the division of the population into Marxist and Maoist categories was futile.
All were equal, they held, and they demanded that government organs
should be elected by general election. Such an election was actually held
in a certain region of Chekiang Province. The army stepped in, of course,
and put an end to this unseemly display of democracy.

It was highly significant that this kind of thing should happen, not only
because it showed disillusionment with the present system, but also—and
this is what interests us here—because it showed that there are political
currents other than those that came from the Soviet Union. For many
people, the word "democracy" still has a meaning quite different from that
given it in such Communist terms as "democratic dictatorship" and "democratic centralism." The explicit demand for, and the attempt to introduce,
universal suffrage under the most difficult conditions of political persecution is testimony to a complex situation. No one can measure public
opinion in mainland China today; but such facts show that Western political ideas are not dead.

Chinese Elements

China will never be able to take a foreign political system and apply it
mechanically. This is not merely a matter of national pride. The innate
intellectualism of the Chinese temperament demands a comprehensive
view of man's life and his place in the social structure. Throughout the
long course of history, China never found it necessary to import political

institutions from abroad. Then came the shock of the nineteenth and early twentieth centuries. For the first time, China had to be pupil, not teacher; this caused a shock from which the country has not yet recovered.

REJECTION OF OLD PATTERNS. At the turn of the century, the great political debate — to which the names of K'ang Yu-wei, Liang Ch'i-ch'ao, and Sun Yat-sen are attached[2] — turned on the retention or rejection of fundamental traditional institutions, among them the imperial throne. The radical view represented by Sun Yat-sen prevailed. In the beginning of this century, societies were formed for the overthrow of the imperial system, and many publications appeared pleading for radical change. Mao Tse-tung grew up in the provincial town of Changsha surrounded by this revolutionary atmosphere. After the Bolshevik revolution, the Russian way had much appeal as a possible answer for China. But it would have been hard, perhaps impossible, to reject the old Chinese system completely. The result was a paradoxical mixture of old and new.

Mao turned against the old. In the Red Army and throughout the history of the Chinese Communist Party, there has been a continuous effort to reject everything that resembled the old rule of the mandarins, the old society in which Mao had grown up. Mao carried in his heart an abiding hatred of the immemorial past. He wanted to create a new China. In the early Red Army, and later under the People's Republic, he carried on an implacable fight against "officialdom." The introduction into the army of the Russian system of ranks, with its marshals and generals, its clear distinctions between officers and other ranks, and its rigid external discipline, was deeply resented. In the later 1950s, this system was widely discussed in China, and there was evident longing for the spirit of the old Red Army. This culminated, in January 1965, in the abolition of the insignia of rank. Again, whenever Mao got the upper hand politically, he insisted that officials should share in the manual labor of ordinary workers and peasants. This was a part of the same idealism, although it also had the practical purpose of ensuring that "no tree should grow to heaven."

It is not clear, however, that all this was as new or as revolutionary as it may have sounded. Along with the fraternization and spirit of equality, there also existed a sharp distinction between the rulers and the ruled. The title of cadre, *kanpu,* put a person into a different class. He was in command even if only in a small workshop. In the army, the distinctions remained even after the insignia of rank had been done away with. Several

[2]K'ang Yu-wei advocated reforms that combined Western knowledge and constitutional government with the best of traditional Chinese culture. Liang Ch'i-ch'ao, a student of K'ang Yu-wei, at first supported the concept of reform within the traditional context of China. In his middle years, he shifted to promoting Westernization and scientific knowledge more vigorously. But after World War I, he came to reject Westernization as too materialist, and sought a return to traditional Chinese values.

stories were published in the Peking press about higher officers going to live for a while with ordinary soldiers, and finding it impossible to avoid the respectful treatment due their rank. Moreover, a certain simple familiarity was never lacking in traditional Chinese society. The Chinese language, unlike Japanese, makes no difference between high and low. Everybody was called *hsien-sheng*—Mr. or Sir—until the day came when everyone was to be called "Comrade."

The Communist Party introduced new names and forms. It did not change the traditional social relations between rulers and ruled, and the party itself became the new mandarin class. Another traditional characteristic persisted: the Chinese sense of dignity. The Chinese dignity is not the pseudo-dignity of haughtiness or ostentatious superiority. It is the opposite of this, a modest consciousness of being somebody, the unassuming reserve of a man who knows how to behave, an attitude that gave scholarly poise to the old mandarins even in the era of imperial decay. This dignity persisted, very perceptibly, under the new system. It invested the administration with an air of imperturbable stability. The leaders of the country looked dignified. Even when they were locked in internal strife, they appeared united. Until the Cultural Revolution, the press never contradicted one day what it had said the day before. No Chinese leader would take off his shoes in public as Khrushchev did. The private life of the leaders was ignored. No one was ever reported ill; sickness was mentioned only in obituaries. Wives never appeared at public functions, except for those who were themselves veterans of the Communist movement.

When all this changed, in the early 1960s, it was a sure sign of decay. The Cultural Revolution destroyed this solemnity, revealing dirty personal stories, even introducing an abusive, vulgar language into the official press. Here was convincing proof of wide cracks in the Communist political structure.

TWO BLUNDERS. The Communist Party made two blunders in dealing with its own people. One was the effort to put an end to "face." The other was the appalling lack of judgment shown in using the means of persuasion.

The Communist Party purposely set about destroying the traditional "face" complex. In China, public criticism is felt to be deeply shameful; it wounds to the depths of self-respect and personal dignity. Under the Communist regime, public criticism and public revelations of the most intimate details of life have been commonplace. To use this method, to apply this Stalinist medicine to China, was a major psychological error; and it remained ineffective. People who have had to take part in such meetings maintain that the participants were usually very careful about what they did and did not say. They said only what they knew they had to say, mostly repeating accusations put forward by the authorities. It would require a special study to answer the question whether this method has changed or even significantly modified Chinese character and social behaviour. The answer probably would be negative. The only certain result was to foster dissimulation. Even in the old China, it was not unknown for men to bow to the authorities, to say what they wanted to hear, to use words not as instruments for expressing thoughts but as weapons for self-defense in face of an overwhelming power. The present system, in which wrong words may bring disaster to oneself and to one's family, has produced dissimulation on a gigantic scale. In short, this campaign against tradition backfired. The attempt to destroy face, which is best described as a sense of honor, instead produced pretence and hypocrisy.

The second major blunder was the misjudgment of Chinese temperament shown in prescribing a dosage of political propaganda far beyond what the patient could absorb. The Chinese are more inclined to accept a doctrine if it is proposed as a vague possibility than if it is presented as an absolute must. It is perhaps a fair generalization to say that intellectual bullying inclines the Chinese temperament to skepticism, and that internal disbelief grows in proportion to the intensity of insistence. The Communists seemed not to know this. Such a mistake would have been understandable if it had been committed by a foreign ruler. But the present regime is Chinese. The Communists had a fantastic belief in the effectiveness of their doctrine. It took them by surprise when, in 1957, universities held mass meetings demanding that the party committees should quit the schools. The reaction of the party leadership was violent: the Communist Party took over the direct administration of the country.

The Cultural Revolution destroyed what little had been accomplished by propaganda in the past. Liu, the respected master of Marxist orthodoxy, was rolled in the mud. The licentious private lives of various party leaders were exposed to the public gaze. Soviet communism was denounced as evil. No new doctrine was put in place of the old, except the worship of Mao, the old man now called "the sun in our hearts." Self-sacrifice and total subjection are demanded in a propaganda that has become more repetitious and oppressive than ever before. The propagandist's law of diminishing returns has not been learned.

By nature, the Chinese people are not difficult to govern. Their patience and endurance are proverbial. They are not prone to engage in rash actions when no worthwhile object is clearly in view. They can hide their feelings without effort. The voices of discontent in 1957, and the defiance of all authority in 1967 and 1968, were altogether exceptional, clear evidence of deep disenchantment. The Communists did not succeed in adapting the methods learned from Russia to the Chinese way of thinking. Now, when Russia has become the enemy, the old Soviet ideals are still being pursued by the Communist regime in China.

Stability and Mobility

Traditional Chinese legal thought distinguishes *jen-chih* from *fa-chih,* rule by man from rule by law. Under *jen-chih,* the human personality of the ruler comes into play, and there is an admixture of what English law calls equity; *fa-chih* is a system of objective regulations, less affected by humanitarian considerations.

The quality of Communist rule over the past twenty years cannot be called *fa-chih.* The country has been ruled not by a body of laws, but by the ever-changing whims of the Communist Party. Ten years ago, people in the Ministry of Justice (which was about to be suppressed) complained: "Today, there is no law; there is only policy."[3] The party believed that "it would be a great mistake to follow a procedure of set, permanent, unchanging rules that would hinder the revolutionary struggle."[4] Constantly changing rules, circulars, executive orders, and instructions were issued, although there were few legislative acts in the proper sense of the word. But neither can it be said, on the other hand, that the country was ruled by *jen-chih,* the rule of man; for this term implies equity and kindness and a deep sense of justice. The new system will not fit into either of the old categories.

In fact, the country has been ruled by shock treatment, by the tremors produced by recurrent political campaigns. This started with the land reform in which the landlords — a term that was broadened to include all enemies or potential enemies of the new regime — were exterminated by organized mass lynching. The campaign against the landlords began before 1949 in the earlier conquered areas, and ended everywhere in 1952.

Simultaneously from 1949 onwards, a campaign for the "suppression of counter-revolutionaries" raged throughout the country. This was carried out quite openly, with public executions in cities and villages. Next came the anti-corruption campaigns, which introduced stricter control over private businessmen. When everything appeared to have settled down at last, and a new constitution was being introduced, there came the purge of Kao Kang; the Communist Party leader in Manchuria. Collectivization of the land was next, although not in the form of a political campaign. It was accompanied, however, by a campaign in the cities called *su-fan,* the "purge of the opposition." Simultaneously, private businesses were taken away from their owners. This was carried out in a gruesome series of well-organized "joyful processions," with the dispossessed owners marching through the streets chanting that they had given their hearts to the party.

[3]*Jen-min Jih-pao,* September 20, 1957.
[4]*China News Analysis,* No. 284 (July 10, 1959).

A period of relaxation was followed by a new and violent campaign in 1957 and 1958, directed mainly against those—many of them government officials—who had voiced their discontent during a short-lived period of free speech in the spring of 1957. Masses of people were once again sent off to forced labor. On the countryside, the collectives had barely been consolidated when Mao suddenly introduced the commune. Emergency party meetings followed one another. In 1959, a year after the introduction of the commune, came the great confrontation within the leadership and the dismissal of the Minister of Defense, P'eng Teh-huai, the legendary military companion of Mao. From that time on, as we now can see, the party leadership was deeply divided. This friction led ultimately to the final break-up in the Great Proletarian Cultural Revolution.

In spite of these hectic campaigns, a certain stability of government was evident. This stability did not manifest itself in set laws and a set system. It had two aspects, the cohesion of the leadership and the maintenance of the same men in the same jobs for many years. Apart from the purge of Kao Kang, there were few changes and no defections at the top. The membership of the Communist Party Central Committee remained stable. There were some changes in the government; but when changing posts, leading party members in the government usually remained in the same type of work. This was a notable feature of the government, and it contributed greatly to stability.

There was less stability among regional administrators, whether in the party or in the government; but the system was largely centralized, and it was the central authorities who counted. This cohesiveness and stability could not have been achieved without an imposing central personality who could keep together men who (as we now know) were diametrically opposed to one another. The stability lasted for ten years. Then internal strife began; and ultimately, in 1966, the Cultural Revolution put an end to the cohesiveness of the group of men who had governed China for seventeen years.

A New Period Begins

The Cultural Revolution raised the most serious questions about the nature of Communist rule in mainland China. It would be naive to accept the "revelations" now being publicized by the new leaders in an effort to explain the past. According to these, not only Liu Shao-ch'i but the whole machinery of the party disobeyed and sabotaged the always correct directives of Chairman Mao. The impression is deliberately fostered that only now are the ideas of Mao being put into practice. This can hardly correspond to reality.

It appears rather that Mao's prestige as a leader was always overwhelming. He was the focus of unity and so much the master of the situation that he could afford to keep even his personal adversaries, men like Li Li-san,[5] in leadership positions. Even the case of Kao Kang may well have meant a strengthening of Mao's power. During the last years of Stalin's life, Kao Kang was the governor of Manchuria. It was there that the Russians first introduced their methods into China, to be extended to the whole country after a period of trial; and this must have been a humiliating prospect for Peking and for Mao.

On the other hand, Mao's visionary ideas were not always accepted promptly. His position had some similarity to that of General DeGaulle, who used to complain that his ideas were not understood by his bureaucrat subordinates. Mao was a real leader who, on meeting obstacles, not of opposition but of a lack of comprehension, knew how to wait until by a sudden stroke he could introduce what he wanted. The documents of Communist Party meetings reveal that this often happened, ever since the Yenan period. The classic examples are the collectivization of the land in 1955, and the much more brutal communization of the land three years later. Both were Mao's personal acts and both were promptly executed throughout the country. It was only after the economic collapse that followed the communes and the Great Leap, that (according to all signs) his prestige was first challenged. But even P'eng Teh-huai, dismissed in 1959, did not start a palace revolt and probably could not have done so. He retired to a minor job in the provinces and disappeared from notice. The same happened to other party leaders who vanished from the public eye after 1959.

In the early 1960s, Mao's prestige certainly declined and his orders were more and more sabotaged or quietly modified. Nevertheless, when he introduced a stern policy once more, after years of relaxation, it was promptly implemented. At the beginning of 1963, the freezing of cultural liberties began, and the first steps were taken to reimpose discipline on the national economy. Whether Mao wanted these things done at a more rapid pace is anybody's guess. His utterances in 1963 and the following years, which reflected deep dissatisfaction, particularly with the leaders of culture and propaganda in the party, were only disclosed during the Cultural Revolution and their real meaning cannot be reconstituted.

Meanwhile, another factor entered the situation: the transition of leadership, the announcement that the revolution was looking for successors. With this came the gradual emergence of a new center of power

[5]Li Li-san was a founding member of the Young China Communist Party in France; and by 1928, he was the most powerful member of the Politburo. He was in Russia during the period 1930 to 1949, and then returned to China to serve in the Chinese labor movement.

on the political scene, the army—or to be more precise, not the army as such but the political body ruling the army, the party organization within the People's Liberation Army. Since the time when Lin Piao replaced P'eng Teh-huai, the party in the army has been built into a body separate from the civilian Communist Party. In 1961, a special selection from the writings of Mao was published for use in the armed forces only. In response, Liu's austere Marxist booklet, *How To Be A Good Communist,* first published in 1939, was republished in 1962 with some modifications.[6] In 1964, the nation—which meant the civilian party machine—was called upon to take the army as a model. Members of the army's organizations began to infiltrate the civilian party. The latter resisted, and a great internal conflict arose. What actually sparked off the conflict of the Cultural Revolution, which led to the abolition of the whole civilian party machine, but left intact the party machine within the People's Liberation Army, is still a secret of recent history.

With this, a new period in the history of Communist China began. At the end in 1957, the party took the civil administration into its own hands. Now it is the army that leads and imprints its image on the whole nation, attempting to rebuild the nation on a military model. An attempt is being made to form workers in the factories and peasants in the villages into units in exact imitation of the military. For a time, the name of Chairman Mao was on everyone's lips. Even in the villages, people were encouraged to gather in the morning in front of Mao's picture "to ask for inspiration," and "to report" to the Master in the evening. Before meals, everyone was reminded that all good things came from Chairman Mao. The strange cult of the old man was quasi-religious. Meanwhile, several provinces were enthusiastically building gigantic monuments to Mao. This made it the more startling when, after the Ninth Party Congress in April 1969, all this stopped. Since then, not a word has been heard about the half-completed Mao monuments in the provincial cities of China.

Mao appears to be the master, but the genuine features of the old Mao are missing; his down-to-earth realism, his ability to bring together people of opposite trends and to maintain a balance, his peasant bonhomie—these peculiar traits of Mao are now all gone. Everything is running on a single track. The country is supposed to conform to a strictly uniform pattern of thought in straightforward military discipline.

But it is not working out this way. Once the hordes of savage youths organized by the military to surround and arrest the leaders of the civilian party had fulfilled their mission, they were expected to disband. But these organizations, and the parallel organizations of young workers that mushroomed throughout the country, have shown an extraordinary vitality. In the fall of 1968, an attempt was made to suppress them. But the "revolu-

[6]Liu Shao-ch'i, *How To Be a Good Communist* (New York: New Century Publishers, 1952).

tionary mass organizations" still exist, and they could hardly have survived without receiving secret support from sections of the military.

Hardly had the army taken over the administration of the country when it began to yield, as the party had yielded earlier, to the temptations of comfort. In 1969, this was called "money and women;" today, it is bluntly termed "corruption." Mao's chosen rebels have been discarded, and Peking has to rely on the old regional military commanders to establish order. In the spring of 1968, the Army Chief of Staff, the Commander of the Peking Garrison, and the Political Commissar of the Air Force had to be purged. The fierce leader of the rebels, Mao's ex-film-star wife, is still listed among the leadership. But her real power seems to have diminished, and this may mean a diminution of the power of Mao himself. The seeds of trouble are still there.

Liu Shao-ch'i is reported to have said in 1961 that two thousand years ago the first emperor, Ch'in Shih Huang-ti, fell because he wanted to build the Great Wall; and that the Sui dynasty, the predecessor of the T'ang, was short-lived because it demanded inhuman sacrifices from the people. Lu Ting-yi, head of the Communist Party propaganda apparatus, recalled that a minister of the T'ang dynasty warned the emperor not to imitate the Sui, who had perished "because too many soldiers were used and the people were overburdened with incessant labor."[7] It is significant that these Communist leaders took their argument not from Marx but from Chinese dynastic history, which is always so much more vividly present to the Chinese mind.

A period of transition from one dynasty to another, from one historical period to another, may have come; and it may last a long time. Chinese reactions are cautious and slow, and it takes time for a new doctrine to crystallize and new leaders to emerge.

The Answer

Looking back, one sees how inept the Chinese Communists were in their efforts to establish a new and lasting political system. In past ages, when a new dynasty came to power, its first task was to work out a stable system of administration expressed in lasting legal codes. The Nationalists, too, did this. Mao found the idea repugnant. Seen with Chinese eyes, Mao's "dynasty" has never been established.

Chinese history in the twentieth century can hardly be explained in Marxist terms. The Communist Party was accepted not because it was Marxist, but because the authority of the Nationalist government had been eroded by war and civil war, and there was no other alternative available. The only aspiration of the nation was to build China into an inde-

[7] *Jen-min Jih-pao,* May 24, 1968.

pendent, dignified, strong country. The Communists seemed competent to undertake this task. Now, after twenty years, all can see their impotence. The party has had to be virtually abolished and then built up again by the military. But no permanent solution is yet in sight.

In the past two decades, there was stability and unified purpose only so long as a foreign model was imposed on the country, only so long as China, in Mao's words, leaned on one side, toward Soviet Russia. This bias was felt in every field. In schools of law, Soviet legal texts were read without even appendices to adapt them to Chinese conditions. The same applied to economic policy, and even to Marxist philosophy and to literature. Such a state of affairs could not last.

China had not been ruled by Chinese since the middle of the seventeenth century. She got her chance early in this century; but in the years that have passed since then, she has not been able to produce a political system capable of ensuring a lasting, stable rule. What China is really laboring with, however, is the transition from an established system that answered the country's needs for thousands of years to a form of rule that is adapted to the demands of the modern world. This is, indeed, the problem not of China alone but of all the nations of Asia. China is going through great anguish in the search for a solution. It is an internal labor that is bound to last a long time.

No return to the past, to Confucianism, is possible. Confucianism presupposes the old, firm, coherent social structure that has now passed away and will never return. Western ideas of democracy have never been fully grasped in China. Democratic freedoms presuppose a basic consensus on the fundamentals, a self-imposed minimum discipline. If this consensus does not exist, the way is open for a clique to impose its will by oppressive secret police methods.

By nature and tradition, China demands a cohesive system of rule that affords a comprehensive interpretation of life and society. Confucianism belongs to history, the book of Sun Yat-sen is obsolete, Marxism led to turmoil and to immeasurable human suffering. It is possible that the time may come when China, disillusioned with the search for a new system, will adopt a more pragmatic approach to politics.

Between 1967 and 1968, militant youths were putting up manifestos proclaiming the need for a new formula of political rule for China. The official press called this the wicked New Trend, *ssu ch'ao,* opposing this term to the Thought of Mao, which in Chinese is expressed by the similar but distinct term, *ssu hsiang.* The New Trend first appeared in the news in the middle of 1967. At the beginning of 1970, this "wicked trend" is still being reported on, and Peking is still battling against it. The New Trend is not the fruit of one unified organization. It is a fermentation in the minds of many, and in the long run it may produce strong wine.

Perhaps the Communist period, which seems to have come to its last stage, will in the long run prove to have been beneficial. In reaction to what has happened, there is now a great desire in China, especially among the younger generation, for a more peaceful, normal life. While their foreign brethren are fomenting "revolution" in the schools, Chinese youth is being blamed by the army for neglecting Marxist politics and Peking's directives. All they want is to study and to be left in peace. The hectic history of the last twenty years has generated a longing for life lived in the tranquility of a stable society. The most important aspect is the acknowledgment of freedom within the family. The Communists have attempted many times to break down family ties; the latest and most preposterous move has been to name as head of the family the son or daughter who proves most loyal to Chairman Mao. But all past attempts to disintegrate the family have failed, and the present one will fare no better.

This tormented history has generated a single fruit, an intense desire for stability, for the rule of law, and for the acknowledgment of the human person. From the crucible through which China is now passing, a consensus may emerge; and after long turbulent years, political rule of a different nature may follow. What it will be, no man can yet tell.

Chapter Four

Party Politics and
the Cultural Revolution

Jürgen Domes

The violent conflict that erupted within the Chinese Communist leadership during the Great Proletarian Cultural Revolution has shaken the very foundations of party rule. Combining the elements of a basic policy dispute and a factional struggle for power, both of which will be analyzed later, this conflict developed into the most severe political crisis that mainland China has experienced since the Communists seized control of the country in 1949. In the years between the Communist takeover and the outbreak of the Cultural Revolution, there have been precursors of such conflict. But they differed significantly in character from the recent—and possibly current—crisis.

Up to the present, the existence of factional disputes in the CCP has been telegraphed by varying signals. One such signal has been the *expulsion* of individual dissenters from the party, without tarnishing too much the monolithic picture which the CCP generally presented to the outside world. Another signal has been the *removal* of dissenters from influential positions, but without their explusion from the party; the outward appearance of party unity was preserved. A third signal of factional conflict, which has characterized developments since 1965, is the *open split* that has destroyed even the outward appearance of party unity. The differences are readily apparent when we examine the four most important conflicts that have taken place within the Chinese Communist Party since 1949: (1) the dispute between 1953 and 1954 that led to the purge of the Chairman of the State Planning Commission, Kao Kang, and of the Director of Central Committee's Organization Department, Jao Shu-shih; (2) the argument over the handling of the Hundred Flowers campaign in 1957; (3) the dispute over the establishment of people's communes, and over Mao Tsetung's policy of the Great Leap Forward between 1958 and 1959; and (4) the conflict that developed after 1962 between the promoters of the Maoist line, and their opponents in the major areas of culture, education, economy, and the style of party work.

Early Party Conflicts

THE EXPULSION OF KAO KANG AND JAO SHU-SHIH. On March 31, 1955, a CCP National Delegates Conference, meeting in Peking, passed a resolution to expel Kao Kang and Jao Shu-shih from the party. At that time, Kao was the fifth-ranking member of the Politburo. He had served as Chairman of the Manchurian Military and Administrative Committee from 1948 to 1953, and concurrently was one of the six vice-chairmen of the Central People's Government. In November 1952, he took over the chairmanship of the newly established State Planning Commission. Jao had served as party chief in the East China Military and Administrative Committee from 1949 to 1953; and after his transfer to Peking, he was appointed Director of the Central Committee's Organization Department.[1] When the fifth plenary meeting of the CCP Seventh Central Committee confirmed these purges on April 4, 1955, it announced that Kao "not only did not admit his guilt to the party but even committed suicide as an expression of his ultimate betrayal of the party."[2]

The purge of these two high-ranking leaders marked the first major leadership crisis in the CCP since 1938, when Politburo member Chang Kuo-t'ao defected to the Kuomintang. It occurred at a time when important changes in domestic policy were taking place. On October 1, 1953, Mao Tse-tung had proclaimed the new "General Line of Socialist Reconstruction," which sparked a countrywide drive towards agricultural collectivization. The year 1953 was also supposed to mark the beginning of the First Five Year Plan for the economic development of China.[3] In June 1954, the Central People's Government decided to abolish the six military and administrative committees that had been established in 1949–50 with strong regional military participation to administer the country,[4] and that had developed into nearly independent bodies. From now on, China was again divided into provinces, autonomous regions, and special municipalities that reported directly to the central government. With the authority

---

[1]Seven minor party leaders, most of whom had worked with Kao in Manchuria, were also censured.

[2]*Jen-min Jih-pao,* April 5, 1955.

[3]This plan generally followed the basic development principles of the Stalinist Soviet Union by stressing the importance of the construction of heavy industry.

[4]*China News Analysis,* No. 43 (July 1954). The six administrative areas controlled by these committees included the following provinces: (1) Northeast (Manchuria): Liaoning, Kirin, Heilungkiang, and Jehol; (2) North: Hopei, Shansi, Inner Mongolia, Peking, and Tientsin; (3) East: Shantung, Kiangsu, Anhwei, Chekiang, Fukien, and Shanghai; (4) South: Honan, Hupei, Hunan, Kiangsi, Kwangtung, and Kwangsi; (5) Southwest: Szechuan, Kweichow, Yunnan, and Tibet; (6) Northwest: Shensi, Kansu, Ningshia, Tsinghai, and Sinkiang.

of the center thus considerably strengthened, a formal constitution was promulgated on September 20, 1954.[5]

The reasons for the purge of Kao and Jao are still not entirely clear. The party leadership accused them of having initiated "conspiratorial activities." Kao was blamed for having "made the Northeast (i.e., Manchuria) an independent kingdom" and for trying "to instigate party members in the army to support his conspiracy against the Central Committee of the party." Jao was alleged to have "protected counter-revolutionaries" in East China, and to have "surrendered to landlords and rich peasants" in that area. After their transfer to Peking, they were said to have created an "anti-party alliance" in order to seize "the power of leadership of the party and the state."[6]

It has been argued that the activities of the two leaders constituted an attempt to establish a new ruling group that would have been more docile in its relations with the Soviet Union, and that, therefore, Kao Kang and Jao Shu-shih were backed by Moscow. There can be no doubt that Kao had established close relations with Soviet authorities when he headed the administration in Manchuria, but the same cannot be said about Jao. On the other hand, some of Kao's colleagues in Manchuria, who had at least as many connections with the Russians as himself (for example, Li Fu-ch'un) were promoted at the same time that he was purged. Moreover, while the possibility of a Soviet attempt to achieve greater influence over the leadership of Communist China through the ascendancy of Kao cannot be excluded, there were at least three areas of domestic policy with respect to which Kao and Jao were in disagreement with the prevailing line in Peking. First, there were arguments over the speed of agricultural collectivization, in which Jao obviously plumped for a slower pace. Second, the regional allocation of investment funds during the First Five Year Plan was sharply debated; and it would appear that Kao, in opposition to the views of leaders from other areas, had worked for special emphasis on the further industrial development of Manchuria. Finally, it has been suggested that Kao, who did not belong to the leadership core that emerged during the Long March, tried to replace Liu Shao-ch'i in the number two position of the central leadership,[7] while Jao was said to be aiming at Chou En-lai's post as Prime Minister. Their alleged attempts to muster support from among the military would have aggravated the misgivings of the central leadership.

[5]The text may be found in Peter S. H. Tang, *Communist China Today,* Vol. 2, *Chronology and Documentary Supplement* (New York: Praeger, 1958), pp. 90–135.

[6]*Jen-min Jih-pao,* April 5, 1955.

[7]Peter S. H. Tang and Joan N. Maloney, *Communist China: The Domestic Scene, 1949–1967* (South Orange: Seton Hall University Press, 1967), pp. 92 ff. See also *China News Analysis,* No. 80 (April 22, 1955).

Thus, disagreements over economic policy and a thrust for personal power, possibly exacerbated by the impact of Soviet influence, had created the conflict. This crisis, however, had limited consequences. The purge affected only two of the 43 full members of the Central Committee; and although these two held fairly influential positions, they were still peripheral figures as compared with the inner core of the leadership that had risen to the top during the Long March. The main results of the purge were to reinforce the trend toward centralized control in the field of organization, and to strengthen the positions of Liu Shao-ch'i and Chou En-lai in terms of individual power distribution. During the course of the next major crisis, these two leaders obviously fell into disagreement.

THE HUNDRED FLOWERS CAMPAIGN. When the purge of Kao and Jao was announced, a new "rectification" campaign was already in full swing among Chinese intellectuals, forcing them into often humiliating "self-criticisms," and aimed at the suppression of independent thought. The intellectuals were badly frightened, and many found themselves unable to do the work which the leadership wanted of them. Sometime around New Year 1956, the central authorities seem to have realized the dangers stemming from this situation. Chou En-lai was the first to call for a shift in party policy; and in a speech delivered at a meeting of the Central Committee in January 1956, he asked the party to treat the intellectuals, and in particular the specialists who were needed for China's economic development, in a more understanding manner.[8] On May 25, the Director of the Central Committee's Propaganda Department, Lu Ting-yi, introduced the slogan, "Let the hundred flowers bloom! Let the hundred schools of thought contend!" And he promised greater freedom of discussion within the party as well as between the party and nonparty intellectuals.[9]

During the nine months that followed, the intellectuals and members of the minority parties in the united front were exhorted to criticize the mistakes and shortcomings of the party. The campaign developed rather slowly; the critics were obviously very cautious. Nevertheless, two trends gradually became visible. On the one hand, some leading figures—most of them prominent in government administration—encouraged criticism. Leaders within the civilian party machine, such as Liu Shao-ch'i, P'eng Chen and others, on the other hand, kept relatively quiet on the unfolding campaign, while continuing to stress party discipline and the importance of collective leadership. At the Eighth Party Congress in September 1956, Liu emphasized the importance of party guidance, and only occasionally referred to the special position and merits of Mao Tse-tung himself and

[8]Chou En-lai, *Report on the Question of the Intellectuals* (Peking: Foreign Languages Press, 1956).

[9]*Jen-min Jih-pao,* June 12, 1956. See also *China News Analysis,* No. 138 (July 6, 1956).

Mao's role in the development of Marxist-Leninist ideology.[10] The Secretary-General of the Central Committee, Teng Hsiao-p'ing, called for a "movement to improve the working style of the party and administration," a term that could be analyzed as supporting the Hundred Flowers campaign; but he also gave special attention to the importance of discipline and collective leadership.[11] In May 1957, P'eng Chen reiterated the importance of clear leadership by the Central Committee.[12] Thus, the major figures of the party machine around Liu Shao-ch'i apparently were highly skeptical about the new campaign, presumably because in their view it threatened the party discipline that they were geared to preserve.

It seems that Mao at this time sided with Chou En-lai's more "moderate" group in government administration. In early 1957, he publicly took sides with the promoters of open discussion within and outside the party. Following his speech before an enlarged meeting of the Supreme State Conference on February 27, 1957, the campaign for freedom of criticism was greatly intensified.[13] Mao might have hoped that this freedom would serve as an outlet for the grievances that had accumulated during the years of strict regimentation of all intellectual activities. Developments soon indicated, however, that from the party's point of view, the "orthodox" critics of the campaign had been right. The movement eventually developed into a formidable threat to the regime, when intellectual criticism was no longer directed only against administrative shortcomings, but turned into a direct assault on Communist ideology, the Communist system, and the top leadership itself. Widespread student demonstrations joined the protest, and even called for the overthrow of party rule. In order to avert the imminent danger of a general uprising, the leadership shifted gears. On June 8, the press stated for the first time that a "counter-criticism" was necessary; and soon the critics were themselves assailed by an intense campaign against "rightist deviationists."

This campaign, however, concentrated on nonparty individuals and members of the minority parties. Very few purges occurred within the CCP itself. Some provincial party leaders, including a few alternate members of the Central Committee, were removed from their positions, while actual expulsions from the party were limited to a number of intellectuals of relatively low party rank. Moreover, while there was obvious dissent

[10]Liu Shao-ch'i, *The Political Report of the Central Committee of the Communist Party of China to the Eighth National Congress of the Party* (Peking: Foreign Languages Press, 1956).

[11]Teng Hsiao-p'ing, *Report on the Revision of the Constitution of the Communist Party of China* (Peking: Supplement to Hsinhua News Agency Release, 1956). See also *China News Analysis,* No. 151 (October 5, 1956).

[12]*Kuang-ming Jih-pao* (Peking), May 5, 1957.

[13]See p. 34, fn. 9, above.

within the leadership on the issue of the Hundred Flowers campaign, agreement on procedures remained intact. All groups still seemed to recognize the decision-making power of the Central Committee and the Politburo. Within the party leadership, a relatively "moderate" group around Chou En-lai faced the opposition of an "orthodox" group around Liu Shao-ch'i. When the hostile activities of the intellectuals intensified in spring 1957, Mao himself decided to change sides; thereafter, he supported the "orthodox" group.[14]

THE DISPUTE OVER DEVELOPMENT POLICY. During the following autumn and winter, the "moderate" and "orthodox" groups again faced each other in a dispute over development policy. Once again the "orthodox" leaders, now with the personal support of Mao, emerged as victors.[15]

During the debates that preceded the formulation of the Second Five Year Plan, administrators and economic managers suggested the continuation of a gradual, "step-by-step" development policy that corresponded to the "objective" economic and social conditions of the country. Mao Tse-tung, his closest supporters, and leading members of the party machine around Liu Shao-ch'i, on the other hand, pressed for stronger emphasis on mass mobilization and for a considerable acceleration of the pace of development, which in their view would lead to the early transformation of China from a Socialist to a Communist society. For them, the outspoken expression of widespread discontent during the Hundred Flowers campaign, despite the economic successes of the regime and a remarkable rise in the standard of living, was evidence enough for the view that thought reform and mass mobilization were more important to the future of China than development in accordance with established principles of economic growth.

By late 1957, there were indications of a victory for the "orthodox," more radical forces behind Mao and Liu. The party leadership started to call for a more rapid pace of development, in "gigantic steps." At the second plenary meeting of the Eighth Party Congress, in May 1958, Liu proclaimed the theory of "permanent revolution" as the guiding principle of the new party line. After violent attacks against "those comrades who would prefer to advance slowly and not quickly," he called for the development of China into a "great Socialist country" within the "shortest possible time."[16] Already during the winter of 1957 and 1958, the Chinese Communists had started in some areas to combine a number of agricultural co-

---

[14]See Roderick MacFarquhar, "Communist China's Intra-Party Dispute," *Pacific Affairs,* Vol. 31, No. 4 (December 1958), pp. 323 ff.

[15]See Donald S. Zagoria, *The Sino-Soviet Conflict, 1956–1961* (Princeton: Princeton University Press, 1962), pp. 66 ff.

[16]*Peking Review,* Vol. 1, No. 14 (June 3, 1958).

operatives into larger production units. This movement became nation-wide in May and June 1958; and on July 1, Ch'en Po-ta, a leading Maoist theoretician, for the first time used the term "people's communes" as the name for this new type of collective.[17] But the new policies were obviously still under dispute during the summer. While Mao, Liu, Ch'en Po-ta, and some other leaders continuously praised the establishment of people's communes as a most important step on the road to a Communist society, Chou, Ch'en Yun (a vice-premier and leading economic administrator), and the Minister of National Defense, P'eng Teh-huai, conspicuously avoided the subject in their public statements.

At the fifth plenary meeting of the Eighth Central Committee, which convened at Peitaiho in August, the decision was taken to force the commune system on the whole nation. The policy of the "Three Red Banners" was proclaimed as the guideline for China's future development; it included the following elements: (1) the General Line of Socialist Construction, which placed equal emphasis on the development of heavy industry and agriculture, and which called for the use of modern and conventional methods of production; (2) the Great Leap Forward, which envisaged a drive to overtake the industrial production of Great Britain within fifteen years, and within the context of which the famous movement to produce crude steel in small backyard furnaces was introduced; and (3) the campaign to establish people's communes throughout China.[18]

After some striking initial successes, however, the new policies of the Three Red Banners proved to be a disastrous failure, leading to organizational chaos, severe economic dislocations, a serious food shortage, and finally to widespread passive resistance among the populace. Thereafter, although Mao himself continued to press for the implementation of this line of accelerated development, the more pragmatically minded leaders launched an effort to bring about a gradual revision of the radical policies. During the winter of 1958 and 1959, three distinct issue-based groups emerged within the party leadership: first, Mao himself and a nucleus of leaders who persisted in promoting the Three Red Banners; second, a group around P'eng Teh-huai, who pressed for the liquidation of these policies and who had at least the tacit support of Chou En-lai and other leading figures in the government administration; and finally, Liu Shao-ch'i, Teng Hsiao-p'ing, P'eng Chen, and other leaders in the party apparatus who, convinced that the Maoist line had failed, now ceased to support the policies of the party leader and formed what might be called a "new right."

[17]*Hung-ch'i,* No. 3 (1958).

[18]The resolution of the fifth plenary meeting of the Eighth Central Committee, dated August 23, 1958, was first published in *Jen-min Jih-pao,* September 1958.

At the sixth and seventh plenary meetings of the Eighth Central Committee, held at Wuhan in December 1958 and Shanghai in April 1959, the majority formed by the latter two groups introduced a drive for a "readjustment" in policy, during which the first moderating changes of the commune system took place. It was in this context that Mao Tse-tung, at the Wuhan plenum, announced that he would not run again for the position of Chief of State; and in April 1959, the first plenary meeting of the Second National People's Congress elected Liu Shao-ch'i as Chairman of the People's Republic.

But the real showdown between these groups did not come until summer 1959, when the Politburo met at Lushan in order to prepare for the eighth plenary meeting of the Eighth Central Committee, scheduled for the first half of August, also at Lushan. During the Politburo sessions, a letter which P'eng Teh-huai had written to Mao on July 14 became known to the leadership. In very polite language, P'eng criticized Mao's policies as departing too much from reality, and even branded some of them as "petit-bourgeois fanaticism."[19] P'eng's attack was made against the background of a growing deterioration of conditions throughout the country. The Lushan plenum, which started on August 2, became the scene of a bitter encounter between Mao and his critics. At a decisive moment, however, Liu Shao-ch'i and Chou En-lai obviously decided to reach a compromise with the party leader. P'eng and his closest supporters, Chief of the General Staff Huang K'e-ch'eng, and Vice-Minister for Foreign Affairs Chang Wen-t'ien were removed from their official posts, although they retained membership on the Central Committee; a resolution of the Lushan plenum blamed them for "rightist deviationism." But at the same time, most of the policy changes proposed by the opposition were adopted.[20] Thus, while the leaders of the party and government apparatus agreed to censure P'eng, they also forced Mao to agree to a thoroughgoing revision of the Three Red Banners policy. The organization of agricultural work along military lines had already been discarded. Now the main responsibility for agricultural production was shifted from the communes to the much smaller production brigades; and in 1961, it was further devolved down to production teams, which comprised on the average ten to 25 families. Before long, farmers were also allowed to retain some of their land for private plots, the produce of which could be sold on the free market from January 1962 on. The campaign to establish backyard furnaces was halted, and the new

[19]*Ke-ming ch'uan-lien,* August 24, 1967. See also Dieter Heinzig, "Von Lushan zur Kulturrevolution," *Berichte des Bundesinstituts für Ostwissenschaftliche und Internationale Studien,* No. 5 (Cologne: 1968), pp. 7 ff; also J. D. Seinmonds, "P'eng Teh-huai: A Chronological Re-Examination," *China Quarterly,* No. 37 (January-March 1969), pp. 120 ff.

[20]*Hung-ch'i,* No. 13 (1967). See also David A. Charles, "The Dismissal of Marshall P'eng Teh-huai," *China Quarterly,* No. 8 (October-December 1961), pp. 63 ff.

policy again stressed a gradual development more in accord with economic realities.

Genesis of the Cultural Revolution.

But in the years following the Lushan compromise, neither the Maoists, who had only reluctantly agreed to the policies of "readjustment," nor the more pragmatically oriented groups that rallied around Liu Shao-ch'i were satisfied with the situation. Out of the conflict of 1958 and 1959, a new crisis unfolded between 1961 and 1962, that led directly to the Great Proletarian Cultural Revolution.

In spite of the revisions that terminated the policy of the Three Red Banners, opposition from intellectuals, economists, and leading party cadres became more and more intense, and eventually developed into a general offensive against the policies of Mao and his supporters in at least five major areas. First, in the field of cultural policy, the opponents—mostly party intellectuals—protested against the regimentation of arts and literature. This opposition began to press for greater freedom of thought and expression, and their efforts were accompanied by acid satirical attacks against the views and even the person of the party leader. Second, in the field of educational policy, cadres in the government and teachers called for a shift of emphasis from irregular institutions such as the work-study schools back to regular educational institutions. High-ranking party and government officials underlined the importance of "expertness" rather than "redness," a tendency that was diametrically opposed to the educational policies of 1958.

Third, in the field of ideology, party theoreticians disagreed with the Maoist interpretation of the Marxist theory of contradictions, and emphasized the importance of the synthesis of contradictions rather than the antithesis between them. This had important political implications. The theory of "combining two into one," which was argued between 1963 and 1964 by Yang Hsien-chen, Deputy Director of the Marxist-Leninist Institute and member of the Central Committee, could provide a rationalization for a Sino-Soviet rapprochement internationally, and for a policy of "co-existence" of state-owned enterprises and individual ownership of the means of production domestically. Fourth, the opposition forces in the party and government apparatus that had succeeded in substantially liquidating the Three Red Banners policy, continued their drive for major policy revisions. In 1962, they called for more private plots for commune farmers, more free markets, and for a further shift of responsibility for agricultural production from production teams to the individual farmer. Finally, in 1965 a debate developed in which the opponents of Mao called for the accentuation of quality over quantity, and for stronger support for those enterprises that produced a profit in their operations.

From another perspective, the conflict that developed between 1962 and 1965 related to the fundamental questions of intellectual diversity *versus* uniformity, attempts at domestic and international reconciliation *versus* the acceleration of domestic and international "class struggle," and predominantly technocratic concepts of development policy as opposed to the Maoist idea of mass-mobilization as the main developmental force. In short, beginning with the debates over the Three Red Banners policy, fairly narrow, issue-based disagreements among the party leaders were gradually transformed into a much more fundamental dispute over basic policy approaches.

In the case of Kao and Jao, the dissenters did not belong to the inner core of the party leadership, although they did hold high-ranking official positions. Moreover, there is evidence that their own relationship was not free from strain: Kao had distinguished himself in Manchuria as one of the main promoters of agricultural collectivization, while Jao in East China was very cautious in this field. The Central Committee's allegation notwithstanding, it is clear that the two did not really succeed in forming a coherent faction. Theirs was a temporary alliance based on an agreement on some but not all issues. Since there was a basic consensus among the inner core of the party leadership on the main political issues under dispute, as well as on appropriate party procedures, the conflict could be resolved by the expulsion of the two dissenters without causing a party split.

This basic consensus on the issues was shaken in the course of debate on the Hundred Flowers campaign; and it definitely broke down in the disputes that followed the failure of Mao's radical approach to the development of China in 1958. The consensus on procedures, however, remained intact. Even when P'eng Teh-huai and his closest supporters were censured, all elements in the party leadership were still agreed on the use of the Central Committee and the Politburo as the appropriate policy-making organs. Nor had coherent, identifiable factions yet emerged. The strategy of Liu Shao-ch'i at the Lushan plenum, in which he supported most of the policies proposed by P'eng while at the same time agreeing to his removal from office, suggests that intra-party disputes were still issue-based and personal affiliations changing. The fact that the Central Committee decided on the removal of the dissenters from their official positions rather than their expulsion from the party, also indicates that expulsion could not be resorted to as a method of conflict resolution in cases where a disagreement over issues was nevertheless still accompanied by a continued agreement over procedures. Moreover, it would also appear that in all these cases the inner circle shared a basic interest in presenting as much of a "monolithic" picture to the outside world as possible.

Thus, expulsion from the party or removal from official position would appear to be the major signals of intra-party conflict before such conflict degenerates to the stage where rival factions begin to take shape.[21] But between 1962 and 1965, disagreement on issues was more and more aggravated by dissent on procedures. The opposing groups began to develop into relatively coherent circles competing for overall control; the dispute reached the stage of factionalism. At this stage, the main signal of intra-party conflict became the open split.

The Great Proletarian Cultural Revolution

During summer 1965, there were growing indications that forces within the party and mass organizations opposed to Maoist policies were again preparing to force a thoroughgoing revision of the aging leader's political line. Since the end of April, and especially during August and September of that year, a number of articles asking for major modifications of policy had appeared in the press, mainly in organs controlled by P'eng Chen's Peking Municipal Party Committee, by the trade unions, and by the Chinese Communist Youth League. It also appears that at least some of the leading oppositionists who were censured in 1959 were making a political comeback. P'eng Teh-huai reappeared as a member of the CCP Provincial Control Commission in Szechuan, while Huang K'e-ch'eng was appointed Vice-Governor of Shansi. Other indications of the growing strength of the "new right" led by Liu Shao-ch'i included an effort by the propaganda machine to build up a "Chairman Liu" image equalling that of Mao, and the fact that P'eng Chen was selected to give the main address at the 1965 National Day celebrations in Peking. Moreover, while the mass media had launched a number of attacks against opposition literary figures and party theoreticians between summer 1964 and spring 1965, most of these attacks were discontinued after May.

At a meeting of the Politburo held in Peking during the second half of September 1965, Mao Tse-tung apparently sensed that the opposition was quickly gathering momentum. To counter this development, he proposed a new, all-out rectification campaign among the intellectuals. At the same time, he pressed for educational reform which would again emphasize political indoctrination rather than professional training. But the majority of the Politburo voted against his proposals.[22] Embittered and possibly

[21]One might even ask whether the acceptance of Mao Tse-tung's decision not to run again for the post of Chairman of the People's Republic, at the Wuhan Plenum in December 1958, represented a sort of removal.

[22]*Hung-ch'i,* No. 9 (1967). See also Franz Michael, "Moscow and the Current Chinese Crisis," *Current History,* Vol. 53, No. 313, (September 1967), p. 147; and Philip Bridgham, "Mao's Cultural Revolution: Origin and Development," *China Quarterly,* No. 29 (January-March 1967), p. 16.

also in poor health, Mao left Peking for the Shanghai area in late October, and was not seen again in public for more than six months (until May 11, 1966).

At this moment, when Mao and his closest supporters seemed increasingly isolated from the sources of power, Lin Piao rushed to their aid by throwing the weight of the military behind the Maoist cause. This enabled the Maoists to launch a counterattack against the opposition. They struck first from Shanghai on November 10 with an article condemning the historian and playwright Wu Han, one of P'eng Chen's deputies in the Peking city government.[23] From that moment on, the development of the domestic political crisis in Communist China can be divided into six stages.

FIRST STAGE. Events during the first stage, which began November 10, 1965, and lasted until May 16, 1966, are still not entirely clear. For several months, two centers of power competed for overall control: the central party authorities and the Peking Municipal Party Committee opposing the Mao-Lin group, which was able to rally support from the East China CCP Regional Bureau in Shanghai. While the Shanghai news media, aided by the PLA newspaper, continued their attacks on Wu Han and soon extended them to other intellectuals, *Jen-min Jih-pao* and the organs controlled by the Peking Municipal Party Committee published articles defending those attacked. Wu's "self-criticism," which was published in Peking at the end of December, sounded more like self-defense;[24] and as late as January 19, 1966, contributions defending Wu and other figures could still be found in the Peking papers. But gradually the voices for the defense were silenced. Articles supporting the ideas of the intellectual opposition ceased to appear. This may have been a consequence of the fact that, meanwhile, a conflict for control of the PLA between Lin Piao and the Chief of the General Staff, Lo Jui-ch'ing, had been decided in favor of Lin. Lo was removed from office in February or early March 1966, and attempted suicide on March 18.

Although the Mao-Lin group's control over the armed forces had become manifest, the party machine still tried to deflect the Maoist effort. In early February, the central party authorities appointed a group of five leading cadres to formulate the basic principles for a rectification campaign among the intellectuals. Four members of this group were decidedly anti-Maoist (P'eng Chen, Lu Ting-yi, Chou Yang, and Wu Leng-hsi), while the fifth, K'ang Sheng, seems to have been undecided at that time and only later joined the Mao-Lin group. On February 13, this group agreed on guidelines for the campaign, according to which the dispute should be treated as a "nonantagonistic contradiction," that is, it should be solved by

---

[23]*Wen-hui Pao,* November 10, 1965.
[24]*Jen-min Jih-pao,* December 3C, 1965.

open discussion and without physical coercion.[25] These guidelines still dominated the proclamation of a "Great *Socialist* Cultural Revolution" at the thirtieth meeting of the Standing Committee of the Third National People's Congress on April 14.

In reaction to this, the Mao-Lin group for the first time used military force to overcome the opposition of the central party authorities. According to a report by Branko Bogunovic, the Peking correspondent of *Tanyug,* armed units of the PLA occupied the premises of the Peking Municipal Party Committee.[26] Then in early May, the army newspaper gave the signal for an all-out attack against the intellectual critics of the 1961–62 period. Wu Han and Teng T'o (Director of the Propaganda Department of the Peking Municipal Party Committee) were denounced as "poisonous revisionist snakes" who had tried to form a "black counter-revolutionary gang" and who, therefore, should be "beaten down until they stink."[27] On May 8, the PLA paper even stated that behind this "black gang" there were "more dangerous freaks and monsters" against whom a "life-and-death struggle" must be waged. This indicated that the Maoist attack would soon be directed toward political figures who ranked much higher than the intellectuals. And indeed, on May 16, a circular allegedly drawn by the Central Committee declared the February 13 guidelines null and void.[28] The conflict was now to be regarded as an "antagonistic contradication," which meant that those who opposed the leader could be suppressed as "enemies of the people."

SECOND STAGE. The May 16 circular can be regarded as a starting point for the second stage, which lasted until the end of July 1966. During this period, three parallel developments took place. First, the Maoists continued their counterattack. Sometime between May 16 and May 25, they succeeded in removing P'eng Chen and seven of the eight secretaries of the Peking Municipal Party Committee. Soon thereafter, the Director of the Central Committee's Propaganda Department, Lu Ting-yi (Vice Premier, Minister of Culture, and alternate Politburo member), and his deputies Chou Yang and Lin Mo-han, were ousted; and the Maoists thereby secured control over the party's propaganda machine.

---

[25]"Instruction Issued by the CCP Central Committee General Office Concerning the Outline of the Summary Report on Current Literary Discussion," February 12, 1966, in *I-chiu-liu-pa nien fei-ch'ing nien-pao* (1968 Yearbook on Chinese Communism) (Taipei: Institute for the Study of Chinese Communist Problems, 1968), pp. 573–577.

[26]Branko Bogunovic, "The Storm in July," Chinese translation from *Politika* (Belgrade), in *Ming Pao* (Hong Kong), January 1 and 2, 1967. It should, however, be noted that *Tanyug* very frequently edits the reports of its correspondents.

[27]*Chieh-fang Chun-pao,* May 4 and 8, 1966.

[28]Circular of the Central Committee of the Communist Party of China, May 16, 1966, *Current Background,* No. 852 (May 6, 1968), pp. 2–6.

Second, having failed to enlist not only the party's support for their rectification drive but also that of the Communist Youth League, the Maoists tried to build up a militant youth organization of their own. As early as April 1966, student representatives at a conference in Tsinan praised the "principles of comrade Lin Piao, which are still not accepted in many schools."[29] In May, the authorities started to close down schools and universities all over China. This measure was confirmed by a circular of the State Council and the "Party Central" on June 13, which postponed entrance examinations for secondary schools and colleges for six months. Political commissars of the PLA began to organize the students, and soon groups of "little revolutionary generals" began to attack prominent members of the intellectual opposition, especially teachers. The term "Red Guards" was first used for the new organization at Tsinghua University in Peking on June 26; and during July, the movement spread rapidly to many Chinese cities.

The anti-Maoists, however, did not remain inactive. They attempted to discipline the Maoist youth by sending teams of experienced party cadres into schools and universities. At the same time, they reportedly made an attempt to convene a plenary meeting of the Central Committee in Peking on July 21, obviously in order to curtail Mao's power. In an attempt to rally support for this plan, P'eng Chen, at the end of June, went to the Northwest and later to the Southwest for talks with party leaders in these areas. Around mid-July, 51 out of 91 full members and 38 out of 87 alternates of the Central Committee were reported to have assembled in Peking to attend the conference. But on July 17, while the Chairman was reportedly engaged in his famous long-distance swim in the Yangtze River, strong military units in combat gear occupied the capital. This move obviously "convinced" Liu and his group not to go ahead with the conference.[30]

Physical control over the capital having thus been secured for the Mao-Lin group by the military, Mao returned to Peking on July 28 after an absence of nine months. At the same time, large numbers of Red Guards, logistically supported by the PLA, began to pour into the capital from various parts of China. On August 1, the Maoists convened the eleventh plenary meeting of the Eighth Central Committee, which met in the presence of delegates from the PLA and the Red Guards, but with more than half the members of the Committee absent.

THIRD STAGE. The eleventh plenary meeting marks the beginning of the third stage of the Cultural Revolution, which lasted until late January 1967. Despite the fact that the Central Committee plenum was packed by Mao's supporters, the Mao-Lin group still had to compromise.

[29]*Jen-min Jih-pao,* April 11, 1966.
[30]Bogunovic, *op. cit.*

The "Decision Concerning the Great Proletarian Cultural Revolution,"[31] which was passed by the plenum on August 8, is one of the most contradictory documents in CCP history. While generally confirming the Maoist line, it also cautions against violence and asks for the "protection of the minority."[32] Decisions of the plenum affecting personnel assured a slight Maoist majority on the Politburo. P'eng Chen, P'eng Teh-huai, Chang Wen-t'ien, and Lu Ting-yi were removed from that body; while T'ao Chu, Ch'en Po-ta, and K'ang Sheng, three politicians who at the time were considered to be supporters of Mao and Lin, joined the Politburo's Standing Committee. Another addition to that group was Li Fu-ch'un, who was regarded as being close to Chou En-lai. Of the six new full and alternate members of the Politburo, five had military backgrounds.[33] Military representation in the top leadership thus rose from almost 35 percent to 46 percent. The most important decision, however, was the demotion of Liu Shao-ch'i from second to eighth place in the official hierarchy, and the promotion of Lin Piao to the position of sole Vice Chairman of the Politburo and the Central Committee. The emerging Politburo majority presented itself as a combination of the military, the group around Chou En-lai (who again in a decisive moment of conflict had joined the victors), and the personal associates of Mao Tse-tung.

The latter faction, rallying around the "Central Cultural Revolution Group" led by Ch'en Po-ta and Mao's wife, Chiang Ch'ing, soon tried to push the Maoist drive even more vigorously ahead. On August 18, they organized (with the support of the military) the first of a series of mass rallies, during which about ten million Red Guards in all gathered to cheer the leader. Following the August 18 rally, the Red Guards began to rampage through the main cities of China, witch-hunting for members of the opposition in intellectual circles and among the civilian party cadres, burning temples and some museums, killing, torturing, and beating up people whom they regarded as "bourgeois." These activities soon met with unexpected but strong spontaneous resistance. As early as August 19 and 20, the Red Guards engaged in street fights with an organization created in Changsha, the capital of Hunan, for the defense of the local leadership against Maoist attacks. On August 25 and September 1, Red Guard units were routed by their opponents in Tsingtao, and during October, sabotage against trains transporting Red Guards occurred in many places.

During the four months following the August 18 rally, two opposing trends unfolded. In the first place, the group around Liu Shao-ch'i and

[31]*New China News Agency,* August 8, 1966.

[32]It could, however, be argued that in this case the term "minority" applied to the Maoists, who in fact constituted only a minority of the CCP Central Committee.

[33]Hsu Hsiang-ch'ien, Nieh Jung-chen, Yeh Chien-ying, Hsieh Fu-chih, and Sung Jen-ch'iung.

Teng Hsiao-p'ing—who were soon joined by T'ao Chu, obviously disgusted by the violence of the Red Guards—did not accept the defeat they had sustained at the eleventh plenary meeting of the Eighth Central Committee. Still strongly entrenched in the provincial party leadership and also having the support of some leading military figures,[34] they tried again to blunt the Maoist drive. In October and November 1966, they attempted to discipline the Red Guards in many areas; and at the same time, they established fake Red Guard units of their own, thus contributing to rising confusion in the country. The central military authorities around Lin Piao, and the government apparatus headed by Chou En-lai, were also becoming more and more concerned about the rampages of the Red Guards. On August 31, Lin admonished the teenage Maoist battalions at their second mass rally "not to beat up anybody."[35] On November 12 and 16, the Red Guards were ordered to leave the capital. This call was not obeyed; it was repeated on November 21, and on December 3, the State Council and the Party Central set a definite deadline of December 27 for their departure.

The extremist wing of the Mao-Lin group, meanwhile, continued its efforts to overcome the opposition of the party machine. While Lin and Chou, in this respect obviously supported by Liu and Teng, were attempting to confine the Cultural Revolution to the schools and universities, the extremists tried to extend Red Guard activities to factories and rural people's communes. In this manner, they hoped to overthrow the strongly oppositionist regional and provincial party leadership as well as the leading organs of the labor unions, which also resisted the Maoist thrust.

While the central leadership was being torn apart by this dispute, most of the regional military commanders tried to take a neutral position. When they were approached for support by competing Maoist and anti-Maoist factions, which in some areas had already turned to armed violence, they issued nonintervention orders to their troops.

But in spite of the party machine's opposition and the attempts of the military to remain neutral, by late November the extremists had temporarily won the upper hand. On November 28, Chiang Ch'ing was appointed as "PLA Advisor for Cultural Affairs," a step which indicated that the central PLA leadership would now inaugurate a period of close cooperation with the radicals. On December 3, P'eng Chen was arrested by Red Guards; and by the end of the month, the extremists had succeeded in forcing their will on the central leadership. An editorial which appeared in *Jen-min Jih-pao* on December 26 called for a "high tide of the Cultural Revolution in industrial and mining enterprises," and the headquarters of the Central Labor Union were occupied by revolutionary rebels three days later. At the same time, wall posters began to appear in Peking and

---

[34]Most prominent among them was Marshal Ho Lung.

[35]*New China News Agency,* September 1, 1966.

other Chinese cities violently attacking Liu Shao-ch'i and a number of leading members of the Central Committee.

Then, during the first days of 1967, the extremists set out to overthrow the provincial party leadership all over China, and scored their first success in Shanghai early in January. But the new Maoist drive for power in the provinces again met with unexpectedly strong resistance. While the proclamations of the radicals became more violent day by day, and while in Peking the first public trials of ousted members of the Central Committee were being held, the workers in many Chinese cities—encouraged by local party and government authorities—went on strike. Lines of communication were interrupted and banks raided. In many places, farmers stormed the commune storehouses, seized grain, distributed land among themselves, and reverted to private agricultural production. Units of Red Guards were attacked by workers and peasants.

In this difficult situation, Mao had to turn to the military for support. For the first time since 1949, he felt it necessary to call on the PLA to sustain his cause in the face of strong popular resistance. On January 17 or 18, he sent the following order to Lin Piao:[36]

It is necessary that the PLA be moved in to support the broad masses of the left wing. Mao Tse-tung.

P.S. From now on, whenever the real revolutionary faction calls on the troops to support and save it, everyone must act in accordance with this call. So-called nonintervention is wrong. Wherever nonintervention has been ordered before, new orders must be issued and the former orders declared invalid. Please act as ordered here.

Although the army had been asked to intervene in the conflict even before January 17 (for example, when broadcasting stations all over the country were placed under its control on January 11), this mandate of the party leader marked one of the most critical moments in the history of Communist China. It called for the armed forces to come out openly—and, if necessary, forcibly—not in favor of the whole party, of which they had been the reliable instrument in the past, but in support of one faction. The party's army, according to the wishes of Mao and his associates, should now become a faction's army. This could not but subject the loyalty and unity of the PLA to dangerous stresses and strains.

FOURTH STAGE. With Mao Tse-tung's mandate of January 17–18, the fourth stage of the crisis began. During this stage, which lasted until the latter part of August 1967, the Chinese scene was dominated on the one

[36]*Tung-fang Hung* (Peking), January 28, 1967.

hand by the unsuccessful attempts of the Maoist extremists to get the Cultural Revolution moving again, and on the other by obvious military reluctance to support the leftist drive. Between the end of January and late April, the Maoists succeeded in overthrowing the local authorities in six of 29 provinces. So-called "revolutionary committees," composed of almost equal numbers of representatives from Maoist organizations, the PLA, and pro-Maoist party cadres, were established in these six provinces to take over control of the party and the administrative and economic apparatus.[37]

At the same time, however, further attempts were made to curtail the activities of the extremists even in the capital. On January 28, the Red Guards were ordered to cease operations in the Tsinan, Nanking, Foochow, Canton, Kunming, Wuhan, and Sinkiang military regions; and several days later, they were similarly barred from all armaments factories and scientific research institutions. On February 11, the military took over police and public security buildings in Peking; and on February 20, warehouses and factories in a number of important cities were placed under military control. An editorial in the March 10 edition of *Hung-ch'i* stated that the revolutionary committees should be established by a "revolutionary triple alliance" consisting of "revolutionary mass organizations," the PLA garrison forces, and "revolutionary cadres" (that is, pro-Maoist party functionaries). In this "triple alliance," the position of the military was obviously regarded as crucial. The editorial continued:

> In all institutions where a seizure of power has become necessary, . . . the participation of PLA and militia delegates in the temporary power organs of the revolutionary triple alliance is indispensable. Factories, villages, institutions of finance and commerce, educational institutions including colleges, secondary, and primary schools, as well as party organs, administrative organs, and mass organizations, must be led with the participation of representatives of the PLA. . . . Where there are not enough PLA representatives available, these positions should better be left vacant temporarily.

In spite of these efforts to stabilize the domestic political situation while at the same time expanding Maoist control over larger areas of China, it was precisely during this fourth stage of the crisis that the leftist offensive collapsed. The response of the PLA to Mao's quest for support remained ambiguous. Lin Piao decided to "play 'possum;" he engaged in no public activities during the period from January 20 through March 20. During the six months that followed Mao's mandate of January 17 and 18, the military supported a Maoist seizure of power in only six of 29 provinces. In five

[37]Heilungkiang (January 31, 1967), Shantung (February 5), Kweichow (February 13), Shansi (March 18), and Peking (April 20).

other provinces, the commanders showed benevolent neutrality towards the leftists;[38] while in nine provinces they adopted a strictly neutral attitude;[39] and in the remaining nine provinces,[40] the local military took sides with the opposition.

Despite these differences of attitude, regional military commanders and political commissars increasingly took over administrative responsibilities throughout most of China. At the same time, widespread violence occurred, and by July had erupted in about ten provinces. Fighting took place not only between Maoist and anti-Maoist organizations, but also increasingly among the numerous competing factions within the Maoist camp. In early May, and again in July, these disturbances reached dimensions which in some areas verged on civil war. On May 25, the Minister of Public Security, Hsieh Fu-chih, said in an address that according to "incomplete statistics," 130 "incidents of bloodshed" resulting in 63,500 casualties were recorded between April 30 and May 10.[41] In Shanghai, there were reports of the establishment of anti-Maoist labor unions; and in South China, Red Guard transports were attacked by local militia. All over the country, the party machine broke down, and the administrative chain of command was seriously damaged.

In this situation, the PLA was the only instrument of power that remained relatively intact. At the beginning of July, the extremists started a new and desperate attempt to revive the revolutionary enthusiasm that had prevailed in early January. This time, however, they were met with energetic resistance not only from civilian party personnel, workers, and peasants, but also from local PLA units. Around mid-July, serious clashes occurred in the vital industrial center of Wuhan. When Hsieh Fu-chih, the Minister of Public Security, and Wang Li, head of the Central Committee's Propaganda Department and a henchman of Chiang Ch'ing, arrived in Wuhan in order to turn the tide in favor of the Maoists, the Commander of the Wuhan Military Region, General Ch'en Tsai-tao, ordered their arrest and brought them before a kangaroo court set up by anti-Maoist organizations. Chou En-lai hastily flew in from Peking to mediate,[42] and finally succeeded in getting the two officials freed. During the following five

[38]Hopei, Anhwei, Kwangtung, Kiangsi, and Fukien. See Domes, *Kulturrevolution und Armee* (Bonn: Studiengesellschaft für Zeitprobleme, 1967), pp. 111–113.

[39]Kiangsi, Kwangsi, Inner Mongolia, Chekiang, Yunnan, Tsinghai, Tientsin, Sinkiang, and Tibet. See *ibid.*

[40]Kirin, Liaoning, Honan, Shensi, Kansu, Hupei, Hunan, Szechuan, and Ninghsia. See *ibid.*

[41]Gordon A. Bennett, "Hsieh Fu-chih, China's Trouble-Shooter," *Far Eastern Economic Review,* Vol. 44 (1968), p. 184.

[42]On the Wuhan Incident, see, among others, *China Quarterly,* No. 32 (October-December 1967), pp. 185–190.

weeks, violent clashes again broke out in at least twelve provinces, and in some places they developed into protracted armed struggles.[43]

The "Wuhan Incident," as the Chinese Communists soon started to call it, can be regarded as the last, decisive turning point in the course of the Cultural Revolution. Soon after his release, Wang Li attacked "power holders within the army" in an article which was published in the August 17 edition of *Hung-ch'i*. The unity of the PLA, which Lin Piao had tried hard to keep intact, was seriously threatened. In order to save the situation, Lin convened a conference of regional military commanders and other high ranking PLA cadres in Peking during the first half of August. Here, a compromise was apparently reached. While the regional commanders agreed to purge some of their colleagues who had gone too far in supporting the anti-Maoist forces, Lin Piao consented to a definite turn against the extreme left. At the same time, the regional commanders acceded to the establishment of more revolutionary committees, but they obviously were assured that military representatives would control these organs. After a Red Guard "occupation" of the Ministry of Foreign Affairs in mid-August, Chou En-lai returned to the policies of "readjustment" which—in another context—he had promoted between 1959 and 1965. Thus, a Lin-Chou coalition with the regional military commanders set out to liquidate Mao's Cultural Revolution in its original form. On August 20, Wang Li was purged, while other henchmen of Chiang Ch'ing were accused of being "Kuomintang agents" and arrested in Peking.[44] The various competing leftist factions were ordered to stop fighting immediately, and the PLA moved in to enforce this order with military power in at least eleven provinces.

FIFTH STAGE. These events opened the fifth stage of the crisis. This stage, which ended in late March 1968, was dominated by military efforts to restore order. On August 14, the Peking authorities ordered that henceforward the Red Guards and other Maoist organizations would be allowed to attack opposition leaders only with their consent and that of the "military control commissions," which now started to supervise mass-organization activities in most areas of China. When Red Guard units seized classified archives in the Ministry for Chemical Industry, this act was condemned in very strong words by the CCP Central Committee, the State Council, the Military Commission, and the Central Cultural Revolution Group in a joint order issued on August 31. In the turbulent days between June and August, Maoist and anti-Maoist organizations had in some places stolen weapons from PLA arsenals, and it also appears that some local commanders had distributed weapons to competing factions. This was now strictly forbidden by another joint order of the four leading organs issued on September 4.

[43]Hupei, Kwangtung, Kiangsi, Chekiang, Kweichou, Yunnan, Kiangsu, Shanghai, Inner Mongolia, Tsinghai, Kansu, and Shantung. See *China News Analysis,* No. 676 (September 8, 1967).

[44]Kuang Feng, Lin Chieh, and Mu Hsin, later to be followed by Ch'i Pen-yu.

A day later, the turning of the tide became even more obvious when Chiang Ch'ing, in an address to delegates of Red Guard organizations from Anhwei, found strong words of praise for the military, which had been attacked by her henchmen only three weeks before, and at the same time called for discipline within the Maoist movement.

Restrictive measures now escalated rapidly. When the joint order of September 4 was published eleven days later, it included an additional statement that the enforcement of central orders henceforward rested with the regional commanders. Thus, for the first time since 1953, the center yielded to regionalist tendencies among the military leadership. The PLA soon started disciplinary actions against leftist organizations. In early October, Red Guards who had gone to the villages were exhorted to participate more than before in agricultural production. A few days later, on October 14, they were ordered to return to school, which they had left between May and August 1966. Such orders had previously been issued without much success in February, March, June, and September. This time, however, the military was entrusted with the task of enforcing them. In Peking, Tientsin, Shanghai, and Tsingtao, PLA units were reported to be "helping" the students to return to school, where in addition military instructors soon took over ideological education from Red Guard leaders. It is possible that similar things happened in other places, too.

At the same time, attempts were made to rebuild the shattered party organization. In October, Hsieh Fu-chih announced that a Ninth Party Congress would be convened sometime in 1968; and on November 27, a joint circular of the Central Committee and the Central Cultural Revolution Group asked the Maoist organizations to "give their opinion" on the procedures to be followed in convoking this conference. On December 2, the Central Committee published a notice on principles for the "readjustment, restoration, and reconstruction" of the CCP. By these and other measures, including a number of conferences that resulted in compromise agreements with regional and local military commanders, the threat of civil war was averted. Sporadic armed clashes continued to erupt, however; Chinese Communist news media reported such occurrences in nine provinces between December 15, 1965, and January 15, 1968.[45]

After the military conference in August, the drive to establish revolutionary committees in the provinces was renewed. But by the end of the year, only three more had been formed;[46] and in these, military partici-

[45]Chekiang, Honan, Kwangtung, Szechuan, Kiangsi, Yunnan, Shantung, Ninghsia, and Inner Mongolia.

[46]Tsinghai (August 12, 1967), Inner Mongolia (November 2), and Tientsin (December 6). Among the 80 standing committee members of the six revolutionary committees formed between January and April 1967, 36.25 percent were "revolutionary cadres," 32.5 percent represented the Maoist organizations, and 31.25 percent the PLA. In the three new committees, 44.7 percent of the 38 standing committee members represented the PLA, 31.6 percent the "revolutionary cadres," and only 23.7 percent the Maoist organizations.

pation was already much more evident than in the six committees that had been formed in spring 1967. The slow progress in the formation of these new provincial power organs obviously forced the central leadership to new compromises with the regional military commanders. Reports of a reception of military cadres by Mao and Lin on December 31, 1967, indicate that another important military conference was held in Peking around that time. Here the regional commanders obviously agreed to accelerate the pace of establishing revolutionary committees. Between early January and the end of March 1968, nine more committees were set up; this equalled the number established during the whole of 1967. Especially noteworthy was the fact that more than half of their leading personnel came from the PLA.[47]

Nevertheless, military unity during this period could not be taken for granted. There are indications that Lin Piao's long time aide, Yang Ch'eng-wu, who was appointed as Acting Chief of the General Staff in 1966, had made attempts to undercut the power of the major regional commanders by trying to appoint his own nominees as leaders of many units, and by denouncing some of the regional commanders as anti-party elements. At another military conference, which convened in Peking around March 20, the regional commanders seem to have won out against Yang. On March 24, the leadership announced that Yang, the First Political Commissar of the Air Force, Yu Li-chin, and the Peking Garrison Commander, Fu Ch'-ung-pi, were accused of having plotted a *coup d'etat* against the central leadership; and they were immediately removed from their positions. The charges against these three leading military figures appear somewhat shaky. The whole context of the purge suggests that Yang and his colleagues were made the scapegoats in a conflict in which the regional commanders succeeded in gaining influence within the central leadership. This theory is supported by the fact that the Commander of the Canton Military Region, Huang Yung-sheng, was appointed Chief of the General Staff; and that his deputy in Canton, Wen Yu-ch'eng, became Vice Chief of the General Staff and concurrently Peking Garrison Commander.

SIXTH STAGE. Growing military influence, disciplinary action against the Maoist organizations, and efforts to restore the party organization dominated the sixth stage of the crisis, which continued through the winter of 1968-69. Between the end of March and the beginning of September 1968, the drive for the establishment of revolutionary committees finally succeeded with the formation of such organs in the eleven remaining prov-

---

[47]Kiangsi (January 5, 1968), Kansu (January 24), Honan (January 27), Hopei (February 3), Hupei (February 5), Kwangtung (February 21), Kirin (March 6), Kiangsu (March 23), and Chekiang (March 24). Among the 130 standing committee members of these nine committees, the three constituent groups were represented as follows: PLA, 56.9 percent; "revolutionary cadres," 23.1 percent; Maoist organizations, twenty percent.

inces.[48] In these eleven committees, overall military representation continued to be very strong. The representation of "revolutionary cadres" was reduced in favor of Maoist organizations.[49] On the other hand, nine of the committees were headed by military men, and two by "revolutionary cadres," so that in none of the 29 committees did a representative of a Maoist organization succeed in reaching the chairmanship. Furthermore, a number of "mass organization" representatives seem to have been hand-picked by the regional military leaders.

In spite of the extension of these new power organs to all the provinces of China, preparations for the Ninth Party Congress did not unfold as the central leadership might have hoped. Although its convocation had been announced for October 1968, the congress did not actually meet until April 1969. Meanwhile, Maoist attacks concentrated more and more on Liu Shao-ch'i and some of his closest supporters. Armed struggle again erupted in a number of areas, particularly in Kwangsi and Kwangtung, in August and September 1968, and caused a great number of casualties. In a further drive to discipline the Red Guards, the central leadership ordered the establishment of "control commissions" consisting of industrial workers in the cities and peasants in the countryside. This decision may have been taken in order to relieve the PLA of some of its now extensive duties in running civilian affairs. But it may also have symbolized the downgrading of Maoist organizations; it was the industrial workers and peasants who had offered the most violent resistance to the Maoist drive in January 1967.

During summer and autumn 1968, the posting of "big character posters" was forbidden in many Chinese cities; and in some areas, notably Kirin, Honan, Szechuan, and Sinkiang, Red Guard organizations were disbanded. Thus, Mao's original intentions in general and the leftist mass organizations in particular, seem to have become casualties of the PLA's drive for unity and consolidation.

These efforts at consolidation reached their apex at the "enlarged" twelfth plenary meeting of the Eighth CCP Central Committee, which convened in Peking on October 11. The communiqué of this meeting did not reveal the number of Central Committee members attending. From accompanying evidence, however, the conclusion can be drawn that only 26 out of 91 full members took part. In addition, about 85 representatives of the Central Cultural Revolution Group and of provincial revolutionary committees, and—more remarkably—135 leading PLA cadres attended the

[48]Hunan (April 8, 1968), Anhwei (April 18), Ninghsia (April 20), Shensi (May 1), Liaoning (May 10), Szechuan (May 31), Yunnan (August 13), Fukien (August 19), Kwangsi (August 26), Tibet and Sinkiang (both September 5).

[49]Among the 203 standing committee members of these eleven provinces; 48.8 percent represented the PLA, 31.5 percent the Maoist organizations, and 19.7 percent were "revolutionary cadres."

plenum. The major decision of this conference was the expulsion of Liu Shao-ch'i, and possibly a number of his supporters, from the CCP and from all posts both inside and outside the party.[50] In addition, the plenum announced the convocation of the Ninth Party Congress for some time in 1969. A campaign was also started to admit "fresh blood" into the party, a measure obviously aimed at bringing in a number of members of Maoist organizations, while at the same time placing them under strict party discipline.

The twelfth plenum ended with the acceptance of the draft of a new party constitution,[51] which in its preamble formally named Lin Piao as the successor of Mao Tse-tung. This draft was adopted without significant change by the Ninth Party Congress, which met in Peking during April 1969. Contrary to earlier Maoist announcements, the number of delegates to the Congress was not in the range of eight to ten thousand; they numbered exactly 1,512, which was comparable to the Eighth Congress and reflected no basic change in political style. Among the 24 leading members of the Presidium, which included 176 delegates in all, eleven were military men and two others had strong military connections. The Congress was conducted behind a screen of strict secrecy, and only three communiques have been published concerning its work. According to the new constitution, the party congress will meet only once every five years, and then only under "normal conditions." It does not provide for any fixed number of Central Committee plenary meetings, but leaves their convocation entirely to the Politburo and its Standing Committee. No provision is made for the establishment of party control commissions, to which criticized members may appeal. The PLA is mentioned extensively in the text, and is given authority to set up party organizations of its own at every level below the central party organs; heretofore, this was only possible at lower levels.

Conclusions

The conflict of the Cultural Revolution produced a fundamental split in the Chinese Communist Party, which led subsequently to a breakdown of the party organization in many areas of China. It also brought about remarkable changes in the methods by which intra-party disputes are resolved.

SYMBOLS. This applies, first of all, to the symbols used by the opposing forces. Until 1959, groups within the party used basically the same language; but as distinct factions began to take shape in the early 1960s, differences in terminology became apparent. Where the Maoists stressed "uninterrupted revolution," for example, the anti-Maoists emphasized

---

[50]For the communique of the twelfth plenary meeting, see *Peking Review,* No. 44, supplement (1968).

[51]English translation in *New York Times,* January 8, 1969.

"step-by-step development." Other pairs of contradictory symbols were: "the Thought of Mao Tse-tung" *versus* "Marxism-Leninism;" the "masses" as against the "party" (or, "the party and Chairman Mao"); "contradiction" *versus* "production" or "consolidation." While the Maoists tended to use the words "right" and "wrong" as decisive criteria in evaluating policies, the anti-Maoists preferred the terms "objective" and "subjective." The Maoists stressed "redness," while the anti-Maoists placed greater emphasis on "expertness." With respect to denunciatory symbols, the leftists used a whole catalog of terms, most prominent among them being "revisionism," "counter-revolutionary," "conservative," and "black." They called their adversaries "powerholders within the party taking the capitalist road," "landlords, rich peasants, counter-revolutionaries, bad elements and rightists," "three-anti-elements" (anti-party, anti-Socialist, and anti-Maoist), and at the height of conflict, even "freaks and monsters," "snakes," "worms," or "rats." Not so well versed in abusive language, the anti-Maoists usually were content to castigate the Maoists as being influenced by "subjectivism," and to apply to them the term "leftist," albeit in quotation marks.[52]

This brief listing of conflicting symbols also indicates that the crisis developed as a conflict on three distinct levels. With respect to *political style,* the Maoists concentrated on open and abusive accusations, which were raised in the context of a general atmosphere of "struggle." Their opponents, on the other hand, preferred to stress consolidation, peace and order, and concentration on the development of the country. In this connection, one should note that many pronouncements by the military and by surviving representatives of the administrative machine after February 1967 seemed to be more in conformity with anti-Maoist concepts of political style than with the Maoist version. Second, the conflict was also a dispute over the *character of the party.* Here, a basic question was whether the party should be regarded as an auxiliary organ to promote the ideas and the power position of a particular individual, or of one or

[52]The quoted terms are mostly, but not entirely, taken from "On Khrushchev's Phoney Communism and its Historical Lessons for the World. Ninth article by the Editorial Departments of *Jen-min Jih-pao* and *Hung-ch'i* commenting on the Open Letter of the Central Committee of the C.P.S.U.," in *Peking Review,* Vol. 7, No. 29 (July 17, 1964), pp. 7 ff.; *Carry The Great Proletarian Cultural Revolution Through To The End* (Peking: 1966); "Hold Still Higher the Great Red Banner of Mao Tse-tung's Thought, Bring the Mass Movement for the Creative Study and Application of Chairman Mao's Works to a New and Higher Stage, and Turn Our Army Into a Genuine, Great School of Mao Tse-tung's Thought," *Jen-min Jih-pao,* January 2, 1967; Lo Keng-mo, "The Character of Rural People's Communes at the Present Stage," *Kung-jen Jih-pao* (Peking), July 19, 1961; "Consolidate the Great Achievements and Strive for New Victories," *Jen-min Jih-pao,* January 1, 1963; "P'eng Teh-huai's So-called 'Letter of Opinion' to Chairman Mao at the 1959 Lushan Conference," *Ke-ming Ch'uan-liu,* August 24, 1967.

two individuals, or whether the individual should be regarded as a servant of an overriding cause led by the collectivity of the party represented by its legitimate leadership organs. Finally, although the Maoists in February 1967 (when they were already under military influence) adopted the slogan of "grasping revolution and promoting production," the Maoist emphasis was clearly on *revolution,* while it was the anti-Maoists who stressed the importance of *production.*

ORGANIZATIONAL WEAPONS. Basic differences can also be discerned with respect to the organizational weapons used in the conflict. Mao and his supporters were the first group in the history of the Chinese Communist Party to rely on newly created *ad hoc* organizations outside the regular party chain of command as a major instrument of factional struggle.

The Red Guards, created in spring and summer 1966, and also the "revolutionary rebels," who appeared at about the beginning of 1967, were mainly groups of people who were discontented with the party machine. Most prominent among them were young people between fourteen and 25 years of age: PLA cadets, children of "reliable" Maoist cadres, and rural youngsters living in boarding schools in the cities formed the hard core. During the early stages of the Maoist movement, this attempt at the mobilization of a group influenced by not-too-well sublimated puberty problems (in particular, the frustrations resulting from a rather rigid educational system), which could easily be converted into aggressions, seemed to be highly successful. Soon, however, the movement developed a considerable number of competing factions; and by summer 1967, it was proving very difficult to control. The basic failure of the Maoist drive thus became apparent: as an attempt at rationalizing the irrational and organizing the unorganizable, it was bound to end in chaotic infighting.

In the early stages of the struggle, the anti-Maoists first tried to apply the same organizational weapon that had proved successful when they practically sabotaged the "Socialist education" movement in 1963 and 1964. Using the regular channels of the party machine, they tried to deflect the Maoist effort by verbally accepting parts of the Maoist program while in practice continuing to pursue their own political platform. When the Maoists turned to the schools in summer 1966 as the main center of their revolutionary activities, the organizational answer of the Liu Shao-ch'i faction was still implemented within the party machine: party committees formed "working teams" which were supposed to discipline the emerging groups of revolutionary youngsters. Only under the impact of the Red Guard rampage in autumn 1966, did the anti-Maoists also turn to organizational weapons outside of regular party channels. Following the Maoist blueprint, they themselves created *ad hoc* organizations, relying mostly on industrial workers who formed militia-type units to fight against the

Red Guards and the "revolutionary rebels." In addition, the opposition also incited workers and peasants to go on strike and to disrupt the agricultural collectives.

ECLIPSE OF THE PARTY. As we have seen, these efforts succeeded in halting the Maoist offensive by late January 1967. It did *not,* however, succeed in overthrowing the Mao-Lin group, nor did it even enable Liu and his supporters to maintain their positions. Astonishingly enough, the powers of resistance of the regular party and the regular mass organizations proved to be rather low. The seemingly well-oiled party apparatus was soon in a shambles. This is to be accounted for by three main considerations.

In the first place, with its restrictive if not oppressive attitude toward many strata of Chinese society, the party had more and more lost the support of the majority of the population. When Mao and his supporters set out to attack the party machine, few Chinese were prepared to give active support to the organization. The general attitude was to "sit down and watch the tiger eating the lion," rather than to defend unpopular party functionaries against attacks by youth and the military. Moreover, it should be kept in mind that the party machine, against which the Maoist thrust of 1966 and 1967 was directed, had undergone a deep and nearly devastating crisis in the aftermath of the Great Leap Forward. In this period, its lines of control had been badly damaged at the basic level. Recuperation from this crisis had been under way ever since 1963, but the recovery was not yet fully accomplished when the new crisis began.

Finally, at the regional and provincial levels, a growing rivalry had developed between the leading civilian and military party cadres. The PLA, therefore, was only too willing to assist the Maoist offensive against the civilian party machine, even if it did not necessarily support the objectives of this drive. But the party machine had not been constructed to deal with demonstrations of military power, and hence its collapse was inevitable.

RISE OF THE MILITARY. With the regular party machine thus shattered, the chain of command of the government administration badly damaged, and the Maoist movement splitting up into a large number of competing factions, the PLA emerged as the only instrument of power that remained relatively intact. After late January 1967, it therefore set out to take over control, at least for the time being. Under the impact of this military drive for power in the provinces, new types of leadership organizations came to the fore. The first of these was the "commune," which was established by leftist organizations in Shanghai on February 5, 1967, and which provided for a committee-type of government following the model of the 1871 Paris Commune. The implementation of this utopian concept of decentralized and direct democracy, however, proved to be impractical.

The commune was, therefore, never fully endorsed by the central authorities, it did not spread from Shanghai to other places, and even in Shanghai it was disbanded after less than three weeks.

Military intervention in most provinces led to the establishment of provisional government agencies which were under undisguised military control. These were called "temporary power organs," and were made up almost entirely of PLA personnel. But their task was transitional, to pave the way for a more durable organ which has now been set up in all Chinese provinces, the so-called revolutionary committees. These committees unite, on the provincial level, the leadership of the administrative and economic structures, as well as of the party and mass organizations, which are now under reconstruction. Although originally conceived as representing an equal coalition of the Maoist organizations, the PLA, and pro-Maoist party and administrative cadres,[53] it is clear from developments in 1967 and 1968 that the military has come out as the decisive factor in them.

This fact is reflected in their numerical composition. Of the 479 standing committee members on the 29 provincial revolutionary committees as of August 1, 1969, a total of 235 or 49 percent were military men, and 109 or 22.8 percent "revolutionary cadres," while 132 or 27.6 percent represented the Maoist organizations. Among the 219 chairmen and vice-chairmen, 100 represented the PLA (45.7 percent), 62 the "revolutionary cadres" (28.3 percent), and 57 the Maoist organizations (26 percent). The picture becomes even more distinct with the 29 chairmen, of whom 22 or 75.9 percent are either generals (thirteen or 44.8 percent) or military commissars (9 or 31.1 percent). Two other chairmen are party cadres who at the same time hold the position of commissar in the PLA. Hence there remain only four out of 29 chairmen with a strictly civilian background.

Most prominent among the emerging regional leadership are the military region commanders. With the army field forces (which comprise about eighty percent of China's total ground forces) already under their direct command, seven of them have also taken over the chairmanship of the revolutionary committees in the most important provinces of their regions.[54] Three others are vice-chairmen of revolutionary committees,[55] and only two remain without an assignment in these power organs.[56] In

[53]See p. 80, above.

[54]Ch'en Hsi-lien (Shenyang) in Liaoning, Hsu Shih-yu (Nanking) in Kiangsu, Han Hsien-ch'u (Foochow) in Fukien, Tseng Ssu-yu (Wuhan) in Hupei, Huang Yung-sheng (Canton) in Kwangtung, Tseng Yung-ya (Tibet) in Tibet, and—most probably now—Yang Te-chih (Tsinan) in Shantung.

[55]Cheng Wei-shan (Peking) in Peking, Wang En-mao (Sinkiang) in Sinkiang, and Liang Hsing-ch'u (Chengtu) in Szechuan.

[56]Chang Ta-chih (Lanchow), and Ch'in Chi-wei (Kunming), the latter most probably already ousted from office.

short, one of the major results of the Cultural Revolution thus far has been a military takeover in most Chinese provinces.

OUTCOME. To the extent that the recent crisis was caused by a basic policy conflict, the result has obviously not been a decisive victory for the Maoist line. Although the political ideas of Mao's principal opponent, Liu Shao-ch'i, were denounced as "revisionist" and ostensibly repudiated, developments in 1968 and early 1969 suggest that a return to more orthodox rather than revolution-oriented policies may well be in preparation. But insofar as the Cultural Revolution presents itself as a power struggle, and most conspicuously as a fight for the succession while the aging leader is still alive, it has resulted in a thoroughgoing purge of the Liu group, at least at the central level. Of 97 full members of the Eighth Central Committee in August 1966, five have since died under normal circumstances,[57] and 54 were apparently purged during the Cultural Revolution.[58] Only 37 were reelected to the Ninth Central Committee,[59] 34 of them as full members and three as alternates; while one,[60] although not reelected to the new Central Committee, still participated in the 1969 May Day celebrations in Peking and is therefore not considered as purged in this context. This leaves only a little more than a third of the August 1966 membership in positions of relatively good standing with the current central leadership; and nineteen of them are military men. Among the 170 full members of the Ninth Central Committee elected in April 1969, there are 68 professional soldiers and 19 military commissars, leaving PLA representation at 87 or 51.2 percent of the full membership. In addition, there are 53 "revolutionary cadres" and 29 representatives of "mass organizations."

The composition of the new Politburo offers some clues to the nature of the coalition that now rules the country:

[57]Wu Yu-chang, Yeh Chi-chuang, Hsu T'e-li, Liu Ch'ang-sheng and Chao Erh-lu.

[58]Liu Shao-ch'i, Teng Hsiao-p'ing, Lu Ting-yi, Lo Jui-ch'ing, P'eng Teh-huai, Liao Ch'eng-chih, Lin Feng, P'eng Chen, Ulanfu, Huang K'e-ch'eng, T'an Cheng, Ho Lung, Yang Shang-k'un, Sung Jen-ch'iung, Liu Hsiao, Li Wei-han, Wang Chia-hsiang, Liu Lan-t'ao, Liu Ning-i, Po I-po, Hu Ch'iao-mu, Yang Hsiu-feng, Shu T'ung, Chang Chi-ch'un, Ch'eng Tzu-hua, Wu Hsiu-ch'uan, Hsiao K'e, Ch'ien Ying, Wang Ts'ung-wu, Ma Ming-fang, Chang Wen-t'ien, T'an Chen-lin, Ch'en Shao-min, Li Pao-hua, Hsu Kuang-ta, Lin T'ieh, Cheng Wei-san, Hsiao Hua, Hu Yao-pang, Ou-yang Ch'in, Hsi Chung-hsun, An Tzu-wen, Chia To'-Fu, Li Li-san, Li Ch'ing-ch'uan, Wu Chih-p'u, Lu Cheng-ts'ao, T'ao Chu, Ch'en Shao-yu, Yang Hsien-chen, Lo Kuei-po, Chang Ching-wu, Yeh Fei.

[59]Mao Tse-tung, Chu Teh, Chou En-lai, Tung Pi-wu, Ch'en Yun, Lin Piao, Ch'en Po-ta, Ts'ai Ch'ang, Li Fu-ch'un, Hsu Hsiang-ch'ien, Teng Ying-ch'ao, Liu Po-ch'eng, Ch'en Yi, Li Hsien-nien, Nieh Jung-chen, Chang Ting-ch'eng, T'eng Tai-yuan, Hsiao Ching-kuang, Su Yu, Wang Shou-tao, Teng Tzu-hui, Yeh Chien-ying, Chang Yun-yi, K'ang Sheng, Ch'en Yu, Teng Hua, Li Hsueh-feng, Wang Chen, Tseng Shan, Hsu Hai-tung, Liu Ke-p'ing, Hsieh Fu-chih, Wang Shu-sheng, Tseng Hsi-sheng, Wang En-mao, Yang Te-chih, Wei Kuo-ch'ing.

[60]Hsieh Chueh-ts'ai.

1. Mao Tse-tung, Chairman of the Central Committee.
2. Marshal Lin Piao, Vice-Chairman of the Central Committee, Acting Chairman of the Central Committee's Military Commission, Vice-Premier, and Minister of National Defense.
3. Chou En-lai, Prime Minister.
4. Ch'en Po-ta, Chairman of the Central Cultural Revolution Group, and President, National Peking University.
5. K'ang Sheng, former Chief of Intelligence, and now Advisor to the Cultural Revolution Group.
6. Chang Ch'un-ch'iao, member of the Cultural Revolution Group, and Chairman of the Shanghai Municipal Revolutionary Committee.
7. General Ch'en Hsi-lien, Chairman of the Liaoning Provincial Revolutionary Committee, and Commander of the Shenyang Military Region.
8. Chiang Ch'ing (Mme. Mao), First Vice-Chairman of the Cultural Revolution Group.
9. General Ch'iu Hui-tso, Director of the General Logistical Department of the PLA.
10. Marshal Chu Teh, Chairman of the Standing Committee, National People's Congress.
11. General Hsieh Fu-chih, Vice-Premier, Minister of Public Security, and Chairman of the Peking Municipal Revolutionary Committee.
12. General Hsu Shih-yu, Chairman of· the Kiangsu Provincial Revolutionary Committee, and Commander of the Nanking Military Region.
13. General Huang Yung-sheng, Chief of the General Staff, and former Chairman of the Kuangtung Provincial Revolutionary Committee.
14. Li Hsien-nien, Vice-Premier, Minister of Finance, and possibly Acting Minister of Foreign Affairs as well.
15. Admiral Li Tso-p'eng, Deputy Commander of the Navy, and possibly Director of the PLA General Political Department.
16. Marshal Liu Po-ch'eng, Vice-Chairman of the Standing Committee, National People's Congress.
17. Tung Pi-wu, Vice-Chairman and now Acting Chairman of the People's Republic.
18. General Wu Fa-hsien, Deputy Chief of the General Staff, Commander of the Air Force.
19. Yao Wen-yuan (son-in-law of Mao Tse-tung), member of the Cultural Revolution Group, and Vice-Chairman of the Shanghai Muncipal Revolutionary Committee.
20. Marshal Yeh Chien-ying, Director of the PLA Training Department.

21. Yeh Ch'un (Mme. Lin Piao), most probably in a leading position in the PLA General Political Department.

Alternate members:

1. Chi Teng-k'uei, Vice-Chairman of the Honan Provincial Revolutionary Committee.
2. Li Hsueh-feng, Chairman of the Hopei Provincial Revolutionary Committee.
3. General Li Teh-sheng, Chairman of the Anhwei Provincial Revolutionary Committee, Commander of the Anhwei Military District.
4. General Wang Tung-hsing, Commander of the Peking Guard Regiment.

This coalition reflects a combination of four main forces: the central military leadership, regional military commanders, the remnants of the old administrative apparatus centering around Chou En-lai, and the Cultural Revolution Group (which considers itself as the central organ of the Maoist organizations). In this setup, the administrative apparatus, decimated in leadership and with a damaged organizational structure as a result of the protracted crisis, appears to be much weaker than it was before 1966. Meanwhile, the power of the Cultural Revolution Group is being increasingly undercut by disciplinary action against the Red Guards and other Maoist organizations. With its two partners thus in precarious straits, the influence of the PLA in the central decision-making process has sharply increased. The position of Mao Tse-tung himself remains unclear. In spite of the outward appearance of triumph over his opponents in the party, the aging leader seems to have lost much of his influence. Although the ruling authorities continue to refer to his "instructions," and although the cult of personality dedicated to him has reached the proportions of apotheosis, one may well doubt whether he really still takes part in day-to-day decision-making.

The Cultural Revolution cannot, therefore, be regarded as having resulted in a Maoist victory. While the strongly centralized leadership structure that prevailed in the country down to 1966 has obviously been damaged, trends towards military regionalism—albeit of a different type from that in the early years of the People's Republic—are clearly detectable. The party split that developed in recent years has thus endangered the prospects for Communist China, and it is still doubtful whether this split can be entirely overcome in the forseeable future.[61]

[61]The author is indebted to Marie-Luise Näth for her assistance with documentation, and for her valuable critical suggestions in the preparation of this chapter.

Chapter Five

The Military: Their Role in the Policy Process

William W. Whitson

Introduction

It is curious that by 1970, so many post-World War II revolutions in Asia and Africa should have "turned right," that is, fallen under the control of men who had become skeptical of the promise that major social and economic achievements could be attained rapidly, even suddenly, at minimal political and human costs. In Burma, Indonesia, South Korea, Pakistan, and South Viet-Nam, twenty years of experience found the heady wine of anti-colonialism, revolution, and independence turning into the stale beer of governmental responsibility and vexatious administrative routine. It is the contention of this essay that the Chinese Communists have now joined this club, having passed from a "liberal" euphoria of the "revolution militant" to a "conservative" sobriety of the "revolution betrayed."

Without forcing false comparisons or contrasts with other Asian countries, it is suggested here that the competition for power among three major functional elites in China over the past twenty years has generated a succession of compromises between revolutionary ideals and political-economic realities. The first of these elites was made up of career military commanders, that is, men whose professional lives since 1937 (or earlier) had focused principally on combat planning, training, or operations.[1] The second elite included the men most responsible for resource management in the civil sphere. that is, the party administrators. The third functional elite was composed of "ideologues," both military ("commissars") and civil (principally members of the party propaganda apparatus). For the purposes of this discussion, which is directed primarily to the role of

[1]For a more detailed discussion of the concept of Chinese Communist military generations, see William W. Whitson, "The Concept of Military Generation: The Chinese Communist Case," *Asian Survey,* Vol. 8, No. 11 (November 1968).

commanders and commissars in the policy process, ideologues are men whose energies have been directed to the task of rationalizing prevailing policies, plans, and programs with Communist ideology.

Through the first ten to twenty years of his career, depending upon the date of his entry into the Communist Party, an individual frequently found himself engaged in a struggle for personal political survival simultaneously in all three spheres of activity: military command, civil administration, and ideology. Especially in the late 1920s and early 1930s, it was often impossible to divorce the dialogue over the philosophical dimensions of communism from a practical concern for its military and administrative dimensions. In Kiangsi or on the Long March, for example, senior figures such as Ch'en Yi, the present Foreign Minister, or Nieh Jung-chen, the Chairman of the National Defense Scientific and Technology Commission, both of whom were educated in France, could be challenged with questions simultaneously demanding their personal responses in all three spheres. Even after 1950, the essential indivisibility of ideology, civil administration, and national defense would underline the fact that no senior leader, whether at the national, regional, military district (province) or even corps level, could be exclusively concerned with one sphere, completely indifferent to the other two.

However, the expansion of the Communist Party and the People's Liberation Army, matched by an expansion of their respective administrative burdens, brought as early as 1931—but especially after 1946—an inescapable requirement for specialization of function and division of labor. Within the military, for example, a recent study has demonstrated that only about ten percent of five hundred senior military leaders in key positions between 1966 and late 1967 had enjoyed equal experience and success as both a commander and a commissar. The other 450 men had specialized in either commissar functions or operational command functions.[2] After 1950, such functional specialization tended to accentuate one sphere of behavior at the expense of the other two, depending on the individual's role.

Thus, civil administrators tended to become increasingly engrossed with rational resource allocation (economic planners and managers) or administration (party and government managers). Military commanders tended to become preoccupied with the creation and potential employment of a combat effective military machine. And ideologues, whether in the party, the government, or the military hierarchy (General Political Department propagandists), dedicated themselves to their role of "institutional conscience"—a priesthood, whether in or out of uniform, engaged in the

[2]See William W. Whitson, *The Political Dynamics of the Chinese Communist Military Elite* (Washington: Office of the Chief of Military History, 1968). As large sections of this study are classified, it is not available for general distribution.

search for and the exposition of a dynamic national ethic, both to inspire and to measure the achievements of commanders and civil administrators.

While the energies and talents of civil administrators and military commanders would focus on the world of reality, that is, the organization of human and material resources for the achievement of visible progress in production and distribution, the ideologues would be measuring those achievements against an ideal model of both personal and institutional behavior. By 1958, the ideologues, including Mao Tse-tung, would detect signs of significant deviation from their own notions of revolutionary ideals. By mid-1968, a decade of effort to revive the *élan* and the mode of a "revolution militant" would end in a climax of "revolutionary" excesses on the part of young Red Guard militants. Their abrupt and ruthless suppression by the late summer of 1968 would reflect the comparative victory of party administrators and military commanders, whose numerical dominance in the new provincial revolutionary committees suggested that ideology and ideologues had been forced once again to compromise with the realities of a major foreign threat coupled with the internal threat to security resulting from the dislocations of the Cultural Revolution. Regardless of propaganda to the contrary, the ensuing mobilization of resources under the pervasive direction of military cadres at all levels seemed to employ the theme of war preparedness (and Mao's thought) to buttress administrative rationality and the notion that it was better for a society to run well than to run fast.

After analyzing the process whereby commanders contributed to the frustration of ideologue initiatives between 1949 and 1970, this essay will conclude with comments on the implications of the 1968 commander-civil administrator ascendancy for domestic and foreign policy, and on the permanence of the present military role in the policy process.

The Revolution Militant: 1949

When the People's Republic of China was established in October 1949, two major field armies were still engaged in massive offensives in Northwest and Southwest China.[3] In the Southwest, the Second Field Army under the joint leadership of Liu Po-ch'eng and Teng Hsiao-p'ing was massing for the campaign against Chungking and Chengtu in wealthy Szechuan province. There remained the burdensome task of conquering Yunnan and Tibet, which would not be completed until mid-1951. Likewise in the Northwest, the First Field Army under P'eng Teh-huai and Ho Lung had just fought the battle of Lanchow, and was engaged in the long march up the Hohsi corridor into Sinkiang. This campaign would

[3]For a useful general treatment of this period, see Lionel Max Chassin, *The Communist Conquest of China* (Cambridge: Harvard University Press, 1965).

also occupy such senior figures as Wang En-mao (still First Political Com-missar of the Sinkiang Military Region and Vice-Chairman of the Sinkiang Revolutionary Committee) and Wang Chen (now Minister of State Farms and Land Reclamation) well into 1951. In East China, Ch'en Yi's Third Field Army had seized Shanghai, but still faced the problem of mopping up Nationalist resistance in the coastal provinces of Chekiang and Fukien. Elements of Lin Piao's Fourth Field Army occupied Wuhan and Canton, having swept across the Yangtze River after breaking out of Manchuria in late 1948 to assist in the conquest of Peking, Tientsin, and Taiyuan.

The 1948 withdrawal of Lin Piao's forces from Manchuria and the April 1949 offensive by the Second and Third field armies across the Yangtze River had marked a shift in the war's center of gravity away from the North-east and North China into the South and Southwest, areas from which Communist influence had largely been absent for fifteen years (since the departure of Communist forces from Kiangsi in October 1934 on the Long March). Thus, while the militant phase of revolution had already been completed in North China and Manchuria, it was still in progress in other areas where older military leaders, with origins principally in four Yangtze River provinces (Kiangsi, Hunan, Hupei, Szechuan), were leading younger northerners on campaigns of conquest and occupation.

A distinction may be drawn between the militant phase and the later "triumphant" phase of the revolution because the roles of commanders, administrators, and ideologues would necessarily experience a shift in emphasis as one phase ended and the next began. At the climax of the revolution militant in 1949, as field armies of nearly one million men con-tinued to maneuver into Northwest and Southwest China, all three elites could agree without difficulty on priorities of resource allocation. In effect, until military victory had been firmly secured, there could be no denial of the resources necessary for the ultimate achievement of that goal. Thus, immediately following the Nationalist surrender at Taiyuan, Nieh Jung-chen's Eighteenth and Nineteenth armies were ordered west and south-west to reinforce the poorly-equipped armies under P'eng Teh-huai. Elements of Lin Piao's Fourth Field Army were moved west along the Yangtze River to provide a reserve for the Second Field Army offensive against Chungking. Until these vital areas had been brought to heel, com-manders would retain first claim on resources; no administrator could conceive of diverting essential manpower to civil, non-operational affairs, and ideologues would continue to accent the primacy of military violence in their revolutionary model.

However, in North China and Manchuria, the revolution triumphant had already brought administrators to the forefront, as nation-building now became the obvious requirement. Consumed by problems associated with the rebuilding of a war-torn economy, these men had already begun to claim the services of capable military leaders, who began to shed their military uniforms in order to tackle very real issues of social, political, and economic organization. Even commanders who remained in uniform could perceive and answer the need for public works, the rebuilding of railroads, highways, and vital communications facilities, and for the support of harassed civil administrators. In such a context, the ideologue was now challenged to translate the slogans of revolution into the reality of reform, indoctrinating all classes with a new vision of national purpose.

The north-to-south transition from the revolution militant to the revolution triumphant thus posed practical administrative questions for commanders and administrators alike. In the political sphere before October 1950, they were confronted by the problems of eradicating residual local opposition, including Nationalist guerrillas, and creating a viable political organization capable of administering the energies of six hundred million people. In the economic sphere, they were challenged to reconstruct a production and distribution infrastructure that had suffered the ravages of thirteen years of warfare. At the same time, they were required to anticipate a rational investment program that might promise maximum growth in minimal time.

While military and civil administrators were wrestling with these questions, the ideologues were enmeshed in the age-old question of loyalty: how to replace traditional loyalty to specific persons and places with a broader sense of patriotism, of obligation to "China." At the same time, they were challenged to sustain a spirit of self-sacrifice and national purpose that had already been overworked in the name of a foreign or domestic threat ever since 1937. Yet the memory of earlier trials and crises must have sustained them at this hour of victory, when their sacrifices would have seemed vindicated, and with the future offering brilliant new possibilities for applying the magic of their pseudo-religious message.

In this 1949 context of confident expectation among ideologues that a new China was undergoing its birth pangs, matched by the preoccupation of commanders and administrators with burgeoning organizational problems, commanders enjoyed unprecedented power and authority. The country had been temporarily divided into six huge regions, each under a military and administrative committee (MAC). In those areas that had not been organized by the Communist Party during the Sino-Japanese War, that is, all of China except the area north of the Huai River in Anhwei Province, field army commanders served concurrently as chairmen of the military and administrative committees (East, South, Southwest and Northwest China committees).[4] Only in Manchuria (Northeast MAC) and North China (North China MAC) had commanders begun to relinquish authority

[4]For an excellent treatment of this period in South China, see John Gittings, *The Role of the Chinese Army* (London, New York, Toronto: Oxford University Press, 1967), pp. 32 ff.

to civil party cadres, in part because many units under Lin Piao's Fourth Field Army and Nieh Jung-chen's North China Field Army had been moved south to reinforce continuing military operations.

Such reinforcements notwithstanding, it is important to remember that each field army had been largely independent in its expansion and civil war operational evolution.[5] This fact is fundamental to any understanding of post-1950 military-political behavior in China. With separate origins in different regions of Central China after the 1927 Nanchang uprising, three of the 1949 field armies (the First: P'eng Teh-huai, Ho Lung; the Second: Liu Po-ch'eng; the Third: Ch'en Yi, Su Yu) were still under the leadership of officers who had retained a distinctive group identity for a period of sixteen to twenty years. For example, most of the senior officers of the First Field Army had occupied leadership positions under Ho Lung since late 1927. Together they had experienced the tragedies of the Long March and the early stages of the Sino-Japanese War, as well as the expansion that had led to the victories of 1946 through 1950. Very few of these officers had been transferred in from other separate systems of career development. In a survey of five hundred senior military leaders in 1967, it was found that only about fifteen percent had shifted from one stream of unit evolution (ultimately leading to the 1949 field army organization) to another. The geographic, political, and economic circumstances of Chinese Communist struggles for survival and ascendancy, first against the Nationalists and, after 1937, against both the Japanese and the Nationalists, had accentuated this tendency toward the phenomenon of what Maoists have called "mountaintopism"—a term derived from the pre-1945 practice of establishing separate "soviet" or "border region" headquarters in remote mountain hideouts.

In contrast with these three field army systems, each of which had enjoyed a relatively separate development for as long as 22 years, the units which would eventually be brought within the overall designation of the Fourth Field Army under Lin Piao had come together for the first time only in late 1945. Many of the military leaders in this field army had served under Lin in Kiangsi in the early 1930s, had endured the Long March with him, and had served with him very briefly at the outset of the Sino-Japanese War. But Lin's wounds forced him to sit out the rest of the war after 1938; and other commanders had split up Lin's old units, expanded them, and enjoyed successes in notable contrast with the defeats that had characterized most of Lin's military operations before 1945.

On the other hand, Nieh Jung-chen's North China (sometimes called the "Fifth") Field Army had started its separate existence in 1937 as the first

[5]For a detailed discussion of the political role of the field army as a "military party," see the author's article on "The Field Army in Chinese Communist Military Politics," *China Quarterly*, No. 37 (January-March 1969).

border region established after the outbreak of the Sino-Japanese War. Known as the Chin-Cha-Chi Border Region (the Chinese shorthand term for Shansi-Chahar-Hopei provinces), this military government soon expanded into a formidable military-political bureaucracy that could provide 47 regular regiments for the August 1940 Hundred Regiment campaign. This success, and the close personal ties among the senior cadres whose collaboration had made it possible, would assume profound political significance 28 years later during the interfactional struggles of the Cultural Revolution.

By mid-1950, these five separate military elites had acquired regional power bases over which their combat forces had superimposed the authority and privilege of conquerors. This status was especially characteristic of local political power in the four large regions, mentioned earlier, where victory remained incomplete and the transition to the revolution triumphant was still in progress. The First Field Army elite was already consolidating its hold over what would become the Sinkiang and Lanchow military regions (see map). The same elite was sharing power with the Second Field Army elite in Szechuan. Additionally, Second Field Army leaders were establishing their hegemony over the Kunming Military Region, and were also mobilizing for the thrust westward that would reward them with control over the Tibet Military Region. The Third Field Army military leaders had shared the political-military spoils among themselves in the East China provinces that would later become the Foochow and Nanking military regions—the areas in which many of them had originated, and where they had fought during the early period of the Sino-Japanese War. Some of these Third Field Army leaders shared power with the Fifth (North China) Field Army elite in Shantung (later the Tsinan Military Region). The remainder of the Fifth Field Army leaders held key posts in what would become the Inner Mongolia and Peking military regions. Finally the Fourth Field Army high command retained partial control of political-military affairs in Manchuria, where they had recruited, organized, and expanded their forces, and where they had enjoyed their greatest successes during the civil war; and in Canton, to which the drive south had brought them for occupation duties by late 1949.

Armed with the formal power of position on military and administrative committees and their own field army high commands, plus the informal power of personal relationships and mutual confidence derived from long association within each of the five relatively independent military elites, these separate power centers proceeded to dispatch their most senior leaders to Peking to occupy key roles at the apex of the military-political bureaucracy. Without exception, each field army commander became a member of the Military Affairs Committee, the top party organ responsible for military affairs. From that vantage point, these leaders divided up the spoils of conquest: the most influential positions in the military and government hierarchies. For example, the First Field Army received representation on what would become the State Council and the General Staff, command of the armed forces, and representation in the General Political Department. Each field army elite received representation presumably commensurate with its military strength, the political and economic importance of its regional base, and the personal eloquence and influence of its chief negotiators. While many military leaders doffed uniforms and moved into formal party and government roles, it must be recognized that their appointments and their continuing source of political power derived from informal career affiliations already established through long-term experiences shared in the evolution of their own field armies. Although it remains to complete research on this feature of the 1949 political-military structure and distribution of power, it would thus appear that party, government, and military chains of command all came to reflect the existence and influence of what might be considered five separate military parties.

Aside from the buildup in Szechuan for the campaign into Tibet, by mid-1950 other military commanders of divisions, corps, and armies were engaged in a variety of missions throughout China, the priorities depending upon the locale and the date that the Communists arrived. In general, the sequence of operations began with counterinsurgency, and led through efforts at mass mobilization to party building. While contributing to mass mobilization, troop units could also direct their energies (as well as the peasants) to war recovery work and the reconstruction of infrastructure. While engaged in party building, the PLA could demobilize many cadres and thus provide a presumably loyal local elite of new administrators from its own excessive ranks. Such reductions in strength did not necessarily foster the earliest release of the best men, since the least combat-effective forces were usually deactivated for assignment to local public security roles or special construction tasks. For example, the majority of the First Field Army was redesignated the Production and Construction Army, and given the task of developing the vast untapped agriculture and mineral resources of Sinkiang.

At this point in time, on the eve of the Korean War, modernization and regularization of the armed forces was necessarily a low priority objective, although the demobilization process was an essential step toward that goal. However, until other more pressing matters had been given attention, particularly in the South, Southwest, and Northwest, even the best units of the PLA would remain an infantry army. Its officers were men whose professional lives had been passed without much familiarity with military technology; even the availability and employment of artillery had been delayed until late 1946. Such complex matters of military management and coordination as joint operations, the armor-infantry-artillery team, close air support, and vertical envelopment lay completely beyond the experience and the capability of most PLA staffs.

On the other hand, the organizing skills of the military, and especially of the military commissars, had been taxed to the limit for at least thirteen years during the many campaigns to mobilize the peasantry in support of regular Communist units. Thanks to those campaigns, the commissars had learned how to utilize the relatively primitive skills of the peasantry to furnish adequate intelligence, personnel, and logistical support services. At the decisive battle of Huai-Hai in late 1948, for example, civil party cadres coordinating with military commissars had mobilized over two million peasants to push wheelbarrow-loads of gasoline, food, and ammunition into the battle area in support of the Second and Third field armies, which together comprised over a million combat troops. It was thus the commissars who had acquired the experience necessary to establish a combat service support system, which was eventually labelled the General Rear Services Department of the General Staff.

The Evolution of Military Roles and Power

Proceeding from this 1949 foundation of unprecedented political power, the impact of professional military perspectives on domestic and foreign policies waxed and waned with the rise and fall of both internal and external threats to national security, on the one hand, and their own capabilities for responding to such threats, on the other.

Although the evidence is slender, it appears that the external threat of the Korean War in the summer of 1950 was matched by an internal threat which may have troubled Mao Tse-tung far more than United Nations victories after the September Inchon landing. This was the threat to central control posed by the system described above. Mao could not have been unconscious of the potential dangers inherent in the 1950 distribution of military and political power among five major field army commanders, each enjoying control of still-effective combat forces occupying and acquiring increasing control over distinctive geographic power bases. With loyal followers at local levels and strong representation at the center, these commanders might so circumscribe central initiatives as to hamstring Mao's personal power, while at the same time delaying the effective political and economic reunification of the country.

In that context, despite Mao's historic preference for "people's war" and the prosecution of a defensive war of attrition against a superior enemy who was coaxed into overextending his lines of supply by an offensive into Chinese territory, the year 1950 found many of the 73 Chinese

Communist regular corps again marshalling for war *beyond the national borders*. Mao may have agreed to such a strategy partly out of a desire to dislocate the dangerous internal distribution of political and military power, which would be eroded by the massive withdrawal of combat forces to the Northeast. Under such circumstances, Mao and his personal followers in the party might then gain an opportunity to consolidate their control over local and regional civil administrative functions.

Certainly other considerations must have entered into Mao's assessment of the situation. One was a fear of American aggression. In addition, the administrators, ideologues, and commanders alike may have appreciated the opportunity to use this foreign threat as a goad to essential internal reforms and sacrifices discussed earlier. In brief, the war could justify a host of organizational measures which might have been more difficult to impose in peacetime. Whatever may have been the Maoist calculus of motivations, costs, and gains, the war did permit party leaders to organize the country ostensibly in support of heroes fighting abroad, while also building a new network of party committees at local and provincial levels in anticipation of the first National People's Congress. This administrative effort was accompanied by a massive mobilization of manpower aimed at the reconstruction of vital national defense industries and communications. In retrospect, the period may be perceived as one of nation-building under forced draft.

In this context of foreign threat and domestic mobilization, however, the Korean War was also the beginning of what might be characterized as "the revolution forgotten." Under such circumstances, even ideologues might rationalize certain ideological irregularities in the name of national security. For example, the need for trained military manpower had to take precedence over class origins, and young men of all classes were welcomed into the Chinese People's Volunteers. Just as Mao may have deliberately thrown some of the most effective troops of his potential rivals into the Korean cauldron, so the majority of former Nationalist troops were also dispatched to silence the United Nations guns.

While Mao may have visualized a Machiavellian objective in these maneuvers (that is, to destroy an internal enemy, whether political or ideological, by sending him against an external enemy), the consequences of this period included a new commitment to professionalization on the part of both party administrators and military commanders, at the expense of the position of party and military ideologues. In the context of a foreign threat, much of the Maoist ideology—whose origins and evolution had been sustained by civil war—proved inapplicable. The perspectives and methods of people's war could never quite come to grips with the terrifying reality of United Nations firepower and the indifference of South

Korean villagers to Chinese commissar sermons.[6] Terrible casualties taught commanders that the professional values first emphasized by Russian advisers at Whampoa in the 1920s and at the Red Army Academy in Juichin in the early 1930s remained fundamentally valid during P'eng Teh-huai's offensive against the "Golden Line" in 1951.[7] Career military commissars could do little more than preach a text that they must have recognized to be inappropriate. Soon the commanders began to ignore the requirement for commissar signatures on operational orders. It was the beginning of hard times for military ideologues.

Meanwhile, at home, practical problems dominated the thinking of party administrators. Production and distribution for the war effort took priority over other concerns normally associated with "class warfare." While there were unquestionably disagreements between commanders and administrators over resource allocation between the home front and the combat front, at least their dialogue was focused on practical issues. Under such circumstances, ideologues could only search for new interpretations to old slogans of the revolution suddenly turned stale.

With the end of the Korean War in 1953, the prewar distribution of military-political power gradually experienced a slight alteration, marked by an erosion of the geographic concentration of power which had characterized the 1949 through 1950 period. In part, this alteration was reflected in the return of units from Korea to new garrison areas. Also, some senior military leaders were separated from their 1950 power bases. But the fact remains that most Korean War units returned to their place of origin, while sixty percent or more of each field army elite remained concentrated in its pre-1950 power base. An additional twenty percent of each elite was located in Peking, and another twenty percent was distributed among military regions as if to perform ambassadorial roles. In the same manner, Lin Piao's former power base in the national industrial center of Manchuria suffered an invasion by units and leaders from both the Second and Third field armies. Military power in the Peking Military Region was likewise shared among unit and personnel representatives of three field armies; while two field armies were represented in the Nanking Military Region, containing the important commercial center of Shanghai.

This redistribution of elite members and units probably reflected a deliberate balancing of power among the five field army "parties," which still constituted a main element in the informal web of Chinese politics. In September 1954, the deactivation of field armies and the reorganization of the

---

[6]For a superb account of the role of the commissars during the Korean War, see Alexander George, *The Chinese Communist Army in Action* (New York: Columbia University Press, 1967).

[7]This was the most advanced line of defense north of Seoul in April 1951.

country into thirteen military regions (see map) only slightly altered the formal structure of military power and authority. Acting through this structure, the new Chief of the General Staff, P'eng Teh-huai, sought to translate the lessons of United Nations firepower into a process of professionalization that was actually a continuation of the Korean War experience. With the input of more Russian advisors and new Russian equipment, Russian drill manuals and organizational concepts, the PLA leadership (principally the commanders) embarked on a campaign to modernize all three services.

In this campaign, it soon became evident that the commissar role would continue to be of marginal importance, as it had become during the Korean War. Despite a 1956 effort to reassert their power, their arguments for people's war and the Yenan spirit of collaboration with the masses fell on the deaf ears of the commanders. By 1960, the indifference of unit commanders and their superiors to their political responsibilities was reflected in the fact that over six thousand companies of the PLA did not have Communist Party branch committees.[8] Commissars complained that they could not obtain jeeps to accompany troops to the field for maneuvers.

Thus preoccupied with professional questions, including the challenging problems of American airpower and nuclear strategy, military professionals probably made a minimal contribution to the 1956 debate over economic plans for the next few years. On the other hand, they were doubtless vitally interested in obtaining their own share of available resources for the expansion of the defense mobilization base, the development of an air defense system, and the creation of an advanced weapons program.[9] In this context, they might not have opposed the concepts of the 1958 to 1960 Great Leap Forward, which promised enormous returns for comparatively small investments. But they soon had ample reason to regret that experiment.

At the Lushan Conference in August 1959, the Chief of the General Staff had the temerity to challenge the wisdom of Mao's vision of mass mobilization. Instead of discussing strategy, P'eng Teh-huai criticized the effects of the many economically disastrous programs of the 1958 to 1960 period. Echoing the feelings and assessments of many party administrators and economic planners, P'eng's speech must have punctuated a crisis of confidence in Mao's leadership. Despite P'eng's removal from his post soon after the conference, and the appointment of Lin Piao as his replacement, Mao evidently experienced a significant personal setback from which he did not begin to recover until the Eighth Central Committee Plenum in September 1962. During that three-year period, China suffered the con-

---

[8]For this and an encyclopaedia of facts about the PLA in 1960, see J. Chester Cheng (ed.), *The Politics of the Chinese Red Army* (Stanford: Stanford University Press, 1966).

[9]For a superior military-economic analysis of the cost of China's first atomic bomb, see James W. Barnett, Jr., "What Price China's Bomb?" *Military Review* (Command and General Staff College, Fort Leavenworth), Vol. 47, No. 8 (August 1967).

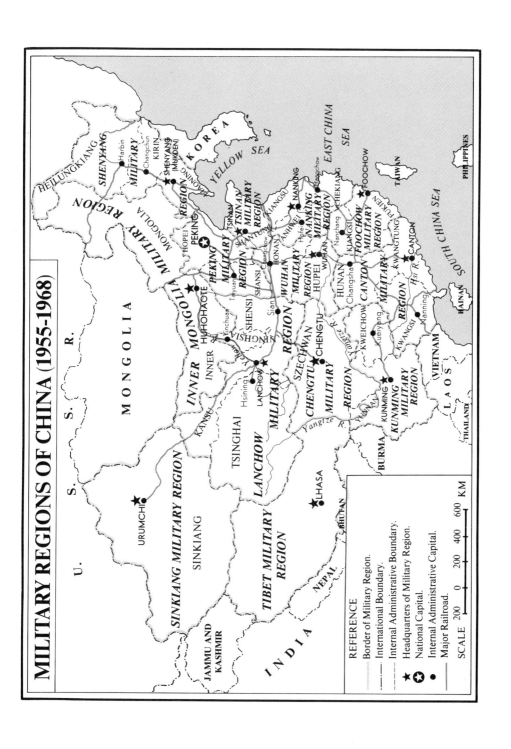

MILITARY REGIONS OF CHINA (1955-1968)

REFERENCE

Border of Military Region.
International Boundary.
Internal Administrative Boundary.
Headquarters of Military Region.
National Capital.
Internal Administrative Capital.
Major Railroad.

★ ✪ ●

SCALE 200 0 200 400 600 KM

sequences of Mao's ambitious plans. So did the PLA, where disease rates climbed and morale dropped to a point that prompted Lin Piao to warn darkly of problems with troop reliability.

In such a context of general economic suffering, an effort to revive the authority and power of the military commissars found expression in many techniques which would later characterize the Cultural Revolution: struggle meetings, "big character" posters, and the little red book of Mao's thought. Faced by morale problems, as well as shortages of gasoline and other material, the commanders may very well have appreciated commissar efforts to revive the *esprit* of troops through such programs as the "Four-Good" and "Five-Good" movements.[10]

But commissar success within the PLA soon captured the imagination of Mao Tse-tung, and probably encouraged him to employ this *military* priesthood against both party administrators and civil ideologues (that is, the party propagandists), whose faith in the Maoist vision had evidently suffered serious doubts after the disastrous consequences of the Great Leap. Indeed, a spate of articles by various senior members of the party propaganda apparatus after 1960 employed Chinese history to criticize Mao, especially his dismissal of faithful men like P'eng Teh-huai. Although these authors never used the names of active leaders, the references to historic figures would gradually become unmistakably synonymous with both current personalities and problems. These writings, together with the increasingly evident inclination among party ideologues to rationalize the status quo in party structure and administrative style, must have aroused Mao's deepest suspicions and resentment.

For Mao could recall other occasions when his attempts to adapt communism to Chinese circumstances had stimulated effective opposition from party administrators and ideologues, and from military commanders. Indeed, beginning with his attempts to consolidate his hold over the military professionals at the December 1929 conference at Kutien, Mao had frequently encountered a fundamental conflict of interest between himself and the military commissars, on the one hand, and party administrators and ideologues and the military commanders, on the other. The conflict has been concerned with contradictory notions of the military

[10]These movements began after the enlarged session of the Military Affairs Committee which met from September 14 to October 20, 1960. The Four-Good Movement set priorities for behavior: the human factor to be first in relations between men and weapons; politics to take precedence over military technique; ideology to be emphasized over other aspects of political education; and practical experience to receive priority over book learning. The Five-Good movement, started at the same time (a revision of a similar program begun two years earlier), called for excellence in political thought, military training, style of work, achievement of missions, and physical education. In practice, the decision to award a Four-Good rating to a unit and a Five-Good rating to an individual probably rested with the party committee at the next higher level of the military bureaucracy.

role generally and commander-commissar roles specifically; and it has also been the effect as well as the cause of disagreements over military organization, strategy, and tactics. Over the past forty years, it has emerged as one of the major sources of disunity within the Chinese Communist leadership.

Almost from the beginnings of the Red Army at Nanchang in August 1927, Mao Tse-tung has conceived of the military as an instrument for domestic political mobilization. The 1964 "Learn from the PLA" and the 1966 "Make the PLA a Great School of Revolution" movements were only the most recent expressions of that ideal, perhaps best articulated by Mao at the December 1929 Kutien Conference. The commissar system, especially after Kutien, has been dedicated to the institutional expression of that Maoist concept; the dual authority between commissars and commanders would supposedly insure that military operations would aim at appropriate political objectives. With his experience at Chingkangshan and in Kiangsi before the Long March, Mao's concepts of military organization, strategy, and tactics were logical extensions of his belief that a disciplined military organization should be dedicated principally to domestic political goals. Large concentrations of military power were to be avoided, except under special circumstances. Instead, Mao long retained a preference for the wide dispersion of military power among small regular units, reinforced by guerrilla forces, in order to mobilize and lead the maximum number of peasants more effectively both in war and peace. For such a military organization, in which the commissar would play a central role straddling and coordinating the military and the political spheres, the obvious strategy against a presumed superior enemy would be a war of attrition. Such a "passive" strategy would avoid pitched battles of position in favor of harassing operations designed to lure the enemy into hostile territory where "sparrow tactics" and the "short attack" might consume his resources and ultimately drown him in people's war.

The alternative military philosophy, with its corollaries on commander and commissar functions, organization, and strategy and tactics, was best articulated at the 1932 Ningtu Conference. Here Mao came under attack from commanders and senior party administrators alike for "adventurism," "guerrilla-ism," and "escapism" (attempting to escape from rather than defend against the Nationalist blockhouse offensive first employed on a small scale during the Fourth Encirclement campaign). At that time, men like Chou En-lai (then Chairman of the Military Affairs Committee) and P'eng Teh-huai, commander of the army, expressed the outlook of their respective functions of party administration and military command. They emphasized the need for specialization between military operations and civil administration, the one to be in the hands of commanders, assisted by commissars, the other to be exclusively under party control with no interference from military commissars. The more professional (and Russian) notion of proper military organization was expressed in Chou En-lai's complete reorganization of the Red Army, which aimed at the creation of a standard table of organization in firepower and manpower. Likewise, strategy called for "active" defense beyond the borders of the Central Soviet Republic, and tactics were disdainful of guerrilla actions by regular forces.

Thereafter, as Mao's personal fortunes rose and fell, it must have become clear that neither party administrators nor party ideologues relished sharing local political power with military commissars—a phenomenon which occurred only when the number of trained party officials was insufficient to cope with an expanding population base. Likewise, the commanders did not like having to share command authority with commissars, except under the special circumstances of civil war when commissar management of guerrillas might support rather than interfere with the unity of command. It was thus logical for the commanders and party administrators alike to prefer an "active" defense strategy, that is, the projection of concentrated military power beyond the borders. Under such circumstances, the commanders would be more likely to have a relatively free hand in maneuvering their troops while party officials at home would also be freed from any necessity for sharing local political power with military ideologues.

Given this admittedly oversimplified set of preferences shared among party administrators and commanders, on the one hand, and the Maoists and commissars, on the other, it is not surprising to find Mao criticizing senior commanders like P'eng Teh-huai in 1967 for planning and executing the highly professional offensive-defensive Hundred Regiments campaign of 1940. That campaign, as well as the offensive-defensive thrust into Korea, the attack on India in 1962, and even the movement of units into North Vietnam in 1965, all reflected fundamental commander disagreement with the Maoist military ethic. It is noteworthy that in moments of national crisis, down to and including the Cultural Revolution, the professional view has prevailed against the Maoist ethic.

The Revolution Revisited

Faced by a party which had apparently lost confidence in his simplism and sloganeering during and after the Great Leap Forward, Mao's December 1963 call for the party to "learn from the PLA" may be perceived as a call for an alliance with the commissars, who in February 1964 began to invade traditional civil party agencies. The earlier "Socialist education" campaign in 1963, which aimed at reviving the revolutionary *élan* of basic cadres, the "Learn from the PLA" movement, and the Cultural Revolution itself must all be considered as related phases of a four-year period which could be characterized as the "revolution revisited." Beginning in 1963 and extending into mid-1967, these various movements and rectification campaigns represented a major resurgence of Maoists and military ideologues against the bureaucratic and professional values, goals, and methods both of the party and the military commanders. It is likely that his offensive was also directed against the power of the regional and field army elites, whose control of resources had seriously restricted the ability of the central government to mobilize surplus resources.[11]

Having been under increasing commissar pressure since late 1959 to reexamine their own post-liberation behavior in the light of pre-liberation aspirations and values, it is probable that the early stages of this revolution revisited found many senior commanders sincerely confused over the historic issues in controversy. Accused, in effect, of abandoning their revolutionary ideals for the appeals of bureaucratic status, power, and privilege, some of them—the veterans of many battles and political struggles—may have suffered doubts about China's evolving style and image at home and abroad. Since 1960, the Russian threat had escalated quietly on China's northern borders. By 1965, the American threat was becoming ominous to the south. There was even the possibility of a Soviet-American conspiracy against China. Many senior leaders, especially those responsible for economic and military mobilization, must have felt that this was no time to permit, much less foster, internal disagreements. Yet, all major issues were under reexamination as Lo Jui-ch'ing, the Chief of the General Staff, apparently appealed in 1965 for a rapprochement with the USSR, serious preparation for war with the United States, and a forward defense in North Viet-Nam. In opposition, the Minister of Defense, Lin Piao, argued for the strategy of people's war.

As suggested above, the arguments of both men emphasized strategy; but they actually held implications for all other issues in controversy, including the domestic political power of the field army elites. In oversimplified terms, Lo was arguing for the professional viewpoint on all questions relating to the role of the military, the authority of commanders versus commissars, military organization, strategy, and tactics. In that argument, he is believed to have had the sympathy of many senior party administrators and most professional commanders. Lin Piao, on the other hand, whether for reasons of political expediency or honest conviction, was echoing Mao's historic position on these issues. He was thus warning both party leaders and commanders at all levels that the domestic political-military

[11]Audrey G. Donnithorne provides compelling economic arguments to support this thesis in her book *China's Economic System* (New York: Praeger, 1967). A much shorter treatment of this theme is given in her testimony before the Joint Economic Committee, 90th Congress, 1st Session, published in *Hearings on Mainland China in the World Economy* (1967), pp. 46–171.

values and organizational concepts implicit in people's war must be accepted as the correct criteria for both personal and institutional performance. Although that Maoist philosophy evidently received a cool reception at a meeting of party and military leaders in September 1965, their own doubts about the correct approach, and a generalized dissatisfaction with the huge party bureaucracy, contributed to Mao's personal determination to rectify the party by employing his allies—the military commissars.

By the spring of 1966, it became evident that, once again, the priesthood of military commissars would have a crucial role in applying Maoist concepts of civil-military relations to an ever-widening circle of party, government and, finally in 1967, military leaders. From Mao's viewpoint, the commissars must have seemed ideally trained for that task. Frustrated since 1944 by both commanders and an expanding civil party bureaucracy, the commissars had found it increasingly difficult to play—in either the military or civil spheres—the role portrayed for them in the Maoist scenario. After 1959, the opportunity to stage a limited comeback had permitted them to experiment with Maoist notions of the politicized soldier. Until late 1963, however, their efforts had been confined to a rectification movement within the PLA. For two years, from early 1964 until late 1965, they had then moved cautiously into the arena of civil administration, clearly threatening civil party power and privilege. With the spring 1966 attack on the Communist Party Propaganda Department and the vital Peking Municipal Committee under P'eng Chen, they moved directly onto the political stage, aiming at the party ideologues whose rationalization of post-Great Leap efforts to revive the economy and encourage production, regardless of compromise with revolutionary principles, must have been tantamount—in Mao's mind—to a betrayal of the revolution.

Spearheading this climax to the revolution revisited, the commissars may have been instrumental in organizing Red Guards and inspiring them with the Maoist call to struggle against the "four olds" and "capitalist roaders," and finally to "seize power." These efforts must be perceived as an increasingly hysterical outburst of ultra-leftist idealism aimed at destroying, or at least altering, a political-administrative system which had returned the national internal style to some semblance of orderly process following the disastrous experiment of the Great Leap. This outburst derived in part from general dissatisfaction with a bureaucracy that was threatening to ossify in its own red tape. But the leftist "revolutionary rebels" soon acquired a vast entourage of people whose dissatisfaction with their daily lives had only a marginal relationship with the presumed ideals of the Yenan spirit of self-sacrifice. Political opportunists and criminal elements, and just about everything in between, used this opportunity to avenge themselves of past grievances. China became a battleground on which the larger issues outlined earlier became translated into petty issues of local politics.

Until late 1966, despite the mounting threat to regional and provincial party leaders by the Maoist-commissar alliance, PLA senior commanders on the Military Affairs Committee and General Staff were able to shield the regular forces from the movement. Only local forces, public security bureaus, and militia had become involved in the question of choosing up sides. By November, however, the Maoists apparently decided to carry their ideological message and techniques of "struggle" back into regular PLA units. In that plan lay the basis of their most dramatic confrontation with the senior military commanders.

For despite disagreement on various aspects of the military ethic (an interregional competition for power and privilege; an intergenerational conflict in which officers under the average age of 48 had not yet been allowed to move into really significant power positions, which were still largely retained by pre-1936 cadres; and a mixed reaction to the revolution in weapons technology, a revolution which would ultimately jeopardize the power status of older leaders with very limited technical military education), these sources of disunity among the commanders were matched by fundamental sources of unity. Perhaps the most important factor making for unity was their personal experience with a China divided against itself. Most of the senior commanders had emerged from a context of warlordism, and fully understand its worst manifestations. Certainly their own power aggrandizement had attained for them the status of "Communist warlords." But the commitment to a central directive authority implied by the word "Communist" had been an important element of their political ethic hammered out through forty years of experimentation. It was, in fact, the apparently lunatic erosion of central authority by Maoist bungling and Red Guard excesses that probably most dismayed commanders and party administrators alike. Regardless of their own ideological shortcomings in the eyes of Maoists and commissars, they had never so threatened the integrity of the formal political system and the informal balance of power process that had kept it viable.

Secondly, commanders at all levels of command shared a career commitment and a professional pride that had been reinforced through countless pre-1950 battles, and by the encouragement of Russian advisors and instructors after 1950 in formal schools set up in Nanking and Peking. The respect for professional organization and modern weaponry that characterized civil war and Korean War veterans was not the monopoly of youth. As early as 1931, Liu Po-ch'eng, who had just returned from two years of study in the Frunze Military Institute in the USSR, could express nothing but disdain for Mao's "museum-piece" notions of warfare. Since 1951, Liu has been the director of advanced military education for senior officers, and his sophisticated concepts of strategy and tactics could only have reinforced the lessons taught by battle experience to the several hundred senior officers who had passed through his hands over the ensuing sixteen years.

Finally, by 1967 a modern communications network permitted senior military leaders to discuss their problems with friends simply by lifting a telephone. No commander had to feel isolated. The military radio and telephone system permitted an exchange of opinions, attitudes, and guidance to anyone who felt confused or guilty about his anti-Maoist reactions to the current assault on internal order and the threatened assault directly on the PLA.

The Maoist-commissar-Red Guard alliance was first resisted by senior members of the Military Affairs Committee, principally by the old fighter Ho Lung, whose personal following was soon humiliated and dismissed from key offices. Between December 1966 and January 1967, the Maoist team found themselves under massive pressures from senior military region commanders at both the local and national levels. While undertaking the brutal suppression of young Red Guard idealists as well as the hoodlums who had joined them, military region commanders in Sinkiang, Tibet, Canton, Foochow, and Manchuria probably also brought the weight of their party status and their local power to bear directly on what they must have considered irresponsible leadership at the center. In that effort, it is important to emphasize the probability that this was a process of negotiation between regional and central authority, wherein informal loyalties became crucial to the task of persuading Mao personally that the "Maoists" and "power-seekers" had gone too far in using Mao's name for their own ends.

It is not only possible but likely that Mao was as prepared to abandon selected members of his personal following as he was later willing to abandon the entire Red Guard organization. For once they had served their presumed purpose of returning Mao to a central role in the power-balancing process, they could all be sacrificed. Mao had been fighting his way back to such a position ever since the 1959 Lushan Conference. His personal ego-satisfaction was thus an essential ingredient in the apparently maniacal Chinese search for what Mao called "revolutionary order"—a curious contradiction in terms that would seem to sum up the whole period of the revolution revisited.

After January 1967, a flow of directives began to emerge from the center calling upon the PLA to "support the left" through direct involvement in the Cultural Revolution, with the primary mission of confining that "revolution" to campuses and nondefense-related institutions. At the same time, military region commanders with the greatest military power were permitted to "postpone" the Cultural Revolution. Although a revival of ultra-left radicalism occurred between April and June, the outright rebellion of the Wuhan Military Region commander in July was an unprecedented expression of commander preoccupation with the larger mission of national defense and their diminishing capabilities for executing such a mission.

It is important to examine the probable perspectives of senior Chinese military commanders in this situation. In their own background, both cultural and experiential, the notion of a tri-polar balance of power may be taken as an ideal political model. Whether speaking of *The Romance of the Three Kingdoms*[12] with which they were all familiar, the Communist-Nationalist-Japanese system of World War II, or the post-1950 USSR-United States-Chinese Far Eastern system of power distribution, their calculus of challenge and response is believed to begin with such a mode. Having established three adversaries, including themselves, all other countries were designated as relatively more or less affiliated with one of the adversaries.

Assuming that such an estimate characterized High Command perspectives toward the international arena (commissars could be expected to suffer from slightly more confused and complex notions of political power), it is probable that commanders perceived the 1967 situation as highly dangerous. The possibility of agreement between the United States and the USSR on such matters as nuclear weapons, policy toward China and Southeast Asia, and trade between the United States and the East European countries, might first isolate China and then threaten her with nuclear attack from the world's major land and sea powers. Such a potential threat must have seemed clear to the Chinese military mind by late 1966. At that time, a logical strategy would have been to stabilize the internal situation, and then to seek a *modus vivendi* with one threat while concentrating major resources against the other.

The impact of the regional political-military power centers on central policy formulated after the July 1967 incident at Wuhan was reflected in Lin Piao's August 9 speech.[13] Appealing in effect for patience on the part of the senior military leaders, Lin publicly denounced the commissars and asserted that the General Political Department had failed. The Director of the General Political Department and all of his deputies were dismissed, and the functions of the department were evidently turned over to a subcommittee chaired by a veteran commander, Yang Ch'eng-wu, the Acting Chief of General Staff. Within a week, Wang Li, one of the most outspoken advocates of "purging capitalist roaders in the PLA," also disappeared. Thereafter, key members of the Central Cultural Revolution Group, the "Maoists" (who must be distinguished from Mao personally), were either

[12]For a standard translation, see C. H. Brewitt-Taylor, *The Romance of the Three Kingdoms* (Rutland, Vt.: Tuttle, 1960).

[13]For this important speech by Lin Piao, see *Survey of China Mainland Press,* No. 4036 (October 6, 1967), pp. 1–6.

dismissed or suffered a significant erosion of power. Mao presumably had been convinced by the commanders that "war preparedness" and the external threat must take priority over the internal threat.

From September 1967 until April 1968, a mood of relative moderation accompanied the creation of sixteen provincial revolutionary committees, of which the chairmen and vice-chairmen were drawn almost entirely from commanders or party leaders long familiar with the problems of these provinces. After another brief three-month resurgence of Red Guard radicalism in April-June 1968, the following month brought a series of directives that authorized commanders to suppress all Red Guard interference with due process. After that, the input of professional military opinion probably became a decisive feature of policy-making in all major spheres. This is not to say that the commanders had created a military dictatorship. But it is to argue that a military junta, probably in sympathy with many of Chou En-lai's concerns for economic growth and administrative rationality, was now capable of injecting the fundamental value of national security into all major policy debates.

The allocation of power and influence among 140 chairmen and vice-chairmen on 29 provincial revolutionary committees by October 1968 was significant. Given the traditional power struggle among military commissars, party administrators and military commanders, it is noteworthy that the alliance of commanders and administrators had emerged with 109 out of 140 positions (52 commanders and 57 party administrators as against 31 commissars). This does not take into account the affiliation of certain party administrators and commanders with the "Maoists," or the apparent loyalty of certain commissars to the "moderates." But, even if we assume (incorrectly) that all 31 commissars were "radical," the addition of 13 "Maoist" administrators and two "Maoist" commanders would find the "left" with only 46 key positions, as against 94 for the "right;" and this balance shifts in favor of the "right" if we revise the estimate on the political leanings of the commissars.

Turning to the question of regionalism and the formal structure of the interregional balance of power, against which we have assumed the Cultural Revolution was partly directed, it is clear that representation on the revolutionary committees confirmed the continuing viability of the regional power centers. The central government had little success in shifting many people from one region to another. Of the 140 men who held power in late 1968, only ten men moved from "other" regions into a new region during the Cultural Revolution. Of the remaining 130, some 89 now held power in the same province in which they had served before the Cultural Revolution. An additional 41 (all military figures) had been serving in the same military region of which the province is a part. Thirteen of these 41 individuals had been either commanders (seven) or commissars (six) of the regular PLA corps stationed in the military region. The other 28 had been assigned to military region headquarters, and had moved down to provincial level to assume control over the revolutionary committees. These regional personalities were assisted in establishing the new organs of power by seventeen commanders, sixteen commissars, and 56 former party administrators who had been serving at provincial (military district) level of the same provinces in which they now served. In spite of the tumult and disorders of the Cultural Revolution, the informal distribution of power among the five field army parties discussed earlier had not been altered radically. Nor had major changes occurred in field army representation among the thirteen major military regions; only the Chengtu and Wuhan military region staffs suffered some erosion of power by the input of outsiders.[14]

With respect to intergenerational conflict, it is interesting to note that out of 107 men on the revolutionary committees whose dates of admission into the Communist Party are known, 102 entered before December 1936; and only five are known to have entered between 1936 and 1940. With further research, it may be possible to identify the admission dates of the other 33 men. However, available evidence suggests that the "Long Marchers" persisted in 1970 in their thirty-year retention of power. On the other hand, it is perhaps significant that only nineteen of Mao's contemporaries (men who entered the party before May 1928) now sit on revolutionary committees, which are dominated by the second generation of party and military leaders.

Conclusions: The "Revolution Betrayed"

The Cultural Revolution seems to have confirmed the essential viability of an interregional, inter-field army "party" balance-of-power system, against which the energies of the Red Guards and the commissar propaganda apparatus ultimately proved ineffectual. The resounding victory of local power figures would suggest that pre-Cultural Revolution regional military and party figures may be expected to prevail in their domination of local political programs and policies, while also imposing serious restrictions on the flexibility of the central government.

While it is dangerous to draw too many conclusions from the available data, the achievement of power by "younger" men (in their fifties) would seem to presage a constantly increasing concern with professional standards of material and management to the detriment of revolutionary *élan*. Exposed only briefly to Maoist notions and methods regarding people's war between 1928 and 1930, these leaders were subjected, after late 1931, to

[14]Much of this discussion is taken from "The Field Army in Chinese Communist Military Politics," *loc. cit.*

strong and persistent doses of Russian-sponsored professional military training in new schools, and to new tactical experiences that stressed the conventional military art (the Fourth and Fifth Extermination campaigns in Kiangsi; the Long March; campaigns of the Sino-Japanese War culminating in the "conventional" warfare of the 1940 Hundred Regiments campaign).

From that foundation of military professionalism, the post-1967 impact of commander perspectives on both domestic and foreign policies may be characterized as the "revolution betrayed;" that is, a clear turn to the "right" away from socially destructive campaigns that ostensibly aim at revolutionary goals but actually erode authority, generate dissatisfaction, and complicate the serious business of military and party administrators. Having survived the violence of the "revolution revisited," commanders and party administrators returned to the process of nation-building, which had been so seriously interfered with by the three-year mania of the Cultural Revolution.

At the heart of that process, military professionalism and a consuming preoccupation with national security appeared to dominate all other policy issues. As we have seen,[15] Lo Jui-ch'ing had unsuccessfully attempted as early as May 1965 to inject the foreign threat into a debate that held far wider implications for China than strategy alone. In January 1967, in the name of war preparedness, selected military regions had been authorized to "postpone" the Cultural Revolution, presumably after demands by the commanders that revolutionary "blooming and contending" be minimized in vital border areas. Despite the eclipse of key military leaders who then challenged the Maoist military philosophy, their fundamental opposition to its dangerous internal implications was soon echoed at Wuhan in July 1967, and reaffirmed in Kwangsi in July-August 1968 when regular military forces ruthlessly suppressed the Red Guards in that province. In short, in the context of what was probably real fear, the High Command moved on the internal stage to rediscipline the Chinese population, suppress all expressions of opposition, reimpose censorship, and in general to mobilize China for national defense.

In late December 1968, the Chinese Communists informed a London newspaper that, although the Cultural Revolution had temporarily set back the advanced weapons program, a fully operational intercontinental ballistic missile would be tested by late 1969. In the same month (December 1968), refugees reported the creation of a new public security system more ruthless than ever before. By spring 1969, the adoption of a new party constitution, replacing the 1956 constitution, provided further (if somewhat

[15]See p. 110 above. For the text of Lo Jui-ch'ing's speech in May 1965 in which he underscored the military achievements of the USSR during World War II and denounced the American threat, see *Peking Review,* Vol. 8, No. 20 (May 14, 1965).

ambiguous) evidence of the military approach to problem-solving in China. Instead of a highly detailed document which clearly defined the respective spheres of action of the military, the party, and the government, the new constitution was a remarkably simple document in which the procedures of "due process" within the party were left vague, and the central authorities retained the widest leeway for rationalizing administration.

In other respects, the rebuilding of the police system, the disciplining of the former Red Guards by a workers provost corps and peasant-worker teams (both under PLA supervision), the mass exodus of more radical youngsters to the countryside, the revival of discipline in the communes, tightened censorship and a clamp-down on the export of publications, and the emphasis on party rebuilding, all characterized a massive organizational effort which could only be labelled "national mobilization." Under military supervision, China was being converted into a defense-oriented polity and economy where there would be no more nonsense about "blooming and contending." Disenchanted with Maoist experiments in economics (the Great Leap) and politics (the Cultural Revolution), both of which had appealed to the masses for vindication, the commanders and the party administrators, working within the existing formal system of thirteen military regions and 29 revolutionary committees, and the informal system of field army affiliations, strove to restore stability and a moderate growth rate to the economy.

In a sense, however, the increasing involvement of Chinese military after 1967 in the day-to-day administration of China might have symbolized a fundamental victory for Mao's notions of the correct military role, that is, a maximum participation by the PLA in mass mobilization. Certainly, by the autumn of that year, the military presence on revolutionary committees at all levels suggested a military concern for local political affairs unprecedented since 1950. But it is the author's belief that the pervasiveness of military and party administrative perspectives and organization reflected their abiding concern for national defense, not their loyalty to the Thought of Chairman Mao.

By November 1968, Chinese fears of a Soviet-American conspiracy found substance in such "evidence" as projected talks on nuclear armaments, the unprecedented visit of a Soviet "newsman" to Taiwan, the escalation of Soviet military power along China's northern borders, the apparent preference of the North Vietnamese for Soviet aid (and, presumably, for Soviet advice at the Paris peace talks on Viet-Nam), and the curious maneuverings of American naval vessels in the Black Sea while Soviet ships moved freely into the Mediterranean. To the Three Kingdoms mentality of a senior Chinese strategist, even one so sophisticated as the old Second Field Army commander, Liu Po-ch'eng, now President of the Advanced

War College in Peking, these events could have demanded a crucial decision about the priority of threats and resource allocation.

The Chinese probably made a decision on these subjects as early as September 1968. They then engaged in the process of translating that decision into political messages, some verbal, but most programmatic. The November republication of Mao's 1949 speech accepting "capitalism" as a temporary expedient;[16] the reaffirmation (also in November 1968) of the five Bandung principles[17] as a basis of co-existence with the United States; the expressed desire to continue the Warsaw talks; above all, the November trip of the Chief of the General Staff to Albania on what was supposedly a diplomatic mission, but which reportedly involved military discussions about aid and bases for China in Albania; all reflected a determination by the Chinese High Command as to priorities of threat. Russian behavior in Czechoslovakia, their distribution of IRBM's on China's northern borders, and the presence of a liberation headquarters in Alma Ata, consisting of former chiefs of minority tribes in Sinkiang, were only three expressions of the danger to some of China's most important industrial (Manchuria), advanced weapons (Lanchow and Sinkiang), and political (Inner Mongolia pointed at Peking) centers.

The threat was dramatized in March 1969 when a skirmish took place between a Chinese infantry unit and a Russian mechanized border patrol unit at Damansky Island on the Ussuri River.[18] Both sides immediately publicized the clash. The Russians claimed that they had lost 31 men killed and fourteen wounded, as against more than two hundred Chinese casualties, and the latter were accused of instigating the incident. The Chinese, in turn, asserted that at least sixteen clashes or intrusions had occurred along the border since January 1967; this statement seemed to focus attention on the significance of a growing foreign threat *after* that date, when military commanders had first moved resolutely to stabilize the domestic situation. The Damansky Island incident thus seemed to be significant primarily as a justification for the mobilization process already under way (in this author's estimation) since mid-1968. After the incident, an increasing volume of Sino-Soviet vituperation was matched by a succession of rallies in China to whip up popular resentment against a "foreign aggressor" and to rationalize new sacrifices at home.

The foregoing combination of internal mobilization and external maneu-

[16]For the most recent text of the English version of Mao's speech, first published in March 1949 as "The Report to the Second Plenary Session of the Seventh Central Committee," see *ibid.,* Vol. 11, No. 48 (November 29, 1968).

[17]For the Foreign Ministry statement on the five Bandung principles of peaceful coexistence and their relationship to the anticipated Warsaw talks, see *ibid.,* Vol. 11, No. 48 (November 29, 1968).

[18]For a discussion of this clash, see *South China Morning Post,* March 9, 1969.

vering not only was a reflection of military emphasis on efficient human
and material resource mobilization, but also may have been aimed at tele-
graphing Peking's estimate of the evolving international situation, encouraging one adversary (the United States) to meet China in some form of
modus vivendi, while identifying the other (the USSR) as its principal
enemy. Chinese military strategy would seem to be clear: minimize the
threat from the Pacific, and concentrate on embarrassing and confusing
the threat from the North.

On the other hand, there is also evidence that the Chinese had thus far
failed to reach agreement on a strategy technique for dealing with an assumed Soviet-American "conspiracy." Chinese Communist speeches early
in 1969 seemed to indicate no change at the propaganda level in Sino-
American mutual suspicion. Chinese sensitivity at that time found dramatic
expression in their sudden cancellation of talks scheduled to begin with
American diplomats at Warsaw in February. It was not until a year later,
in January 1970, that Sino-American talks were finally resumed.

In spite of a three-year tirade of Maoist invective against their "revisionist" tendencies and the existing distribution of power among multiple
regional centers and informal field army "parties," the latter have clearly
weathered what was probably the last major Maoist effort to appeal to the
masses for a revival of revolutionary pace. In doing so, the commanders
and party administrators reinforced what was likely to remain a relatively
permanent "federal" structure of political power, one in which professional military influence had remained at least vocal, and usually significant, throughout the forty-year history of controversy among Maoists,
commissars, commanders, and party administrators. By 1967, the voices of
military professionalism, in support of experienced party administrators,
had become—and were likely to remain—dominant.

As if to underline the probable permanence of the professional ethic and
style now ascendant in China, more Liu-ist than Liu Shao-ch'i had ever
been, the 1969 party constitution named Lin Piao as Mao's successor.
Whether or not that actually assured power to Lin personally or to a collective military junta, it seemed to symbolize the likelihood of the continuing dominance of professional (but also Chinese) military thought in
China's policy process. In so doing, it brought Chinese military leaders
abreast of other Asian military figures who, for similar reasons under similar provocations of internal political bungling and external threat, had
ultimately gained ascendancy over policy in their countries.

This did not mean the destruction of the commissar system or the abandonment of Mao's thought, which also remained in the new party constitution. It only meant that, for the foreseeable future, the commissar
system and Mao's thought would probably be tools in the hands of a com-
mander-party administrator alliance determined to thwart any further

challenges by ideologues to their notions of the proper role of the military, its organization, strategy, and tactics. It also seemed likely that national security would inevitably influence the new political structure, all resource allocation, including the scheduling of imports and exports, the choice of trading partners, an accelerated pace of nuclear weapons development, the design of a "practical" education system, the forced-draft improvement of key transportation and communications facilities, and the further development of industry, all probably aimed at the potentially costly but alluring goal of autarky, with which Mao personally had expressed sympathy after 1960.

While the influence of experienced bureaucrats like Chou En-lai might condition such a thrust, particularly if popular resentment against heavy-handed military discipline increased, the long memories of the commanders argued for their firm resistance to any future ideology-laden initiatives that lacked potential for a visible return to national security. In their calculation of realistic costs versus returns, Chinese senior commanders might also approach the international arena with a concern for their still limited military capabilities. Thus, it would not be surprising to find the Chinese provocation of Russian patience and military power kept within bounds, pending the improvement of China's internal situation and military potential, and the clarification of American policies abroad.

On the home front, the Cultural Revolution had already tested China's capabilities for defense mobilization. The mass movements of Red Guards; their attacks on one another and on public security and even regular PLA units; the general atmosphere of crisis; the disappearance of key party and military leaders; the disruption of the country's production and distribution systems; and threats from abroad; all had taxed the institutional and decision-making capabilities of Communist China to the utmost. Chou En-lai has even characterized the Cultural Revolution as a vast defense mobilization exercise. But the setback to defense production and the advanced weapons program, the loss of training time, the disorganization of the chain of command, and the commitment of regular forces to non-military functions, have been among the many costs imposed by that "exercise" on military commanders and party administrators. Reports of increasing peasant dissatisfaction with military rule in early 1969 suggested that the high command still faced serious problems in restoring stability and mobilizing internal resources. In such a context of continuing domestic dislocation, major aggressive foreign adventures (as distinguished from aggressive propaganda aimed at a foreign audience) seemed unlikely.

Furthermore, Sino-Soviet military clashes on the Ussuri River in March 1969, and the increasing tensions in Sino-Soviet relations throughout 1969, had reinforced professional military arguments that war preparedness must not be interrupted or damaged by internal political conflict. By

October 1969, when negotiations between the Chinese and the Russians began in Peking, the need for countrywide preparations for war was reflected in press reports of precautionary digging around major cities all over China. Apparently convinced that their major enemy—for the moment—lay to the north, the Chinese finally agreed to meet with the Americans in Warsaw almost one year later than the meeting originally scheduled for February 1969.

In further confirmation of the power of the military over China's fate, the Ninth Party Congress, elected in March 1969, contained 65 percent military versus only 35 percent civilian members. Among the military members, there were more than twice as many commanders as commissars (57 active commanders versus 27 commissars). Finally, the power of regional commanders was reflected in the fact that only sixteen percent of the members with reliable biographies (131 out of a total of 170 full members) had spent their careers primarily at the center of the Chinese Communist movement, that is, with Mao Tse-tung. Some 84 percent came from the provinces. These figures are in contrast with figures for the Eighth Party Congress (37 percent from the center; 63 percent from the field armies) and the Seventh (52 percent from the center; 48 percent from the field armies). China's future indeed seemed to lie in the hands of her generals.

Chapter Six

The Economy After Twenty Years

Yuan-li Wu*

On the eve of the Communist takeover in 1949, the Chinese economy was in total chaos. Indeed, economic chaos was a principal contributing factor to the political success of the Communists. The long hostilities with Japan and the subsequent civil war, the disintegrating and demoralizing wartime and postwar hyperinflation, Soviet removal of industrial equipment from Manchuria, and the general breakdown of government authority and social order — largely as a result of inflation and war — had brought production to a low ebb. The fragile fabric of political unity and the long hoped for integration of a national economy and market had burst asunder. The almost inevitable outcome in the circumstances was the establishment of a new regime.

Twenty years later, in 1969, the governing party and the central authorities were again in trouble. Both the Communist Party and the Communist government now found themselves thoroughly undermined by the Great Proletarian Cultural Revolution and internecine political strife. The administration and organization of the national economy have again broken down. Order is maintained only to the extent that the People's Liberation Army can exercise control. These difficulties are compounded by the continuing dispute with the Soviet Union, which precludes the benefits that a helping hand from abroad might otherwise be able to offer. While there are no comparable developments in war devastation and hyperinflation, the Cultural Revolution and the activities of the Red Guards and other "revolutionary groups" have exerted a demoralizing and disintegrating influence that may be no less profound. Economic conditions today may not be as chaotic as they were in 1949, but production has suffered severely. In the circumstances, what are the prospects for the Chinese economy? Further, what political future will the Chinese Communist Party have if economic order and growth cannot be restored?

There are some striking parallels between the current situation in Communist China and the conditions that prevailed twenty years ago. Yet the

*The author, Professor of Economics at the University of San Francisco, is at present on leave for service with the United States government. This essay was written prior to his departure, and does not necessarily reflect the views of the government or any of its agencies.

123

parallels are not complete, and the differences between the two situations are no less important. The significance of this general observation will become clear as we examine some of the developments in the Chinese economy during the past two decades in greater detail.

A Note on Methodology

To begin with, let us consider some basic methodological issues. First, a simple and apparently straightforward assessment of the Chinese economy can be undertaken by selecting a number of indicators, comparing their values at different dates, and drawing conclusions on the basis of such a comparison. Methodologically, this is "comparative statics." Such an assessment would yield an overview of specific "cross sections" in the continuum of time. Yet the findings could be quite misleading because, unless the developmental paths are uniform for all sectors of the economy, and unless both the direction and the rate of growth (or decline) are constant over time, different impressions would be obtained by choosing different beginning and ending dates.

On the other hand, a partial compensation for this shortcoming can be made where the dual condition of "proportional" and "monotonic" growth is absent, as is the case of Communist China, by choosing more than one set of beginning and ending dates on the basis of special benchmarks. If the "benchmark" dates for the majority of the indicators are chosen on the basis of statistical data, they are likely to be points of discontinuity. If the dates are selected on some other basis, such as the occurrence of important policy or institutional changes, the same kind of discontinuity is likely to be found at or about these dates. In either case, the benefit of comparing the economic situation at more than two dates stems from the greater light the method would cast on the nature and process of the economic change.

If we designate the beginning state of the Chinese economy, say, in 1949, by "O" (to denote "origin"), and the conditions of the economy at the ending date, say, 1969, by "E" (to denote "end"), in comparative statics we would compare E with O. However, we must not lose sight of the fact that during the two decades in question, the Chinese economy was supposed to be centrally directed and its activities closely controlled, and that a system of increasingly comprehensive economic planning was laboriously established during the period of the First Five Year Plan (1953–57).[1] Thus,

[1]For a fuller discussion of the development of the planning apparatus, see Yuan-li Wu, *The Economy of Communist China: An Introduction* (New York: Praeger, 1965), pp. 18–46.

we cannot ignore the distinct possibility that there is another set of economic conditions ("T" to denote "target") which the final decision-makers would like to have seen at the ending date and that T and E are not the same. To the extent that T and E are different, a possible implication is that the general policy as well as the specific development strategy adopted (including the economic organization and institutions) have been inappropriate in the light of the historical background, the external environment, and the quantity and quality of the resources available. It is also possible that certain component elements of T, being totally unattainable, would have defied any realistic policy and development strategy that might have been conceived. It is even quite likely that some of the official economic goals were really inconsistent with one another. Thus, we must seek to identify the components of T and compare them with those of E if we wish to understand and evaluate the manner in which the economic process has been carried out. In our particular case, this means that we must analyze the nature of the economic goals of the Chinese Communist Party and the means employed to attain them. Such an examination will serve to show why objective and accomplishment have often diverged so widely. It will also bring to light the nagging question whether certain goals which we impute to the Chinese Communists, because they are such obvious and widely held objectives of economic development, have really been sincerely held by the Communist leaders who made the final decisions, or whether the requirements of these objectives have been fully grasped. The question of priority and of deciding what adjustments to make if initial plans fail will be an integral part of this discussion.

If an analysis of Chinese policy and development strategy will explain the divergence between T and E, it will inevitably raise the question whether alternative end results (or, symbolically, "AE") might not have been possible. More than one set of alternatives may exist. In the first place, if there is mutual compatibility in the economic objectives, an alternative end result would mean greater or lesser divergence from T. A relevant question is whether Communist China could not have been more efficient in pursuing the economic objectives she had set for herself. Secondly, where mutual compatibility of some of the objectives is in doubt, a different combination might have led to a quite different end result. In the latter case, more than the degree of efficiency in planning and execution will be involved. This leads us then to the next logical question: Where can, and will, Communist China go from here?

The last part of this essay will, therefore, be devoted to a comparison of the economic alternatives open to Communist China twenty years after the establishment of the present regime, with the possibilities facing her in 1949. In this connection, it would be useful to bear in mind the analogy of a railroad built at great cost in order to develop a gold mine which turns out to be disappointingly poor. The original decision to invest in the railroad was bad and the railroad may never serve any useful purpose. However, it is just possible that some other opportunity of economic development will turn up in the neighborhood of the railroad which, albeit built by mistake, will then become quite useful to the future project. Such a development could be regarded as fortunate especially if the cost of the past investment were ignored. But is it proper to ignore the past entirely? For Communist China, the important questions for the future are whether the decision-makers can learn from past experience, what lessons they will draw from experience, and whether their choices will not in some sense be preordained because they are what they are. It is, therefore, conceivable that while more and better options may now exist than before, the decisions that will most likely be made in the end will not be any better.

An Assessment in Comparative Statics

In the Chinese case, aside from the beginning year 1949 and the ending year 1969, or 1965 if we exclude the period of the Cultural Revolution for want of more recent information, the major "benchmark" periods are 1952-53, 1957-58, 1959-60, and 1962. The significance of these years needs to be explained briefly. First, 1952 was the last pre-plan year; it is also generally regarded in Communist China as the year when economic recovery from the 1949 low succeeded in restoring production to the previous peak levels.[2] On the other hand, it was in 1953 that the Communist program of land redistribution was completed, so that in the agricultural sector it may be more meaningful to treat 1953 as the dividing line. The Korean armistice, a critical factor in Peking's economic planning, was also signed in 1953. The year 1957 saw the completion of the First Five Year Plan, and also heralded the end of the period of conscious and total emulation of Soviet economic planning in China.[3] The following year marked the introduction of the agricultural commune and the adoption of a decentralized, labor intensive, small industry drive, together with the continued development of the modern economic sector. Next, 1959 saw the initial decline of agricultural production, largely as a result of the failure of the commune movement; while 1960 witnessed the wholesale withdrawal of Soviet technical assistance from China and, with it, a general retreat in industrial production and investment which had been preceded by the collapse of the small industry drive (exemplified by the disastrous failure of the "backyard

---

[2]This is generally true only in terms of current output, not in terms of installed capacity.

[3]This description does not mean that Soviet-style development of the modern sector was abandoned with the completion of the first plan. Actually much of the success in 1958-60 was under the second plan. However, the dualistic approach to economic development was introduced in 1958, and its adverse effect soon overshadowed the more positive accomplishments in the modern sector.

furnace" for iron smelting).[4] The ensuing severe depression bottomed out with the main fall harvest in 1962, when industrial production also began to recover. There is some uncertainty about the date when full economic recovery was achieved. However, the balance of the Soviet loans was apparently paid up in 1964, and the long postponed Third Five Year Plan was scheduled to begin in 1966, although details of the plan have thus far not been revealed. The Cultural Revolution was also launched in the winter of 1965–66. Thus, 1965 should clearly be regarded as another benchmark date.

In order to answer the question how the Chinese economy stood at the different benchmark dates, we may turn to Table 1. The indicators chosen all reflect "current output," so that by comparing the figures for any two dates, one can tell whether the results of the specific economic activities were better or worse at the later date. The comparison can be made either in aggregates or in terms of the corresponding *per capita* estimates. The second approach would indicate whether output grew faster than population and, therefore, whether the latter could be regarded as "better off" in the sense that more goods were available at the later date for allocation to each person (even if there should be no increase in actual *per capita* personal consumption, which would, of course, be a more direct measure of an individual's current economic well-being). The first approach (that is, employing aggregates) would, on the other hand, indicate whether more could be made available at the later date for disposal by the government for some special purpose, such as export, defense, or investment, if the authorities were able and willing to impose the necessary controls in spite of population growth.[5] Without attempting to be exhaustive, the indicators selected are meant to reflect (1) total output, (2) industrial output in general and in the modern sector, (3) output in selected producer and consumer goods industries respectively, (4) food grain production as an index of agricultural development, and (5) total foreign trade turnover.

A plus sign in Table 1 indicates that the figure at the ending date was higher than at the beginning date; a minus sign denotes that the opposite

[4]For a discussion of the "backyard furnace" failure, see Yuan-li Wu, *The Steel Industry in Communist China* (New York: Praeger, 1965), pp. 80–90, 236.

[5]The point that an increase in the size of the aggregate output without an increase in *per capita* output may be the determining factor in permitting a larger volume of defense spending, is often overlooked. For instance, let us assume that both total output and the population are represented by one hundred and that defense spending is eight percent of total output or eight. This would give us a civilian output of 92 (.92 per capita). If total output now rises by two percent to 102 while the population also grows by two percent, then there can be an increase of one in defense spending (or a 12.5 percent increase), with a resultant *per capita* civilian output of .9117 (<u>102-9</u>), which is only 91/100 or one percent less than before.
                    102

Table 1.
Increase (+) or Decrease (−) in Production
as Measured by Selected Indicators for Different Time Periods[a]

		1949-65	1952-65	1949-52	1952-57	1957-60	1960-62	1962-65	1958-65	1959-65
Producers' Goods										
Coal	Total	+	+	+	+	+	−	+	+	+
	Per Capita	+	+	+	+	+	−	+	+	−
Electric Power	Total	+	+	+	+	+	−	+	+	−
	Per Capita	+	+	+	+	+	−	+	+	−
Crude Oil	Total	+	+	+	+	+	+	+	+	+
	Per Capita	+	+	+	+	+	+	+	+	+
Raw Steel[b] (Ingot)	Total	+	+	+	+	(+)	(−)	+	(+)	(+)
	Per Capita	+	+	+	+	+	−	+	+	+
Consumers' Goods						(+)	(−)		(+)	(+)
Cotton Cloth	Total	+	+	+	+	+	−	+	−	−
	Per Capita	+	−	+	+	+	−	+	−	−
Food Grain Official	{ Total	+	+	+	+	+ (1957–59)	−	+	−	−
	{ *Per Capita*	+	+	+	+	+ (1957–59)	−	+	−	−
O. L. Dawson	{ Total	+	+	+	+	− (1957–59)	+	+	−	+
	{ *Per Ca...*	+	−	+	−		+	+	−	+

Foreign Trade (Total Turnover)								
Total	...	+	+	+	+	−	+	−
Per Capita	...	+	...	+	+	−	+	−
Gross National Product								
Total	+	+	...	+	+	−	+	+
Per Capita	+	+	...	+	+	−	+	+
Industrial Output								
Official Total	+	+	+	− (1960–63)	+ (1963–65)	+	+	−
Per Capita	+	+	+	− (1960–63)	+ (1963–65)	+	+	−
Y. L. Wu [c]								
Total	...	+	+	+	+	+	+	+
Per Capita	...	+	...	+	+	+	+	+

a For the original data and sources, see Appendix.

b The signs in parentheses refer to modern steel production only.

c Refers to modern industry only.

was true. As can be seen, where information permits comparison, for the periods of 1949-52, 1952-57, 1957-60, and 1962-65, as well as the entire period of 1949-65, there are plus signs only in all sectors except food grain production. This is true both in the aggregate and on a *per capita* basis. On the other hand, for the period of 1960-62, minus signs dominated the scene. Of all the indicators employed, only crude oil and food grain showed an increase during this period, reflecting production from new oil fields and a recovery of production with the 1962 harvest. Because of the decline during the 1960-62 period (a decline on a slightly less broad scale was also registered for 1958-62 and 1959-62, neither of which periods is shown in Table 1; see the Appendix at the end of this chapter), inclusion of the depression in a somewhat longer time span, such as 1958-65 or 1959-65, would also produce a checkered picture. All of this confirms the point made earlier, namely, that the choice of the period is crucial in assessing Communist China's economic performance, and that much more needs to be known about the causes of the movements before the production statistics can be interpreted meaningfully.

While interpretation of the Chinese production statistics cited is a little complicated, estimates of personal consumption present an apparently simpler record. According to T. C. Liu, although aggregate personal consumption rose from an index of 99.4 in 1952 to 123.4 in 1957 (1933=100), the corresponding *per capita* index increased from 87.3 to only 96.9, thus falling short of the level reached nearly a quarter of a century earlier.[6] According to the author's own estimates, if the depression in the early 1960s is taken into account, total personal consumption may have risen at an annual rate of 1.4 percent for the 1952-62 period.[7] A third estimate by Edwin F. Jones, covering the 1957-65 period, thus inclusive of the depression and the subsequent recovery, shows an increase in private consumption from $44.2 billion in 1957 to $50 billion in 1965, which kept the *per capita* figure more or less constant.[8] These results are in clear contrast to the increase in production registered in a number of periods mentioned above.

Divergent results can also be obtained if we compare the different production sectors with one another. For instance, during 1959-65, the decline of production was much greater and the subsequent recovery much slower for cotton piece goods than for the products of heavy industry listed. The

[6]See Ta-chung Liu, "The Tempo of Economic Development of the Chinese Mainland, 1945-65," in *An Economic Profile of Mainland China* (Washington: Government Printing Office, 1967), Vol. 1, p. 63.

[7]See Yuan-li Wu, *The Economy of Communist China: An Introduction,* p. 91. These personal consumption estimates were made as a residual after government consumption and investment had been subtracted from the GNP.

[8]See Edwin F. Jones, "The Emerging Pattern of China's Economic Revolution," in *An Economic Profile of Mainland China,* Vol. 1, p. 96.

same may be said of foreign trade, because a high proportion of exports consisted of goods of agricultural origin while, on the whole, imports had to be financed by current exports. For the interested reader, a detailed comparison of the original data in the Appendix would bring out these contrasts very clearly. For instance, while the production of cotton cloth declined from 7.5 billion meters in 1959 to three billion meters in 1962, a drop of sixty percent, the corresponding decrease in electric power production was from 41.5 billion kwh. to thirty billion kwh., a 28 percent decrease only. On the other hand, the production of cotton piece goods rose by thirty percent to 3.9 billion meters in 1965, while that of electric power increased at the slightly higher rate of 33.3 percent to forty billion kwh. Obviously, the differential rates of change in different sectors, similar to the unequal rates of change over time, must be a consequence of both policy and other circumstances. But to go into them any deeper would require that we go beyond comparative statics.

Economic Performance in Terms of Goals and Their Fulfilment

THE HIERARCHY OF ECONOMIC GOALS. Having demonstrated the limited significance of static comparisons, let us examine Communist China's economic performance in terms of her ability to realize her own goals. This presupposes, in turn, that the goals can be identified. In this connection, there are certain economic conditions which the Chinese Communists have plainly desired to create, and these definitely may be regarded as among their stated goals. At the same time, there are other conditions which could well be, and from time to time are said to be, their goals, but which seem to enjoy such a low priority that one often wonders whether they are desired in earnest at all. The record shows that in the hierarchy of Communist China's economic goals, those that are ideologically and politically motivated take precedence, while the normal objectives of economic development, especially for an underdeveloped country, often seem to be of secondary importance only, even though occasionally a different interpretation is possible.

At the very beginning of Communist rule, the most important ideologically-motivated objective was the establishment of a Socialist society and the transformation of the pre-Communist institutions of private property and private decision-making in economic activities into state ownership and decision-making by the state and state-controlled agencies. Beginning with the introduction of the commune in 1958, the general ideological objective—for the Maoists especially—has become, with a far greater sense of urgency than before, the creation of "Communist man." The "Communist man" is a puritanical, dedicated revolutionary who seeks perpetual class struggle as a way of life, and who is at once an industrial worker, a farmer, and a pliant instrument of the Communist Party, always responding with alacrity to normative — rather than material — incentives by working harder and harder. For the economy, this means a tendency toward somewhat more decentralized control — which is not the same as giving individual initiative full play, less emphasis on expertise and more on being "red," and greater reliance on ideological incentives and therefore less regard for personal consumption. The basic objectives of socialization and state control of the economy were clearly stated in the 1954 constitution of the People's Republic of China, and only slightly more tentatively in the 1949 Common Program. The more "fundamentalist" Maoist version of continuing revolution and "participatory communism" has become increasingly clear since 1958. Following an eclipse of a few years (1960–65), this particular ideological outlook has been virtually sanctified during the Cultural Revolution in the form of the Thought of Mao Tse-tung, which is supposedly capable of inspiring the discovery of solutions for any and all problems, economic ones included.

The politically motivated goals of the country's economic effort are all linked to Communist China's ambition to become a great world power. This means, in the first place, the adoption of a policy to industrialize the economy and, more specifically, to build up the capital goods and weapons-related industries as fast as possible. China's past military defeats at the hands of the more industrialized powers, the more recent example of the emergence of the Soviet Union as a great military power, and the belief that a certain minimum threshold of technological and industrial development is essential for the acquisition of nuclear weapons (a symbol of the ultimate and absolute in international status), all point in the direction of industrialization by forced draft, with primary emphasis on a few industries. Secondly, the status of a great power is associated with the idea of sovereignty and independence, an ability to "go it alone," if necessary. This means the attainment of self-sufficiency and self-reliance as an economic goal, and of technological independence from foreign countries. Lastly, since Communist China aspires to leadership in the Afro-Asian world, she has always wanted to demonstrate to other underdeveloped countries through her own economic success the superiority of the Chinese model of economic development. The objective, therefore, is to provide a convincing record of steady economic growth.

The predominantly economic objectives can be considered under two categories, a rapid increase in national output and a more equal distribution of wealth. These are essentially the common objectives of most underdeveloped countries. Moreover, a rapidly rising output, advancing without interruption, would also provide the economic image needed for purposes of international political demonstration. The desire to increase the national product at a rapid pace is not, however, accompanied by a comparable desire to increase consumption. While consumption is ostensibly to be increased, it is to rise slowly so that the rate of investment can be further stepped up, thus causing the national product to rise even faster. The Chinese goal of rapid economic development is not, therefore, the same as the rapid promotion of economic welfare when the latter is measured in terms of personal consumption. Rather the approach is that of all Soviet-type economies, as well as of some non-Communist underdeveloped countries which are extremely impatient with the rate of increase in their national product.

Finally, a more equal distribution of income and wealth is a necessary measure to redress past economic injustice. To the extent that such a redistribution has already taken place, it is used as a reminder of the benefits bestowed by the new regime. In this sense, therefore, redistribution is also a politically motivated objective. Furthermore, because a change in distribution toward greater equality is supposed to be able to set free enormous productive forces which would greatly increase the productivity of labor—the Chinese Communists have never ceased to affirm this proposition as if it were an article of faith—one may also regard this objective as an intermediate step to increase the level of production.

CHANGING ECONOMIC INSTITUTIONS AND BEHAVIOR. Looking back over the past twenty years, it is quite clear that Communist China has scored considerable success in realizing some of her objectives but has failed miserably in other respects. Moreover, even within the same area of ideological, political, or economic interest, her record has not been consistent.

First, let us consider Communist China's record in socialization, nationalization, and the establishment of a controlled economy. In this general area, the redistribution of land without compensation from the "landlords" and "rich peasants" to the "poor peasants" and landless farm workers was pushed through energetically in the newly occupied areas after the establishment of the Communist regime.[9] In spite of the vast size of the country and the millions of farm households involved, this "land reform" was by and large completed before the end of 1953. In many parts of the country, it had been carried out even earlier. The main step toward socialization, that is, the replacement of the small private farm by the collective or cooperative farm, was taken immediately thereafter. While the entire process of collectivization was supposed to have taken a number of years and be carried out in two stages, at the behest of Mao Tse-tung it was accelerated and virtually completed by the end of 1956. In the non-agricultural sectors, the formation of "joint state-private enterprises" took place rapidly between 1952 and 1956. During the same period, the numerous small busi-

---

[9]For a fuller description of this process, see Yuan-li Wu, *An Economic Survey of Communist China* (New York: Bookman Associates, 1956), pp. 113–153.

nesses in urban areas were either amalgamated or forcibly converted into cooperatives, while other state-sponsored marketing and producer cooperatives were simultaneously established. The record before 1957 was, therefore, one of considerable success in bringing about the institutional changes desired by the Communists.

Yet, beginning with establishment of the communes in 1958, the Chinese Communists have been singularly unsuccessful in carrying out the more "advanced" forms of Communist reorganization of man and society. Furthermore, the economy has simply refused to respond in the ideologically correct manner. The peasants were unable to maintain their enthusiasm and productivity in the face of long hours and the small material rewards they received. They did not show the same concern for property. They could not see why disparity in work should not be reflected in a differential pay scale. The direct participation of the people in industrial production— as exemplified by establishment of the numerous "backyard furnaces" which dotted the countryside between 1958 and 1959, like the massive application of labor in such activities as manure gathering and deep plowing, —proved unable to unlock the promised mythical reservoir of potential productivity or to alter the technical conditions for smelting iron and growing crops.

Even worse than this failure to make the economy operate according to ideologically correct precepts, the population actually seemed to respond with enthusiasm to all the wrong incentives and institutions. Farm production began to pick up when the commune was progressively downgraded during 1961 and 1962 as the agency of farm management and income distribution among farmers. More poultry and pigs were raised and more vegetables were grown as soon as small private plots were restored and farmers were allowed to sell on a limited free market what they could produce on their own. This economic behavior was, to Mao Tse-tung and his followers, renascent capitalism. From 1963 on, it was to become first the object of "Socialist education" and then of the Cultural Revolution.

Finally, during 1966-68, while trying to stamp out "economism," often reflected in the existence of "underground factories" and other illicit private enterprises and in the alleged corrupt behavior of Communist Party cadres and government officials, the Cultural Revolution succeeded in crippling a large part of the structure and procedure of economic planning and management. It failed, however, to create in their place the all-round Communist man whose emergence would presumably have made child's play of orderly and coordinated economic planning and operation by a centralized agency, if not wholly eliminating them as altogether unnecessary.

Without going into the detailed circumstances surrounding the successive successes and failures, we may note some common factors which appeared to be present. The success in carrying out "land reform," collectivization, and even the initial establishment of the communes, and in bringing private business under direct state ownership or control, was a tribute to the remarkable abilities of the Chinese Communist Party in mass organization. Success was made possible by the many party cadres who were experienced in revolutionary tactics and in the management of large numbers of people. It was made easier by political stratagems[10] which divided the Communist Party's potential opponents, neutralized large numbers of persons by taking advantage of their very natural desire to save their own skins, and established political controls that, once in place, could not be readily dislodged. These successes were also scored in the first decade of Communist rule. During this period, the general public—weary of both war and inflation—was ready to accept at face value the Communists' professions of good will. By 1958, however, many of these advantages, except the party's ability to organize, had been dissipated; and organization by itself was not a strong enough substitute for material incentives, technical competence, and, in the case of agriculture especially, the dependence of production on the farmer's intimate knowledge of local conditions. Last but not least, organization could no longer offset the desperate tenacity with which the peasant clung to his last trace of private property. In other words, once the initial changes in economic institutions had been accomplished, the further changes that Mao Tse-tung wished to see could not help but outrage the Chinese farmer's minimal demands for personal "freedom" and private ownership. Finally, in the case of the communes, Mao Tse-tung committed a tactical error in taking on the whole countryside virtually at once. In doing so, he violated his own cardinal rules of strategy and good politics.

SUCCESS IN SELECTED INDUSTRIES *versus* FAILURE IN ACHIEVING TECHNOLOGICAL INDEPENDENCE. Efforts to attain the several politically motivated objectives were not equally successful in each case. On the one hand, what Peking probably regards as one of its most prominent accomplishments, the development of a nuclear capability in advance of foreign expectations, showed quite clearly that Chinese planners were able to organize production in a number of mutually supporting industries. They were able to mobilize the necessary resources for the development of specific goods when sufficient priority and urgency were accorded to the goal. The very rapid growth of such industries as steel, petroleum, coal, power, and, more recently, chemical fertilizers points to the same conclusion. Communist China could and did achieve a high rate of growth for

[10]The Common Program resembled the Russian NEP. It was adopted to placate Chinese industrialists and modern businessmen whose services were needed. In a similar manner, "land reform" served the purpose of winning over large segments of the poorer farmers. It was used as bait in carrying on "class struggle" that eliminated the Communists' opponents.

a few selected industries. As will be argued a little later, breakthroughs on such a selective basis were at the expense of other industries and, indirectly if not directly, of personal consumption as well. However, in so far as the few high priority goals were realized, the reported success was often emphasized as evidence of the superiority of the Chinese economic system. How convincing this claim can be made to appear depends on the period and indicators chosen. It would be more convincing if made before 1960 and if some of the capital goods industries are employed as illustrations.

As for the objective of achieving economic and technological independence, Communist China has been unsuccessful in some respects. Although the entire Chinese experiment in economic development has been financed by domestic savings alone (if we take into consideration the whole period 1949-64),[11] Peking's success in industrial development during the early years of this period was to a considerable extent due to Soviet aid in equipment and technology. Communist China's technological dependence upon the Soviet Union was most dramatically revealed when many unfinished investment projects and scientific and technological programs, as well as current production in some cases, had to be curtailed or discontinued in mid-1960 when Soviet technical assistance was suddenly withdrawn. The Chinese Communists were dismayed that they had to pay, in their dealings with the Soviet Union, the same bitter penalty that they had tried to avoid by not relying upon the capitalist West. With economic recovery in the early 1960s, they have had to reverse themselves and to seek new technology from Western Europe and Japan. Objectively speaking, Communist China probably accomplished as much in learning from the Soviet Union as anyone could reasonably expect, but the initial decision by Mao Tsetung to rely upon the Soviet Union for new technology was obviously a poor political decision. Misplaced trust in the Soviet Union as a dependable source of "fraternal Socialist assistance," and in the "internationalist duty" of the more advanced Socialist countries toward the less advanced ones, were apparently responsible for this error in political judgment.

FLAWS IN COMMUNIST CHINA'S DEVELOPMENT STRATEGY: EXCESSIVE SPEED, UNBALANCED GROWTH, AND INSTABILITY. The information on aggregate outputs contained in Table 1 presents a picture of overall growth for the entire period 1949-65. These dates do not, however, tell the whole story. Even the *per capita* figures, which have taken population growth into account, are inadequate because they do not allow for the passage of time and the changing rates of growth within the entire period or, in some cases, for the direction of the movement itself. Changes in rates of growth and direction are brought out when we examine the annual rates of change for varying lengths of time. The information for such a comparison is contained in Table 2. (Data for the 1966–68 period have

[11]Repayment of China's debt to the Soviet Union was probably completed in 1964.

been excluded from Table 2 because of the effects of the Cultural Revolution, which will be discussed separately.)

In general, the data indicate that with the exception of the initial period of economic rehabilitation, the highest growth rates were attained during the 1957-60 period of the Great Leap, followed by the rates in 1952-57 or during the First Five Year Plan. Furthermore, the annual rates for the entire 1952-65 period were, with minor exceptions, below the levels reached in 1952-57.

Perhaps the most significant fact in China's growth record is the relatively low annual rate when sufficiently long periods of time are examined. The results also vary a great deal depending upon whether the economic decline in 1959-61 is included within the total period in question. It should be borne in mind that although the Chinese Communists have stressed industrial production much more than the growth of GNP as a whole, at no time did they contemplate an *absolute* decline in total output.

Mao Tse-tung's thesis that economic progress should proceed in a wavelike motion envisages only an occasional slowdown in the rate of growth for purposes of "consolidation;" it does not postulate a recession or depression of any magnitude. Therefore, the great slide back of the economy after the Great Leap was unanticipated, and its occurrence could be regarded as a definite indication that steady economic growth was not realized. For our purpose, therefore, the important question is whether the "depression" was an inevitable outcome of the preceding expansion.

It is the contention of this essay that, in spite of some external factors — such as unfavorable weather, which affected the farm sector, and the termination of Soviet assistance, which had a severe impact on the non-agricultural sectors — and the sheer incompetence and ignorance of certain Communist cadres in production planning management, the fundamental causes of instability were political and ideological in nature.

For several reasons, Communist China had adopted the "big push" approach in the development of a few selected industries. There was the Soviet example of overwhelming emphasis on heavy industry; and Soviet advisors, as well as material and technical aid, played a significant role in Chinese planning, especially in the First Five Year Plan.[12] The experience of Chinese Communist leaders during the revolutionary war was perhaps an even greater influence in this direction. Their practice of concentrating large forces for a massive assault on a few military targets was carried over into economic planning, and the leaders seemed confident that a succession of such all-out efforts would be able to lift the Chinese economy onto higher and higher plateaus. This state of mind accounted for (1) the continual acceleration of the planned rates of growth, which led to an accelera-

[12]The Second Five Year Plan also owes a great deal to Soviet participation, both in formulation and in its execution before mid-1960.

Table 2.
Annual Rates of Growth of Production
as Measured by Selected Indicators for Different Time Periods[a]

		1949-65	1952-65	1949-52	1952-57	1957-60	1960-62	1962-65	1958-65	1959-65
Producers' Goods										
Coal	Total	15.25	12.70	27.00	14.10	40.80	−14.80	6.25	4.60	1.05
	Per Capita	13.10	10.60	24.55	11.50	38.00	−15.97	5.10	3.15	−0.29
Electric Power	Total	14.90	14.10	18.95	21.66	34.45	−20.12	10.10	5.50	−0.61
	Per Capita	13.70	12.00	21.65	9.55	50.85	−21.20	8.85	4.00	−1.95
Crude Oil	Total	31.80	27.25	53.30	27.30	55.60	11.20	13.70	23.60	18.00
	Per Capita	30.20	24.45	58.70	23.50	51.50	9.55	12.60	22.00	16.50
Raw Steel[b] (Ingot)	Total	32.90	20.35	104.40	24.30	51.10 (30.90)	−26.43 (−8.70)	14.45	4.40 (9.40)	2.00 (9.70)
	Per Capita	30.20	18.35	97.20	29.20	47.80 (28.00)	−27.48 (−10.00)	13.30	2.90 (7.80)	0.60 (8.20)
Consumers' Goods										
Cotton Cloth	Total	4.60	0.13	26.55	5.70	5.90	−29.29	9.10	−5.28	−10.30
	Per Capita	2.65	−1.79	24.15	3.10	3.70	−30.50	8.05	−6.69	−11.60
Food Grain Official	Total	3.90	2.00	12.60	3.70	9.00 (1957-59)	−3.00	4.80	−3.14	−1.60
	Per Capita	2.00	0.13	10.45	1.30	6.80 (1957-59)	−4.34	3.60	−4.53	−2.86
O. L. Dawson	Total	1.60	0.75	5.30	1.10	−2.79 (1957-59)	6.00	2.35	−0.86	1.65
	Per Capita	−.29	−1.08	3.20	−1.23	−4.82 (1957-59)	4.60	1.20	−2.28	0.30

Foreign Trade (Total Turnover)	Total	...	4.10	...	10.10	9.80	−20.25	7.45	−2.31	−5.20
	Per Capita	...	2.20	...	7.70	7.45	−21.14	6.00	−3.88	−6.90
Gross National Product	Total	...	4.45	...	5.80	6.50	−5.24	7.20	2.80	1.90
	Per Capita	...	2.55	...	3.30	4.30	−6.51	6.00	1.25	0.58
Industrial Output Official	{ Total	16.70	12.85	34.80	17.95	44.00	−17.87 (1960–63)	12.90 (1963–65)	3.45	−1.50
	{ *Per Capita*	14.50	10.80	32.10	15.20	41.00	−18.92 (1960–63)	11.70 (1963–65)	2.00	−2.86
Y. L. Wu[c]	{ Total	...	12.80	...	18.50	27.30	−8.18	5.60	7.55	2.95
	{ *Per Capita*	...	10.70	...	15.70	24.70	−9.50	4.40	6.00	1.60

a For the original data and sources, see Appendix.
b The figures in parentheses refer to modern steel production only.
c Refers to modern industry only.

tion of the planned rate of capital formation; and (2) the unbalanced expansion in selected sectors, with emphasis on heavy industry and capital goods before 1961. These policies had the effect of repressing the very natural tendency of peasants and workers to demand a larger share of the output for personal consumption. They also created bottlenecks and cutbacks in economic sectors which had lower priority, including the consumer goods industries and agriculture. The bottlenecks were further accentuated as a result of the massive, uncoordinated expansion attempted under the backyard furnace campaign, which was by no means limited to iron smelting alone. Party leaders, especially Mao Tse-tung, apparently failed to recognize the limited endurance of the population under conditions of low consumption. They failed to do so because in their ideological conception of economic behavior the "proto-Communist man" should respond to normative incentives alone. When the workers and peasants could not do what they were ideologically supposed to do, productivity declined and the accumulated result of past errors finally caught up with the Chinese Communists.

Although the same ideological approach to economic planning prevailed before the Great Leap, albeit not to the same degree, the Chinese economy benefited from two other important conditions in the first few years of their rule which were no longer present later. The earlier plans probably placed a less stringent demand on China's available resources. This may have occurred unwittingly. In agriculture, for instance, the restoration of transportation and new railroad construction unlocked agricultural surpluses in previously isolated provinces. Current production of grain before 1956 was probably also underestimated,[13] so that more may have been available than the economic plans accounted for. Furthermore, there was the factor of Soviet assistance, which could be called upon to help bridge some critical gaps in output. These circumstances made it possible for Communist China to exceed the objectives of the First Five Year Plan. By the time of the Great Leap, however, the "reserves" which had cushioned the demands of heavy investment and the unbalanced growth in the economy had been used up. Yet the self-confidence of the Chinese Communist leadership had grown in the meantime, and there seemed to be a greater urgency for even faster economic growth.

The sense of urgency for accelerated growth was partly political and partly economic. The basic political need to speed up economic growth was, of course, always present; it merely reflected the desire for great power status. The economic factor, however, reflected the effect of population growth, which was aggravated by improved transportation facilities and the consequent availability of surplus food in deficit areas, for the

[13]See Yuan-li Wu, *The Economy of Communist China: An Introduction,* pp. 143–144.

"Malthusian constraint" of starvation had been temporarily removed. However, even this apparently economic phenomenon of population growth was not independent of Communist ideology. Because there should not be a demographic problem under socialism, it was not until the end of the First Five Year Plan that the need to curb population growth was consciously recognized in active government policy.

Even the "external" factors which hampered economic growth were not entirely independent of government policy and practice. The sharp decline in agricultural production during 1959–61 was partly a result of unwise efforts to increase output through deep plowing and irrigation. The withdrawal of Soviet technical assistance in 1960 was in direct response to Chinese policy preceding the open Sino-Soviet dispute. The mistake made by the Chinese Communists was to have placed their trust in the Soviet Union, and then to have crossed the wishes of certain Soviet leaders. As mentioned before, this was an error of political judgment which had its roots in Chinese ideology.

All in all, therefore, the instability exhibited in Communist China's economic development was an outcome of a development strategy which suffered from the ideological and political attitudes of Communist China's leaders. To put the matter in a nutshell, too much haste in becoming a great power, unquestioned and frequently misplaced faith in the ideological appeals of communism, too little understanding of the deepseated desire of the Chinese peasant and worker to own some property, overconfidence on the part of the leaders in their ability to adapt revolutionary military tactics to the solution of economic problems, and undue reliance upon the "fraternal goodwill" of the Soviet Union—these were the principal factors underlying China's economic failures. All of these factors were either political or ideological in content and origin. Technological backwardness and managerial errors only served to make the failures worse.

THE QUEST FOR ECONOMIC JUSTICE. Finally, let us consider briefly the goal of achieving greater economic equality. Mention has already been made of the program of nationalization and socialization. A by-product of this policy has been the reduction of the relative importance of income from property. While the level of wages and the income of peasants have been kept back in order to raise the rate of capital formation, the share of wages and income from work has undoubtedly risen in relation to that from property. The practice of maintaining class labels to denote the family origin of individuals has also raised the relative social standing of those who were formerly poor. The equalizing process which tends to reduce differences in income and wealth has, therefore, gone a long way. To the extent the change was desired as an economic goal, the Chinese Communists may be considered quite successful.

The same, however, cannot be said of equality in a different sense. For both agricultural collectivization and nationalization in the nonagricultural sectors have effectively reduced the number of decision-making units. As is characteristic of all administratively controlled economies, the degree of concentration of economic power has increased. Greater power is vested in a new managerial class, which consists of select party cadres and technocrats. Even when the communes were downgraded during the early 1960s, the number of economic decision-makers remained much smaller than before the Communist revolution. Mao Tse-tung probably had some of this development in mind when he tried to rejuvenate the hidebound party and government bureaucracy during the Cultural Revolution. One aspect of the "economism" which Mao abhorred and which he tried to eradicate was probably the effect of this tendency toward economic concentration without an adequate check-and-balance system within the power structure of the Chinese Communist Party. Unfortunately for China, it seems that Mao has tried to do this only by arrogating even greater power to himself, and that he may have succeeded only in putting greater power into the hands of the military commanders.

WHAT MIGHT HAVE BEEN. If Communist China was in reality not able to attain all the objectives she had set for herself, could she have done better by following a different development strategy, or simply by being more efficient? The answer to the second question is relatively easy, for some of the problems that Chinese planners faced were the result of erroneous information, while others were created by technological and managerial backwardness. These deficiencies could have been lessened.[14] On the other hand, it is far more difficult to imagine that politics and ideology would not "take command" under a Communist regime.

Communist China could hardly have been expected to give up the emphasis on heavy industry, certainly not in the beginning of her development planning. Nor could the Chinese Communists have openly welcomed foreign capital from the West. Nor would they have foregone collectivization and socialization entirely, although less damage might have been done had the rate of change been slower. Given the political leadership of the Chinese Communist Party during the last twenty years—and one must bear in mind that Mao Tse-tung was not the entire party leadership—it is difficult to see what radical departures from China's actual experience could have taken place as long as the Communist Party was in power. One suspects that the very qualities which made the top Communist Chinese leaders good revolutionaries and fighters also make them poor political leaders for economic development.

---

[14]See Yuan-li Wu, "Planning Management, and Economic Revolution," in *An Economic Profile of Mainland China,* Vol. 1, pp. 97-119.

Conditions for Economic Growth

THE PRINCIPAL FAVORABLE CONDITIONS FOR A NEW START. If we compare 1969 with 1949, assuming that the worst phase of the Cultural Revolution is over and that renewed economic development can take place, are the present conditions more favorable to economic development than they were twenty years ago? In order to answer this question, let us first see where the Chinese economy now stands. In this connection, we must now look not at the level of current output at these two dates, but at the stock of available resources, the state of technological knowledge, the size of the population which the economy must support, and the alternative development policies which one can realistically regard as possible.

Both the resource base and the level of Chinese technology present a much more favorable picture today than they did in 1949. In the first place, we know that China has far more natural resources, with the exception of arable land, than she was known to have in 1949. Both iron ore and petroleum are in much more abundant supply than they were thought to be. The same applies to a number of other metals. The raw material base for a large chemical fertilizer industry, of great importance to the future of Chinese agriculture, is also present. The intensive work in geological survey and prospecting during the 1950s has definitely produced some tangible results.

In the second place, China today has a much larger capital stock in industrial plants, transportation facilities, thermal and hydro-power plants, and irrigation installations than she had in 1949. The following figures may serve as an illustration:

	1949	1952	Present
Annual Capacity of Ingot Steel (Rated) (million metric tons)[a]	0.6	1.6	30.1* (1960)
Railway Trackage (thousand kilometers)[b]	23.6	25.1	52.6 (1963)
Electric Power Capacity[c]	1.8	2.0	15.0 (1967)

* Including some planned figures.

a Yuan-li Wu, *The Steel Industry in Communist China,* pp. 265–266.

b Yuan-li Wu, *The Spatial Economy of Communist China* (New York: Praeger, 1967), p. 129. New construction in 1964–68 is estimated at 1500 km. of trunk lines.

c Yuan-li Wu, *Economic Development and the Use of Energy Resources in Communist China* (New York: Praeger, 1963), p. 14. For 1967, see Chu Chiang-huai, "Ta-lu Tien-li Kung-yeh Chih Yen-chiu" (The Electric Power Industry of Mainland China). *Ta-lu Ching-chi Yen-chiu* (Economic Study of Mainland China), No. 25 (Taipei: Ministry of Economic Affairs, January 31, 1968), p. 4.

In the third place, developments in rail and road transportation have brought modern industry from the eastern third of the country to the central third. No longer is the coastal fringe of China, plus southern Manchuria and the lower reaches of the Yangtze, the only industrialized and modern sectors of the economy. It is now physically possible to replace the erstwhile regional markets by a much larger national market, thus taking advantage of the benefits of scale and of "comparative advantage" on a regional basis.

A fourth favorable factor is the tremendous expansion of the research and development industry of China, which reached a record high on the eve of the Cultural Revolution. The number of research and technical personnel increased from an official estimate of 9,300 in 1952 to 99,000 (preliminary) in 1964. The state science budget rose from 64 million yuan in 1953 to about 1.5 billion yuan in 1963.[15] Total expenditure on "science," including research and development for new weapons systems, is believed to be three to four times the size of the state science budget. There has also been a tremendous growth in the number of institutions devoted to research and development, including a large number of design institutes[16] whose primary function seems to be the replication of new technology embodied in industrial and other equipment imported from Western Europe and Japan. Because of the long time lag between research and application, China may be rapidly reaching a point in time when the positive results of indigenous research could begin to be felt.

There are also some intangible advantages today that were not available to Chinese planners in 1949. These are the lessons which could be learned from the experience of the last twenty years. On the positive side, it is now known that it would be organizationally possible to devote about twenty percent of the country's current output to capital formation. It has also been clearly established that both the peasants and the workers are not only hard-working, a fact that has been generally known for a long time, but that they are also responsive to technical innovation and rational, material incentives. On the negative side, ample evidence has been adduced to convince any disinterested observer that Maoist ideological and political doctrine and its derivative approach to economic development will not work. It is also clear that there are certain limits beyond which even the very patient Chinese population cannot be pushed. Thus Chinese planners should not count on a rate of capital formation much higher than twenty percent for any length of time without experiencing serious political reverberations.

[15]See *Organization and Support of Scientific Research and Development in Mainland China* (Washington: Surveys and Research Corporation, 1967), especially Ch. 6, p. 19, and Ch. 7, p. 27.

[16]See *A Directory of Selected Scientific Institutions in Mainland China* (Washington: National Science Foundation, forthcoming).

THE PRINCIPAL UNFAVORABLE FACTORS FOR A NEW START. Given a larger potential in resources and technology, and the knowledge of what kinds of mistakes to avoid, is there any reason to question Communist China's prospects for economic growth? Is it possible for these prospects to be anything but significantly better than they were in 1949? There are several reasons to believe that the prospects are by no means assured in spite of these apparently favorable circumstances.

First, the present Chinese population is about two hundred million larger than it was in 1949, and continues to grow at about two percent a year. For the entire 1952–65 period, the average rate of growth in GNP was probably not more than 4.5 percent a year, which yields an annual growth rate of about 2.5 percent *per capita*. In order to achieve a higher *per capita* rate, some or all of the following developments will be necessary: (1) large downswings of the GNP must be avoided; (2) the growth process must not be stalled for long periods, even if any serious downswing is ruled out; and (3) the growth of the population must be slowed down. Since the last development is not readily controllable, let us consider the first two possibilities.

Whether large downswings can be avoided will probably hinge upon the nature of the political leadership and its economic policy. A Maoist economic policy as characterized by the Great Leap will in all probability produce another sharp reaction. Muddling through economically, which can probably best describe the conditions during the first two years of the Cultural Revolution, will result in a stall, if not worse. The effect of the Cultural Revolution on current output was relatively minor in 1966. By 1967, however, disruptions had caught up with industrial production, and there was a noticeable decline. Although only preliminary information is available, there is good reason to believe that the decline continued during at least a part of 1968. If population growth continues, the need to halt the slide and to resume expansion will become progressively more urgent. In this respect, the Chinese economy is certainly in no better position today than it was twenty years earlier.

Second, even if the end of the Cultural Revolution should coincide with the immediate appearance of a united national leadership, the Chinese economy will suffer from the fact that the entire structure and apparatus of economic planning and management have been seriously undermined. From the very beginning, the Cultural Revolution aimed its attack on the government and party hierarchy, including many cadres who held responsible positions in economic planning and operations. In their effort to resist the attacks of the Maoists, they had to resort to means which caused the controls to disintegrate further.[17] All of these controls would have to be reconstituted by the post-Cultural Revolution leadership. Furthermore, it is doubtful that the planners will have the necessary statistical and other

---

[17] This point will be more fully discussed in a forthcoming article by the author.

information required for efficient planning. Their need to reorganize and staff a planning apparatus and to provide it with adequate information would, in effect, repeat Communist China's experience when the regime was first established. There will, however, be a major difference. While the Chinese Communist Party rode the crest of a successful revolution in 1949 and, therefore, enjoyed unquestioned authority in the progressive development of its planning apparatus, it is far less certain whether a new leadership, Maoist or otherwise, can reconstitute the shattered authority required for planning in a unified national economy, and whether it can do so within a short period of time.

THE BALANCE. When the favorable factors are arrayed against the unfavorable ones, it would seem that the prospects of resuming economic growth depend upon the degree of pragmatism the post-Cultural Revolution leadership will possess. If it is pragmatic but remains Communist, then the prospects for continued growth would depend upon whether a Maoist leadership might not rise again after some time to supplant the new leadership. (The outlook under a non-Communist leadership is not considered here, inasmuch as a totally different set of economic possibilities would then emerge. The practical possibility of a non-Communist leadership, however, cannot be dismissed if the post-Cultural Revolution regime again runs into serious economic difficulties or if national unity cannot be restored.)

Compared with 1949, Communist China's economic prospects in 1969 were, therefore, even more uncertain than they must have appeared twenty years ago. Any crucial difference between the two situations would not be economic; rather, it may be the lack thus far of an immediate political alternative to the Chinese Communist Party. The Chinese Communists themselves constituted such an alternative in 1949. If there were a similar alternative today, the parallelism between 1949 and 1969 would be virtually complete.

Conclusion

One can quite seriously raise the question whether Communist China has really had a chance to undergo the full experience of comprehensive economic planning. The First Five Year Plan was not a complete and fair test; the apparatus of central planning was not fully developed until the latter part of the period, and there were some rather favorable circumstances which made for relatively easy success. However, let us assume that an annual growth rate of just under six percent, which was reached between 1952 and 1957, is possible for the Chinese GNP in the long run. How would this compare with the record of other countries? On the basis of statistics developed for a similar comparison involving the Soviet Union[18] and six other developed countries, the Chinese growth rate of 1952–57 would be higher than the corresponding rates for the United Kingdom, the United States, France, and Italy in the period from 1950 to 1958, but below the rates attained by Japan, the Soviet Union, and West Germany. The United Kingdom had 2.4 percent or the lowest of the seven countries, while West Germany had 7.6 percent, which was the highest rate. For the period between 1958 and 1962, of the same seven countries, Japan, Italy, and West Germany again had higher annual growth rates than the Chinese rate between 1952 and 1957. The range was 13.2 percent (Japan) and 2.8 percent (the United Kingdom). What this comparison means is that, to say the least, the record of Communist China was not in the upper half of the range, or even particularly impressive. If we were to employ the 1952–65 period for China, the annual growth rate of the Chinese GNP would be closer to 4.5 percent, which would put the rank of Communist China in the lower half of the range of the seven countries.

Of course, one could find underdeveloped countries that showed a worse record, which would put Communist China's in a more favorable light. However, even in such a case, the same general result would obtain. For instance, of the twelve underdeveloped countries given by Chenery and Strout that satisfied their "savings and trade criteria" between 1957 and 1962, the GNP growth rate varied from four percent (Korea) to 11.1 percent (Jordan), with a median rate of 6.7 percent.[19] The Chinese rate of six percent would be slightly below the median level. Specifically, one may also compare Communist China's record with the 7.4 percent attained by Taiwan during the period between 1957 and 1962.

Furthermore, the Chinese production record in modern industry for the period between 1952 and 1965—an annual growth rate of 12.8 percent—would also have a relative standing, when compared with that of other countries, only a little better than the GNP comparison. For instance, from 1953 to 1958, the annual growth rates of industrial production were 15.8 percent in Pakistan, 11.3 percent in the U.S.S.R., 10.1 percent in Japan, 9.2 percent in Taiwan, 8.7 percent in West Germany and 6.7 percent in India. On the other hand, for the 1953 to 1966 period, the rates were Pakistan, 13.8 percent; the Soviet Union, 9.9 percent; Japan, 12.7 percent; Taiwan, 11.8 percent; West Germany, seven percent; India, 7.2 percent.[20] The comparison would become much more favorable for Communist

[18]See *Annual Economic Indicators for the U.S.S.R.* (Washington: Government Printing Office, 1964), p. 95.

[19]See H. B. Chenery and A. M. Strout, "Foreign Assistance and Economic Development," *American Economic Review,* Vol. 51, No. 4, Part 1 (September 1966), pp. 708–709.

[20]Derived from *Statistical Yearbook 1967* (New York: United Nations, 1968), pp. 158–164.

China only if we choose the 1952–57 period, when large Soviet aid and other favorable conditions for development were present.

A much more *un*favorable comparison would be obtained if we took *per capita* personal consumption. While there was little improvement in mainland China in this respect during the entire period, *per capita* personal consumption rose at a high rate in both Japan and Taiwan, two of Peking's closest rivals. The annual growth rates were 13.1 percent (1952 to 1957) and 8.7 percent (1957 to 1965) for Taiwan, and 8.5 percent (1953 to 1958) and ten percent (1957 to 1965) for Japan.[21]

If Communist China's overall economic performance during the past two decades, including that of the First Five Year Plan, was surpassed by many other countries under widely divergent conditions, it would seem that the Chinese model has no particular claim to superiority. Add to this the tremendous human cost that has accompanied China's economic achievements, such as they are, as well as the great uncertainty which surrounds the economic future of Communist China today, and one cannot but conclude that from the point of view of the Chinese population, the whole effort could hardly be considered worthwhile. It is true that Communist China now has nuclear weapons. It is also true that the Chinese population, including millions of China's youth, have now had the experience of living through and participating in a revolution. How much value should be assigned to the bomb and the "revolutionary experience?" Obviously, these questions cannot be answered without presupposing a particular system of values. It is fair to say, however, that unless very high values are assigned to the political and ideological "achievements"—as has been pointed out, these are highly questionable even within their own terms of reference—the Chinese effort must have yielded a rather low rate of return. Unfortunately, the population of mainland China was never offered an opportunity to choose with full knowledge of the consequences. The economic consequences of Mao Tse-tung have already been far more onerous than any single generation of men should reasonably be expected to bear.

[21]See *Statistical Abstract of the Republic of China* (Taipei: Directorate-General of Budgets, Accounts and Statistics, 1961), p. 30; 1968, pp. 38 and 744–45; and *Monthly Statistics of Japan* (Tokyo: Bureau of Statistics, Office of the Prime Minister), No. 1 (July 1961), p. 3; No. 6 (December 1961), p. 122; No. 89 (November 1968), pp. 3 and 118.

Appendix

for

Chapter 6

Appendix
Estimated Output of Selected Products and Indices of Output

Year	Coal[1] (Modern Mines) Total (1,000 M.T.)	Per Capita** (Kg.)	Electric Power[2] Total (Million K.W.H.)	Per Capita** (K.W.H.)	Crude Oil[3] Total (1,000 M.T.)	Per Capita** (Kg.)	Steel Ingot[4] Total (1,000 M.T.)	Per Capita** (Kg.)	Cotton Cloth[5] Total (Million Meters)	Per Capita** (Meters)
1949	30,980	57.2	4,310	7.0	121	0.2	158	0.3	1,890	3.5
1952	63,530	110.5	7,260	12.6	436	0.8	1,349	2.3	3,830	6.7
1953	66,570	113.2	9,200	15.6	622	1.1	1,774	3.0	4,690	8.0
1957	123,230	190.5	19,340	19.9	1,458	2.3	5,350	8.3	5,050	7.8
1958	218,860	331.1	27,530	41.6	2,264	3.4	11,080 (8,000)*	16.8 (12.1)*	5,700	8.6
1959	281,720	417.4	41,500	61.5	3,700	5.5	13,350 (8,630)*	19.8 (12.8)*	7,500	11.1
1960	344,250	500.4	47,000	68.3	5,500	8.0	18,450 (12,000)*	26.8 (17.4)*	6,000	8.7
1962	250,000	353.6	30,000	42.4	6,800	9.6	10,000	14.1	3,000	4.2
1965	300,000	410.4	40,000	54.7	10,000	13.7	15,000	20.5	3,900	5.3

Year	Grain Official Estimate[6] Total (Million M.T.)	Per Capita** (Kg.)	O. L. Dawson[7] Total (Million M.T.)	Per Capita** (Kg.)	Foreign Trade[8] Total (Million Yuan)	Per Capita** (Yuan)	Industrial Output Official Estimate[9] Total (Billion of 1952 Yuan)	Per Capita** (Yuan)	Y. L. Wu (Modern)[10] Total (Billion of 1952 Yuan)	Per Capita** (Yuan)	GNP[11] Total (Billion of 1952 Yuan)	Per Capita** (Yuan)
1949	108.1	199.4	150	276.8	...	...	14.02	25.9	...	...	...	...
1952	154.4	268.5	175	304.3	6,460	11.2	34.33	59.7	8.2	14.3	75.6	131.5
1953	156.9	266.8	166	282.3	8,090	13.8	44.70	74.8	10.3	17.5	78.9	134.2
1957	185.0	285.9	185	285.9	10,450	16.2	78.39	121.2	19.2	29.7	100.0	154.6
1958	250.0	378.2	205	310.1	12,870	19.5	130.30	197.1	23.6	35.7	110.0	167.5
1959	220.0	325.9	175	259.3	15,440	22.9	181.50	268.9	33.0	48.9	119.1	176.4
1960	185.0	268.9	160	232.6	13,845	20.1	233.80	339.8	39.6	57.6	120.7	175.4
1962	174.0	246.1	180	254.6	8,803	12.5	129.50 (1963)	181.1 (1963)	33.4	47.2	108.4	153.3
1965	200.0	273.6	193	264.0	10,925	14.9	165.30	226.1	39.3	53.8	133.5	182.6

* Modern Steel.
** The population estimates (in millions of persons) used in computing the per capita figures are: 1949, 542; 1952, 575; 1953, 588; 1957, 647; 1958, 661; 1959, 675; 1960, 688; 1962, 707; 1965, 731. For 1949-53 figures, see *T'ung-chi Kung-tso* (Statistical Bulletin), No. 11 (1957), pp. 24-25; for 1957 figure, see State Statistical Bureau, *Ten Great Years—Statistics on Economic and Cultural Construction Achievements of the People's Republic of China* (Peking: Foreign Languages Press, 1960), p. 8; for 1958-65, see Yuan-li Wu et al., *The Economic Potential of Communist China* (Stanford: Stanford Research Institute, 1963), Vol. 1, p. 28.

Sources:

1. The 1949-57 figures are from *T'ung-chi Yen-chiu* (Statistical Research), No. 4 (April 1958), pp. 19-22: *Jen-min Shou-ts'e, 1957* (People's Handbook, 1957) (Peking), p. 429; People's Handbook, 1958, p. 457; and Y. I. Berezina, *Toplivno-Energeticheskaia Baza Kitayskoi Narodnoi Respubliki* (The Fuel and Power Base of the Chinese People's Republic) (Moscow: 1959), p. 10. For 1958-60, see Yuan-li Wu, *Economic Development and the Use of Energy Resources in Communist China* (New York: Praeger, 1963), p. 241. For 1962 and 1965, see K. P. Wang, "The Mineral Resources Base of Communist China," in *An Economic Profile of Mainland China*. (Washington: Government Printing Office, 1967), Vol. 1, p. 174.

2. The 1949-58 figures are from *Ten Great Years*, p. 95; the 1959 figure is from *New China News Agency*, April 9, 1960. For 1960-65, see John Ashton, "Development of Electric Energy Resources in Communist China," in *An Economic Profile of Mainland China*, Vol. 1, p. 307.

3. The 1949-59 figures are from *Ten Great Years*, p. 95. The 1960 figure is from K. P. Wang, "The Mineral Industry of Mainland China," in *Minerals Yearbook 1963* (Washington: Bureau of Mines, 1963). The 1962 and 1965 figures are from K. P. Wang, "The Mineral Resources Base of Communist China," *loc. cit.*, p. 174.

4. The 1949-58 figures are from *Ten Great Years*, p. 95. The 1959-60 figures are from Yuan-li Wu, *The Steel Industry in Communist China* (New York: Praeger, 1965), p. 66; and K. P. Wang, "The Mineral Industry of Mainland China," *loc. cit.* The 1962 and 1965 figures are from K. P. Wang, "The Mineral Resources Base of Communist China," *loc. cit.*, p. 174.

5. The 1949-58 figures are from *Ten Great Years*, p. 88. The 1959-65 figures are from Robert M. Field, "Chinese Communist Industrial Production," in *An Economic Profile of Mainland China*. Vol. 1, p. 294.

6. The 1949-58 figures are from *Ten Great Years*, p. 105. For 1959-60, see Yuan-li Wu et. al., *The Economic Potential of Communist China*, Vol. 1, p. 85. For 1962 and 1965, see Edwin F. Jones, "The Emerging Pattern of China's Economic Revolution," in *An Economic Profile of Mainland China*, Vol. 1, p. 93.

7. Owen L. Dawson, *A Constraint on ChiCom Foreign Policy: Agricultural Output, 1966-1975*, (Stanford: Stanford Research Institute, 1967), p. 71.

8. The 1952-58 figures are based on *Ten Great Years*, p. 155. The 1959 figure is taken from *China Yearbook, 1961* (Tokyo), p. 228. The 1960-65 figures are from Robert L. Price, "International Trade of Communist China, 1950-65," in *An Economic Profile of Mainland China*, Vol. 2, p. 584.

9. The 1949-58 figures are from *Ten Great Years*, pp. 87, 94. The 1959 figure is from *Press Communique on the Growth of China's National Economy in 1959* (Peking: 1960), p. 1. For 1960, see *Jen-min Jih-pao*, March 31, 1960. For 1963, see *Jen-min Jih-pao*, October 27, 1963. For 1965, see *Survey of Chinese Mainland Press*, No. 3370 (January 5, 1965).

10. The 1952-60 figures are from Yuan-li Wu et. al., *The Economic Potential of Communist China*, Vol. 1, p. 241. The 1962 and 1965 figures are preliminary estimates from Yuan-li Wu's unpublished study.

11. For 1952-60, see Yuan-li Wu, *The Economic Potential of Communist China*, Vol. 1, p. 241. The 1962 and 1965 figures are preliminary estimates from Yuan-li Wu's unpublished study.

Chapter Seven

Agrarian Problems and the Peasantry

E. Stuart Kirby

Mainland China is approximately the size of the United States, and contains a great variety of conditions and problems. It has a gigantic population that is very preponderantly rural in location, livelihood, and outlook, whose material estate is overwhelmingly poor and whose needs are urgent. Chinese communism—ultimately like everything else in China—was agrarian in origin and conditioning. Proposing tremendous changes on this complex background, the Communists have not been able to follow a straight-line course. They have "zigged" and "zagged," changed or compromised priorities from time to time, taken (like Lenin) "two steps forward, one step back." Not having the resources to meet all their prodigious tasks at once, the Communists have concentrated on one "front" at a time.

The first section below defines the main perspectives of rural China, to see how they have changed over the past two decades. The second section traces the aims, efforts, and experience of Chinese communism on the countryside. The third deals particularly with problems of agricultural management. The fourth attempts to summarize conclusions and prospects.

The Rural Giant

THE PREDOMINANCE OF AGRICULTURE AND VILLAGE LIFE. The Chinese Communist government produces practically no fully econometric or sociometric data, such as most other countries (including other Communist countries) nowadays normally do. Such material is "security" information in Communist China, and the attempt to collect or analyze it is considered "espionage." Nevertheless, there is a flood of detailed information and commentary available: the printed flow without which no state can work, the reports of refugees and travellers, information from the channels of trade.

Everyone agrees on the fact of rural preponderance. In his fundamental treatise *On New Democracy,* published in 1940, Mao Tse-tung said:[1]

[1]*Selected Works,* Vol. 2.

It is the common knowledge of every primary schoolboy that eighty percent of the Chinese population consists of peasants. Therefore the peasant question becomes the fundamental question of the Chinese revolution, the force of the peasantry is the main force of the Chinese revolution.

Investigations in the 1930s showed that seventy percent of China's population were directly and fully agricultural (compared with five to ten percent in advanced Western countries). Another fifteen percent, however, were also to be found in villages, including handicraftsmen, traders, and so forth. Many of these were at least partly dependent on agriculture, which was, indeed, the basis of the whole nation's subsistence.

The only modern, scientific census ever conducted on the mainland was carried out by the Communist authorities in 1953. It gave only the demographic particulars in such broad categories as sex and location, and included no occupational, income, or other socio-economic data such as are usual in national censuses. This census showed 62 percent of the population as "agricultural," another 26 percent as "rural," and twelve percent as "urban." The extent of the actual rusticity is, however, only fully realized when it is noted that about half of the "urban" twelve percent were in "towns" of less than ten thousand inhabitants.

No census, even within this simple demographic frame of reference, has been made since then; the 1953 exercise was not repeated at the decennial in 1963. The authorities have, however, naturally kept a keen eye on this very basic question, and have made some public, if partial, observations and calculations. There are clear indications from these materials, as well as from general inference, that the proportions have not changed; 1969 shows very much the same distribution as 1953. The agricultural category is now very slightly reduced, to perhaps sixty percent, the "other rural" figure is still about 26 percent, while the urban figure has apparently risen to fourteen percent. Mao's dictum that it all depends on the peasants remains entirely valid, not only from the point of view of manpower, but also because mainland China still does not produce an excess of food (in recent years, she has changed from an exporter to an importer of food grains), and because her industrialization plans are vitally dependent on agricultural raw materials.

POPULATION PRESSURE. The population is estimated to have been roughly five hundred million in 1933. The census gave 581 million in 1953. It is now about eight hundred million. The total has risen in the order of forty percent since 1952. The *annual* increase in the 1950s was roughly equivalent to the whole population of Australia, and by the 1960s, to the population of New York State. The one billion mark will be reached, probably, around the Orwellian year 1984. Such a number is hard enough to envisage in the abstract, let alone to manage and to provide for on the spot.

The rate of increase is apparently over two percent *per annum*. Birth rates are not high; government policy restrains them, not by encouraging contraception so much as by enforcing late marriages and encouraging a general atmosphere of puritanism and work worship, and by the lack of the necessary personal privacy. Meanwhile, death rates fall, with the aid of public health measures and relatively simple new medications. The Communist leadership (who, like most people, had been giving distinctly lower estimates) were evidently startled not only by the absolute figures shown in the 1953 census, but also by the rate of increase. Obviously, on this broad-based population pyramid, the rate of increase itself is likely to rise, along with the rising proportion of people of reproductive age. The ratio of dependents to people of working age, which is also rising, is another heavy consideration for a poor country. The increase is clearly in the rural-based 85 percent of the population, which is the locus of the most serious human pressure, in the view of Communist and non-Communist observers alike. The agricultural population has increased since 1952 by a little less than the national average (by about 37 percent), the rest of the rural population by about the average (39 percent), and the urban population proportionately much less (29 percent).

POVERTY AND LAND SHORTAGE. The area of China, which is approximately the same as the United States, may contain a comparable wealth of resources, but in some respects they are less favorably patterned. Mainland China's natural resources are still largely unexplored or unconfirmed, although great claims are made both for the potentials and the actuals. Optimism must, however, be sharply tempered by translating the estimates into *per capita* terms. With the population doubling between the pre-World War II period and the 1980s, the average personal level can only be raised by results even more miraculous than have been claimed. Chinese Communist statements about increases rarely give absolute figures, dealing in percentages based on 1949 or on the "highest prewar year." However, 1949 was the nadir of wartime dislocation, and the whole preceding period was similarly abnormal; any increase from such a low level shows as a disproportionately large percentage. In terms of *per capita* national income, the most optimistic assessments show a level at the beginning of the Communist period about one-fifteenth that designated in the United States as the poverty line, rising possibly to one-tenth that level at present.

Mainland China is not closed to the "demonstration effect." In one way or another, people learn of better standards and opportunities elsewhere. Indeed, the Communist authorities themselves publicize the gains of industrialization in China. Some seventeen million Chinese live overseas, and do communicate with the mainland, especially through Hong Kong, which is a glittering showcase of capitalism and consumerism right on China's doorstep. Many thousands of Russian, East European, and other visitors, books, broadcasts, and movies, all have provided ample data and standards of comparison and expectation, even though these are available first and primarily in the cities.

The crux of the problem is the high man-land ratio. A large proportion of the mainland is considered to be uncultivable: as much as seventy percent in pre-Communist estimates, which further showed most of the remaining area (27 percent, or about 250 million acres) as already cultivated. This is, of course, a circumstantial judgment. Marked technical improvements could change the picture. Maximum Peking claims are for an average annual increase of approximately two percent in the cultivated area since 1950 (except for 1950 and 1960, when there was admittedly regression). Thus the cultivated area hardly increased in proportion to the increase in population. Some experts consider that the cultivable area per member of the farm population may have increased slightly since before World War II, from around a third of an acre to half an acre. Though the farmers are now organizationally agglomerated into communes, this estimate shows the small basic factor-scale and the high labor-intensity of Chinese "garden" style farming. In the United States, the cultivated area per member of farm households is about eight acres. The size of farm per family is about three acres in China, forty in Denmark, eighty in England, and 160 in the United States.

The insecurity of this production base is marked. Much of China's land has been cultivated intensively for centuries, and its fertility is maintained only by heavy and constant manuring. This means mainly animal and human manure, since the supply of chemical fertilizers is small. Pesticides and other adjuncts are also in short supply. Chinese agriculture is the theater of prodigious human effort.

Millions of people have been mobilized for work on irrigation and water conservancy projects. Great improvements were possible, particularly on minor waterworks; but the Communists hankered for large-scale and multipurpose projects. Some of these were never completed, especially after the withdrawal of Soviet aid at the end of the 1950s; others failed through planning errors. As dikes were built higher and larger, damage was more extensive when breaches or overflows did occur. The less spectacular improvement of local facilities might have been better. Bitter experience has, of course, taught much. Many mistakes have been corrected, especially in the 1960s when official pressures on the peasantry eased. This applies also to intensive cropping. Many acres have long been planted to two crops a year, some to three. Double cropping has further increased;

but in this, too, Communist grandiosity led to extreme errors in over-deep plowing, over-close planting, and the like.

Besides these proximate causes of continuing rural poverty, two other basic factors must be mentioned. The competition of cash or market crops with food crops, long a crucial matter for the peasantry, has been newly intensified in the Communist drive for industrialization, for which home-produced agricultural raw materials are essential. Last but not least, Chinese agriculture is chronically and drastically undercapitalized. Its equipment and financing are scanty and primitive. In the Communist period, this problem has not been adequately dealt with. The lion's share of all investment has gone to industrialization. In 1952, forty percent of total investment went to industry, eighteen percent to transportation and communications, and only fourteen percent to agriculture. By the 1960s, industry's share had risen to above fifty percent, transport and communications remained at fifteen to eighteen percent, while agriculture was down to ten percent. (In both periods, agriculture included forestry, water conservancy, and meteorology.) Meanwhile, the peasantry still forms the main tax base. Their taxes as such are slight, but the state absorbs most of the "surplus value" from their produce by levies in kind and by fixing prices.

Official data showed that in 1955, the urban worker enjoyed a total personal consumption equivalent to about US $80 a year. The corresponding rural figure was about $45. In the following decade, these levels rose substantially (except for the disturbed period between 1958 and 1960, when they fell back). By now, the urban worker's level may have roughly doubled, while the rural figure rather less than doubled. To be sure, price levels in China for the range of simpler commodities in question are very much lower than in the United States. For that reason, it may be reasonable to double the Chinese figures, in order to give a truer comparison; but they still remain pitifully low, in relation to other countries.

Table 1 gives key agricultural production statistics taken from official statements.

Potatoes, including the inferior sweet potatoes or yams grown in poorer soils, are lumped together with cereals in Communist returns in a way that is downright obscurantist. Firmly comparable figures after 1960 are not available. It is clear that the 1959 claims were not fulfilled. But by about 1967, actual results caught up with those claimed for about ten years earlier, so that the 1960 figures may be taken as roughly the 1968 actuals. Note that the sown area under the key crops in this table increased by about twenty percent, but the yields nearly trebled; this shows the extreme intensification. Cereals and potatoes increased about fifty percent in area, but more than doubled in output; cotton doubled in area, but multiplied six times in output. Food still occupies nearly all the energies of the country-

Table 1.   Main Agricultural Results

	1949 actual	1952 actual	1959 claim	1960 claim
Principal crops:				
Area (million hectares)				
Grains and potatoes	102	112	121	120
Soy beans	8	12	13	13
Cotton	0.3	0.5	0.6	0.6
	110	125	135	134
Yield (million tons)				
Grains and potatoes	108	155	270	297
Soy beans	5	10	12	12
Cotton	0.4	1.3	2.3	2.5
	113	166	284	312
Yield (tons per hectare)				
Grains and potatoes	1.0	1.4	2.2	2.1
Soy beans	0.6	0.8	0.9	0.9
Cotton	1.3	1.6	3.8	4.2
Livestock (millions)				
Horses, donkeys, mules	16	20	20	—
Cattle and water buffaloes	44	57	65	90
Pigs	58	90	180	243
Sheep and goats	42	62	113	—
	160	229	378	—

side. Chinese agriculture remains, to the extent of ninety percent, a question of subsistence.

The Struggle on the Land

THE AIMS OF THE CHINESE COMMUNISTS. In his basic treatise *On New Democracy,* Mao stated what still remains his purpose:

> The aim of all our effort is the building of a new society and new nation of the Chinese people . . . [in which] there will be not only a new political organization and new economy, but a new culture as well.

This statement is thoroughly nationalist and populist. Over eighty percent of the Chinese people are rural and peasant. Maoist communism developed among the peasantry, had most of its early experience there, and came to power through a broad peasant movement. Mao himself is rural in origin and character—the son of a poor peasant who became rich at about the time this son was born, in the thoroughly (though idiosyncratically) agrarian province of Hunan.

In the 1920s and 1930s, Mao and his associates made surveys and studies in Hunan, and in other areas sporadically held by the Communists. The sufferings of the people in Hunan and elsewhere became their general frame of reference. Mao brooded further on this *Weltanschauung* in the remote vastness of Yenan, his headquarters during the Japanese War, and he came to see the peasant majority as the class by, through, and for which his revolution would be made. From the beginning, his main power base was the peasantry. After its success in China, his strategy of "the countryside" encircling the "cities" was applied to the wider world revolution, in which the "countryside" of the underdeveloped lands in general would besiege, then storm, the "cities" of the industrialized world (which in Mao's current view may well include, besides capitalist states, the "backsliding" Soviet Union).

The Maoists came to power on a broad "common program," with a "united front" embracing all "progressive" elements and ostracizing only the imperialists, reactionaries, and the Kuomintang. They promised gradualism and reasonableness; Mao himself spoke in 1950 of communism as "a hundred years off," although he stressed that internationally he would definitely "lean to one side," the side of the Soviet Union. All these assurances were to be broken in the first two decades.

LAND REFORM (1950–52). In 1949, there were over half a million villages in China, largely isolated, containing about a hundred million families of about five persons each, half of them of working age. Some 46 percent of these households were landowners, about thirty percent were tenants, and 24 percent were part-tenants (owning part of their land and renting part).

Thus the great majority owned some land. But few had much, the average being about three acres per household; and ownership was very unevenly distributed: half the cultivated land was owned by less than one-tenth of the farm population, while two-thirds of the population owned less than one-fifth. Rents and interest rates were atrociously high; they ranged up to sixty percent of the produce, and thirty percent *per annum,* respectively.

It was not the Communists who invented land reform. Long an obvious necessity, it was a main plank of Sun Yat-sen's program and of the Republic he founded in 1911. The Nationalists made efforts to implement land reform, and so did the Communists in the areas they held at various times during the 1920s and 1930s; but in this period of civil war and Japanese occupation, all such efforts were transitory. As the Communists "liberated" larger areas during 1948 and 1949, they made further experiments in land reform. Shortly after achieving national power, they decreed a nationwide land reform in June 1950. Some 120 million acres (about forty percent of the total cultivated area) were taken from four million landowners (an average of about thirty acres from each), and redistributed fairly equally to about fifty million small holders and non-owning households (on the average, less than two and a half acres went to each).

This did not raise as much enthusiasm as the Communists expected. The first general reason was that these handouts of land, even though they nearly doubled the landholdings of many peasants, were still not large enough to appease the existing land hunger, or to permit the desired scale of family operation. Secondly, the distribution only created or highlighted other kinds of problems. Most households could not take much advantage of their accretions of land, because they were short of capital. They often lacked tools even to work their former holdings. They needed more equipment, more labor, and credit to work the additional land effectively; but none of these was forthcoming. One peasant refugee commented at the time that "they gave us some land—and ten thousand difficulties." Thirdly, it was apparent to shrewd peasants that this step—the creation, in fact, of a much larger class of peasant-proprietors than previously existed—was the very opposite of the real aims of the Communists, which were collectivization and the abolition of private property. The Communists would certainly revert to their true ideological course before long. As another refugee commented, "The tiger flexes before pouncing." If any villagers were more sanguine and believed, with some Western observers at that time, that the Chinese Communists were just "reformers," they were immediately disabused by the Communist decision to launch a bitter and violent class war on the countryside.

Everyone was classified into four official categories: landlords, rich peasants, middle peasants, poor peasants and laborers. No clear definitions were given of these. Normally, property status was basic; but the social behavior, political sentiments, standard of living (on such simple criteria as how many times per month a family could eat meat or noodles) were all taken into consideration on the basis of complaints and denunciations by "the masses."

The second phase of this class war brought out clearly what the Communist were struggling *against;* it was significantly termed the "divide the family" campaign, and its objectives were obviously more important to them than even the support of the peasantry. The practice, ever since followed, was established of having everyone gather in mass meetings and "speak bitterness" and "struggle," voicing complaints and criticisms against designated persons or attitudes. Party cadres spent days or weeks preparing mass meetings, which were conducted *crescendo,* in public-trial fashion. So-called "third-class objects of struggle," who were accused of minor faults or offenses, were punished by minor social and economic ostracism. "Second-class" culprits were barred from the favored work groups, and their children from school. "First-class struggled-againsts," the worst offenders, suffered the same punishments, and in addition were placarded as "enemies of the people" and the like. Some were executed on the spot (half a million up to 1957, according to Mao himself;[2] his opponents say many millions). Such "struggle" has continued in mainland China ever since; these methods were still characteristic during the Great Proletarian Cultural Revolution in the late 1960s. Each reader must judge for himself how far the average Chinese, given what is known of his temperament and the deeprooted culture of China (which is rather moralistic and dignified), finds all this to be inspiring, creditable, or satisfactory.

Within a couple of years, however, the "heat" of this campaign on the peasantry was turned off for the time being. The land reform had raised about half the rural population from the status of "poor" to "middle" peasants. A short period of consolidation followed, during which the First Five Year Plan was prepared, the priorities of which were to be overwhelmingly in favor of industrial development.

COLLECTIVIZATION (1952-58). At the end of 1951, the Government launched the next stage: a drive for collectivization. Farmers were organized into mutual aid teams which pooled their manpower, implements, oxen, and land. Two years later, the rules for this step were formalized and made nationwide. The Communist regime was now ready to embark on the kind of revolution it really wanted on the countryside. It had fully formed its cadre organization and gained the necessary experience. Moreover, the regime established a government monopoly of all key economic activities, including trade in the principal agricultural products.

[2]See Dick Wilson. *A Quarter of Mankind: An Anatomy of China Today* (London: Weidenfeld and Nicolson, 1966), p. 25.

In 1953, Peking declared that the course was now straight ahead to a Socialist society. As the next step, the mutual aid teams were to be transformed into full-fledged collective farms, called agricultural production cooperatives, in which the land and the equipment, hitherto still legally the private property of the peasant members, would henceforward be common or public property. Between 1954 and 1957, the cooperatives multiplied rapidly all over the country. A single cooperative typically comprised several villages and a hundred or more households. The government's "model rules" for the cooperatives stressed their "voluntary" character. Although the cooperatives must operate under the guidelines of the state economic plan, members could withdraw with their land and equipment at the end of any output-year. Hardships would be compensated out of the unit's common fund, while cemeteries and private dwellings would be respected.

The more voluntary a movement is in Communist China, the more extensively and clamorously it is organized. Tremendous mental and organizational pressures were applied to ensure that the change was made with spectacular enthusiasm and alacrity. The demands of state planning were heavy, as soon became apparent in the day-to-day working of the collectives. Huge increases were demanded in output and in crop levies by the state. A twelve-year agricultural program introduced in 1956 (by which time the Communist Party was able to claim that it had a "cell" or contact in ninety percent of the villages of China) presented even higher targets. There was resistance in proportion to the pressure. The better-off peasants were often unwilling to pool their resources with others whom they might consider, not always unreasonably, to be lazier or less efficient than themselves. The class of "kulaks" proper (that is, the wealthy landowners and moneylenders) had been eliminated by the land reform, but such a class was already re-forming. *Jen-min Jih-pao* noted editorially in December 1954, for example, that rich peasants "wrecked the cooperatives' tools and irrigation equipment, destroyed grain and livestock, murdered party officers, spread chaos and terror." In 1956, when the harvest was bad, it was officially reported that "many" collectives "disbanded themselves;" in Canton province, half a million were stated to have left "temporarily." A government survey in 1965 recorded that forty percent of the peasants had joined cooperatives "spontaneously," 32 percent after "encouragement," and twenty percent because they "feared the consequences of refusing." It was officially admitted that during the first seven months of 1957, by which time the whole nation was supposed to have been completely and enthusiastically cooperativized, there were a hundred cases of agricultural sabotage in one small county alone (Shantai in Szechuan). These are a few instances, among myriads.

Nevertheless, despite this resistance, cooperativization was decreed complete by 1957; and Mao Tse-tung declared that there was a "high tide" of irresistibly enthusiastic peasant support for a Next Great Step towards socialism.[3] This was clearly tantamount to a decree that such a step was impending, but the nature of the move was not divulged until the spring of 1958. Meanwhile, if anyone had been under any illusions about the quality of the "new democracy" introduced by the Communists, a succession of more or less ferocious "drives" against one group after another of the people, from 1957 on, brought rapid understanding. It is impossible to detail all these turmoils here; every few months there was a drastic new nationwide "campaign" against something or someone.

The period of collectivization was a time of transition to the promised way of living. The whole economy was subjected to national planning. The First Five Year Plan (1953–57) emphasized industrialization almost exclusively, within the broad aim of socialization. It began as a very loose framework, indeed; half the plan's course had run before any schedule-figures were announced. In the second half, however, the plan was more abundantly statisticalized. For the five-year period as a whole, overall economic growth of 25 percent was claimed, and twenty percent in food-grains. Analysts in other countries believe the overall growth rate was in the order of three percent a year rather than four, and emphasize that the starting point was low.

Planning concentrated also on transport, particularly the building of railroads. These were, however, largely of strategic significance, or useful primarily on an interregional scale. They were to benefit industrial development primarily, rather than more localized peasant interests. One of the published results of the plan graphically illustrates this. The volume of traffic carried by the railroads increased fifty percent, but that of goods carried by "traditional means of transportation"—by small boats, carts, pack animals, and by human portage—more than doubled.

The Second Five Year Plan (1958–62) proposed a rising rate of development, to an overall increase of about fifty percent in five years; it laid even more stress on major factory construction, the centralization of decisions, and increasing state ownership. The concomitant twelve-year agricultural program, for the period between 1956 and 1967, spelt out a good deal of progress in agriculture, too, but distinctly as secondary and subordinate to the industrialization program, and as a much longer term, less pressing issue. None of the details of these need be gone into here, for neither the Second Five Year Plan nor the agricultural program was ever implemented. They disappeared from view completely with the launching of a tremendous new scheme, the Great Leap Forward, in 1958. A brief account of this development must now be given.

[3]See Mao Tse-tung, *The Question of Agricultural Cooperation* (Peking: Foreign Languages Press, 1956).

THE GREAT LEAP FORWARD OF 1958, AND THE CRISIS OF 1959-61. Marxism is a dialectic of two conflicting components: determinism (believing that techniques, the material system of production, decides everything), and voluntarism (appealing to the will of the people to change everything). The Chinese Communists, poor in the material means of production, have stressed voluntarism, alternating freely between emphasis on the need to be "red" or "expert," or both, but suggesting in any case that the will of the people (duly organized) can resolve anything, and can even create the necessary material means. The peasant has too much knowledge and experience of natural forces on the one hand, and of the agro-technical decisions of city folk on the other, to be very sanguine about schemes for suddenly transforming rural life and production. In Communist China in 1958, however, the collectivized peasants were mobilized like an army for an offensive of that kind.

One million civilians from the cities were drafted out to the countryside to assist the Great Leap Forward in agriculture. Very few of them had any knowledge of agriculture; but under them and with them, the whole rural population went into action. Between 1957 and 1958, a record amount of manure was applied to the soil. The cultivated area was greatly expanded. Deep plowing (several feet deep), early sowing, close planting (inches apart) and other measures of ultra-intensification were the technical basis of this effort. Investment in agriculture was increased forty percent in a single year (from ten percent of all national investment to fourteen percent). The aim was indeed to "storm heaven," to achieve a fantastic and immediate breakthrough in agricultural production, unprecedented in all history.

Since a sudden, large dosing of capital was out of the question, this meant a prodigious intensification of labor on the existing basis of technology. The other element, paramount in the Communist view, was the belief that organization was the essential factor, in combination with labor. Downgrading capital, or lacking it entirely, the Communists substituted their concept of organization. The cooperatives were rapidly merged, by order, into vast communes, typically merging about a hundred villages (fifty thousand persons) each. Possessions and resources were largely pooled, in some cases down even to kitchenware. Communal mess halls were quite usual. In some cases, separate dormitories for men and women, nurseries for children, and the "free supply" of food and clothing were instituted; but as a general rule, the organization of individual households remained as before, while labor and time were totally mobilized and regimented.

The commune had a significance that went far beyond its function in agricultural production. It was to be "the basis of socialism" on the mainland: that is, the basic unit of local government, a military unit, a unit in the system of law courts, and also for security, tax collection, and other activities, besides serving to break down once and for all the old social and personal relationships. The peasantry not only had to perform miracles in agriculture; they were to help with industrialization and transportation projects, too. The best known, though extreme, example is that of the "backyard furnaces," which were set up anywhere and everywhere to produce iron by crude and simple processes. Urban communes were also instituted.

All this was implemented with the utmost frenzy during 1958, only one year after cooperativization was declared complete. The whole program was an utter fiasco in many practical respects. Grandiose, often virtually incredible, results were announced at first; evidently there were many participants who vied in sending astronomical claims and perfervid accounts of success to Peking. Fortunately the weather was rather good; there might have been a bumper crop in any case. But when a grain harvest of 375 million tons was announced, double the preceding year, hardly anyone in any other country, Communist or capitalist, believed it. Eventually the Peking authorities reduced this claim to 250 million tons. Most of the backyard furnaces and many other projects were a total failure; their output was unusable. The transportation system became clogged, communications and administrative processes confused. Techniques such as deep planting and close seeding were largely unproductive, often even counterproductive. On the material side, at least (as many people unkindly said), the Great Leap fell flat on its face. All its innovations were abandoned the following year—except the communes, which were, however, greatly modified. The country took several years to recover from the practical and psycho-political effects of this fantastic diversion. The entrenched egoism of the Chinese peasant—or simply his realism—was immeasurably deepened.

Table 2 sums up the failure of the Great Leap, in terms of key agricultural items. Thus the original 1958 target for cereals and potatoes was first claimed to have been overachieved by nearly two hundred percent, but later the claim was scaled down to about 28 percent overfulfilment. The target for 1959 was set astronomically high, at two and half times the target for the preceding year. Never in all history has any country achieved such a sudden increase. In the end, the result was admitted to have been an increase of eight percent over the claimed actual harvest in 1958. The target for 1962 (three years later) had to remain at the presumed actual for 1958. Even by 1968, the claims remained around the 1962 level, which may thus be taken broadly to represent the present position. The same applies to the other crops in Table 2; and the number of pigs, similarly, fell much below anticipations.

The organizational and other experience gained from the Great Leap was, however, useful in part. The communes, in particular, were signif-

Table 2.   The "Great Leap Forward" in Agriculture

	1958			1959			1962
	Original target	Original claim	Final claim	Original target	Original claim	Revised target	Target
Grains and potatoes (million tons)	196	375	250	525	275	270	250
Soy beans (million tons)	10	13	11	15	15	12	12
Cotton (million tons)	1.7	3.3	2.1	5.0	2.3	2.4	2.4
	208	391	263	545	292	284	264
Pigs (millions)	180	200	160	280	180	n.a.	250

icant for future developments. They were organized on a three-tier system. Below the commune were production brigades, which were roughly equivalent to the former cooperatives; and under these came production teams, each typically covering a village or a locality. During the Great Leap, all of these were used *en masse* in general operations, like battalions and companies in an army; but subsequently, this structure provided a framework for devolving functions in some significant ways. The situation was perforce one of a new start.

UNEASY PROGRESS IN THE 1960s. The Communists had no choice but to beat a wide retreat on the agrarian front after the downfall of the Great Leap—a disaster which coincided with the sharp ideological breach with the Soviet Union, involving the sudden and pointed withdrawal of Russian assistance from Peking's industrialization plans. Throughout the 1960s, a relative calm was to prevail on the countryside, with slower but more even progress. Moreover, rural China was less affected than the towns by the next major upheaval, the Great Proletarian Cultural Revolution. There continued to be broad and varied pressures on the peasantry; but with many tactical variations, which represented in sum a substantial relaxation of Communist aims and demands, and which reflected concessions to the profit-oriented and personal-incentive instincts or motivations of the peasantry. These non-Communist or anti-Communist propensities of the peasantry are strong and persistent. In Lenin's own formulation:[4]

> Small production engenders capitalism and the bourgeoisie, continually, daily, hourly, spontaneously, and on a mass scale.

[4]V. I. Lenin, *Polnoye Sobranie Sochinenii* (Complete Collected Works) (Moscow: State Publishing House, 1960), Vol. 40, p. 5.

The physical unit of agricultural production in mainland China continues to be small. The communes are huge, but they do not operate by extensive farming methods; they are simply large collections of village and household operations. "Engendered" capitalism is still the endemic tendency. An uneasy balance is maintained between it and the commitment to press on toward communism, toward Mao's "new society," "not only a new political organization and new economy, but a new culture as well." In the 1960s, the pressure towards communism had to be relaxed in many directions, in order to keep agriculture operating well enough to give the whole economy a firm floor. In the aggregate, in the view of some critics, these concessions to the self-interest of the peasants are tantamount to a Chinese Communist NEP, or New Economic Policy, comparable to the first great retreat from direct and immediate communization in Russia in the 1920s. In the USSR at that time, "war communism" was abandoned, private property in land, various kinds of private enterprise, and private markets were all permitted—until this course was reversed under Stalin, who instituted the First Five Year Plan in 1928.

This retreat is the cause of deep anxiety to the Peking authorities, who quite bluntly acknowledge that the future of their revolution is at stake, that the forces and "persons who would take the capitalist road" are so powerful that there is a real crisis for the regime and the system. The peasant masses, as they did nearly twenty years earlier, see the current concessions as being against the grain and will of the Maoists. The latter are struggling for power against their own internal opposition, and they are perfectly prepared to resort to any adventure in order to secure the succession to Mao and the continuance of his policies. Mao did not hesitate to throw the whole country into a flux with his Cultural Revolution; he could act as drastically again. Another Great Leap Forward is quite possibly the form such a venture would take. One could not be optimistic about the prospects of the Communist regime to survive another convulsion of that kind.

Problems of Agricultural Management

Such are the broad perspectives. We turn next to a closer examination of the more immediate problems of agricultural management, especially as seen from the peasant's point of view.

Systematic state control of peasant production began in 1953 with the decree on the state procurement and "planned supply" of food and other farm produce. The peasants were allocated their own rations and a stock of seed and fodder; taxes were levied on them in kind (at around thirty percent of the yield), and any surplus remaining was to be sold to the state at set prices. This was followed, early in 1955, by the stricter "Three-Fixes" system; the authorities determined the amount the peasant should pro-duce, the amount to be levied from him by the government, and the amount remaining for sale to it on its own terms. After the 1955 harvest, cooper-ativization was decreed. At that stage, the peasant at least knew where he stood; the state would take all but his subsistence allowance, and might reward him, at its own discretion, for any surplus over his own subsistence plus the taxes he owed. Concessions to provide an incentive to produce were made principally by raising the prices given for the surplus.

During the Great Leap, direct or "command" relationships prevailed, on a completely communistic basis. After the collapse of the Great Leap, more incentives had again to be conceded to the peasants. Production planning devolved first from the communes to the brigades, and then—closer to the point of individual peasant decision and self-interest—right down to the production teams. Now a "Four-Fixes" system was applied to the teams. Besides the former three "fixes," an additional rule was that each team would have a more permanent allocation of land, draft animals, and tools for its own use. These developments spread between 1960 and 1962. From 1963 on, teams tended to become even smaller, comprising in some cases as few as two families—that is, still nearer to an individual-household scale of operation.

Monetary and other direct incentives were reinstituted and greatly in-creased. As early as 1961, two-thirds of the peasants' income was in cash, and only one-third in "free supply" (that is, in kind). In 1964, the Com-munist Party specifically denounced "egalitarianism," and stated that "he who does not work shall not eat; but he who works more shall receive more." The party journal *Hung-ch'i* made quite clear, however, that this was a sugared pill; it was the best way to build up basic production for a time, so that the agricultural communes could fatten up sufficiently to become strong enough to shift management back to the higher echelons, the brigades and the whole communes, then ultimately to "broad feder-ations of communes," thus resuming the march toward "pure" communism.

Private plots of land were also restored. Between 1953 and 1958, the cooperatives had set aside about one-twentieth of their whole cultivated areas for households to grow vegetables. To some extent, pigs could also be kept privately. The average size of private plots was just a few square yards; but they contributed very disproportionately to output, since they were tended with loving care and devotion. In the Great Leap, they were amalgamated into the communes; but private plots were restored in the following year, and subsequently they have been enlarged and facilitated. Since 1962, at least ten percent of mainland China's food supply, and half of its pigs, have come from these private holdings and are sold on "free" markets (the term must be put in quotes, as it is relative), with the owners pocketing the proceeds. The private plot and pig owners also keep a proportion of their non-communal output for their own direct consumption. Table 1 above shows how the (fifty percent privately owned) pig population has nearly trebled since 1952, whereas the yield of such fully collectivized items as cereals less than doubled. The private plots are so outstandingly green and flourishing amid the generally collectivized landscape of China that they commonly serve as landmarks: "Old Wong's house? It's the third private plot on the right." All this private production represents a considerable breach in the dikes, from the Communist point of view. It was a desperate concession forced, like its prototype NEP in Russia, by the acute food shortage and the highly disincentive effects of the preceding Communist measures.

The crops failed in three successive years, from 1959 to 1961. As early as October 1959, there was an official injunction to "alternate liquid meals with solid ones," followed by others recommending the gathering of edible herbs, and so forth. In 1961–62, the average daily food intake appears to have fallen to between 1,300 and 1,600 calories a day, which is the barest subsistence level, and about half the level necessary for health. The figure is now somewhere near the minimum for health, that is, over two thousand calories a day. There was general malnutrition around 1961; the fact that relatively few actually died was due to the extent to which the people were already inured to shortage, to the degree to which they reduced their work-effort, and to the fact that the government resorted to the large-scale importation of food. Two million food parcels a month were sent by private persons from Hong Kong and Macao to the mainland in 1961. From 1960 onwards, the government began to import five million tons or more of wheat a year. This is still continuing; Peking has long-term contracts for years ahead with Canada, Australia, and other countries.

The disasters of 1959 through 1961 were blamed by the authorities on adverse weather—"the worst floods in a century" and unprecedented droughts, which together affected twenty percent of the farming area. Incidentally, this gave the lie to previous propaganda about wonderful achievements in irrigation, which (it had been claimed only a year before) had made such disasters "a thing of the past." Nature was in fact adverse, sufficiently so for older peasants to mutter that "the Mandate of Heaven" had been withdrawn from this new dynasty; but the situation was much more a failure of the Communist system. Farming in Hong Kong, for example, recorded losses of around ten percent owing to the bad weather, as against 25 percent announced for adjacent Communist areas just across the border. More significantly, perhaps, Hong Kong's crops returned completely to normal within a year, whereas normalcy was not claimed on the mainland until at least five years later.

In the 1960s, a great deal of *laissez faire* had to be permitted on the countryside, if the masses were to survive—and if the economy, which was also sustaining large military forces, developing a nuclear weapons capacity, and investing heavily in industrialization, was to continue along those lines. The relaxation gave considerable scope to the more enterprising. Some peasants (the pushful, the competent, and the good manipulators) faired distinctly better than their neighbors. Indeed, the state credit system, which was originally set up for the communes, in 1964 was instructed to lend directly to poorer peasants, as they needed help in their "class struggle" against the richer peasants. There were many inquisitions against party cadres for arrogance, despotism, and incompetence; their power was curbed, and many were "sent down" to manual labor. In the more tranquil conditions of the countryside during the 1960s, with an economic revival going forward under NEP-like dispensations, and with comparative freedom from the disruptions of the Cultural Revolution, relative prosperity returned. Diets were comparatively adequate, incomes about double 1949, the dire shortage of consumer goods mitigated.

Some areas of the country were better off than others. In the confusion of the Cultural Revolution and the power struggle over the succession to Mao, a great deal of provincial and regional autonomy also developed in practice, within which various groups and factions contended for power. The erstwhile "monolithic" solidity of the regime had so far disappeared that it seemed not impossible that the country and the economy would revert to a kind of fragmentation not altogether unlike that of the ill-famed "warlord" period of the 1920s and 1930s.

That is still a possibility, although ostensibly pro-Mao revolutionary committees reportedly regained power all over the country toward the end of 1968. The political position of these organs is unclear; all factions proclaim exactly the same slogans, but they differ widely in concept and intention. In this situation, the position of the food surplus and raw material surplus areas is strong, as compared with the deficit areas; the former have, in fact, bargained hard with the latter on broad interprovincial issues. Communes in the vicinity of major cities, which afford them ready markets for their vegetables, fruits, and other produce, and offer a relatively good supply of manufactures, do especially well at the present time. To some extent, it is the turn of Mao's own towns to be "surrounded" by the Chinese "countryside." In the more isolated countryside, the contrast between the standards and privileges of the country folk and the cities is greater than ever. It is, for example, very unusual for a peasant to have any housing provision made for him by the government; the townsmen increasingly have public housing and rent-controlled accommodations.

Conclusions

The Chinese peasant, like peasants everywhere, is most literally and emphatically a down-to-earth person. He has a very keen eye for the broad political tides and changes which may alter the setting of his life. Mainly, however, he is concerned with more local and immediate issues. He is not interested in land for some mystical reason, but for the security and the standard of living he may be able to get from it. He judges on practical grounds, whatever lip service he may have to render to the theories and propaganda of those in political and administrative power. He judges by current results, the goods actually delivered and those that can be seen in the pipeline. He wants results for 1969 and 1970, plus something foresee-able and calculable for 1973 and 1980. The "great days" of 1949 or earlier, the "guerrilla ethic" so dear to the Thought of Mao Tse-tung, the Old Guard's nightmares of a dreadful past, the tales of Foreign Devils—all these are necessarily matters of ancient history. They have limited rel-evance for the young majority of the nation, who have no personal expe-rience at all of twenty years ago, or for the rural masses, who are closely tied to the unchanging soil from which they must constantly struggle to wrest a living day by day.

There is some evidence that youth in China is not much more impressed by the reminiscences and admonitions of their grandparents than is the youth of Western countries. The Communists complain abundantly about this, and make tremendous efforts to counter the apathy and self-centered-ness of the younger generation. What the Communist revolution has aimed at from the beginning is modernization; and this has not been viewed in terms very different from what other peoples have had in mind in the twentieth century. The Chinese people want modern techniques and amenities, very much as people nowadays do everywhere. Chinese agricul-ture has many needs, all of them acute, none of them as yet very substan-tially met by the spate of words and the bewildering alternation of policies thought up by the present regime. The peasants will judge according to how their true needs are met. We may rank these needs in something like the following order, governed by a careful balance between the feasibilities and the urgencies.

Chinese agriculture needs an intelligent and complex policy of water-works, starting rationally from the base upwards, not from the spectac-ularist *a priori* conceptions of the Communists. It wants tools and equip-ment, starting (similarly) with the simplest, with designs and methods con-ceived out of knowledge and respect for local conditions. Overall planners in distant cities cannot consider local details; and in China's case, heavy industry has very much higher priority than the provision of "elementary" types of farm implements. Of course, the peasants would welcome more sophisticated machinery as well. Tractors? By all means! Especially in the northern half of the country, in the plains and wheatlands. These areas require one million tractors right away, to make any adequate provision. In 1965, the total number of tractors in mainland China reached fifty thousand—that is, approximately one per commune, or one per five thousand acres, or for 12,500 peasants. These were, however, concentrated in a few areas, and especially on state farms. It is still common to see plows or other equipment drawn by human beings. In the southern, rice-growing half of the country there are other, multiple complications, which can only be mastered by close attention, long experience, and deep respect for the environment—all of which communism rejects. A 1966 report on experimental mechanization in rice production concluded that "in quality, mechanical plowing (of rice fields) proved no better than plowing with buffaloes." It added, moreover, that the peasants reacted badly from the Communist point of view: finding that tractor-plowing had the advantage of taking much less time, though it did not do any better quality of work, the peasants merely enjoyed their new-found leisure, instead of going joyfully to work at something else instead.

Another huge requirement, of similar urgency, is for fertilizer. Chemical fertilizer plants are expensive items; their construction (or the alternative of importing fertilizers) competes with steel works and other projects, which stand much higher in Communist preferences. A few plants have nevertheless been built since 1957, with a total productive capacity of over five million tons. This is perhaps ten percent of the nation's needs. The application and use of fertilizers once they are produced, is another complex matter, and this too has been a source of widespread mistakes and shortfalls.

Last, but possibly not least, the Chinese farmer requires personalized, locally-based credit facilities. At present, these are totally unavailable to him from official sources, since such individual dealings are anathema to the Communist system. Recently, the farmer has again begun to find such facilities in or through the private sector. It is uncertain how long this (very partial) capitalistic revival may last, or in what manner the Communists may move to crush it. Mao himself has declared that he is uncertain whether China will continue under communism, but he has made clear that he hopes by some great final effort, the nature of which is not yet defined, to ensure that it does.

The peasant also wants to go forward—but not, as he has clearly shown every time he has had the chance, to communism. The traditional system of China is largely broken. It had, indeed, been broken by 1949, after generations of misery, upheaval, invasion, civil war, disaster, and dislocation of every kind. These were the reasons why the Communists came to power. But the Communist system has not been able, in agriculture especially, to inaugurate a sure, complete, or satisfactory alternative. The peasants have watched a kaleidoscopic variety of changes, efforts, experiments, pressures, adventures, ups and downs, assertions, and confessions through these two decades of Communist power. They still want what they have wanted for at least half a century: that is, modern equipment, modern methods and facilities, modern living standards and amenities. They have a clear and practical conception of all of these. They also want firm and dependable prospects, some definite basis on which to work into the future. Communism has brought much turmoil, but hardly anything in the way of modernization or sure prospects.

If a system or a set of methods fails, the Chinese peasant wants to change it, to try another that looks more sensible. That is why he supported the overthrow of the pre-Communist system. If the Communist system fails to deliver the goods, the peasant can devise alternatives; witness his present enthusiasm for the "private sector" available to him. But the Communists cannot envisage alternatives, except as temporary concessions. If Communist methods fail, their only recipe is—more Communist measures.

Above all, the Chinese peasant wants peace. He has all the problems—and hopes—he can cope with on his own land. He wants to be given the means, and then to get on with the job. Political adventures mean little to him. Upheavals at home are a great nuisance; involvements abroad are evidently risky. It is not unknown on the countryside that people in foreign countries do have a greater measure of modernization and better material opportunities than the Chinese peasant has. It is not unknown that in the other China, Taiwan, rural problems have been dealt with more successfully, more peacefully, and more decently. On the mainland, communism has put the peasant through a welter of convulsions, stresses, and uncertainties in two short decades, at the end of which everyone is uncertain what happens when Mao dies. The gap between the peasantry and the city has grown in many respects, rather than diminished. Unlike Soviet Russia in Stalin's time, the peasants have not been driven massively into industry and the urban areas. On the contrary, before they were organized into communes, hundreds of thousands of peasants who migrated to the cities were deported back to the countryside (as were city cadres who failed in their duties). Thus Stalin used force to move the country into industrialism, whereas Mao exerted force in the opposite direction, to keep this huge population predominantly on the land.

Skilled operators among the Chinese peasantry, in the present NEP-like period of partial economic freedom, and in the present political confusion resulting from the rivalry of innumerable groups and factions, are outwitting the Communists at many points. The rest, the mass of the farming people, are laboring on, surviving. They have prospered precisely to the degree that, at the points where, and in the periods when the drive towards communism, measures of a Communist character, and attempts to apply Communist principles have been relaxed or modified. This is now clear for anyone to see. The Chinese peasants have seen some progress; but generally in an inverse ratio to the application of Communist methods. Many of them would agree with the conclusion of Michael Borodin, then representative of the Comintern in China and adviser to the Chinese Nationalist government, in 1929 that "the only communism possible in China today is the communism of poverty, a lot of people eating rice out of an almost empty bowl."[5] Some of Mao's own basic formulations still strike the same note; he calls China "poor and blank," the rural areas "a rope of sand."

Maoism glorifies austerity as a superior way of life. Deprivation is, however, the one thing the peasant wants to escape from; he does not want to go back to the older forms of poverty, or forward to the newer form that communism seems to offer. He wants a way out of poverty, an orderly, dignified, humane, clearly signposted way, and as quickly as possible. Hoping that some such opening may lie somewhere beyond all this turmoil, the Chinese peasant will labor on, outlasting the present regime in Peking, as he has outlasted—and in the fullness of time helped to replace—so many regimes before it.

[5]Quoted in Chiang Kai-shek, *China's Destiny* (London: Dennis Dobson, 1947), p. 329.

Chapter Eight

Education in Communist China

Theodore Hsi-en Chen

The Place of Education

The Chinese Communist regime relies on a combination of coercion and persuasion to maintain its position. The Communists talk much of the "mass line" and put a high value on mass support. This support cannot be obtained by force alone. It is necessary to win over the people by argument, however devious or specious it may be, and to convince them of the worthiness of the Communist revolution and the "absolute truth" of Communist ideology. To convince by argument is, in the Communist way of thinking, a form of education.

When the Communists talk about mass support, they mean enthusiastic, wholehearted support. They are not satisfied with passive acceptance, which may imply no more than the absence of overt opposition. They demand active support without reservations. Mao Tse-tung early expressed his scornful attitude toward neutrals. In the revolutionary struggle, he maintained, one is either for or against it; "there is no third road." Superficial compliance is not enough. What the Communists want goes beyond action, and extends to attitudes, emotions, and thought. The task of changing these is the work, not of the police or the firing squad, but of education.

It is true that terrorism, purges, and mass executions have been a part of the story since 1949. But the Communists have understood that force alone is not enough to win popular support or the acceptance of ideas by the masses. Mao Tse-tung voiced this realization in his famous speech of February 1957, *On the Correct Handling of Contradictions Among the People.*[1] After more than seven years of vigorous effort to remould the thought and behavior of all sectors of the population, using methods ranging from indoctrination to violent attack and relentless pressure, he warned his comrades that "the only method to be used in this ideological struggle is that of painstaking reasoning and not crude coercion." He continued: "You

[1]See p. 34, fn. 9, above.

may ban the expression of wrong ideas, but the ideas will still be there . . . it is only by employing the method of discussion, criticism, and reasoning that we can really foster correct ideas and overcome wrong ones."

This does not, of course, rule out the use of force. Harsh methods of suppression and the physical elimination of opponents still remain as important means of control. But whenever possible, force and coercion are held in abeyance in order that "persuasion" and "education" may have a chance to do the job. The Communists call their regime a "democratic dictatorship," which Mao explained as follows:[2]

> The people's democratic dictatorship has two methods. Toward the enemy, it uses the method of dictatorship, namely: it does not allow them to take part in political activities for certain necessary periods; it compels them to obey the law of the people's government and compels them to work and to remould themselves into new men through labor. Toward the people, it is the opposite, it does not use compulsion, but democratic methods, namely: it does not compel them to do this or that, but uses democratic methods in educating and persuading them.

It is, therefore, unnecessary to make any apology for the terrorism and bloody purges that have marked the twenty years of Communist rule. But force and coercion are not used all the time. Where the Communists feel that they have a chance of winning people over, they employ the methods of persuasion and education; according to their definition, this is the practice of democracy.

The combination of coercion and persuasion can obtain a large measure of submission. Persuasion can be very effective when it is known that coercion is only temporarily held in abeyance and may be used as soon as persuasion does not produce results. At the same time, the extensive use of persuasion—indoctrination, propaganda, education—considerably reduces the need of direct coercion. From the standpoint of both theory and practical necessity, the Communists assign a strategic role to education. Education is a major vehicle of the Communist revolution. It is also a major instrument of control.

EDUCATION AS A REFLECTION OF GENERAL POLITICAL TRENDS. Education furnishes a key to an understanding of the Communist regime, because the course of educational development mirrors the rise and decline of the regime in the last two decades. Just as the regime gained substantial popularity in its first decade and ran into serious difficulties in the second, so the impressive expansion of education in the 1950s con-

[2]Mao Tse-tung's Report to the Party Plenum on June 6, 1950. See *People's China* (Peking), Vol. 2, No. 1 (July 1, 1950).

trasted with the turmoil and deterioration brought by the Great Proletarian Cultural Revolution. The general policies of the regime in the first decade coincided, to a considerable extent, with the hopes and aspirations of the Chinese people for a strong modern nation with a sound economy and the prospect of a better life for all. In the second decade, however, the Communists moved beyond popular nationalism to goals dictated by ideology. The drive toward collectivization, communes, and other ideological extremes generated skepticism and passive resistance. Similarly in education, the initial extension of educational opportunities met with popularity in a land where education has always been highly esteemed; but the campaign for "Socialist education" and "class education" in the second decade was not greeted with enthusiasm.

Education mirrors the general course of events in another way. All phases of Chinese Communist policy have been marked by vacillations between hard line, doctrinaire approaches, and more realistic appraisals of what is workable in the light of actual conditions and the state of mind of the people. When doctrinairism is in the ascendancy, there is an aggressive push toward socialism, collectivism, and more rigid control. In education, such periods have been marked by greater emphasis on politics and indoctrination, the disregard of academic standards, and the suppression of intellectuals. Occasionally, however, the realists in the party hierarchy have been able to implement more moderate policies designed both to appease the masses and to get things done in the practical world of economics and politics. Their reluctance to support hasty moves toward dogma-dictated goals was expressed in attempts to slow down the drive toward agricultural collectivization, and their later efforts to modify the commune system by granting private plots to peasants and material incentives to all workers. In education, the occasional assertion of realism was seen in shortlived attempts to reduce the political activities required of students and teachers, and in the recognition, now so severely condemned by Maoists, that "white experts" and "old-time intellectuals" might be of some service until such time as there were enough "proletarian intellectuals" to take over their work.

EDUCATION IN THE CURRENT TURMOIL. If education has loomed large in the general evolution of the last two decades, it has played an even more crucial role during the Great Proletarian Cultural Revolution. The main issues at stake in the Cultural Revolution are in large part ideological and educational in nature. Mao's erstwhile comrades are now denounced as "revisionists" primarily because they do not see eye-to-eye with him in regard to the course of the revolution. They are dedicated Communists, too, but their experience in and responsibility for daily administration and bureaucratic control make them more aware of the public state of mind and more cognizant of the dangers of blind adherence to dogma. The origins of the current ideological dispute are to be found in the reactions of the Chinese people to the Communist program of socialism and collectivism. When they saw that the real goals of the regime, dictated by Marxist doctrine, were quite different from what they had originally hoped for, they became unenthusiastic and uncooperative. Awareness of their state of mind made the realists turn to practical measures to mollify the people.

But the Maoists argued that instead of modifying the Socialist system, it was more important to change the public state of mind by methods of "persuasion and education." The Maoist logic seems to be that if, after years of Communist education, the Chinese people are still not ready for socialism, the fault must lie with education and those in charge of education. In order to carry out a Socialist revolution in accordance with Maoist dogma, there had to be a thoroughgoing reform of education. The nature of this reform will be discussed in subsequent pages. When the Red Guards were let loose to spearhead the Cultural Revolution, their slogan was to destroy old ideas, old habits, old customs, and old culture, and to supplant them with a new mentality. The task of changing ideas, habits, customs, and culture is essentially the work of education.

Characteristics of Communist Education

It is not easy to describe Chinese Communist education. It does not lend itself to the treatment that students of comparative education ordinarily accord to other educational systems. Norms of form and content have little significance here. Description of school curricula and classroom methods is likely to miss the heart of the educational program. Indeed, what is considered in other countries as the essence of education may be rejected by the Communists as bourgeois nonsense, whereas what the Communists value as central to the process may be considered in the West as outside the pale of education. The very word "education" holds a different meaning.

As far as the schools are concerned, they are at present in a state of flux and subject to frequent and abrupt changes. Courses of study, their duration, the requirements for admission and graduation—these are trivial details to the Communists. And today, they are being changed so often that a diagram of the school system, showing the relation of one type to another, would be of little value. New schools are introduced and abolished according to their usefulness to the revolution. To understand Communist education, it is more important to note its special characteristics and to examine its major aims and policies.

Since education is one of the methods of persuasion, according to Communist definition, it is not distinguishable from indoctrination or propaganda. Any attempt to draw a line between education and propaganda is condemned as sheer hypocrisy. The schools and the propaganda agencies of the state are engaged in the common task of remoulding the thought and behavior of the people; their methods are interchangeable and, indeed, often identical. In his short treatise, *Oppose Stereotyped Party Writing*, published in 1942, Mao Tse-tung said:[3]

> Who is a propagandist? Not only is the teacher a propagandist, but all our cadres in all kinds of work are also propagandists. Take for example the military commander . . . when he talks with the soldiers and deals with the people, what is he doing but carrying on propaganda work? Any person engaged in talking with another person is, in effect, engaged in propaganda. . . .

In other words, the communication of ideas in any form is propaganda. In the Communist view, to identify education with propaganda by no means reduces its importance or lowers its status. Schools are an integral part of the Communist methods of propaganda and "culture," which includes all forms of art and literature, and all the varied channels of communication. Press, radio, mass meetings, museums, the stage, all serve the same purpose and pursue the same goals: they all teach and educate. The schools are not fundamentally different from the others.

This concept of education is, of course, very different from what is generally held in non-Communist countries. In China, the schools are only a part of the educational program. Indeed, what goes on outside the schools may be more important and recognized as of greater educational value than formal instruction in the schools. The "mass campaigns," for example, ranging from the discovery and denunciation of "counter-revolutionaries" to the collection of fertilizers, and political demonstrations and parades are considered to be educational activities even more important for the making of revolutionaries than school. There is, therefore, no hesitancy to dismiss regular classes for days and weeks on end in order to enable students and teachers to take part and gain experience in "revolutionary action."

The primary concern of education is not the acquisition of knowledge, but the remoulding of behavior, attitudes, emotions, and thoughts. If at any time activities outside the schools can do a better job in forging the character and emotions of the revolutionary man, the schools should yield to them. The distinction between formal and informal education disappears. As far as the school itself is concerned, what is known as extracurricular activities in other countries often becomes the main show, with class work having a supporting and supplementary function. Youth organ-

---

[3]*Selected Works,* Vol. 3.

izations play a major role in the schools, and the general atmosphere of the schools is created and controlled by these youth organizations and the resident party representatives.

The Form and Content of Education

There are today three main types of schools in Communist China: the full-time school, the work-study school (in which time is divided between work and study), and the spare-time school (which holds classes after work hours). It is the declared intention of the government to make the work-study school the major type of the future, with the spare-time school as the most useful kind for adults, and the full-time school reserved only for those few who qualify and prepare for more advanced education.

Special institutes and short-term courses have also been established to train cadres for such tasks as the agrarian reform, the implementation of the marriage law and the electoral law, and so forth. There are new "colleges" for the remoulding of intellectuals, industrialists, and capitalists to turn them into supporters of socialism. Many of these institutes or colleges are dropped when they have served their purpose or when they prove to be ineffective. The form and content of education are subject to quick changes in the light of political and economic needs. The closing of schools in 1966 provides further evidence of the readiness of the regime to scrap the entire system once it is found inadequate to produce the results expected of it.

A directive on educational work issued by the Central Committee of the Chinese Communist Party in 1958 spells out a set of guidelines for the schools.[4] The directive lays down three basic principles: (1) education must be combined with productive labor; (2) it must serve proletarian politics; and (3) it must be under the firm and sure direction of the Communist Party. These constitute what might be called the three "P's" of Communist education: production, politics, and party control.

LABOR AND PRODUCTION. The Communists attach great importance to labor. They talk about the sanctity of labor, and call themselves the vanguard of the working class, which is synonymous with the laboring people. From the standpoint of theory, they teach that man evolved from the lower animals by dint of the use of his hands; hence the most precious heritage a man has is his ability to use his hands in labor. Labor, moreover, has a therapeutic value in ideological remoulding. By engaging in labor, even compulsary labor, individuals can be reformed and transformed "into new men."[5] Not only are landlords, reactionaries, and recalcitrant intellectuals sent to labor camps for long-term labor, but students, teachers, office

[4]The text of the directive appears in *Jen-min Jih-pao*, September 20, 1958.

[5]See earlier quotation from Mao's *On the People's Democratic Dictatorship.* These words are also found in the Common Program of 1949, which served as a sort of constitution for the new regime until 1954.

workers, and other white-collar groups are regularly sent to farms, factories, and mines for periodic labor service in order to "learn from the laboring class" and "acquire the viewpoint of labor."

Primers for little children contain lessons on labor. One elementary reader reads: "I have hands, you have hands, all have hands, all should use hands." Another reader contains the following: "Daddy does farming with his hands; Mamma cooks with her hands; Sister washes clothes with her hands; little friend, what can you do with your hands?" Textbooks used at higher educational levels dwell on the role of labor in human society and the contributions of labor to mankind.

Labor and production are often mentioned in the same breath. In recent years, the two words have been joined to form the concept of "productive labor," which has become a major theme of education.[6] After the 1958 directive, schools at all levels were ordered to explore various ways of making production an integral part of their program. A major innovation was to have schools and universities establish farms, factories, machine shops, or department stores on school grounds so that students might regularly engage in production as a part of school work. These production units are not meant to be laboratories to give students practical experience; they are regular business enterprises carrying on business just like production units unconnected with schools. At the same time, in further pursuit of the idea of combining production with education, farms, communes, and factories have been encouraged to establish schools so that peasants and workers may combine study with work. As a result of this two-way development, the Communists claim, schools and universities become centers of production as well as centers of learning, while farms and factories become centers of learning as well as of production.

Emphasis on the combination of education with production led to the rapid growth of the work-study school as the major type of educational institution. The central idea is that a student is at no time removed from active production; study and work are considered essential parts of an integrated experience. Theoretically, study is planned to be of assistance in the solution of production problems, while work provides opportunity for the application of knowledge to the improvement of production. The work-study plan is carried out in a variety of ways; work and study may be scheduled on alternate days, or in alternate weeks, or in other alternate periods of time.

The combination of education with productive labor is thus supposed to serve practical and ideological purposes at the same time. From the practical point of view, there is an immediate boost in manpower and productivity. Ideologically, the Communists claim that they are thus bridging the gap between mental and physical labor. They quote Lenin to the

---

[6]See Lu Ting-yi, "Education Must Be Combined with Productive Labor," *Peking Review*, Vol. 1, No. 28 (September 9, 1958).

effect that combining education with productive labor is "one of the most potent means for the transformation of present-day society;" and they also refer to the stipulation of the Communist Manifesto of 1848 concerning the "combination of education with industrial production."

POLITICS IN COMMAND. The second cardinal principle of education is that it must serve proletarian politics. Education apart from politics has no meaning. Just as bourgeois education serves bourgeois politics, so proletarian education must at every point serve the needs and goals of the proletarian revolution. The commanding role of politics is expressed in the curriculum, in school life, and in the aims and purposes of education. Political study is the most important subject of the curriculum from the kindergarten up through the university. Even in literacy classes, where illiterate adults learn to read and write, the political theme is dominant. The content of political study includes current events, the speeches of Communist leaders, official documents explaining the policies of the government and the viewpoint of the Communist Party, and the writings of Marx, Engels, Lenin, Stalin, and, more and more in recent years, the Thought of Mao Tse-tung. Political indoctrination is, in large part, ideological indoctrination. Political reliability presupposes ideological orthodoxy. Among the ideological concepts, class and the class struggle are considered of supreme importance. In the 1960s, intensified ideological indoctrination took the form of "class education," which stressed the importance of continued and resolute struggle against class enemies.

The acquisition of knowledge is not enough. Knowledge must be applied to action, and (to use the Communist cliché) be tested in action. In addition to classroom study, students and teachers must engage in political activities in and out of schools. The activities must be chosen from among an approved list issued by the Communist Party. They may take the form of criticism and self-criticism in group meetings, or the denunciation of students and teachers accused of unproletarian ideas or behavior. They may involve participation in mass campaigns outside the schools, when the school population joins the masses in parades, demonstrations, production drives, or construction projects. All activities must be in support of the ongoing programs of the party and the state.

Politics also determines the aims and goals of education. The central purpose of education is to train politically dependable activists. For teachers as well as students, political qualifications are considered even more important than academic achievement. The crucial importance of the political qualification is expressed in the term "red expert." The country needs experts, to be sure—men and women who have the technical ability to carry on production and various forms of "Socialist construction." But to be effective in his work, an expert must be thoroughly "red," that is, politically dependable and unswervingly loyal to the party and the state. The aim of education is to produce the new Socialist man, and the qualities of this new man are prescribed by "proletarian politics."

PARTY CONTROL. Completing the triumvirate of cardinal principles is the dictate that all education, in and out of schools, must be under the direction and control of the Communist Party. This is, in effect, no more than an elaboration of the second principle; for the meaning of proletarian politics at any given time is defined by the party leadership. The party is the leader and the guardian of the proletarian revolution, and the interpreter of its ideology. The best way to "serve proletarian politics" is to serve the Communist Party and obey its instructions. In every school or university, there is a representative of the party who becomes the resident supervisor, vested with the authority of the party. He and his associates are referred to as the "leadership," and it has a controlling voice in all matters affecting the institution. In the early years of the regime, it was customary to have a non-Communist as the titular head of a school, and a Communist as vice-principal or vice-president; but from the beginning, no one had any doubt that real authority rested with the Communist officer rather than the titular head.

The "leadership" sees to it that all phases of the curriculum and school life are managed in such a way as to serve proletarian politics. It makes rulings in regard to the political acceptability of students and teachers. It presides over the continuing process of ideological remoulding, which engages students and teachers in group criticism and self-criticism, and "thought reform" through study and action. It pronounces judgment on the progress, or lack of progress, in the ideological remoulding of individuals. It directs the activities of the youth organizations, which play a major role in school life. Teachers as well as students seek the advice of the "leadership" in connection with personal as well as academic problems. They submit their teaching plans to it for approval; and they consult the "leadership" before they make any important personal plans.

Students of inferior academic record have been promoted and given honors despite the contrary recommendation of their teachers, because they are activists with a good political record. On the other hand, students judged by teachers to be superior have been passed by for scholarships or for study abroad because they are not considered to be sufficiently "red." It is constantly being pounded into the minds of youth that their supreme duty is to obey the call of the party. They are reminded again and again that the purpose of study is not to fulfill personal ambitions or advance personal interests, but rather to serve the revolution under the direction of the party. Each year, members of the graduating class are pressured to sign pledges vowing their readiness to accept any job or position assigned to them by the party and the state, no matter how far removed from personal plans or how distant from home.

SCIENCE AND TECHNOLOGY. Science is promoted for both ideological and practical reasons. Ideologically, the Communists claim that Marxism is a scientific philosophy, and that its materialistic outlook is based on a scientific view of life and society. The scientific view, they say, is opposed to the superstitious or mystical view. The scientific man thinks in terms of the laws of nature and human development, and does not need to resort to mystical or supernatural explanations. Hence, he has no need for religion.

From the practical point of view, science is essential to industrialization and material progress, which are major objectives of Communist planning. The study of science is, therefore, important for all who are to contribute to production, and to the various phases of social and economic reconstruction. The place of science in the Communist scheme of things was expounded by Mao Tse-tung in a speech, *Rectify the Party's Style of Work*, delivered in 1942. He said:[7]

What is knowledge? From ancient times to the present, there have been only two areas of knowledge in the world: the knowledge pertaining to the production struggle and the knowledge pertaining to the class struggle, including the material struggle. Is there any other area of knowledge besides these two? No. Natural science and social science are the crystallization of these two areas of knowledge, and philosophy is the generalization and summation of the two. Aside from these, there is no other knowledge.

It may be noted in passing that Mao did not recognize art and literature as independent fields of study, and that the humanities have no place in his concept of the curriculum. Moreover, what is known as social science in China today is really nothing but dogmatic Marxism interpreted and, more recently, expanded by the Thought of Mao Tse-tung. What is germane to the present discussion is that what the Communists recognize as science consists largely of applied science. The Communists decry "knowledge for its own sake," and theory that is not applicable to action. The study of theoretical science, therefore, does not receive as much attention as engineering and the applied sciences. When the Communists talk about science, they actually mean technology.

The preponderant emphasis on technology is reflected in student enrollment. According to one compilation of enrollment figures in institutions of higher learning, the state plans for the year 1957 to 1958 called for 177,600 students in engineering, nine hundred thousand in agriculture, forestry, and medicine, but only 27,100 in the natural sciences.[8] The Com-

[7]*Selected Works,* Vol. 3.

[8]See Chu-yuan Cheng, *Scientific and Engineering Manpower in Communist China, 1949-1963* (Washington: National Science Foundation, 1965), p. 38.

munist State Statistical Bureau reported that among graduates of higher institutions in 1958, 17,499 were in engineering, 8,916 in agriculture, forestry, and medicine, and 4,645 in the natural sciences.

Just as "art for art's sake" or "knowledge for its own sake" are ideological deviations, so there is no room for "science for its own sake." Science must meet the practical needs of production and national defense. Since nuclear science is essential to military defense, it has received special attention and support. Even in this field, however, it is probable that there has been greater achievement in engineering and the application of known scientific principles than in the basic research that explores and extends scientific frontiers.

Nevertheless, there is a much larger output of scholarly writings in scientific and technical fields than in social science or the humanities. It is probably fair to say that most of the young scientists in China today are working in different areas of technology; and that among the top scientists, a large number received their education and training before 1949. An investigation of the educational background of seven hundred prominent scientists and engineers in Communist China in 1962 revealed that 373 had received degrees from American universities, 207 from British and European universities, and fifteen from the USSR.[9] Among 422 of the seven hundred who had attained the Ph.D. or Sc.D. degree, 269 had studied in the United States, 167 in Britain and European countries, and three in the USSR. There are, therefore, a large number of scientists with a solid background in theoretical science; but they are the products of "bourgeois scholarship," and they are often attacked as such in periods of political stress.

Soviet influence dominated science and education in the first few years of the regime. A deliberate policy was adopted to shut off Western influence and to condemn Western scholarship. By 1956, during a period of relative moderation and liberalism, scholars were permitted to get books and journals from Western countries, and scientists were enabled to resume their contacts with the world of science abroad. But in general, access to foreign scholarship and the flow of scientific knowledge from the outside world are limited by political restrictions; and the severity of such restrictions varies with the swing of the pendulum between political doctrinairism, with its attendant stifling of intellectual effort, and realism, with an attendant relaxation of control during such a period. At times, the restrictions become very severe.

Achievement

The first decade of the Chinese Communist regime was marked by positive achievement in many areas of national reconstruction. It was also

[9]See *ibid.,* p. 122.

a period of educational growth and expansion. According to official figures, student enrollment in higher institutions rose from 155,000 before 1949 to 660,000 in 1958; in technical middle schools, from 383,000 to 1,470,000; in middle schools, from 1,496,000 to 8,520,000; in primary schools, from 23,683,000 to 86,400,000; and in kindergartens, from 130,000 to 29,501,000.[10] As might be expected, the development of spare-time education was even more spectacular. Official statistics reported 150,000 enrollees in spare-time institutions of higher learning in 1958, five million in spare-time middle schools, and 26 million in spare-time primary schools.[11]

Spare-time education is an imaginative approach to the problem of adult education, and has proved a useful means of reducing illiteracy. There are many forms of spare-time education; their distinguishing characteristic is the provision for study after work hours so that there is no interruption of productive labor. Workers attend classes at the end of the work day, and peasants attend classes or "winter schools" during their lax season. Spare-time classes have also been organized for the crews of steamers in domestic waterways and for other adult groups normally denied the opportunity of schooling.

Educational development in general has been more impressive at the basic levels than at the top, more noteworthy for its quantitative dimensions than for qualitative growth; and this is also true of spare-time education. What the Communists call spare-time secondary schools and higher institutions should not be taken too literally. The curricula and length of schooling are quite flexible, so that it is difficult to identify tangible standards of achievement. The terms "primary," "secondary," and "higher" indicate relative levels rather than specific standards; any instruction beyond the rudimentary level is likely to be called secondary, and any form of relatively advanced training would be labeled as higher learning.

Much has been done to combat illiteracy. Statistical reports on the increase of literacy do not give very precise information, because there is no clear definition of the terms "literate" and "semi-literate" and no stipulation of the number of hours or days of learning required for classification as literate. Moreover, intensive literacy drives are often limited to selected areas, and the accomplishments of such crash programs cannot by considered typical of the country as a whole. Assessment of success is further complicated by the fact that, due to the lack of follow-up and the scarcity of appropriate reading materials, those who have barely emerged from illiteracy have little motivation to keep up their newly acquired skills

[10]See State Statistical Bureau, *Ten Great Years—Statistics on Economic and Cultural Construction Achievements of the People's Republic of China* (Peking: Foreign Languages Press, 1960), p. 192.

[11]See *ibid.,* p. 198.

and easily slide back into illiteracy. Despite these difficulties, however, it is safe to say the regime has made a genuine effort to raise the literacy level of the population, and that substantial progress has been made in the reduction of illiteracy.

LANGUAGE REFORM. An important aid to the popularization of learning has been the language reform. This is not a totally new program; phases of it had been in effect for some years prior to 1949. The reform consists of three major aspects: the unification of the spoken language, the simplification of the written characters, and the introduction of an alphabet. The unification of the spoken language was pushed with vigor and much success by the Nationalist government, and was greatly aided by the radio and by increased travel between the dialect-speaking areas and the rest of the country. Before the Communist takeover, what is known in the West as Mandarin had already become the national spoken language of China, the *kuo-yu* (literally, national language), and was the medium of instruction in all schools. In this phase of the language reform, therefore, the Communists have merely continued the effort of previous years.

The simplification of the written characters, though not a completely new idea either, is a more radical innovation. It consists of reducing the number of strokes that make up complicated characters, so that they may be more easily recognized by the beginner, and certainly much easier to write. It is well known that the Chinese written language is much more difficult than the spoken language. For centuries, popular usage had developed certain abbreviations for complicated written characters; they were *ad hoc* improvisations following no system and generally considered unacceptable in formal writing or in schools. What the Communists have done is not only to give official sanction to the abbreviated forms, but to adopt them in place of the more complicated forms. Official lists of abbreviated forms have been published and are used in books, newspapers, and official documents; in other words, they now have become the standard and the only form of writing. A few of the old abbreviations remain on the lists, and would be easily recognized by any Chinese not familiar with the Communist reform; but there are many new forms which are not readily recognizable. At the same time, there is a generation of new learners to whom the old complicated characters are largely unknown.

The third phase of the Communist reform, the adoption of an alphabet, is the most radical change proposed. The Nationalist government had adopted a system of phonetic symbols to aid in the learning of written characters; the symbols were printed along with the written characters to indicate the pronunciation. The Communists, however, prefer a Latin alphabet, with some modifications to suit Chinese sounds; moreover, their declared intention is the eventual abandonment of the written characters and the complete "latinization" of the written language. This radical proposal has met with resistance and opposition from the scholars, who feel that the neglect of the written characters would result in the loss of China's rich literary heritage. Because of this opposition, and also the practical difficulties of enforcement, the Communists have decided for the present not to push the latinization program. An alphabet has been adopted, but it is not yet widely used; at best, it is employed as an aid to learning the pronunciation of the written characters, in the same manner that phonetic symbols are used in Taiwan today.

The history of the language reform may suggest that it is difficult to enforce innovations which have no roots in past developments. The unification of the spoken language has been carried out with the least difficulty because it is a continuation of the past. Abbreviated written characters have also been accepted; and this idea, too, was not altogether new. All in all, in view of the quiet and unannounced postponement of latinization, the abbreviation of the written characters has become the most important phase of the language reform. Since the abbreviated characters are indeed easier to learn, they constitute a positive step in the direction of simplifying the task of learning for the masses.

WORKER-PEASANT EDUCATION. Needless to say, broadening the base of education benefits most directly those sectors of the population previously deprived of educational opportunities, especially workers and peasants and their children. The Communists have paid special attention to the education of workers and peasants not only because workers and peasants constitute China's "masses," but also because Communist ideology leads them to accord a high status to these classes. They say that their regime is based on a "worker-peasant alliance." Theoretically, the proletarian revolution is led by the working class; but in China, the working class is weak and ineffective and must ally itself with the peasantry. From the beginning of the Communist regime, therefore, worker-peasant education has engaged the attention of the planners.

Special schools for workers and peasants appeared on the scene at an early stage. They were designed for workers and peasants who had had no schooling at all, and enabled them, by attending evening classes and taking accelerated courses of study, to emerge from illiteracy and learn specific skills or prepare for "higher" institutions. It was argued that production experience and general maturity enabled the workers and peasants to encompass the essentials of elementary and secondary education in less than half the time required of young learners. The courses of study were, of course, greatly abbreviated and stripped down to bare essentials; but they did give many workers and peasants an opportunity to join the ranks of the "proletarian intelligentsia."

At the same time, the regular schools and universities were ordered to accord priority to workers and peasants and their children in their admissions policies. Although this has led to a rapid decline of educational standards, the Communists are proud of the increasing percentage of worker and peasant students attending all levels of schools. According to official statistics, the proportion of worker and peasant students to the total number of students in institutions of higher learning rose from 19.1 percent in 1951 to 48 percent in 1958; in technical middle schools, from 56.6 percent to 77 percent; and in middle schools, from 51.3 percent to 75.2 percent.[12] Among new students admitted into higher institutions in 1958, 62 percent were of worker or peasant origin, while in the primary schools and kindergartens more than 99 percent were from worker or peasant families. While the figures may not be accurate, the general trend seems unmistakable.

From the Communist point of view, the growth of worker-peasant education is a major contribution to the proletarian revolution. It increases the ranks of the "proletarian intelligentsia," and paves the way for a society in which the proletariat will exercise leadership in intellectual pursuits as well as all other areas of activity. The program to elevate the workers and peasants to the status of the intelligentsia has been accompanied by a parallel effort to bring the "old-time intellectuals" to the farm and the factory and make them a part of the laboring class. This is the ideological basis for requiring students and teachers to participate in labor and production; the object is to transform them into proletarian intellectuals. By enabling workers and peasants to become educated, and by requiring "old-time intellectuals" to become laborers, the Communists claim that they are moving toward the Marxist ideal of a proletarian society in which there is no distinction between mental and physical labor and no gap between intellectuals and laborers. Education thus contributes directly and immediately to the success of the proletarian revolution.

AROUSING THE MASSES. Aside from ideological claims, there is no doubt that worker-peasant education has brought schooling to many people who would not otherwise have had such an opportunity. Indeed, the Communists have so stimulated the popular appetite for education that the state has been unable to satisfy the demand. More than once, the regime has launched campaigns to tell the people that, while some education was good, it was not always desirable to seek schooling beyond a certain point; and that, for the sake of the party, state, and Socialist society, it was often more important to heed the call for production than to satisfy a personal desire for more education.

There is another facet to popular education worth noting. The Communists talk about their "propaganda" and "cultural" networks, which reach out to the small towns and villages of China (as well as the cities) by means of radio, travelling propaganda teams, exhibits, group meetings, mass

[12]See *ibid.,* p. 200.

campaigns, and other media of communication. These programs reach far more people than the literacy classes and spare-time schools. They bring to millions of people a continuous barrage of messages from the party and the state. They are messages of propaganda and indoctrination, to be sure, and they convey only what the regime wants the people to know. But they do produce a new political consciousness on the part of the people, and an awareness of what goes on in the nation and the world. The net result is that people who used to have little concern for happenings beyond their tiny communities now hear and talk about Cuba, Albania, Viet-Nam, as well as "Socialist construction," production drives, and the class struggle against reactionary elements on the home front.

Shortcomings

The educational growth of the first decade suffered a setback during the 1960s. With the onslaught of the Cultural Revolution, the expansion of the earlier years was arrested and education plunged into chaos. But even during the first decade, there were indications of basic weaknesses. One source of deep concern was the apparent disregard for qualitative growth and the decline of educational standards. If the neglect of quality was only a temporary phenomenon resulting from preoccupation with popularization and quantitive expansion, the problem would not be so serious. But the neglect of quality was often the result of deliberate policy, and was justified by ideological dogma.

When illiterate adults attend part-time schools for a few years, and then are pushed into institutions of higher learning for "advanced study," the level of study must necessarily be adjusted to the kind of academic preparation such students have had. Despite the claim that more mature students are capable of deeper understanding than young people, their accelerated preparation inevitably omitted some of the basic studies that constitute the necessary foundation for advanced scholarship. In consequence, higher institutions have had to lower their academic requirements and to simplify the content of the curriculum. It has already been noted that the Communists are skeptical of theory that is not immediately or clearly applicable to action. The distrust of theoretical knowledge, and the fear that any form of knowledge "for its own sake" might lead to a "professionalism" that stands aloof from politics, have resulted in a disdainful attitude toward systematic scholarship. Moreover, systematic scholarship and the pursuit of fundamental studies call for lengthy training, while the trend on the Chinese mainland has been to shorten the period of schooling. In the early years of the regime, there was a pressing need to produce cadres and trained personnel as quickly as possible. In consequence, short-term institutes and accelerated courses were almost a practical necessity.

But when, at the height of the Cultural Revolution in 1966, Mao Tse-tung again called for a shortening of the period of schooling and for "fewer and better" courses, it was evidence of a continuing trend toward educational short-cuts. Such devices cannot afford to be too particular about established standards.

BOURGEOIS SCHOLARSHIP CONDEMNED. Distrust of intellectuals is another factor that tends to lower educational standards. The Communist attitude toward China's intellectuals has shifted at times from attack and condemnation to relative tolerance and relaxed control; but unfortunately the liberal periods have been brief and infrequent. There have been occasions when the regime admitted that "old-time intellectuals" could still be of service to the new society; until there were enough "red experts" to meet all needs, there would still be room for "white experts."[13] There were also times when the products of short-term institutes and accelerated training were found inadequate for the responsibilities assigned to them,[14] and the authorities urged that more attention be given to systematic learning and old-fashioned "book knowledge."[15] But these were brief interludes punctuating the longer and more enduring policy of slighting the intellectuals and their "bourgeois scholarship."

In his pronouncements on education, Mao Tse-tung has repeatedly ridiculed "bourgeois scholarship," by which is meant time-consuming, systematic study, prolonged periods of schooling, and elaborate courses with content based on prerequisites and prescribed sequences. To the Communist, these are tricks used by bourgeois society to keep education as the privilege of the few and beyond the reach of the masses. They are rejected as valid measures of educational achievement. Even in the promotion of science, the Communists have exalted "worker-peasant scientists" who have shown ingenuity in technological improvements. The implication is that one can become a scientist without long years of study; and the slogan "science is no mystery" was proposed to dispel the notion that years of prolonged study were necessary. The current glorification of "barefoot doctors" is another expression of the same viewpoint, namely, that activists and those motivated by revolutionary zeal need not be burdened with the non-essential knowledge so highly valued by bourgeois scholarship. In such circumstances, the Communists are not likely to be disturbed by academicians who deplore declining standards of education.

THE DOMINANCE OF POLITICS. The dominance of politics lies at the root of many difficulties of Communist education. Early in the regime, the attention of the authorities was drawn to the fact that political require-

[13]See Ch'en Yi's speech in *Kuang-ming Jih-pao,* September 3, 1961.

[14]See Theodore H. E. Chen, "Education and the Economic Failures in Communist China," *Educational Record,* Vol. 44, No. 4 (October 1963).

[15]See *China News Analysis,* No. 407 (February 9, 1962).

ments were crowding out the academic functions of the school. It was becoming impossible to maintain a regular schedule because, in addition to "political study" as a core subject of the curriculum, there were frequent calls for mass meetings and for "criticism and self-criticism" sessions for students and teachers, on top of the requirement that every one had to participate in "revolutionary action" in and out of the schools. Political activities took so much time and energy that students were left physically tired and mentally exhausted. To rectify the situation, the authorities issued orders to limit political activities; but this restraint was short-lived. So long as politics is dominant, academic learning must take a back seat. So long as the party controls the whole process of education, schoolmen have no chance to suggest ameliorative measures. So long as education is the handmaiden of politics, there can be no stability in education. Without stability and continuity, there can be no long-range planning and little educational progress.

Impact of the Cultural Revolution

Political interference and dominance were carried to even greater extremes during the Great Proletarian Cultural Revolution. Despite all the changes that had been introduced, Mao Tse-tung and his associates still felt that education did not adequately serve proletarian politics. No matter how much had been done to popularize learning and to provide schooling for the many, education had failed because it had not brought into being the "new man"—the unselfish, self-effacing, collectivist man ever ready to heed the call of the party and the state at whatever sacrifice to his personal interests and ambitions.

After more than a decade of the new education, the Communists found that the intellectuals had not yet given up their bourgeois notions. Writers and educators were still spreading ideas which were now labeled as revisionist. Young people, presumably products of the new regime, were still animated by personal ambition and the desire to seek a more satisfying personal life. They did not readily accept the job assignments of the regime.[16]

The masses, too, still anticipated the incentives of material rewards and personal benefit. The new Socialist man, the goal of Communist education, was very slow to make his appearance, while the old man, the product of feudal and bourgeois society, was still very much alive. Drastic changes in education were imperative.

In June 1966, the Central Committee of the Chinese Communist Party

[16]A report in the *New York Times* (November 5, 1968) quoted the influential Shanghai newspaper *Wen-hui Pao,* which deplored the lack of devotion of young people "as though they think that love, marriage, family and individual happiness are the aims of life."

and the State Council ordered all institutions of higher learning to postpone the enrollment of students for the following school year, in order to
allow time for a thorough reorganization of education. This order, said
Jen-min Jih-pao on June 18, marked "the beginning of a complete revolution in the entire educational system." What happened in the ensuing
months went far beyond the original order of the government. Lower
schools were also closed after the summer of 1966; and a virtual educational blackout descended upon a land known for its traditional respect for
learning.

The disruptive and destructive antics of the Red Guards are now a
familiar story. Closure of the schools made it easier for young revolutionaries to roam the country. The movement soon gained its own momentum,
and pushed far beyond the limits originally intended by the Maoists. After
a few months, the authorities saw the need for some restraint, and decided
to herd the rampaging students back to the classrooms. Early in 1967, an
order was issued to reopen the schools. The wording of the order indicates
that the government was really more concerned with containing the ram-
bunctious youngsters and getting them off the streets and trains than in the
resumption of academic work. The call was to "resume classes and make
revolution." Statements by responsible authorities exhorted young people
to continue their revolutionary activities, but to combine them with study.
The study, meanwhile, must be centered on the class struggle, the writings
of Mao Tse-tung, and the decisions of the Central Committee of the
Chinese Communist Party regarding the Cultural Revolution.[17]

But the order to reopen the schools fell on deaf ears. The youngsters
seemed to be enjoying their life of freedom and political importance, and
they were in no hurry to settle down again. Teachers who had been the
targets of attacks by their students and other self-appointed guardians of
pure revolutionary thought and conduct were not anxious to return to
their duties, not knowing how they would be treated by students still engaged, with official sanction, in attacking bourgeois intellectuals. According to one newspaper report, the government found it necessary in
October 1967 to call on the army to help force the Red Guards back to
school.[18] Primary schools did gradually reopen in the latter part of 1967.
Secondary schools were much slower; and as late as 1969, higher institutions were still trying to find a *modus operandi* that would be both
acceptable and practicable.

There is no question that drastic changes are in store for schools and
universities at all levels. If Mao's ideas are to be carried out, the new
schools will be very different from the past and from the established schools

[17]See, for example, a leading editorial of *Wen-hui Pao*, reprinted in *Kuang-ming Jih-pao*,
February 18, 1967.
[18]See *Los Angeles Times*, October 24, 1967.

in other countries. There are as yet no detailed regulations for schools and universities that have reopened, and wide variations exist in the manner in which school work has been "resumed." But a fairly clear pattern is emerging. The new programs of the reopened schools all follow the basic guidelines laid down by Mao Tse-tung during the course of the Cultural Revolution. These guidelines may be summarized as follows. The period of schooling must be shortened; revolutionary activities must be continued; the school program must include productive labor and military training; study must center on political and ideological subjects; the influence of bourgeois scholars must be destroyed; and workers, peasants, and the army must take over the control of education.

CURTAILED SCHOOLING. Shortening the period of schooling was reemphasized in 1966 as one of the major reforms demanded of education. Prolonged schooling, it is argued, is a trick by which the bourgeois scholars make education unattainable to the masses. It also keeps young people away from production for too many years and alienates them from the masses. The period of schooling is to be shortened by concentrating on the essentials—that is, subjects of practical value to production and political remoulding—and by simplifying the content. In its famous sixteen-point decision concerning the Cultural Revolution, the Central Committee of the Communist Party directed:[19]

> The period of schooling should be shortened. Courses should be fewer and better. The teaching material should be thoroughly reformed, in some cases beginning with simplifying complicated material.

Since academic studies constitute only a part of the new school program, the further "simplification" of content will necessarily result in the drastic reduction of academic subject matter. The authoritative *Jen-min Jih-pao* editorialized as follows in regard to reopening the schools:[20]

> To reopen classes and make revolution means holding classes in Mao Tse-tung's thought and the Great Proletarian Cultural Revolution. . . . The lessons will consist mainly of the study of Chairman Mao's works and his quotations, of documents related to the Great Proletarian Cultural Revolutions, and the criticism and repudiation of bourgeois teaching material and method. . . . It is necessary to revise the work previously done in mathematics, physics, foreign languages. . . .

Proposals have been made to reduce elementary education from six to five years, and secondary education from six years to four years. In higher

[19]*Peking Review,* Vol. 9, No. 33 (August 12, 1966).
[20]*Jen-min Jih-pao,* March 7, 1967.

education, Mao's "Latest Directive" in August 1968 lays down the following principles:[21]

> It is still necessary to have universities; here I refer mainly to colleges of science and engineering. However, it is essential to shorten the length of schooling, revolutionize education. . . . Students should be selected from among workers and peasants with practical experience, and they should return to production after a few years' study.

The course of study in higher education is therefore to be shortened also. There will be little use for liberal arts, or for the humanities and social sciences; science and technology will be the major concern. The admission of large numbers of workers and peasants will inevitably call for further "simplification" of the curriculum, and shorter courses will insure an early return to the production front.

Take medical education, for example. The medical colleges will stress more practical studies and knowledge applicable to common diseases of the rural areas. They will waste little time on theoretical studies.[22] Again, admission must be offered to workers and peasants rather than to the bourgeoisie, who are likely to indulge in professionalism and remain aloof from politics. The Shantung Medical Center is reported to have reduced its course from five to three years. A medical college in Tsinghai province has adopted a program of part-time study and part-time farming.[23] Workers are sent to hospitals for the study of specific aspects of medicine; and it is claimed that after two months, they are able to diagnose diseases, detect cardiac murmurs, and perform appendicitis operations.[24] According to a report from Hong Kong, the "barefoot doctors" whom the Maoists now exalt as the new type of proletarian doctors, have had no more than nine years of formal schooling, and in some cases less than three.[25]

Downgrading the Intellectuals

The demotion of intellectuals is a policy which the Communist regime has pursued for two decades. There have been intermittent periods of relative leniency, but on the whole the Communists have distrusted the "old-time intellectuals" and attempted to destroy their traditional prestige in Chinese society. Since the advent of the Cultural Revolution, China's intellectuals have been subject to even more severe criticism. Now the stated

[21]*Peking Review,* Vol. II, No. 31 (August 2, 1968).
[22]See *Far Eastern Economic Review,* (October 31, 1968).
[23]See *Survey of China Mainland Press* No. 4229 (July 31, 1968).
[24]See *New York Times,* March 2, 1969.
[25]See *Los Angeles Times,* November 15, 1968.

policy is not merely to condemn the individual failings of "bourgeois scholars," but to terminate their dominant influence in education and to discredit the "bourgeois scholarship" they represent.

The downgrading of intellectuals by such methods as thought reform, confessions, "heart surrender," and hard labor in farms and factories needs no recapitulation here. Since the Cultural Revolution, the anti-intellectual climate has become still more oppressive. Commenting on the cult of mediocrity, a French journalist formerly on the staff of *Peking Review* wrote that an academic degree was a handicap for cadres on account of the taint of bourgeois scholarship.[26] Mao Tse-tung once praised the Shanghai Machine Tools Plant because "old technicians trained before liberation" constituted only five percent of the six hundred engineers and technicians in this training institute. Technical personnel promoted from among the workers are said to be better than those with college degrees. *Jen-min Jih-pao* ridiculed a technician who had studied abroad but had made no significant achievement despite more than twenty years of schooling, and compared his record to the outstanding performance of "a worker who began as an apprentice at the age of fourteen" and studied for only four years in a technical school. The conclusion was that intellectuals with many years of schooling compared unfavorably with workers promoted to be technicians, and that "the domination of our schools by bourgeois intellectuals should by no means be allowed to continue."[27]

THE PROLETARIAN INTELLIGENTSIA. The prestige and authority of scholars were shaken when students were encouraged to attack the reactionary views of their professors and write syllabi and textbooks more in harmony with official dogmas. The position of scholars was further compromised when workers and peasants walked into the classrooms to teach and lecture, and were declared to be more competent than the "bourgeois scholars." During the "class education" campaign that marked the "Socialist education" movement prior to the Cultural Revolution, lectures on the class struggle were given by "old workers and peasants" who recounted their experience of exploitation and oppressive treatment by capitalists and landlords, and who tried to make vivid to the young the evils of the old society. The role of the worker-peasant teachers in the reopened schools has become even more important. Moreover, Mao has now decreed that workers and peasants should not only serve as teachers, but should also take over the control and administration of the schools.

In the latter part of 1968, millions of workers and peasants, reenforced by army cadres, were organized into "Mao Tse-tung Thought Propaganda Teams" to go into the schools and universities and make sure that the new

[26]See Maurice Cianter, "A Gilded Cage," *Far Eastern Economic Review* (August 8, 1968).
[27]*Peking Review,* Vol. 11, No. 31 (August 2, 1968).

educational reforms were being thoroughly enforced. Besides wresting control of education from bourgeois intellectuals, the Maoists may also have been motivated by the need to suppress the excessive exuberance of the Red Guards and to enforce order and discipline in the schools. In March 1967, Mao had issued a directive ordering the army to help reopen the schools and to take charge of military training in schools and universities.[28] Now the worker-peasant-soldier teams were to take over the schools completely. They were to determine major policies, supervise the ideological cleansing of students and teachers, and give lectures in the classroom.

In the cities, these teams consist of workers and soldiers; in the country, they are made up of "poor and lower-middle peasants" and soldiers. It is obvious that they have radically changed the nature of the schools. Although they have had little training, the workers and peasants are showing the scholars and bourgeois intellectuals how to run the schools and universities. A team of workers, peasants, and soldiers entering a university might have as many as a thousand members, each armed with a copy of the writings of Mao Tse-tung. Among 350 workers sent to Hangchow University to direct this institution of higher learning, one was an illiterate man of 57 who had never attended school.[29] In Shanghai, where ten thousand workers, backed by military personnel, penetrated the schools and universities, one team member was an elderly woman who "asked people to teach her to read so that she could propagandize Mao's directives among college students."[30] Another woman serving on a university team was asked how an illiterate person could run a university. Her reply was, "With the backing of Mao Tse-tung, anything can be attained."[31] The Communists insist that the assumption of educational leadership by workers and peasants is a permanent reform, and that the propaganda teams are to remain indefinitely in the schools and universities.[32]

RE-EDUCATION OF INTELLECTUALS. The re-education of intellectuals is also a longstanding Communist policy, but the methods have varied from time to time. The most recent measure, ordered by Mao himself, is to send intellectuals into the rural areas for re-education by poor and lower-middle peasants. Millions of students, intellectuals, Red Guards, and graduates of secondary and higher schools have been dispatched to the countryside for long periods of time. The poor and lower-middle peasants not only teach them how to work, but also how to study Mao's works, especially

[28]The text of the directive may be found in *ibid.*
[29]See *China News Analysis,* No. 731 (November 1, 1968).
[30]Peggy Durdin, "The Bitter Tea of Mao's Red Guards," *New York Times Magazine,* January 19, 1969.
[31]*Los Angeles Times,* December 19, 1968.
[32]*Jen-min Jih-pao,* August 29, 1968.

such simple but celebrated articles as *In Memory of Norman Bethune, Serve the People,* and *How the Foolish Old Man Removed the Mountains.*[33] The magnitude of the exodus may be judged from one report that, within a period of months, some fifteen to twenty million people were uprooted from their urban homes and sent to lifetime jobs on farms, factories, and on reclamation and reforestation projects in frontier areas.[34]

Conclusion

To summarize, education on the Chinese mainland is in the midst of drastic and violent change. Despite repeated orders to reopen, and the use of the army to enforce the orders, not all the secondary and higher institutions are yet in operation. Those that have reopened are carrying on with a minimum of watered-down academic studies. "Making revolution" and political study occupy the center of the stage. Lessons on class struggle are taught by workers and by poor and lower-middle peasants. The schools and universities of the past are condemned for over-emphasis on bourgeois scholarship, and the new proletarian education is to move in a different direction. The voice of the scholars and educators has been silenced. The politicians and ideologues are in control.

The wholesale dispatch of youth to the countryside seems to mean that relatively few people in the future will have training beyond primary school. And in the higher schools, there is no longer a normal instructional program. A report on a secondary school in Kweichow province states that 58 percent of the lessons were devoted to Mao's thought and the class struggle, 21 percent to "learning from workers, peasants, and soldiers," and the remaining 21 percent to "basic subjects."[35] In the Kiangsi Industrial College, the major part of the daily schedule was devoted to Maoism, military training, and anti-revisionist criticism and self-criticism.[36]

How long will this neglect of serious study continue? How long will the harassment of intellectuals go on? The Communists declare that the re-education of intellectuals and the educational leadership of workers and peasants are permanent policies. It may be argued that destruction must precede construction and that, as Mao once said, excesses are inevitable in an early stage of the revolution. Nevertheless, in 1969, Communist China was still a long way from the establishment of an orderly and systematic program of education designed to produce trained and educated people needed to take up the manifold duties of nation-building.

[33]Known as the Three Great Treatises, these pieces are now required reading for ideological rectification. They may be found in *Selected Works,* Vols. 3 and 4.

[34]See *New York Times,* January 19, 1969.

[35]*Far Eastern Economic Review* (December 5, 1968).

[36]See *China News Analysis,* No. 684 (November 10, 1967).

Chapter Nine

Literature and Art Under Mao Tse-tung

C. T. Hsia

Ever since the launching of the Great Proletarian Cultural Revolution in 1966, nearly all those hitherto responsible for the creation and supervision of literature and art in Communist China have not been allowed to function in their professional capacities. A great many leading writers, playwrights, actors, and directors have been purged, and several have reportedly met death in the process. But even those spared public humiliation and punishment have been effectively silenced. So far as we know, except for *PLA Literature,* all literary journals intended for domestic consumption have suspended publication. Even Western observers well informed about the repeated purges of intellectuals since 1949 were unprepared for this massive demonstration of the Communist leadership's total distrust of the intellectual class. In any meaningful assessment of the literature and art of the last twenty years, this phenomenon should claim our first attention.

This essay is concerned primarily with literature and only cursorily with the theater and cinema, although it must be emphasized that the leading practitioners of the fine arts have suffered the same fate as the more prominent literary and theatrical workers—because they are in the eyes of the Communist leadership equally unreliable. With all their past contributions to communism, these people are now anathema to the regime principally because they have refused to sever their ties with the modern tradition of Chinese culture.

Literature and the Leftist Tradition

That tradition, as every student of modern China knows, first crystallized in the May Fourth Movement of 1919, with its dual concern for the self and the nation. Beyond all its linguistic and formal departures from traditional literature, modern Chinese literature differed from it in essence in its advocacy of the claims of the individual and its patriotic concern with China as a land of darkness paralyzed by inhumanity and impotence. Romantic or sentimental in his demand for love and freedom, the modern Chinese writer was at the same time a satiric and humanitarian realist in his passion to expose the ills of Chinese society and to depict the sufferings of the Chinese people. Though his initial hospitality to diverse Western ideologies eventually hardened into a leftism in the main endorsing Communist prescriptions for China's cure, he never lost sight of his twin goals of personal emancipation and national rejuvenation. It is precisely because communism was believed to endorse these goals that a dominant group of writers, and nearly all the progressive elements in the theater and cinema, embraced the Marxist faith in the late 1920s and early 1930s. Immediately before and during the war of resistance against Japan, the Chinese Communist Party won further recruits among writers and intellectuals because it seemed to speak for an unqualified patriotism that promised a brighter future for the nation.

By adopting leftism,[1] of course, Chinese writers cut themselves off from a great portion of the Western heritage that could have deepened their

---

[1]As used here, the term "leftism" refers to the various leftist ideological influences and literary fashions dominant in the late 1920s and 1930s which conditioned not only Chinese writers but also writers in Japan and much of the Western world. In China, after the May Thirtieth Movement of 1925 and especially after the debacle of the so-called Great Revolution (the brief period of the Communist-Kuomintang alliance) in 1927, writers tended to be leftist in sympathy and outlook even if they were not members of the Chinese Communist Party. They agreed that imperialism and feudalism were endangering the Chinese nation, and argued that the Kuomintang under Chiang Kai-shek had betrayed the cause of patriotism in its subservience to imperialism and its ruthless persecution of the Communist Party. As writers, they advocated "proletarian literature" or "revolutionary literature." In 1930, the leftist dominance of the literary world culminated in the establishment of the Chinese League of Left-Wing Writers, a Communist organization which camouflaged its Communist character by its advocacy of a leftist rather than a Communist literature. "Leftism" was more acceptable to writers because it served to bolster their hope that their "twin goals of personal emancipation and national rejuvenation" could be realized. By 1932, the Soviet doctrine of "Socialist realism" was adopted by the League. This doctrine endorsed both the realistic exposé of the ills of China and the roseate depiction of a future when its proletarian classes would be emancipated. The good leftist writers were all satiric and humanitarian realists in their concern with China's plight and the misery of its people; hence they could retain their integrity as writers without putting their Communist faith to the test.

A main theme of the present essay is that these leftist writers were at heart the inheritors of the modern tradition of the May Fourth Movement. Their superficial or untested allegiance to communism would be placed on trial once the party repudiated leftism and spelled out specific programs for the writers to follow (as Mao did at the 1942 Yenan Forum on Literature and Art, discussed below). Insofar as these programs emphasized the writer's complete docility to party discipline and restricted his freedom of expression in regard to social and political ills in China, he could no longer retain his "petit-bourgeois" freedom to seek personal emancipation and to indulge in protest and exposé for the good of the country, as he could in the leftist period. One by one, all the leftist writers and even the party faithful were severely tested as they tried to reconcile their personal beliefs dating from the May Fourth period with the party requirements which they now had to observe.

understanding of man and society. But they did avail themselves of Western literature since the Romantic movement, especially the classics of so-called critical realism ranging from Balzac through the Russian giants to Gorky—writers of liberal and humanitarian faith who have maintained their high position in the Soviet canon.[2] This reading could only confirm Chinese writers in their belief in the necessity for realism, in the universality of love and sympathy that transcends classes, and in their prerogative to combat the dark forces of society. Thus their potential rift with the Communist Party, which could not tolerate these intellectual luxuries once it assumed power over a sizable territory, was widened. As is well known, at the Yenan Forum on Literature and Art in 1942, Mao Tse-tung explicitly warned his corps of writers and artists against their partiality for such luxuries. In a sense, he had eventually to launch a Cultural Revolution because his warnings had had no effect.

Even before the Yenan Forum, many writers in prewar Shanghai or wartime Chungking and Yenan had felt the sting of Communist criticism for their adherence to a leftism that was deemed subversive of the aims of the party. When some 650 delegates attended the first National Congress of Literary and Art Workers in Peking in July 1949, which was convened to greet the impending establishment of the People's Republic, to assess their own work in the past and to map their plans for the future, a sizable number among the writers and theatrical and cinema workers present probably had few illusions about a genuine cultural renascence. They had already undergone self-criticism and self-remoulding and seen the purge of a few of their comrades, notably Wang Shih-wei in 1942 and Hsiao

[2]Soviet literary doctrine prizes "realism" almost to the exclusion of all other literary modes such as "symbolism" and "romanticism," although romanticism is never completely repudiated inasmuch as Soviet criticism insists on the depiction of a bright future and the affirmation of the optimistic in the present. Mao Tse-tung, by endorsing the slogan of "combining revolutionary realism and revolutionary romanticism" (see below), has done much to enhance the dignity of romanticism. But in the main, Soviet and Chinese Communist critics alike have emphasized realism. The realism of the Soviet period (and corresponding Chinese writing of the same period that is considered worthy of praise) is designated "Socialist realism," as distinguished from the "critical realism" of the nineteenth and early twentieth centuries. In most Communist countries, writers still study the literature of critical realism even though it is not ideologically correct by today's standards. The Russian giants of critical realism are, of course, Gogol, Turgenev, Dostoevsky, Chekhov, and Tolstoy. Dostoevsky was suspect in the Stalinist period, and is regarded as a somewhat dangerous writer even today; but his status as a giant of critical realism is secure. Tolstoy was Lenin's favorite, and he has fared much better in Soviet Russia than Dostoevsky. In China today, however, none of these writers can be held up as models, as they were in the 1930s. The strength of leftist writing, as distinguished from Maoist literature since 1942, lies in the fact that writers could then safely study and imitate these classic authors. Their passion for social justice and personal emancipation partly reflected the influence of these giants. Gogol was Lu Hsun's favorite, and most fiction of the love vs. revolution variety popular in China's leftist period showed the pervasive influence of Turgenev.

Chun in 1948.[3] The prominent non-Communist artists invited to attend the conference, such as the painters Ch'i Pai-shih and Hsu Pei-hung, the opera singers Mei Lan-fang and Chou Hsin-fang, and the musician Ma Sitson (Ma Ssu-ts'ung), would seem to have had better cause for rejoicing in their innocence of politics.[4]

But whatever their personal causes for dissatisfaction or complaint, the writers and artists at the Congress had no alternative but to avow their allegiance to the Communist regime. During the years of civil war, they could have left for Hong Kong, Taiwan, or some other place; but none did. Even the disillusioned among them were willing to compromise their artistic integrity and abide by Communist discipline in exchange for tangible gains: a stronger China and a happier proletariat. They were soon to learn, of course, that the kind of repression that stifled the voice of intellectual freedom would also crush the strivings of the people. But at the Congress everything went smoothly. Kuo Mo-jo and Mao Tun, senior leftist authors enjoying the highest national prestige,[5] served respectively as Chairman and First Vice-Chairman, although everyone knew that it was the Second Vice-Chairman, Chou Yang, who would be in effective charge of culture in the period ahead.

The career of Chou Yang is especially interesting in the present context. He is perhaps the ultimate case of a docile Communist who eventually awakened to his responsibilities as a modern Chinese intellectual reared in the traditions of the May Fourth Movement and the literature of leftism. Chou had served in the middle 1930s as the Communist Party's spokesman among writers and artists in Shanghai, and as Mao Tse-tung's ideological watchdog during the Yenan days. Soon after the 1949 Congress of Literary and Art Workers, he enlarged his network of control by filling key bureau-

[3]On Wang Shih-wei and Hsiao Chun, see the author's *A History of Modern Chinese Fiction, 1917-1957* (New Haven: Yale University Press, 1961), pp. 273-80.

[4]The renowned contemporary painters Ch'i Pai-shih and Hsu Pei-hung both died before the Cultural Revolution, and hence were spared the humiliations visited upon their younger colleagues. In its earlier years, the Communist regime made much of Ch'i as a people's artist; the fact that he was born a poor peasant undoubtedly helped. But after his death, and even before the launching of the Cultural Revolution, he had come to be held in less esteem and subject to attack. Hsu was a French-trained artist most famous for his paintings of horses. The opera singer Mei Lan-fang needs no introduction; he died before the Cultural Revolution. Chou Hsin-fang performed during the early 1960s in one of the newly written operas about the upright Ming Official Hai Jui (see below). He was assaulted by Red Guards in the first flush of the Cultural Revolution, and has been subjected to severe criticism ever since. Ma Ssu-ts'ung was one of the most prominent musicians of the Communist regime and a leader in the field of musical education. He defected from China during the Cultural Revolution.

[5]Mao Tun is best known for his novels and short stories. He was removed from his post as Minister of Culture a year or two before the Cultural Revolution. Kuo wrote poetry, fiction, essays, and criticism; he was also a student of ancient Chinese thought and civilization, and a translator. Since 1949, his main role has been as a toady to Mao. Before the advent of the Cultural Revolution, he said publicly that all his books should be burned.

cratic positions in the literary and art sphere with his Yenan colleagues as well as with old friends lately stationed in Shanghai, Hong Kong, or the Nationalist interior. There can be no question that Chou Yang was Mao's deputy in cultural affairs before the Cultural Revolution, although he always served nominally in much more subordinate capacities: as Deputy Director, under Lu Ting-yi, of the party's Propaganda Department; Vice-Minister of Culture, under Mao Tun; and Vice-Chairman, under Kuo Mo-jo, of the Federation of All-China Literary and Art Circles.

During the 1950s, Chou Yang appeared as an implacable persecutor of his fellow intellectuals and artists. For those harboring illusions about Mao's benevolence, it was especially tempting to believe that Chou had gone beyond his superior's wishes in his excessive harshness. But now, thanks to the wealth of information disclosed since the fall of Chou himself, we know that all the purges and rectification campaigns staged in connection with such events as the repudiation of the movie *The Life of Wu Hsun* in 1951, the criticism of Yu P'ing-po's studies of the novel *Dream of the Red Chamber* in 1954, the "unmasking" of Hu Feng and his counter-revolutionary group in 1955, and the denunciation of Ting Ling, Feng Hsueh-feng, and other rightists in 1957, were initiated at the instance of the party's Central Committee with Mao's concurrence.[6] Chou Yang had merely obeyed orders.

It is true that Chou, who had been a translator and literary theorist of no particular brilliance in the early 1930s, owed his rapid rise in the party hierarchy to his unquestioning obedience to the Communist leadership and his determination to carry out its every whim. It may also be true, as some scholars have charged, that in the 1950s, Chou regarded Hu Feng, Ting Ling, and Feng Hsueh-feng as rivals who could challenge his power position, and that he therefore persecuted them with personal vindictiveness. But in view of the immense output of denunciation that has followed every purge, it is perhaps unfair to single out Chou Yang for disapprobation when it was the duty of every unscathed writer to excoriate the victims. Lao She, a non-Communist author noted for his humor and personal warmth,[7] was no less vehement in his abuse of Hu Feng or Ting Ling, although his simulated zeal did not save him from being lynched by the Red Guards in 1966. It is only because it was Chou's duty to write a long and prominently publicized summary toward the conclusion of every purge or rectification campaign that his role as persecutor appeared especially conspicuous.

Whatever his personal failings, we know for certain that Chou was extremely loyal to his associates and protégés, and that he went out of his way to help discredited writers of the Republican era, such as the essayist

---

[6]On these episodes, see *A History of Modern Chinese Fiction, 1917–1957*, Ch. 13.

[7]The novelist Lao She is best known in the United States for his *Rickshaw Boy* (New York: Reynal & Hitchcock, 1945). He also wrote several plays under the Communist regime.

Chou Tso-jen[8] (Lu Hsun's younger brother), and to provide them with work and income. We also know that, even in his Yenan days, he would act upon his own literary convictions whenever it was opportune to do so. And as he grew more powerful in Peking, he became emboldened to encourage the production of a literature and art more to his own liking, despite his public adulation of Mao. There is also evidence that by the late 1950s, he cared increasingly for traditional Chinese culture, and provided expert editorial guidance for the publication of literary classics, source materials, and textbooks that would enable the student to understand China's past with minimal ideological distortion.

Upon the conclusion of the anti-rightist campaign in 1958, Chou Yang and his group began to assume an anti-Maoist position. Like their purged colleagues, the Chou group had the modern leftist tradition in their bones, and they could not forever tolerate Mao's gross violation of that tradition. During the anti-Hu Feng campaign, critics young and old attacked Hu for his anti-Maoist crimes. Yet in a matter of years, all of these critics — Ting Ling, Feng Hsueh-feng, Ch'in Chao-yang, Pa Jen, Ho Ch'i-fang, and Shao Ch'uan-lin[9] (the last two held high posts in the literary establishment as Chou Yang's closest associates) — were attacked for making almost the same demands as Hu had insisted on: a certain degree of freedom for the writer, and his right to depict the truth as he sees it, to affirm a classless human nature, and to portray real characters divested of their strait jackets of heroism and villainy.

When Shao Ch'uan-lin and several veteran playwrights who had been Chou Yang's close associates in the 1930s came under attack in 1964, Chou himself was doomed. Two years later he was purged, and his establishment crashed with him. In the end, even Chou Yang, for so many years the Maoist spokesman on literary matters who appeared so harsh in his treatment of erring writers, proved that he, too, was a product of the same tradition as Hu Feng, Ting Ling, and other Communist writers whom he had earlier purged. Only his awakening took place later than theirs, in part because he was entrusted with official responsibility, and in part because he was more of a doctrinaire theorist and critic who — since he himself did not have to

---

[8]A leading essayist of the prewar period, Chou Tso-jen collaborated with the Japanese and was imprisoned after the end of the war. He was released soon after the Communists came to power, and thereafter managed to write two books about Lu Hsun and to translate a Japanese classic in his declining years.

[9]Ch'in Chao-yang, Pa Jen, Ho Ch'i-fang, and Shao Ch'uan-lin are all critics who were purged — or, at least, found themselves in deep trouble — because of their writings demanding greater realism or more freedom for the writer. The attack on Shao in 1964 was a prelude to the downfall of Chou Yang. It was subsequently revealed that in the early 1960s, the latter had taken a common stand with Shao on various important questions, although at the time Chou was spared public attack.

write in a creative fashion—at first found it easy to promote slogans and impose orders.

The Maoist Formula and the Persistence of Realism

Mao Tse-tung had never been a Communist intellectual in the sense that most leftist writers are. Brought up on the Chinese classics and history, he had delighted in traditional Chinese novels as a youth, but in his ignorance of foreign tongues he had never developed a fondness for Western literature. Of all modern Chinese writers, Lu Hsun had the greatest appeal for men of traditional taste, and we may assume that Mao did enjoy his miscellaneous essays and classical poems even though his public praise of Lu in 1940 was mainly dictated by political expediency. But Mao could not have found the Western-slanted literature of the modern leftist tradition to his liking; and as early as 1938, he called upon cultural workers to utilize the "national forms" of literature and art in explicit repudiation of that tradition. Just as he had earlier turned to the peasantry instead of the industrial proletariat as the source of his power, so in the Yenan period he demanded the kind of folksy literature and art that would far more effectively serve the purpose of propaganda among the peasantry. But in speaking at the 1942 Yenan Forum to his corps of writers and artists, whose spirit of leftist protest had already proved alarming, he would have failed to offer a cure for their petit-bourgeois dissidence if he had simply admonished them to become folksy propagandists, and he would also have appeared to lack cultural statesmanship. So he gave them a hard pill to swallow for their ideological and artistic betterment: to discard their petit-bourgeois ways of thinking and feeling, to learn Marxism-Leninism, to live among the workers, peasants, and soldiers, and to learn their proletarian life at first hand so as to become better equipped to serve and educate them.

Mao's *Talks at the Yenan Forum on Literature and Art*[10] appears to pay

[10]A standard translation may be found in *Talks at the Yenan Forum on Literature and Art* (Peking, Foreign Languages Press, 1960). Insofar as the Yenan *Talks* have not been revised, they are presumably as much holy writ in 1970 as they were in 1942. But the *Talks* can be reinterpreted to suit the times. This was done, for example, at the Forum on Work in Literature and Art in the Armed Forces, held in Shanghai in February 1966. I quote from K. H. Fan (ed.), *The Chinese Cultural Revolution: Selected Documents,* (New York and London: Monthly Review Press, 1968), p. 90:

> This Forum was presided over by Mao's wife, Chiang Ch'ing, who was "entrusted" with the task by Lin Piao. The fact that the "Summary of the Forum" was adopted only after being three times personally examined, revised, and approved by Mao himself and that on March 22, 1966, Lin Piao transmitted, with his personal letter, this document to members of the Standing Committee of the Military Commission of the Party Central Committee indicated its importance, although it was not made public until June, 1967.

The "Summary of the Forum" is reprinted in Fan's book, pp. 99-114. A comparison of this document with the Yenan *Talks* shows that, whereas in 1942 Mao still defers to the people the highest possible tribute to the common people—the worker, peasant, and soldier masses—since he asserts that only by living among them can the writer or artist discover the real essence of Communist life. But it is an ambivalent compliment in that Mao makes no bones about the real mission of literature and art, which is to instruct and educate the people. The people are backward, illiterate, and unenlightened. But in the same breath Mao declares that, by virtue of their class status, they are inherently filled with the proper revolutionary spirit and Socialist zeal; and it is the duty of the writers and artists, with their unfortunate education and class status, to imbibe that spirit and zeal from them.

It was, perhaps, easy for Mao to maintain these two somewhat contradictory views. But the writer is faced with a real dilemma in attempting to apply the Maoist formula. The convenient solution, inevitably, is to single out a few among the people as the Communist *avant-garde*—noble, selfless, filled with immense hatred for the old society and infinite gratitude to the party—and to depict the rest as in need of varying degrees of ideological reform. The cadres who have to work among the people are similarly divided into two categories: the heroes, and those still in need of reform for their incorrect political outlook or working style. Quite often the writer has to portray members of the enemy class who are properly outside the pale of the "people": landlords, reactionaries, Kuomintang agents and saboteurs. The latter two types serve as especially convenient scapegoats to account for the temporary disruption of Socialist construction despite the dedicated endeavors of the *avant-garde*.

(workers, peasants, soldiers) as the "teachers" of the writers and artists, the educative role is now reserved for the Communist Party and Mao himself; that, whereas in 1942 Mao refers to Marx, Lenin, and Stalin as infallible guides, Mao now sees his own thought as the only guide to truth; that, whereas the workers, peasants, and soldiers receive equal attention in 1942, the very fact that the new Forum was sponsored by the armed forces indicates the new importance of the PLA and the model soldier as an example for others to follow; that, whereas Chou Yang and company were in 1942 the enforcers of the Maoist line (though this fact is not mentioned in the *Talks*), the new document refers to the persistence of the "black line" (a term that is synonymous with the Chou Yang leadership); that, whereas in 1942 Mao merely deplores certain trends found in earlier leftist literature (love, human nature, and so forth), the new document totally repudiates leftist literature and art: "We must destroy the blind faith in what is known as the literature and art of the 1930s (in the Kuomintang areas of China)." (Fan, p. 106.) This last point bears out the main contention of the present essay. Also, in 1942 the classics of critical realism were still respected; in 1966 the classics of Europe and Russia and of old China are much less relevant to the needs of China. The "Summary" says: "We must destroy blind faith in Chinese and foreign classical literature. Stalin was a great Marxist-Leninist. His criticism of the modernist literature and art of the bourgeoisie was very sharp. But he uncritically took over what are known as the classics of Russia and Europe and the consequences were bad." (Fan, p. 107.) In 1942, Mao would not have dared to criticize Stalin.

The Song of Ou-yang Hai, which is discussed below, is a concrete example of the new literature written in compliance with Mao's new demands. Nevertheless, the Yenan *Talks* remain a bible, and have never been officially downgraded.

Mao Tse-tung did not prescribe these categories of fictional character. But given his analysis of Chinese society, his stress on self-remoulding, and his affirmation of the party and the proletariat, the writer actually has no choice but to rehearse the victory of the *avant-garde,* the self-improvement of the middle groups, and the punishment of the wicked. Periodically he goes among the workers, peasants, or soldiers to learn about Communist life, and yet he cannot report what he observes there if it contradicts the prescribed social reality of Mao's China.

The earlier leftist literature also conformed to certain predictable clichés. But in the absence of stringent party discipline, the revolutionary hero (who was usually drawn from the petit-bourgeois rather than the proletarian class) could fall passionately in love, kill a personal enemy, and embark on many other kinds of adventure denied his present-day Communist counterpart. He was also free to ponder a wide range of thoughts and feel a wide range of emotions. Even if he was often too idealized or romanticized to be real, the hostile society against which he contended was usually recognizable with its contrasting scenes of capitalist depravity and proletarian squalor; and it is invariably in the depiction of this dark society under warlord or Kuomintang rule that the gifted leftist writer compels our admiration for his satiric power or humanitarian passion. The same writer, now much older, still sees darkness about him. But not only is he denied the right to expose the kind of evil that will discredit the Communist Party; he is not even allowed to depict the elemental passions of man in their true colors. Except for his love of labor and his adoration of Mao, the Communist hero in recent literature is virtually passionless.

While Western scholars are understandably much concerned about the fate of writers who made their reputations before the 1930s, such as Kuo Mo-jo, Mao Tun, Pa Chin,[11] and T'ien Han,[12] because their names are more familiar, the stunted careers of those who began to attract notice in the 1930s and contributed significantly to the literature of the 1940s are perhaps even more tragic. Among novelists, one could name Ai Wu, Lu Ling (purged during the anti-Hu Feng campaign), Sha T'ing, Shih T'o, and Tuan-mu Hung-liang;[13] and among playwrights, one might mention an even greater number who enlivened the wartime stage in Chungking and occupied Shanghai. For all these authors, their thin volume of publications since 1949 contrasts sadly with their prolific output of greater artistic integrity before that date.

[11]Pa Chin was a prolific and popular novelist and storyteller known for his anarchist sympathies. Under the Communist regime, he served as a correspondent in the Korean and Vietnamese wars, and retained an important position among writers. He was subjected to vehement attack during the later stages of the Cultural Revolution.

[12]A veteran playwright, T'ien Han wrote an anti-Mao historical play in the early 1960s which later brought about his purge.

[13]Ai Wu, Lu Ling, Sha T'ing, and Tuan-mu Hung-liang are briefly discussed in *A History of Modern Chinese Fiction, 1917–1957,* Ch. 13; and Shih T'o in Ch. 17.

Ai Wu was luckier than most in that before the Cultural Revolution he was little victimized by the various rectification campaigns and maintained a modest pace of productivity. A talented author showing great signs of maturity in his postwar novels, he had specialized in worker fiction since 1949 and written some of the technically most competent stories among the approved literature; they are collected in the volume *Homeward Journey* (1958). Their themes, however, are predictably trite, and this contrast between narrative skill and trite theme is especially pronounced in his major work of the Communist period, *Steeled and Tempered* (1958), which is generally regarded as the best novel about industrial life ever published in Communist China.

Ai Wu places his story in a factory town in the Northeast, and ably builds up the tensions existing among three steel workers on the one hand, and between the party secretary at the factory and its manager on the other. The principal hero, Ch'in Te-kuei, is a selfless worker who has repeatedly made steel in record time. Of his two co-workers in charge of the same furnace on different shifts, the elder one, also a labor hero, is resentful of the upstart and unwilling to share his hard-earned experience with others. The other rival more than anything else simply wants to get by without overexerting himself, and he also fancies after a girl worker in a neighboring factory who, needless to say, is in love with Ch'in. As for the feud on the higher level, the manager wants to speed up production at all costs; he has nothing but contempt for the party secretary's indirect and time-consuming approach to the problem by trying to raise the morale of the workers individually and collectively. Both sets of circumstances help precipitate a crisis at the factory during which Ch'in Te-kuei has to risk his life to save it from being blown to pieces. Severely burned and in a coma for days, he could have died, and his self-sacrifice would have at least taught a lesson to the reckless manager and spurred the other furnace chiefs to a greater zeal for production. But Ai Wu prefers to end his novel on a false note. We are supposed to believe that neither the lazy furnace chief nor the manager was ultimately responsible for the accident; it is solely the handiwork of a Kuomintang saboteur in the employ of the factory. This cheap surprise ending is apparently designed to prove that no serious conflicts could have arisen among builders of socialism despite their varying attitudes' toward work; only an enemy agent could have wanted to wreck the new China as symbolized by the factory.

Steeled and Tempered is a novel written to formula in that it upholds the *avant-garde* (Ch'in Te-kuei and the party secretary), attests to the self-improvement of the less enlightened (Ch'in's co-workers and the manager), and exposes the enemy (the saboteur). But since Ai Wu actually lived among steel workers for years, he does tell us a great deal about their life at home and in the factory, and about the process of steel-making. Although it is one of the best Chinese Communist novels (as in the Republican period, fiction has remained the most fruitful and successful branch of literature), the conscientious realism of the work is seriously compromised by the formulaic requirements of Maoist propaganda.

Great Changes in A Mountain Village (1958), a peasant novel of exceptional distinction, further proves the point. Like Ai Wu, its author Chou Li-po was schooled in the leftist tradition in the thirties; but Chou went to Yenan during the war and became one of Mao's most obedient students in trying to learn peasant life at first hand. *The Hurricane* (1948), his Stalin Prize-winning novel about land reform in the Northeast, brought him fame. Although he could not report all the cruel truth about the persecution of a landlord in that novel, he did describe in great detail the persistent attempts of party cadres to whip up mob fury among the peasants. And he also tried his hardest to reproduce the dialect of the region. (One incidental benefit of following Mao's admonition to writers to live among the people has been their improved command of peasant speech. Ting Ling's *The Sun Shines Over the Sangkan River* and Ou-yang Shan's *Uncle Kao* are other notable examples drawn from the late 1940s.)

In the mid-1950s, Chou Li-po was assigned to his home region in Hunan to observe the launching of an agricultural production cooperative. *Great Changes in A Mountain Village,* which embodies his findings, gives further proof of his astonishing ability to render dialect; and the same kind of realism informs his descriptions of the village. In Chapter Three, for example, Chou gives a vivid account of a meeting of party cadres and village leaders. It begins at 9:00 P.M.; and after a break during which the participants amuse themselves with card games and other forms of relaxation, it resumes at eleven:

> People came in again, sitting informally round the table. The director of women's work, who always arrived late, had only just come. She put her baby, not yet weaned, on the table, and let him crawl all over it. The little creature had on a pair of padded trousers, split in the middle, exposing his fat little white bottom, with a blue birth-mark. As soon as he saw the clock, he tried to get hold of it. The director of women's work shouted at him so loudly to stop him that he was frightened and cried. She had to take him into her arms, opened her dress and stuffed a nipple into the little yelling mouth.

Unlike the American reader who would never associate breast-feeding with a business meeting, the witnesses around the table are too inured to such scenes to be shocked. The novelist has, furthermore, sided with them in chiding the woman for being chronically late; and yet what is truly shocking is that she should have carried her baby with her at this late hour in performing her assigned duty, however perfunctorily. (Incidentally, in English the phrase "not yet weaned" implies that the baby is old enough to be weaned; the Chinese text carries no such connotation.)

In his conscientious fashion, therefore, Chou Li-po presents enough real scenes of the village to make a non-Communist reader want to sympathize with all those reluctant peasants forced to give up their own holdings and join the cooperative. Even with respect to members of the *avant-garde,* one feels that they pay too high a price for their selfless dedication. Because of his almost total neglect of his home in attending to his duties, Liu Yu-sheng, the head of a mutual aid team (a smaller agricultural cooperative unit), is divorced by his uncomprehending wife, whom he evidently loves very much. Though he is eventually matched to a more public-spirited widow, the plight of the tradition-bound woman in going through with the divorce, and the pain and suffering endured by Liu are depicted with genuine feeling.

Before the cadres succeed in persuading the villagers to join the agricultural cooperative, a rumor has spread among them that the trees on the mountain will be expropriated. In the words of the late T. A. Hsia, who was the first Western scholar to emphasize the merits of the novel:[14]

A panic sets in on a night when they go out in mass, including the very old and the very young, to protect their trees from expropriation. They succeed in denuding the hills, as more than one thousand trees are cut down. Thus they suffer losses, but at least the trees won't go to the collective. Then, on page 270, only fifteen pages later, the cooperative is established, ostensibly with the consent of the majority. As a pure propagandist, Chou Li-po is hardly convincing with his hurried account of the transformation of the peasants' "political awareness," while he describes their resistance at greater length and with far more precision. But as a propagandist at war with the artist within him, he perhaps can do no more. An anti-Communist novelist would be tempted to put in a melodramatic scene of armed revolt; but the cruel fact of submission, so poignantly rendered by Chou Li-po, is a more powerful accusation of the terrible reality in Communist China.

Like Ai Wu, Chou Li-po asserts the might of the Communist *avant-garde* and the reformability of the less enlightened. But since he ends his novel in a far less contrived manner (although still somewhat clumsy), it leaves us with a much stronger impression of "the terrible reality in Communist China." Without imputing to the author any conscious desire to criticize or embarrass the regime, it would seem that his very endeavor to experience the life of the people has made him less effective as a propa-

[14]T. A. Hsia, "Heroes and Hero-Worship in Chinese Communist Fiction," *China Quarterly,* No. 13 (January–March, 1963), pp. 117-118.

gandist. Indeed, it would have made things far easier for all concerned if, at the Yenan Forum, Mao had told his writers and artists to be simple propagandists exempted from the necessity of learning from the people. But in 1942 and for many years afterwards, perhaps Mao seriously believed that any true depiction of the life of the people would inevitably confirm their joy in communism and their love for Socialist construction. In any event, he was then too much influenced by the Soviet doctrine of Socialist realism to do otherwise. As long as feudalism and imperialism were rampant, one could agree with Mao that it was possible for writers to depict the actual reality without compromising their faith in communism. But if the people remained unhappy even after the presumed obstacles to Communist success—Japanese aggression, Kuomintang misrule, landlord and bourgeois domination of the national economy, American imperialism in the form of the Korean War—had one by one been removed, the Communist government itself stood exposed as the cause of China's continuing misery. Under the circumstances, to exhort writers and artists to observe reality would not be in the best interests of the party and government. Consequently, a new cultural policy was launched in 1958—the year of the Great Leap Forward.

1958: New Trends in Cultural Policy

The anti-rightist campaign of the previous year had confirmed the continuing dissidence of a great many writers and artists, and the depiction of Socialist realism by even the most loyal supporters of the regime tended to affirm the Communist cause only at the cost of disclosing serious conflicts in society. It would be far better, the planners of the Great Leap must have thought, for writers and artists to ignore such conflicts, and to spur the people to greater heights of zeal and productivity by emphasizing the past achievements of the party and its even more glorious future. While Mao's Yenan *Talks* remained an oracle, and while a great many writers and artists continued to be assigned to villages, factories, and barracks to observe reality, the new formula for the Great Leap Forward period emphasized "the combination of revolutionary realism and revolutionary romanticism."

This approach stressed, on the one hand, the greater cultural role of the masses themselves spontaneously singing their zeal for production and their faith in the future without benefit of literary middlemen (the "mass poetry" movement); and, on the other hand, the greater freedom allowed to professional writers and artists in their choice of subject matter so that, instead of being bound to contemporary reality, they could now depict the whole history of modern China in order more effectively to praise the heroic record of the Communist Party in bringing about the nation's rejuvenation. It should be noted, however, that while both aspects of this approach embraced revolutionary romanticism in their praise of past and future Communist achievements, in fact they led to contrary trends: one encouraging literary production that was still further removed from the leftist tradition in its unprofessional naiveté and undisguised eulogistic intent, and the other fostering a literature closer in spirit to the earlier leftist product if for no other reason than their thematic affinity—the depiction of a China in the clutches of feudalism and imperialism.

With equal enthusiasm Chou Yang praised both trends, which must have been approved by Mao himself. With the wisdom of hindsight, it would appear that, while it was consistent with Mao's deepseated distrust of the intellectuals to attempt to turn millions of workers, peasants, and soldiers into part-time singers and poets, he must have later come to regret the other trend even if at the time he thought it a good idea to generate enthusiasm for the party by depicting its heroic past. On the other hand, the priorities of Chou Yang and his colleagues must have been just the reverse. With their commitment to professional standards and to the leftist tradition, the Chou Yang group could not have sponsored the mass poetry movement with much real enthusiasm, while they must have genuinely welcomed the opportunity to promote a literature which, if still having a superficial aspect in its obligatory praise of communism, would have the richer appeal of the leftist tradition. And even if they did not seriously intend to revive leftism, they would still have wanted a literature and art with greater audience potential. As the nation's cultural director, Chou Yang had to be concerned with the popular appeal of new books, movies, plays, concerts, and museum displays. Their educational value would have had little impact if they had attracted only a few people. The Hundred Flowers movement of 1956 was launched partly to combat audience indifference to Communist literature and art; and the situation was hardly improved by the anti-rightist campaign of the following year. It would be no harm, so Chou Yang could have reasoned, to let the people escape for a few moments into a bygone world of more varied and colorful humanity so that they could return to their daily tasks refreshed in spirit.

The year 1958 saw the publication of several very popular novels which signalized the start of the new romantic genre, notably Liang Pin's *Keep the Red Flag Flying,* and Miss Yang Mo's *The Song of Youth;*[15] and this trend continued with vigor for a few years. While Yang Mo's novel is a self-contained work about the autobiographical heroine's political awakening in the 1930s, most other novels recalling the late Ch'ing and Republican periods were conceived by their authors as multi-volume projects that should have ended with the Communist victory in 1949 and after. But with

[15]Both works are discussed in *ibid.*

the subsequent shift in cultural policy, none of these projects was even completed.

The Three-Family Lane (1959) is perhaps the finest work of this nostalgic genre. Its author, Ou-yang Shan, planned it as the first part of an ambitious pentalogy entitled *A Generation of Heroes.* In 1962, he completed the second part, *Bitter Struggle;* but two years later he was purged. A veteran leftist novelist who published his first book in 1927, Ou-yang Shan went to Yenan in 1941, and subsequently established himself as the ranking author of his home province when he became Chairman of the Kwangtung branch of the Writers' Union.

The Three-Family Lane traces the fortunes of three families related by marriage from the last years of the Ch'ing dynasty down to the revolutionary debacle of 1927. It is reminiscent of such family chronicles with a regional setting as Pa Chin's famed *Torrent Trilogy,* [16] but it is finer than they in its rich evocation of place (Canton) and period. In fact, the author seems to have patterned his work after China's supreme domestic novel, *Dream of the Red Chamber.* [17] Its handsome hero, Chou Ping, is by design a Chia Pao-yu of the proletarian class, ingenuous and candid to the point of idiocy and adored to distraction by two beautiful cousins. The proletarian cousin, Ch'u T'ao, deserves the intended comparison with Bright Cloud; but whereas the guileless maid of the classic novel dies a victim of feudalist oppression, her modern counterpart is felled by an imperialist bullet as she marches with her comrades in the forefront of a workers' demonstration. Just as Chia Pao-yu loses his gaiety after the death of Bright Cloud and increasingly meditates on his religious vocation, the grief-stricken Chou Ping, too, becomes a changed person and decides to turn Communist to avenge his cousin's martyrdom. The bourgeois cousin, Ch'en Wen-t'ing, is in some ways suggestive of Chia Pao-yu's maid, Pervading Fragrance, although she may be intended to embody the qualities of Precious Clasp as the latter is popularly understood. She, too, avows selfless love; but after the hero has gone into hiding as a Communist worker, she loses courage, yields to family pressure, and marries a rising member of the Kuomintang. Chou Ping hardens himself in the face of this double deprivation of love, and embarks for Shanghai for a more active revolutionary career.

The Communist viewpoint, while pervading the whole novel, becomes prominent only in the second half where, in depicting the Communist set-

[16]On the *Torrent Trilogy,* see *A History of Modern Chinese Fiction, 1917–1957,* Ch. 10; and Olga Lang, *Pa Chin and His Writings: Chinese Youth Between the Two Revolutions* (Cambridge: Harvard University Press, 1967).

[17]For a critical discussion of China's greatest novel, see C. T. Hsia, *The Classic Chinese Novel: A Critical Introduction* (New York: Columbia University Press, 1968), Ch. 7. The characters Chia Pao-yu, Bright Cloud, Pervading Fragrance, and Precious Clasp are dealt with therein.

backs in Kwangtung between 1925 and 1927, the author consistently caricatures the bourgeoisie and the official-gentry class by not allowing a single member of them to become a Communist. But in the first half of the work, he has not only depicted the youth of the May Fourth period with sympathy and understanding, but invested their manners and aspirations with a nostalgic reality of rare charm. With all his romanticized goodness and purity, Chou Ping is nevertheless one of the truly noble characters of modern Chinese fiction, although his eventual conformity to Communist discipline diminishes his archetypal significance as a proletarian Chia Pao-yu.

The popularity of revolutionary chronicles (and the plays and movies based on them) soon brought about a recrudescence of historical drama. During the early 1960s, plays and operas celebrating defiers of tyranny in the feudal past became the rage, even though very few novelists and screen playwrights appropriated historical topics beyond the late Ch'ing period. The Peking opera, of course, has always drawn its stories from history; and during the late 1950s, there had been a few historical plays designed to arouse fervor for national construction. But the systematic creation of new historical plays and operas with satiric or critical references to the Communist regime was certainly a bold gesture toward cultural independence. Just as during the war years in Chungking, the leftist playwrights had staged historical plays to stimulate patriotism and satirize the Nationalist government, now the historian Wu Han and several veteran writers like T'ien Han and Meng Ch'ao again invoked history and legend to make veiled attacks on Mao at the precise time when the consequences of his blunders in economic policy had made him most vulnerable to criticism.[18]

Whether the Chou Yang group had shifted its allegiance to Chief of State Liu Shao-ch'i during this period of cultural liberalization is for our purpose immaterial. What is of decided interest is that, given the conditions of more relaxed control, professional writers and artists should have returned to the kind of sentiments prevalent in prewar Shanghai and wartime Chungking, and reasserted the humanitarianism and satire explicitly repudiated in Mao's Yenan *Talks*. During the same period, the Chou Yang group also sponsored publications affirming the leftist achievement in literature, cinema, and theater, and thus making possible a better understanding of current literature and art in the broader perspective of the modern tradition.

Literature and Art Sponsored by the PLA

In June 1964, Mao Tse-tung, who a year earlier had indicated his displeasure with the current cultural product, issued a directive accusing

---

[18]The attack on Wu Han and his play *The Dismissal of Hai Jui* signaled the start of the Cultural Revolution.

nearly all members of literary and art organizations of being aloof bureaucrats in danger of falling into revisionism, and decrying their failure to
implement the policies of the party over the past fifteen years.[19] Chou
Yang again had to fall in line and start a rectification campaign. Although
— according to his later accusers — he did this with perfunctory enthusiasm,
he still had to sacrifice two of his closest allies, Shao Ch'uan-lin and Hsia
Yen,[20] and also Ou-yang Shan among other important writers.

Mao's 1964 directive amounted to a confession of almost total failure
since 1949 to remould writers and artists in accordance with his Yenan
Talks. His distrust of the Chou Yang group would appear to have taken
shape as early as 1960. In that year, he ordered Defense Minister Lin Piao
to reeducate the armed forces so that they might become a model for the
whole nation. Although in 1942 Mao had decreed a worker, peasant, and
soldier line for literature and art, by 1960 he seems to have preferred the
soldier to the worker and peasant because of his greater docility and political reliability. In remoulding the PLA, Lin Piao deified Mao to the point
where his writings have apparently come to replace the classics of Marxism-
Leninism as the sole repository of truth. In particular, three of Mao's short
essays which are innocent of Marxist philosophy but highly inspirational in
their stress on altruistic love of country and party and one's readiness to
embrace martyrdom, were made the objects of unremitting study.[21] The
soldiers of the PLA were urged to grasp Mao's thought through constant
study, and to use it in every conceivable situation to enhance their zeal,
productivity, and intelligence. In short, just as Mao had earlier abandoned
the Soviet model of Socialist realism for literature and art, by 1960 he had
also realized the irrelevance of Soviet-style Communist ideology for the
remaking of man. The latter miracle could only be accomplished with the
aid of Mao's own thought. Chinese culture of the feudal and Republican
past was also totally irrelevant; it sufficed for the soldiers (and the population at large) to recall at regularly scheduled meetings the "bitterness" of
the pre-liberation years in order to reinforce the myth that, with all its
shortcomings, the present was infinitely preferable.

Far more than the literature and art sponsored by Chou Yang, the kind
produced under the auspices of the PLA is designed to supplement the
study of Mao's thought. It consists mainly of biographies, novels, movies,
and plays about model soldiers who have sacrificed their lives for country
and party, and selections from their diaries. In 1963, an utterly selfless soldier named Lei Feng, who had died in an accident a year earlier, was made

[19]The directive is one of "Two Instructions Concerning Literature and Art," issued in
1963 and 1964, and first made public in May 1967. For the text, see *Peking Review,* Vol. 10,
No. 23 (June 2, 1967).

[20]Hsia Yen, a prominent playwright for both stage and screen, was also — until his downfall — a powerful literary bureaucrat in Shanghai.

[21]The essays are *Serve the People, In Memory of Norman Bethune,* and *How the Foolish
Old Man Removed the Mountains.* They may be found in *Selected Works,* Vols. 3 and 4.

an object of national emulation. Since then, a long succession of young martyrs (plus a few living heroes) have been similarly glorified. Their diaries and biographies are hardly literature, but the fact is that there has been virtually no other literature produced in China since the Cultural Revolution.

The most ambitious literary work sponsored by the PLA has been Chin Ching-mai's *The Song of Ou-yang Hai,* a novel about the life and self-sacrifice of the title hero. First serialized in magazines in 1965, the book was launched with great fanfare; and by the time of its second edition, April 1966, a million copies were in print.[22] Like other such biographical novels, *The Song of Ou-yang Hai* begins with a chapter of unbelievable sentimentality which stresses the stark destitution of the Ou-yang family at the time of the hero's birth and during his early youth. Having thus emphasized his ideal proletarian background, the novel nevertheless goes on for the remaining nine chapters to concern itself almost exclusively with his steady spiritual improvement under the guidance of the party and the Thought of Mao Tse-tung.

In tracing the evolution of Chinese Communist literature from the early Yenan period down to *The Song of Ou-yang Hai,* one is struck by the complete reversal of the roles of the party and the individual hero. In *The White-haired Girl* (1946), the first Communist opera to achieve great popularity, the heroine is passive throughout. Raped and made pregnant by an evil landlord, the peasant girl goes into hiding until she happily rejoins humanity with the liberation of her village by the Red Army and the punishment of the wicked landlord. Nothing is expected of her; she is entitled to her share of the blessings of communism simply by virtue of her past sufferings as a member of the oppressed class. (It is interesting to note that in the subsequent revised version of the opera, the heroine has become far more militantly class conscious, and she volunteers for army service at the end!)[23] In all the novels about land reform, the peasants are given land; and all they have to do is to obey the cadres and muster up enough courage to denounce the landlords.

But in subsequent years, in proportion as the government has had less tangible benefits to bestow upon the people in return for their strenuous participation in various programs of socialization, the stress has been increasingly upon the people's own political awakening and voluntary enthusiasm for building socialism. To have gained an education under the guidance of the cadres and the Thought of Mao is their sufficient and only reward. In *The Song of Ou-yang Hai,* the party's expectations for the hero are so high that he cannot even enjoy himself for doing good, since such

[22]An abridged English translation is available in *Chinese Literature,* Nos. 7-11 (1966).

[23]The revision of *The White-haired Girl* is discussed in K. S. Karol, *China: The Other Communism* (New York: Hill and Wang, 1967), pp. 257-258.

complacency would promote vanity or pride. Whereas his prototype Lei Feng had a wonderful time doing good deeds and was constantly getting recognition and praise, Ou-yang Hai is repeatedly misjudged by his fellow soldiers and superiors. The author makes it quite explicit that the hero's very desire to excel has to be crushed before he can transform himself into a worthy pupil of Mao, and do the bidding of the party and anonymously perform good deeds on his own without the least trace of self-importance. Ou-yang Hai achieves the true humility of a saint at the end; but it is almost a relief to see him sacrifice his life to prevent a train wreck, because his constant struggle to match his conduct against the word of Mao and the demands of the party is finally brought to an end.

The Song of Ou-yang Hai is not a psychological novel in the Western sense. The hero, though a young bachelor of sturdy health, is incapable of a single frivolous or wayward thought, or even a momentary interest in the opposite sex. But it is definitely a novel of moral introspection in its strikingly neo-Confucian obsession with disinterested virtuous conduct. The problem of how to become a good Communist has almost replaced the problem of how to achieve a Communist society as the overriding concern of the Mao-Lin leadership.

No new novels have been published during the frenzy of the Cultural Revolution. The constant study of Mao's works seemingly displaced the need for any other kind of literature. A few ballets and modern-dress Peking operas produced under the personal supervision of Mao's wife, Chiang Ch'ing, and at the request of the PLA, have been given immense publicity as evidence of a new theater liberated from all bad influences, traditional Chinese as well as modern Western. A group of clay sculptures known as "The Rent Collection Compound," portraying the oppression and revolutionary fervor of poor peasants under Kuomintang rule, has been proudly hailed as an example of the art inspired by Mao's thought.[24] But few other art projects have received similar attention from the press.

Prospects for the Future

In the present lull of cultural activities, it may be instructive to ponder the prospects for literature and art in Communist China, especially in the light of the Cultural Revolution. The purge of the Chou Yang group and the repudiation of nearly all professional writers and artists certainly seems to indicate that the Mao-Lin leadership has been thoroughly disenchanted with culture. The intent of the Cultural Revolution, when viewed in detachment from the political struggles that have occasioned it, is to destroy

---

[24]Photographs of these sculptures appear in *Chinese Literature,* No. 3 (1966), under the title, "The Compound Where Rent Was Collected."

all culture incompatible with Mao's thought: not only the feudal culture of the past, but the modern and leftist traditions upon which Communist culture itself was built.

The need for such drastic action is quite obvious. To the extent that culture implies a respect for man's past and a curiosity about what is going on in other parts of the world, it will be antithetical to the requirements of a political system which intends to remould man from scratch, uninfluenced by the past or by contemporary cultural modes elsewhere. The repeated purges and rectification campaigns prompted by the loyalty of writers and artists to the leftist tradition and their awareness of growing intellectual freedom in the Soviet bloc have demonstrated the impossibility of building a new culture tailored to Maoist requirements so long as such loyalty and awareness remained unextinguished. Mao's growing reliance on part-time writers and artists from among the ranks of the people for the manufacture of a culture compatible with his thought would indicate his belief that, precisely because these amateurs are culturally disadvantaged, they will be the more reliable. While Mao had earlier intended to rescue the Chinese people from their poverty and backwardness, by the late 1950s he appeared to delight in their condition of material poverty and cultural "blankness" precisely because it facilitated the task of totally remoulding them.[25] But no people of China's antiquity, however poor and illiterate, could be culturally blank: hence the necessity to obliterate all signs of historical culture that could remind them of their past.

While cultural orthodoxy is at present maintained by the intense propagation of Mao's thought and the decorative efforts of part-time writers and artists to affirm that thought, one wonders if professionalism—in both the creation and supervision of culture—will not revive with the gradual stabilization of the present regime. So long as there is need for culture to embellish Mao's thought and occupy people's minds when they are not engaged in productive activity, culture, in that sense, will remain a vast enterprise requiring planning and control. Of the new cultural leaders who have effectively replaced the Chou Yang group, Chiang Ch'ing is Mao's wife and Yao Wen-yuan[26] is his son-in-law, and they can be counted on to do his

---

[25]Schwartz makes the following observation: "Precisely because China was 'poor and blank,' precisely because its masses lived a simple, austere life and were fundamentally loyal and amenable to the spiritual influence of their Communist leadership, they might achieve industrial development even while bypassing the corruptions of modern Western industrial civilization. The aims of Robespierre's dictatorship were to achieve the reign of virtue. To Mao the reign of virtue had become both an end and a means. It was an end in itself but it could also be used as a means of achieving an economic leap forward." Benjamin Schwartz, "China and the West in the 'Thought of Mao Tse-tung,'" in Ping-ti Ho and Tang Tsou (eds.), *China in Crisis* (Chicago: University of Chicago Press, 1968), Vol. 1, p. 376.

[26]A key member of the Cultural Revolution Group, Yao Wen-yuan was elected a member of the Politburo at the Ninth Congress of the Chinese Communist Party, held in April 1969.

bidding so long as the Chairman remains alive. But, like the Chou Yang group, the new establishment would in time acquire a degree of autonomy in implementing the cultural line, and they would train a large corps of subordinates to oversee the production of literature and art. And insofar as their obligatory allegiance to the Mao-Lin leadership could not totally extinguish their genuine liking for literature and art, could we not predict that at least some members of the new establishment, like the dissident literary bureaucrats of the 1950s, would want to preserve certain values antithetical to the regime and clamor for a more truthful cultural product incompatible with the aims of Communist education?

Or take the case of Chin Ching-mai. He was originally a member of one of the innumerable cultural units in the PLA. With several others, he wrote a short biography of Ou-yang Hai, and then was assigned the task of writing a full-scale novel about that hero. Now he has become famous and has attended several writers' conferences in Peking. Such conferences are unavoidable since delegations from Albania and several Afro-Asian nations still arrive in Peking to exchange ideas and views with Chinese writers and artists; and since the old guard can no longer attend such sessions, the presence of Chin Ching-mai and other new faces is highly desirable. Is Chin now a professional writer? And given the publicity and attention, will he not in time take himself too seriously as an artist and invite criticism and purge? So long as new professionals are needed for the production and supervision of culture, their inadvertent disobedience and potential dissidence can never be discounted.

For the past twenty years, the making of literature and art has been mainly the responsibility of those who had received their training in pre-Communist days. Prior to the Cultural Revolution, all the important singers in the Peking opera, with the exception of Tu Chin-fang,[27] had been stars before 1949. Among stage and screen actors victimized by the Cultural Revolution, the prominent ones had all achieved great popularity in wartime Chungking or postwar Shanghai. Even among writers who had not published before 1949, most had received their education in the 1930s and 1940s. Since the last twenty years have not produced an abundance of young talent, with the removal of these old professionals the prospects for literature and art look bleak indeed.

When addressing a group of textbook editors in 1961, Chou Yang warned that in breadth of knowledge and culture, his own generation was inferior to that of Liang Ch'i-ch'ao and Hu Shih.[28] And it looked as if "each

[27]Miss Tu Chin-fang was a member of the Peking Opera group which toured France and Canada, among other places, in the 1950s. Other members of the group included such famous singers as Li Shao-ch'un, Yeh Sheng-lan, and Yuan Shih-hai. According to unconfirmed reports, Li Shao-ch'un killed himself in 1966, a victim of the Cultural Revolution.

[28]Both were prominent modern Chinese intellectuals and scholars.

generation will be inferior to the preceding one if you are even less learned than we." He was, of course, speaking the truth. Those who have received all their education under the Communist regime will be even worse prepared. Recent visitors to Communist China like K. S. Karol and Alberto Moravia have revealed the incredible ignorance of the younger writers and artists. Karol met theatrical workers who had never heard of Brecht, Sartre, Ibsen, and Shaw. Totally untrained in Western literature, the younger writers are only slightly better acquainted with their own literary heritage. During the early 1960s, writers were encouraged by Chou Yang to study the approved national classics, but this policy was soon reversed. Today a writer, like everyone else, has very little to read except the works of Mao and a few national newspapers and magazines. Even if he has access to a well-stocked library, he will probably be too busy or too prudent to make much use of it. Even a potential literary genius cannot thrive on a steady diet of Mao and jargon-filled journalism.

In view of the cultural isolationism that deprives the young of their proper intellectual nourishment, the steady deterioration of educational standards, and the probable maintenance of the cult of Mao even if Mao himself passes from the scene, the future health of literature and art on the mainland seems likely to depend solely on the continuing resilience of the human spirit to maintain its sanity, skepticism, and creativity under the most deadening circumstances. But, on the other hand, it would be cruel of us in the West to continue to expect the emergence of dissident writers and artists to demonstrate the survival of that spirit, when the punishment visited upon them and upon all those implicated in their crime will only crush them without alleviating in the least the suffering of their fellow countrymen. Actually, since literature and art in Communist China are designed as a means of education to fill the vacant hours of the people and to reconcile them to the regime, the disappearance of such literature and art or their further deterioration until nobody pays them any attention is, after all, not such a tragedy as some scholars would suppose. It is only when people can freely express their real feelings and thoughts again that it would be realistic to expect the rebirth of a genuine literature and art. As conditions now stand, such a prospect is unlikely.

Chapter Ten

The State of the Intellectuals

Vincent Y. C. Shih

The greatest tragedy is the death of heart; the death of the body is a minor one.

Confucius, Chuangtzu, Ch. 21.

Not to be overwhelmed by riches and honors, not to waver in purpose because of poverty and humbleness, and not to surrender to power and force—these make a MAN.

The Book of Mencius, Vol. 3, Ch. 2.

For over two thousand years, Chinese scholars—the elite of Chinese society and the traditional counterpart of modern intellectuals—struggled against falling into the state Confucius talked about, and stoutly held to the ideals that Mencius formulated. There have been many failures; but there have also been many examples of heroism, fortitude, integrity of character, and martyrdom. Whatever changes may have taken place in modern Chinese society, a great deal of this heroic spirit survives. This is seen especially in the lives of those now confronted with difficulties unparalleled in Chinese history, and who have faced up to them with courage and strength. Undoubtedly many Chinese intellectuals have succumbed to the tyranny of the Communist regime and as such they have ceased to function as intellectuals. But there are a few who fight on with the tactics they know best. It is with them that this essay is chiefly concerned.

During the past twenty years, one of the chief concerns of the Chinese Communist regime has been the intellectuals, how to deal with them, and how either to remake them or to annihilate them. With the exception of the very early period, hardly a year has passed without campaigns of one kind or another aimed at thought reform; and thought reform campaigns have been directed exclusively at the intellectuals. In fact, these ideological campaigns can be taken as a barometer indicating the climate of Communist Chinese society. The fury and deadly seriousness with which they have been carried out not only shows the importance with which the Chi-

221

nese Communists view the problem of the intellectuals; it also indicates both the independent spirit of the intellectuals and the utter determination of the regime to stamp out that spirit. So deep is the antagonism between the Chinese Communists and the intellectuals that there appears to be no future for the latter under the present regime. Such mutual distrust must ultimately work against the regime itself.

The Role of the Intellectuals

Most intellectuals we are dealing with here come from families with a tradition of learning. Many of them are the descendants of the gentry class of traditional China. Many are also returned students from abroad. Most of them have occupied important positions in government, in the academic world, or in other scientific and technical fields. A few are professional writers and playwrights. This last group has been especially prominent as a target of ideological or thought reform campaigns. The intellectuals have lived through tumultuous times; many of them witnessed the tragic events that took place in the first decades of the twentieth century.

They knew that they were the elite, and the most articulate sector in Chinese society. They were proud of their status, and independent of thought. Sensitive to the ugly features of Chinese society around them — political corruption, social injustice, and the plain vulgarity and meanness of people in their dealings with one another — they were aroused by an idealism and a desire to do something about these problems. Their impatience and inevitable frustration generated in them a sense of alienation from the existing regime, and oriented them toward revolution and socialism. But their deepseated, traditional habits of mind never completely forsook them. Imbued with some wisdom and grace because of their education, they tended to be less emotional when confronted with difficult situations, believing that all difficulties should be solved under the guidance of reason. The influence of the West also caused them to value individual freedom and to believe in the dignity of man. They cherished a sense of pride and self-respect. In the modern context, they were particularly sensitive to China's national disgrace, and they had a burning desire to see the dignity of their country restored. This patriotism made them vulnerable to political propaganda and intrigue. Their response to what they considered to be a repressive regime was generally to withdraw to academic life or to careers as artists or writers. A few, however, turned revolutionary, and thought they were fighting for personal freedom.

Throughout Chinese history, Chinese scholars always had a clear vision of their role in society. It was to serve the state and the people. This same vision characterizes the modern Chinese intellectual. For similar reasons, both the traditional scholar and his modern counterpart experienced more frustration and alienation than success. But there are significant differences between them. It is true that most traditional scholars were greatly concerned with the welfare of the people. The Confucian conception of *jen* is an eloquent plea for benevolent government in the interests of the people. But the absolute loyalty which traditional scholars felt for the ruler or the dynasty tended to confuse them in choosing a course of action. In the case of modern intellectuals, there was no such confusion. For them, the state was the people; and being more articulate and more discerning of the causes of things, they felt it was their duty to speak for the people. This sense of responsibility to the unfortunate, of messianic mission to work for the welfare of the people, was awakened in them by the sight of "a people who had suffered untold misery in muted silence for thousands of years."[1] The ancient precept to "love the people" still rang in their hearts, without their realizing that such an idea might be anachronistic in the modern world. They became at once bitter critics of the existing government, and advocates of reform and new directions to meet the changing tides of the world. They considered themselves idea men, whose task was to point out a new course.

But being deeply rooted in the past, they often vacillated between an attempt to preserve traditional values, and an all-out effort to bring in a new order. Their nostalgia for home, their love and respect for their parents and the members of their families, their memories of the security and comforts of home in their early years, combined to make them doubtful assets to the Communists. They considered themselves leaders in the fields of art and literature, and of culture in general; they set the norms of taste. But at the same time, they recognized the aesthetic freedom of each and every person to create according to his inner light. If there was any utilitarian tinge to their theory of art and literature, it was so generally conceived that the theory did not become a strait jacket to creativity.

The Intellectuals and the Communists

The Chinese Communist concept of intellectuals and their role in society offers them no significant future under a Communist regime. For two reasons, the Communists have looked upon the intellectuals with suspicion: because of their class origins, which made them a target for class struggle; and because of Communist political philosophy, in the light of which the intellectuals did not inspire complete confidence. Mao Tse-tung has made a number of observations about the intellectuals. He comments that they had a keen political sensitivity. They were seldom satisfied with the status

---

[1]Vincent Y.C. Shih, "China's Heritage," in *China* (San Francisco: Association for Sino-American Cultural Cooperation, 1967).

quo, usually opposed the existing regime, and loved to ventilate their pent-up frustrations. But they knew only what they learned from reading; theirs was a bookish knowledge, idealistic and impractical. They cultivated a subjective individualism and self-conceit. They were proud of their status, and unwilling to cooperate with workers and farmers. At one time, they were useful to the Communists and offered real assistance in the struggle for power. But because of their bourgeois background, they tended to change course at critical moments. It is conceivable that they might even become the enemy of the proletariat; and, indeed, some of them have already done so.[2]

Such is Mao's opinion of the intellectuals. The first emperor of the Han dynasty despised scholars; Mao, in addition, hates them. And he, in turn, has earned their eternal hatred. There is no point in discussing Mao's misconceptions about the intellectuals; in China today, whatever comes from Mao, be it truth or falsehood, has to be accepted as gospel. In the light of such views, what future can the intellectuals expect in Mao's China?

To begin with, it is difficult to imagine why the intellectuals ever allowed themselves to be drawn into the Communist quagmire. On the other hand, it is perhaps the wisdom of hindsight to see the impossibility of the survival of intellectual integrity under Communist rule. When the Communists took over in 1949, the intellectuals had little direct experience with them. Their naive idealism and patriotism led them to believe that all the ills of the country had come to an end with the change of regime. Partly in response to Communist propaganda, and partly because of their own naiveté, they allowed themselves to hope that the Communists would provide the leadership to bring about the unity of the country, to restore its dignity among the family of nations, and to eliminate corruption and do away with injustice. Non-Communist political parties joined with the Communists in a coalition government; scientists flocked home from abroad; journalists and writers, some of whom had fled to Hong Kong and elsewhere, came back and offered their services for the rebuilding of China. Even the "national industrialists," as the Communists called them, stayed on to operate their factories as usual.

As for the Communists themselves, they have never wavered in their fundamental policy toward the intellectuals. As early as 1939, they said:[3]

Intellectuals and semi-intellectuals who are *useful in various degrees* and who are basically *loyal* should be given appropriate work, *trained*

[2]See Wang Chang-ling, "Mao kung ti chih-shih fen-tzu cheng-ts'e" (Mao's Policy Concerning the Intellectuals), *Fei-ch'ing Yueh-k'an* (Communist Information Monthly), Vol. 11, No. 9 (October 1968).

[3]Quoted in Mu Fu-sheng, *The Wilting of the Hundred Flowers* (New York: Praeger, 1963), p. 213. Emphasis added.

adequately and *led* gradually to *correct* their weaknesses in the course of our sustained struggle, in order to enable them to *remould* themselves to *adopt* truly the point of view of the people and to *get along* with the veteran party members and other members of worker and peasant stock.

Looking back from the vantage point of 1970, we can see with crystal clarity that the Chinese Communists meant every single word they uttered in 1939. But few intellectuals had the prophetic vision to see things which, in the light of what has happened since, were so clearly indicated by these words. Of course the Communists needed the intellectuals; but their idea of the role of the intellectuals differed radically from what the intellectuals themselves aspired to. The initial harmony did not last long. From 1951 on, scarcely a year has gone by that has not witnessed "movements" of one sort or another aimed at remoulding the intellectuals in conformity with the image the Communists had already cast for them in 1939. There is no need here to retell the sordid story of "brain-washing." What did the Communists intend to accomplish by their thought reform movements, and in what sense did their method of brain-washing differ from the traditional self-examination which some writers have sought to identify as the source of inspiration?

No political machinery can function properly without the service of the intellectuals or their equivalent. At the outset of a new regime, the Communists recognized that they needed the assistance of the intellectuals to man the bureaucracy. They also knew very well what the reaction of the intellectuals would be when they found out what they were in for under the Communist regime. To forestall the possibility of a rebellious reaction, the Communists sought to transform the intellectuals into willing puppets who followed the Communist line with blind obedience and even a show of enthusiasm. This meant that they had to root out the qualities that were most distinctive of the intellectuals, and to do so by means ruthless and relentless enough to assure success. By group criticism and self-criticism, by forced confessions both written and oral, by insults and humiliation, by threats and cajolery, the Communists sought to kill the intellectuals' pride and self-respect. For days and weeks and months on end, they would be kept in suspense about their fate, until at last they became nervous wrecks, or as the Communists would put it, a rebirth or a new sense of values dawned upon them. After having been so thoroughly remade, the Communists thought that the intellectuals would then "willingly" and "voluntarily" offer their "hearts" and service to the party without any further reservations. In other words, the Communists expected the intellectuals to negate their own scale of values, and redirect their loyalty to the Communist regime. Undoubtedly many intellectuals did succumb to such treatment. But as we shall see, not a few reacted in a way that drove the Communists finally to purge them all and to launch a new attempt to train their own brand of intellectuals.

It is tempting to compare Communist brain-washing to the traditional self-examination we find in the Confucian *Analects,* or in neo-Confucianism. In view of the purpose and some of the results, there seems to be enough similarity, if not to identify them, at least to classify them together as instances of the same principle. But in reality, the similarity is only apparent. The conditions under which the examination is carried on vary so radically that they are in fact two entirely different methods for bringing about a change in human nature. Traditional self-examination was conducted under complete self-control, without the application of coercive force. Such freedom is completely absent in Communist thought reform. Here, with the sword of Damocles hanging over their heads, the intellectuals either have to succumb — or else.

Some Victims of Thought Reform

Fung Yu-lan, a philosopher of considerable depth and originality, had to confess that everything he wrote was wrong. In his later writings, phrases like "feudal morality" and "the struggle between materialism and idealism" are met at every turn. To him, the history of Chinese philosophy has now been reduced to a simple conflict between the materialist and idealist schools. Mencius and Lu Hsiang-shan,[4] representatives of the idealist school, emerge as proletarian prophets simply because Mencius once said, "Every man can become Yao and Shun,"[5] and Lu once said, "In the street all people are sages." Without showing the classical reason behind these statements, Fung goes on to argue that, "From this point of view (that is, from the fact that they considered the people to be sages), the philosophy of the school of Lu Hsiang-shan and Wang should not be simply denied in its entirety."[6] Fung's intention is reasonably clear. Despite the autocratic nature of the regime, the Communists would like the outside world to believe that there is real freedom in mainland China. Fung's vindication of idealism, even though only a partial one, served to give substance to that claim; while the emphasis placed on the "people," however shallow in thinking, conformed to the Communist line. But for Fung, there must have been a private satisfaction in showing up the eagerness with which the

[4]Mencius (371–289 B.C.) and Lu Hsiang-shan (1139–93) were both Confucian idealists.

[5]Yao and Shun were legendary sages.

[6]Quoted in Wing-tsit Chan, *A Source Book in Chinese Philosophy* (Princeton: Princeton University Press, 1963), p. 779. Wang Yang-ming (1472-1528) was an idealist philosopher of the Ming dynasty.

Communists accepted rubbish for truth, provided only that it had some relationship to what was dear to their hearts.

Chin Yueh-lin, another philosopher of great renown, wrote a "confession" in 1951 entitled *Criticizing My Bourgeois Pedagogical Ideology*.[7] In actuality, this document is as clever as Liu Shao-ch'i's in 1966,[8] and Li Ssu's in 208 B.C.,[9] for all of them, while ostensibly denouncing their mistakes, were taking stock of their merits in the very process of self-incrimination. Chin categorically condemned himself as a confirmed individualist whose "extremely depraved epicurean, liberalist, and bourgeois ideology of striving after individual freedom" was the source of the numerous crimes he had committed against the people. He denounced himself for his bourgeois views on education and for turning out such students as Yin Fu-sheng, Shen Yueh-(Yu-)ting and Wang Hao, all brilliant logicians. "From now on, however, I shall strive to become a new man and a teacher of the people in substance as well in name. I shall exert myself to study, as well to work, for one year, two years, three years, or even five or ten years. Provided I am able to keep up my efforts, I shall ultimately succeed." His guilt-laden language in explaining why the new Communist curriculum had taken so long to put into effect at Tsinghua University speaks well of his courage, as Dean of the College of Arts and Chairman of the Department of Philosophy, in resisting the party's determined effort to transform Tsinghua into a training ground for the dissemination of Marxism-Leninism. Indeed, insofar as his "confession" was presented without supporting evidence, he lost none of his intellectual integrity despite the extravagance of his language. In the mind of a discriminating reader, his statement makes a mockery of the Communist effort at thought reform.

Intellectuals within the Communist Party have not been overlooked when there was any evidence of unorthodox thinking. Whether he was a member of the party or not, Hu Feng had always been considered a comrade, and had worked for the party against the Kuomintang since the early 1930s. But he was one of those who could not shed his aesthetic conscience completely, even though he thought of himself as a faithful follower of Mao and the Communists. His opposition to the stifling control that the party bureaucrats imposed on literary and artistic production may be called a loyal opposition. All he wanted to bring about was a little more freedom for writers and artists to express themselves, because he believed that excessive literary control would inevitably suffocate the vitality of art and lit-

---

[7]Chin's "confession" is reproduced in Robert Jay Lifton, *Thought Reform and the Psychology of Totalism* (New York: Norton, 1961), pp. 473–484.

[8]See "Self-Criticism" (October 23, 1966), in *Collected Works of Liu Shao-ch'i, 1958–1967* (Hong Kong: Union Research Institute, 1968), pp. 357–364.

[9]See Ssu-ma Ch'ien, *Shih-chi* (Historical Records), T'ung-wen edition, Ch. 87, pp. 19–20.

erature. He had at one time compared the various forms of control to five knives, threatening to snuff out creative activities in China. Hu Feng was not opposed to the party or its leadership; but he could not remain silent. Like the censors of imperial times, he was willing to risk his life for beliefs in remonstrating against the ruler. Confident that his past services to the party would win for him the support of the Communist leaders, and apparently unaware that these leaders were more autocratic than the most dictatorial traditional rulers, he presented a report to the Central Committee in 1954 which ultimately proved to be his undoing.[10]

In this report, he offered his own definition of communism as a flexible system of ideas responding to the ever-changing needs of the people. He viewed Socialist realism in terms of humanism and a humanistic concern with man and his emancipation. And he considered everything and everyone as suitable themes for writers, not just the lives of workers, peasants, and soldiers, provided only that the subject was approached in a way not extraneous to art and literature. Hu Feng also thought that literature should be concerned with the sufferings of the people, and not just with the bright side of things. Thus he denied the Communist claim that in a Communist society everything always went well, and there was nothing to expose and everything to praise and glorify. Finally, he believed that organized thought reform should not be directed at the writers, who should be liberated from dogmatism and given greater freedom to develop their talents.

All this was anathema to the Communists, and Hu's purge was slow but certain. Before the presentation of his report, he was always referred to as Comrade Hu, and he was criticized for nothing more serious than being "erroneous," a state considered to be salvageable by a return to the orthodox line. After the report, he was labelled a counter-revolutionary who attacked the party and its policies, and who had worked as a leader of the imperialist and Kuomintang secret services and as a commander of the anti-Communist, anti-masses underground. Eventually he was arrested, and he has never been heard of again. Nonetheless, criticism of his sins has continued with intensified fury; and those who have failed to join the chorus have been questioned for keeping silent. Commenting on the Communists' utilization of Hu's purge as an object lesson to the intellectuals, Robert Guillain states that the pressure "was so great . . . that many people's nerves gave way; suicides were frequent, for instance, in the cultural organization where I am employed." And again, ". . . certain intellectuals, well-known professors, . . . were in a terrible state. I've seen them tremble like leaves. They lived in terror of these compulsory sessions."[11]

---

[10]Hu Feng's report has never been published. His ideas are culled from *Hu Feng wen-i ssu-hsiang p'i-p'an lun-wen hui-chi* (Criticisms of Hu Feng's Literary and Art Theories) (Peking: Workers Press, 1955).

[11]Robert Guillain, *600 Million Chinese* (New York: Criterion Books, 1957), p. 176.

Ting Ling, a winner of the Stalin prize in 1948, followed the path of Hu Feng to oblivion in 1957, because of her beliefs in individualism, the importance of intrinsic literary merit, and freedom from bureaucratic leadership. Doubtless she also suffered because of her animosity toward Chou Yang, who was the Communist literary tsar until he himself was purged (along with many of his cohorts) during the Great Proletarian Cultural Revolution. Ting Ling was accused of involvement in a conspiracy against the party, removed from all her official positions, and deprived of her rights as a writer and citizen. In the end, she was sentenced to two years of labor reform in northern Manchuria.

The Hundred Flowers Movement

What lay behind the Hundred Flowers movement is only partially clear. The Communists, like everyone else, recognized that working under repressive conditions was bound to affect the efficiency of the intellectuals; and they were too valuable to the regime simply to ignore the problem. Furthermore, it was possible to reason that the intellectuals had been cowed to the extent that the promise of a little more freedom might at last induce them to cooperate voluntarily. Or the Communist leaders, Mao in particular, might have concluded that the silence of repression was not healthy for the state. With the recent Hungarian and Polish uprisings still fresh in the minds of the intellectuals, a chance to let off a little steam would ease their anxiety and give them at least the illusion of enjoying the freedom of speech they valued so much. Or Mao might have thought that the regime had become so firmly established both politically and ideologically, and had achieved such success in the field of national reconstruction, that the cause of the Communists had been vindicated beyond challenge. Also, the intellectuals would have seen the light, and would come out willingly to do honor to the regime by singing its praises. Or again, the Hundred Flowers movement may have been a sinister scheme on the part of the party leaders to smoke out the dissenters in order to mark them for liquidation. At any rate, there was no danger that there would be too much deviation from the party line, since the conditions for the expression of opinion were set in such a way that criticism was not to be directed against either the party or the party line.

The pandemonium which followed came as a complete surprise to the Communists. Beginning with mild criticism, the chorus of dissent gradually grew in intensity, until at last it assumed tempestuous proportions in which all restraint was thrown to the winds. Criticism turned into accusation, and much of the protest showed a definite rebellious intent. The total failure of the Communist regime to remake the intellectuals, and the depths of their hostility toward it, was demonstrated beyond the possibility of doubt. The confessions, self-criticisms, and self-denunciations were seen to be a mere charade enabling the intellectuals to comply outwardly with what the regime had required, while within them the spirit of independence still remained strong. The outburst also demonstrated how completely the Communists had misjudged the intellectuals, and this is difficult to understand when we recall that many of the Chinese Communist leaders were once intellectuals themselves.

The protests came from a wide range of intellectuals, including journalists, scholars, medical doctors, students, writers, civil servants, members of the surviving non-Communist parties, leaders of various religious and national minority groups, besides businessmen, peasants and workers. But for their protests, the outside world would never have known the extent to which the intellectuals have been subjected to suppression, and the intensity of their feelings against the regime. In general, their allegations may be summarized under two main categories, ideological and political. The main ideological criticism was that Marxism-Leninism, like every other philosophy, does not embody the whole truth. Blind faith in it regardless of specific circumstances constitutes formalism and doctrinairism, both of which the Communists themselves were supposedly trying to get rid of.

Political criticisms formed an endless list. Some called for genuine opposition parties to keep watch over the way the Communists were handling the affairs of state. Others complained that the constitution was treated as a scrap of paper. There were no legal safeguards for civil rights. The democracy promised by the constitution should be implemented forthwith. The press criticized the way in which the regime flagrantly manipulated the news. Newspapers were no more than gramophones or bulletin boards for official news releases. The whole concept of thought reform was attacked. One critic said, "I find thought reform rather repulsive. . . . I am not aware that there is anything wrong with my thought." The practice was described as "rotten to the core," an "assault on the person."

The Communist Party was called upon to admit its mistakes in humiliating, imprisoning, and even executing many thousands of innocent people. Relations between the Communist leadership and the people were denounced as comparable to those between masters and slaves. Criticism itself was seen to be a joke. To invite criticism "within the party line" was like sealing one's mouth while asking one to speak. Non-party people were said to be discriminated against in terms of job opportunities, salary, and promotion. Professional people complained about the interference of party cadres in their work. Members of non-Communist political parties in the government protested that they were treated as rubber stamps, and that all power was concentrated in the hands of Communist Party members.

Ko P'ei-ch'i of the China People's University expressed the sentiment of many when he said:[12]

> When the Communist Party entered the city in 1949, the common people welcomed it with food and drink and looked upon it as a benevolent force. Today, the common people choose to estrange themselves from the Communist Party as if its members were gods and devils. . . . The party members behave like plain-clothes police and place the masses under their surveillance. . . . If the Communist Party distrusted me, the distrust would be mutual. China belongs to 600,000,000 people including the counter-revolutionaries. It does not belong to the Communist Party alone.

A Professor Yang Shih-chan addressed a ten-thousand-word letter to Chairman Mao detailing the grievances of the intellectuals, of which the following are two pertinent excerpts:[13]

> Our constitution provides that citizens "enjoy freedom of residence and freedom to change residence." In fact, we have not given any of the 500 million peasants the freedom to change their residence to a city. . . .
> Again, our constitution provides that "freedom of the person of citizens is inviolable." During the campaign for the suppression of counter-revolutionaries in 1955, an untold number of citizens throughout the country were detained by the units where they were working. . . . A great many of them died because they could not endure the struggle . . . this was after all a serious violation of human rights. . . .
> This is tyranny! This is malevolence!
> . . . the articles of the constitution on human rights have become a sort of window-dressing to deceive the people.
> . . . We have simply become ballot-casting machines. . . .

After reporting the fact that many intellectuals now bitterly regretted that they had not listened to the advice of friends to flee to Taiwan at the time of the Communist "liberation," the letter continues:

> In the last seven years, they [the intellectuals] have lived like a girl being brought up under her future mother-in-law in the home of her fiance, constantly trembling in fear. . . .

[12]Quoted in Roderick MacFarquhar, *The Hundred Flowers Campaign and the Chinese Intellectuals* (New York: Praeger, 1960), p. 87.
[13]Quoted in *ibid.,* p. 94.

We have applied to intellectuals methods of punishment which peasants would not apply to landlords and workers would not apply to capitalists. During the social reform campaigns, unable to endure the spiritual torture and humiliation imposed by the struggle . . . the intellectuals who chose to die by jumping from tall buildings, drowning in rivers, swallowing poison, cutting their throats or by other methods were innumerable. . . . Comparing our method of massacre with that adopted by the fascists of Auschwitz, the latter appeared more clumsy and childish . . . but more prompt and "benevolent." If we say that Comrade Stalin has not escaped from condemnation in history for his cruel massacre of comrades, then our party, in my opinion, will also be condemned for our massacre of intellectuals . . . who had already "surrendered" themselves to us. Our party's massacre of intellectuals and the mass burying alive of the *literati* by the tyrant, Ch'in Shih-huang, will go down in China's history as two ineradicable stigma.

The tone of this letter, and the allegations listed in it, give some impression of the state of the intellectuals in Communist China in the mid-1950s.

The Fate of Scientists and Writers

Scientists, like other intellectuals, are needed by any regime. But for the same reasons that all other intellectuals have been considered suspect by the Chinese Communist regime, the scientists, too, are held to be unreliable. They, too, have had to go through thought reform in order to be considered worthy of the regime, or to be able to serve the people. Although the Communists, before the Hundred Flowers period, reluctantly acknowledged the classless nature of science so as to induce scientists to join the movement, their subsequent policies show this to have been simply a tactical move. The scientists have been accused of bourgeois liberalism, individualism, and entertaining "above politics" and "purely technical" viewpoints. Through criticism and self-criticism, the Communists have tried to make them see that science, like everything else, is a handmaid of politics, and that technical expertise should be subordinated to "redness." Theory in itself has no value unless it is employed in the service of production under the leadership of the party. All scientific work should be integrated under a master plan worked out by the state. Unless it is directly relevant to the political life of the state, basic research, theoretical inquiry, higher mathematics, and the like are all evidence of bourgeois thinking and have no place in a Communist society.

Concrete cases abound in Communist newspapers and learned journals reporting self-criticism and confessions by scientists and their determination to get rid of their wrong attitudes, such as a belief in expertise before "redness," or individualism and the desire for personal fame and profit, and, before the split with Moscow, unwillingness to learn from the Russians. All self-denunciations agreed on the all-important point that scientists should accept the leadership of the Communist Party and that science must be integrated with production. Many scientists were told to learn from "countrified experts," that is, from those who possessed practical ingenuity rather than theoretical knowledge or understanding. In reality, what the Chinese Communists are really looking for is not science but applied technology.

The ideological struggle against the scientists was especially intense in relation to the problem of "redness" versus technical expertise. While the party repeatedly emphasized the absolute necessity of having science under political leadership, the scientists constantly voiced their concern about the state of science if party ignoramuses should be allowed to dominate the scientific scene. During the Hundred Flowers period, a group of scientists presented a program which later came to be known as the "Anti-Party Anti-Socialist Scientific Program." This program implied sharp criticisms of party control over science. It appealed for greater freedom in research along specialized lines, and for the encouragement of younger students by placing greater emphasis on academic achievement than on political qualifications when they were being considered for job opportunities or for promotion. In 1958, an editorial in *Kuang-ming Jih-pao* called for a campaign "to liquidate the bourgeois medical tradition, to establish the proletarian science of hygiene, to pull down the white flag and raise the red flag." When even medicine has to submit to political control, one can imagine what was taking place in other scientific and technical fields.

A few examples of confessions made by scientists will show the state they were in, and also the kinds of subterfuge they employed to counter the Communist onslaught. The head of the Department of Electrical Engineering at Tsinghua University made the following confession:[14]

In a recent forum, I said, "The party sometimes treats us with courtesy, at other times with indifference, and it is hard to understand why ... I used to think that the party stood in front to lead, now I feel that it is standing behind us and driving us with a whip. . . ." In another forum, I said, "Most of the cadres are not familiar with problems of teaching; if we rely on them entirely for the administration of the school, the people of the nation will suffer a big loss and the schools will not be well run." I now realize what a lowly creature I have been. I belong to the people. I resolve to give myself to the people, to surrender my heart to the party.

[14]Quoted in *ibid.*

What is really interesting about this statement is not the author's new-found resolution, but what he had to say at previous forums.

Hua Lo-keng, who spent some time with Einstein at the Institute for Advanced Study at Princeton, had this to say in a confession made to atone for his part in the drafting of the scientists' Anti-Party Anti-Socialist Scientific Program:[15]

> Our Communist Party is the political party of Marxism and Marxism is the universal scientific truth. Consequently, the party itself is the product of science, and by virtue of its pronounced scientific nature, it can surely lead the people of the whole world toward victory in every part of the struggle.

Hua's ultimate purge in the 1960s indicates that the Communists did not forgive him for this satire of syllogistic reasoning. Mao I-sheng, Director of the Institute for Railway Science, had to write a confessional article in 1957 entitled *The Party is Completely Capable of Offering Leadership to Science*. The title of his paper speaks for itself.

Ch'ien Hsueh-shen, once Professor of Aerodynamics at both M.I.T. and the California Institute of Technology, resorted to vituperative invective in his condemnation of a fellow scientist. "He is a liar and a time-server," he said. "He has not the least spirit of a scientist. He is a most noxious and virulent Machiavellian." We shall see that Lao She, one of the group of writers to be dealt with next, used the same tactic in attacking Wu Tsu-kuang, a playwright, as a "rightist." Why did they do it if they did not mean what they said? To say that there is no right to silence, as Dr. Hu Shih did when his son condemned him, is only half the answer. The other half lies in a profound subterfuge which will be discussed below in connection with the writers.

In all the Communist attacks on the scientists, the nuclear scientists were treated with special consideration. Even during the Cultural Revolution, the latter were—for awhile, at least—immune from the attacks of the Red Guards. But recently they, too, have found themselves the targets of violence. Ch'ien San-ch'iang, head of the Atomic Energy Institute, has been accused of being a "secret enemy agent." The Institute's Deputy Director, Wang Kan-ch'ang, has also been criticized. Marshal Nieh Jung-chen, Chairman of the Scientific and Technological Commission—the man most responsible for coordinating the nuclear weapons program—is another victim. Hua Lo-keng, Director of the Institute of Mathematics; Pei Li-sheng, Vice-President of the Chinese Academy of Sciences; and Tu Jun-

---

[15]See his article in *Jen-min Jih-pao,* June 8, 1969; and his "Chairman Mao Points Out the Road of Advance for Me," *China Reconstructs* (Peking), Vol. 18, No. 11 (November 1969).

sheng, Secretary-General of the Academy, all have been arrested. The charges against them are vague and general, and the attacks appear to be a part of the general anti-intellectualism campaign. The current attitude is typified by the widespread quotation of a Maoist axiom to justify the campaign: "The lowly are most intelligent; the elite are most ignorant."

In any society, the writers have always been the most articulate of all intellectuals. In the Chinese tradition, too, the power of the pen is more awesome than the sword because, unlike the effect of a sword which is limited to the present, a pen cuts deep into posterity in the form of an historical verdict. Mao Tse-tung's literary and artistic views, as expressed in 1942 at the Yenan Forum on Literature and Art, are discussed elsewhere in the present volume.[16] It is against this ideological background that the opinions expressed by the writers during the Hundred Flowers period are interesting as indicating the intensity of their hostility to the regime, and the failure of the Communists to make them over into faithful cogs in the Communist machine.

Their criticisms can be briefly summarized. Mao's literary pronouncements at Yenan in 1942 could no longer be considered valid in the 1950s. To limit the subject matter of literature only to certain aspects of the lives of workers, peasants, and soldiers was pure doctrinairism and paralyzing to creative activity. Literature and art could not be made to play the mechanical role of serving a certain policy. One writer asked:[17]

> Do we mean to say that the workers, peasants, and soldiers have no "domestic affairs and boy-and-girl romances?" Do we mean to say that we must only use the following type of subject matter when we are writing about workers: "The furnace fire is flaming red, the wheel of the engine is turning, the iron press is clanging. . . .?" Do we mean to say that in writing about the peasants we can only use the following type of subject matter: "Ahem! Ahem! Ahem! Let's exert ourselves and work with renewed vigor, so that the produce will be an inch taller?"

For them, there could be only one answer. The true value of literature was determined by its intellectual significance expressed through artistic forms, as well as by its power of persuasion.

Nearly all the writers complained about party control, which explained why most of them remained silent. Party leadership was described as "uncouth and tyrannical, ignorant but pretentious." There were too many political distractions, too many "pay attentions" and "considerations" in one's head, so that "one's personal intentions get smaller and smaller." Dramatists, too, complained about party control. "The road block in the way of progress of dramatic groups today is the fact that certain leading

[16]See pp. 205–206, above.
[17]Quoted in MacFarquhar, *op. cit.,* pp. 179–180.

comrades are ignorant of the arts, and they do not lead a dramatic group in a manner appropriate to the special characteristics of artistic organizations."

Some writers were worried about the cultural heritage of China, and the general disregard for the country's cultural treasures. One commented that "hundreds and thousands of books have been dumped in stores to rot without being sorted; this is really heartrending." It used to be thought that the Communists had done well in the publication of classical literary works and art catalogues. Now we begin to see that the purpose of these publications was economic rather than cultural. The regime looked upon these publications primarily as a source of foreign exchange. What would these writers say about the depredations of the Red Guards and Mao's current rejection of anything that is traditional?

The anti-rightist campaign came to a temporary halt in 1960 and 1961. Schools and colleges were asked to reinstate their teachers and old professors. The interruption of education during the campaign was seen to have damaged the reconstruction effort. People with technical knowledge were desperately needed, and the schools were not turning them out fast enough. Moreover, the regime was beset with difficulties in both the agricultural and industrial sectors. Even Mao could not afford to rock the boat in such circumstances. But this thaw turned out to be merely a lull before another storm swept across the mainland with unparalleled fury, leaving in its wake chaos and confusion. What interests us here is neither the Red Guards and their destructive activities, nor even the Cultural Revolution itself. We are mainly concerned with the reassertion of the heroic spirit, which Mencius held up as the proper ideal of man, in the lives of many writers during this tragic episode.

Even before the storm broke out, intellectuals were already feeling renewed political pressure. In May 1962, Pa Chin published a rigorous complaint against political interference in literary activity. According to him, small groups of people turned up from nowhere the moment anyone opened his mouth or picked up his pen, with a hoop in one hand and a club in the other, the hoop to trap him with and the club to hit him on the head. Because of this interference, fear was generated in the minds of many writers, including himself. Pa Chin deplored the fact that he had not written much, but at the same time he felt uneasily fortunate in not having written much. Like so many other writers, his main concern was not in what he could achieve but in how he could avoid faults. This fear of exposing oneself to the fault finders paralyzed all creative impulse. It forced writers to act cautiously. Pa Chin then urged his fellow writers to muster enough courage to throw off this fear and to write creatively again. In an apparently sincere and serious tone, he declared: "I must do some serious writing and attach importance to writers' courage and sense of responsibility. . . .

Writers of New China in particular, should be concerned with more important things than merely avoiding faults."[18]

The Writers and Political Criticism

Political criticism has been an important literary function since the time Han scholars began to write their commentaries on the *Book of Odes.* A late classical scholar wrote:[19]

> Poetry may either praise or censure. Censure poetry takes many forms, each with its own distinct pattern; it may criticize directly, or by subtle satire, or by giving unreserved praise. A praise-censure poem may sound like any other praise poem; but the discrepancy between the factual course of events and what the poem portrays would make it obvious that it is intended to be a criticism.

Another form of criticism in traditional China was "cursing the locust while pointing to the mulberry," a picturesque way of describing an oblique satirical attack, usually under the cloak of another era in history.

The writer Lao She used both forms of criticism with great skill; and his work may be taken as representative of the genre. His play *Hsi wang Ch'ang-an* employs direct criticism. The title, a partial quotation from a line of Li Po's poem, is a satire in itself.[20] By suppressing the second half of the line and by substituting a homophone for the last character, Lao She turned a nostalgic line into a satirical jibe. Instead of "Looking west to Ch'ang-an I do not see my home," it now reads, "Looking west to Ch'ang-an, nothing is good." Ch'ang-an, the capital of the T'ang dynasty, was located in the same general area as Yenan, the wartime capital of the Communists. The implied message is: Communism is no good.

Lao She also criticized while hiding behind the cloak of history, as in the play *Ch'a-kuan,* which is the name of a famous teahouse in Peking. As one commentator puts it:

> The teahouse is used to link three periods in modern Chinese history. . . . Through the words of the customers who frequent the teahouse and the ever-declining fortune of the teahouse itself, the author unrolls before the audience an increasingly sad picture of China, demonstrating the truth of a statement which the Communists have tried hard to

---

[18]Quoted in Vincent Y.C. Shih, "Enthusiast and Escapist: Writers of the Older Generation," *China Quarterly,* No. 13 (January–March 1963), p. 107.

[19]Wang Hsien-ch'ien, *Shih san-chia-i chi-su* (Collected Commentaries on the Interpretations of the Three Schools of Poetry), photo-lithographic edition (Taipei: 1957), Vol. 1, p. 1.

[20]Li Po (699–762) was a famous poet of the T'ang dynasty.

combat during the Anti-Rightist campaign: "The present is not as good as the past." The activities of secret service men, the lack of food, the tragic circumstances of one's inability to even heed the sick and the hungry, the plight faced by the national industrialists whose factories are confiscated, these and many other conditions portrayed combine to give a picture more fittingly applicable to the present than to the old.

Lao's use of the technique of censure by praise is found in the following case, which is really an indirect jibe at Mao Tse-tung himself. After praising the poetry of Shakespeare in the West and Tu Fu and Li Po in China,[21] he cites a modern doggerel praising Mao Tse-tung as equal to all of them in beauty and profundity. The jibe is obvious when one contrasts the vulgar quality of the poem and the extravagant language Lao She uses to enumerate its "exquisite" qualities.[22]

Lao She could bring in criticism where it was least expected. In a discussion on rhetoric, he said:[23]

> A sentence is in itself a complete entity. . . . Take for example: "For the convenience to exercise control, use the intellectuals like slaves." Every word in this sentence is all right, and as a sentence, it is not bad either. But it is not complete, and cannot stand alone as a complete entity. "Who" is working for this convenience to exercise control, and "Who" use the intellectuals like slaves? Since the author does not make these points clear, we have to guess, and the sentence becomes a riddle.

In illustrating how to make a long-winded sentence concise, Lao She used this example: "[This] not only deprives people of their wealth, a physical robbery; besides, [this] also deprives people of their spiritual food." The corrected sentence: "[This] not only deprives people of their physical wealth, it deprives them of their spiritual food as well." There can be no question of Lao She's satirical intent in using these examples.

During the Anti-Rightist campaign, Wu Tsu-kuang, a playwright, came under fire because he objected to the "leadership" of cadres who did not know anything about dramatic art. Lao She picked up the party line and lambasted Wu:[24]

---

[21]Tu Fu (712-770) was also a T'ang dynasty poet.

[22]Lao She, *Fu-hsing-chi* (Peking: Peking Publishing House, 1958), p. 32. The doggerel runs (in translation):

> The East is red,
> The sun rises,
> In China appears a certain Mao Tse-tung.

[23]*Ibid.*, pp. 37-38.

[24]*Ibid.*, p. 204.

Wu Tsu-kuang, you who have been called a bright star in a muddy world! Formerly you had no prospect, now you have even less. In the old society there was a toilet pit, so maggots could thrive. In our new society there is not only no public toilet pit, neither are there any maggots. All flies will also be destroyed. Wu Tse-kuang! Repent!

Obviously there is more here than meets the eye. By allying himself with the Communists and speaking for them, the writer's stupidity really becomes theirs. With one masterful stroke, he succeeds in holding up the imbecility of the Communist regime for all to see.

The playwrights T'ien Han and Wu Han both used historical themes to criticize the regime. In 1956, T'ien wrote *There is a Need to Show an Earnest Concern Regarding the Livelihood of Artists and a Desire to Improve It.* This article was an effort to bring the plight of actors and actresses to the attention of the authorities in the hope that something could be done about it. In it, he exposed the sad situation which had led some actors in local guilds of Hunan and Kwangsi to commit suicide. And in 1957, when Wu Tsu-kuang was liquidated, T'ien showed a great deal of sympathy for Wu. His play *Kuan Han-ch'ing,* written a year later, contained such lines as these: "Grievance and injustice like this are repeatedly reenacted even now;" and again, "This is indeed a rotten time. Evil ones live on in countless number but good fellows are picked off one by one." For such commentary, T'ien had been subjected to severe party criticism. But with the appearance of *Hsieh Yao-huan* in 1961, his work became marked as a poisonous weed, symbolic of the counter-revolutionary spirit.

In *Hsieh Yao-huan,* T'ien Han sings the praises of Hsieh Yao-huan, a woman official during the reign of Empress Wu of the T'ang dynasty. Hsieh Yao-huan has memorialized the throne to take speedy measures to help a severely harassed people. As the play proceeds, T'ien Han describes how the officials treat the people like fish and meat in their effort to deprive them of their land, in consequence of which the air was filled with resentment. Empress Wu is criticized for listening to the sycophants, while victimizing the loyal and upright ministers; for her love of travel, which drains the state treasury; and for her unquenchable ambition manifested in the attempt to erect a huge memorial to herself by collecting metal from the people, including even their ploughs and hoes, making it impossible for them to farm their land. It is perfectly clear that T'ien Han intended to use the historical theme to criticize the present regime. The Communists themselves were quick to label the work as "cursing the locust while pointing to the mulberry."

Criticisms of the government can also be made by expressing opinions seemingly in line with the regime, by upholding its policies, and by extravagant praise. Ping Hsin provides an excellent example. In her *Visiting*

Ch'ing-lung ch'iao for the Second Time, she portrayed in glowing terms the joy and happiness of the youth who had been sent to work in this agricultural commune as part of the *hsia-fang* movement. According to her, they were there "to conquer nature and reform their thought." She described the life of university students sent to work in a mountainous region in the following words: "How lovely and how fortunate these young people are! How beautiful a strip of mountain land have they received for 'greenization!' " It was common knowledge that the commune movement was a disaster and that *hsia-fang* was meant to be a punishment for the recalcitrants. Ping Hsin certainly knew of the failure of the one and the suffering entailed in the other. The only way to understand her is to interpret these phrases as satire.

Wu Han, an important historian and a Deputy Mayor of Peking under P'eng Chen, came under fire because of his historical play *The Dismissal of Hai Jui,* written in 1960. Hai Jui (1515-1587) was a respected official in the Ming dynasty. He did much for the people in building irrigation systems, bringing relief to districts devastated by flood and famine, and, in particular, by cracking down on the local gentry, and forcing them to return land to the peasants. The Communists were quite right in concluding that Wu Han really meant his plays as a criticism of the regime. In *The Dismissal of Hai Jui,* there is a pervasive spirit of justice, a virile determination to perform one's duty at all odds; and it is no wonder the Communists called it a "poisonous weed." Such a spirit is also manifest in a poem by Teng T'o, who was also accused of "singing the praises of the past and condemning the present"; and whose *Evening Talks at Yenshan* was also dubbed a poisonous weed.

We are not sure of the fate of these intellectuals. From reliable sources, we know that Lao She was dead, probably as the result of a beating at the hands of the Red Guards. Ping Hsin and her husband Wu Wen-tsao were said to have committed suicide by taking poison.

Chien Po-tsan, a historian and Vice-President of Peking University, was accused of four mistakes: advocating "historicalism" against class struggle; distorting and slandering the peasant revolution while singing the praises of emperors, kings, generals, and ministers of the old society; and propagating tolerance for feudal society. In other words, Chien was condemned because he refused to rewrite history along Communist lines. Chou Ku-ch'eng, another historian of renown, was purged because he failed to recognize the importance of class feelings, and taught that only art could inspire true feelings. Hua Lo-keng, the mathematician, was accused of a number of sins: he was a worshipper of Western science; one of those responsible for drafting the Anti-Party Anti-Socialist Science Program; against the study of Maoism, and in favor of technical training; against using the slogan "politics in command" as a norm for recruiting graduate students; advising students to learn technical skills; and criticizing Chiang Ch'ing, Mao's wife, for being muddle-headed.

Li Ta, one of the founders of the Chinese Communist Party and a former President of Wuhan University, died during the early stages of the Great Proletarian Cultural Revolution. On September 5, 1966, *Jen-min Jih-pao* revealed his crimes. Li was regarded as a renegade, a discredit to the nation, an old anti-Communist hand and exploiter of peasants. The paper accused him of being a double dealer: on the one hand, he called himself a "senior revolutionary," "senior party member," and a "philosophical authority on Marxism," while on the other, he engaged in "criminal activities" against the party, socialism, and Mao Tse-tung's thought. An editorial summed up his crimes: "Li Ta viciously attacked the party's proletarian educational policy, opposed the revolutionary movement in teaching, and opposed party leadership. He practiced bourgeois dictatorship at Wuta, implemented the bourgeois line of 'having professors administer the school,' and repelled and attacked cadres of worker-peasant background and revolutionary students. He wanted to turn our Socialist universities into positioning for a conspiratory comeback by the bourgeoisie." The case of Li Ta makes clear that no one showing any sign of an intellectual's normal critical discontent can be safe in Communist China.

In the recent past, workers have been told to go into schools and colleges to take up positions of leadership. This obviously represents an attempt on the part of the Communists to create their own brand of intellectuals after realizing their failure in remaking the old intellectuals. *Jen-min Jih-pao* editorialized: [25]

In all 29 provinces (with the exception of Taiwan), municipalities, and self-governing districts, revolutionary committees have been established. This indicates that the Great Proletarian Cultural Revolution has developed to a stage in which "struggle, criticism, and reform" are taking place. Under the new directives of Chairman Mao, the great army of workers have methodically under guidance moved into schools and other units in the superstructure level, units where there were no "struggle, criticism, and reform," to promote "struggle, criticism, and reform." This not only opens up new vistas for proletarian education, but also hastens the process of remaking the intellectuals in the image of the workers themselves. When workers enter into cultural and educational ground, their main targets are the intellectuals. To master correctly the party policy toward the intellectuals is a sure way of winning the struggle.

[25]*Jen-min Jih-pao,* September 7, 1968.

But, one must have grave doubts as to the success of the Chinese Communists in attempting to create their own brand of intellectuals. In the 1950s during the Hundred Flowers movement, high school students raised in the pattern of Mao's thought were among the noisiest and bitterest critics of the regime. In the late 1960s, the Communists had no better chance of success. It was reported, for example, that colleges and technical schools in Shanghai staged strong protests against the take-over of their campuses by workers. Unable either to keep the old intellectuals from deviating or to raise a new crop of intellectuals in their own image, the Chinese Communist leaders face a bleak future in this respect.

The Communist regime being what it is, there is really no place for the intellectuals in China today. But there is enough spark left to rekindle the genius of the intellectuals if and when conditions change. The intellectuals being what they are, no force—however cynical and strong—can snuff them out completely. They will rise again whenever conditions permit. And if conditions do not permit, we will find their heads bloodied, perhaps, but still unbowed.

Chapter Eleven

Peking and the National Minorities

Robert A. Rupen

Communist China has no nationalities or minorities problem comparable to the Soviet Union. The so-called Han Chinese make up some 95 percent of the country's total population. Of the approximately 35 million non-Han, perhaps 25 million have either been strongly acculturated and Sinified over a long period of time, thus minimizing their unique character, or they comprise ethnic islands completely surrounded by the Han sea. The remaining ten million, however, combine non-Han characteristics and aspirations with a strategic location on China's borders, which gives a significant political dimension to their ethnic and cultural peculiarities. The most important of these non-Han minorities are the "native" populations of Inner Mongolia, Sinkiang, and Tibet; and this brief survey deals primarily with them. More cursory treatment is also given to the strategically located minorities of China's southwest.

Inner Mongolia, Sinkiang, and Tibet[1]

SOME BROAD COMPARISONS. By 1949, the Han population of Inner Mongolia already outnumbered the Mongols. Sinification had caused a

[1]The area and population of these territories are as follows:

	Area (in 000 sq. mi.)	"Natives" (in millions)	Han Chinese (in millions)
Inner Mongolian Autonomous Region	500	1.5	8.5
Sinkiang	640	4.0	4.0
Tibet	470	2.0	0.5

N.B. Population statistics for China and the Chinese are notoriously unreliable, and those for the national minorities are even more so. Estimates for Tibet are probably the most suspect of all; hard estimates for Sinkiang are almost equally difficult to obtain; while the totals for Inner Mongolia are perhaps a bit more dependable. But none of these figures should be taken as really reliable.

243

substantial proportion of the Mongols to shift from nomadic livestock herding to sedentary farming, from living in felt yurts to mud huts, and often even from speaking and writing Mongolian to using the Chinese language; although the nomadic way of life, animal husbandry, and Buddhism still characterized many Mongols. And by 1949, political power was already concentrated in the hands of a Sinified Mao-oriented Mongol Communist, Ulanfu.[2]

Compared to Inner Mongolia, far fewer Han Chinese had settled in Sinkiang by 1949, and Chinese politicians and "warlords" were able to dominate the area only because the indigenous population was disunited and lacked a common national consciousness. Moslem religious identification inhibited the natives from any significant relationship, political or cultural, with their Buddhist Mongol neighbors to the east or their Buddhist Tibetan neighbors to the south. Vast distances and a sparse and scattered population also contributed to the absence of unity or sense of common identity. Significant Russian influence was also felt in Sinkiang, while this was completely absent from Inner Mongolia and Tibet. Before 1949, several thousand Russians were living and working permanently in Sinkiang. Native Communists were often Russian-trained and Moscow-oriented; the most notable of them was Saifuddin.[3]

Almost no Han Chinese lived permanently in Tibet in 1949, nor was there any other significant non-Tibetan minority. The office and person of the Dalai Lama, representing at once the religion of Tibet, its history, culture, and even Tibetan "nationalism," gave unity and cohesion to the country. Peking's writ ran not at all in Tibet.

Taking a conceptual "great leap forward" to 1969, a significantly larger number of Chinese were settled in Inner Mongolia as compared with twenty years before, acculturation and Sinification continued, the Buddhist religion had been emasculated, a new university and other educational and cultural institutions had been established, and a rail connection to the

[2]Ulanfu was the top official of the Inner Mongolian Autonomous Region even before the formal establishment of the Chinese Communist regime at Peking in 1949. The Cultural Revolution brought about his downfall, and it has been reported that he is now imprisoned in Peking. The first personal attack on Ulanfu was launched in September 1966, and the campaign against him mounted throughout the course of 1967. A pro-Ulanfu backlash reportedly occurred in 1968, but he was not reinstated. See Robert A. Rupen, *Mongols of the Twentieth Century* (Bloomington: Indiana University Press, 1964), Vol. 1, p. 267, fn. 18; and Paul Hyer and William Heaton, "The Cultural Revolution in Inner Mongolia," *China Quarterly*, No. 36 (October-December 1968).

[3]Saifuddin was reported in July and September 1969 to be Deputy Chairman, Sinkiang Regional Revolutionary Committee, and Deputy Commander, Sinkiang Military Region, under a Chinese Chairman and Commander, Lung Shu-chin. In September 1969, a former colleague of Saifuddin's, Burkhan Shahidi, was castigated as an agent of Liu Shao-ch'i in Sinkiang. See also fn. 6 below, concerning Wang En-mao. These various changes may have related to "loyal" or "treasonous" attitudes taken in border disputes with the USSR.

Mongolian People's Republic constructed. But essentially, Inner Mongolia remained much as before: Han numerical and political dominance continued; there was no Russian presence or influence to speak of, and little contact with the Mongolian People's Republic.[4] Revolutionary changes had taken place, but Inner Mongolia's relative place in the Chinese scheme of things had changed less than Sinkiang or Tibet.

Sinkiang in 1969 had ten times the Han population of 1949; a formerly small Han minority probably now equalled the indigenous non-Han population. The Russian presence had been eliminated. A new railroad tied the province to China proper; petroleum production had become significant; nuclear weapons development had created a vast new industry. No great economic takeoff had occurred, but things were in motion. Sinkiang had become more definitively "Chinese."

Tibet had changed most of all by 1969, while paradoxically it probably looked much the same as ever. What had been an autonomous province, almost an independent country, was now a Chinese satrapy, a "colony." Chinese military occupation held the country in tight control. Han Chinese had begun to settle on the land. The Dalai Lama and Panchen Lama,[5] and perhaps ninety percent of the religious hierarchy, were dead, under *de facto* arrest, or refugees abroad. The political, religious, and cultural complexion of Tibet was forever changed; a kind of genocide had been committed. But the physical signs of change were much less striking: a few new highways and airfields, no factories, mines, or railroads—at least, not yet.

An assessment of these territories in 1969 must also take account of the consequences of the Cultural Revolution, which has toppled the long-time Communist leaders of Inner Mongolia (Ulanfu) and Sinkiang (Wang En-mao),[6] and brought about the transfer of the top Chinese Communist

[4]The Mongolian People's Republic has an area of 600,000 square miles, and a population of approximately one million (mostly Mongols and almost no Chinese).

[5]Long before 1949, Peking had attempted to play on differences between the Dalai Lama at Lhasa and the Panchen Lama at Shigatse. In the complex of twentieth century developments in Tibet, the then Panchen Lama spent the years from 1923 until his death in 1937 in and around Peking, while the Dalai Lama dominated the country. The Chinese chose the next Panchen Lama as a rival to the Dalai Lama; and when the Dalai Lama fled from Tibet to India in 1959, the Chinese Communists appointed the Panchen Lama as nominal leader of Tibet and Honorary Chairman of the Chinese Buddhist Association. But the Panchen Lama apparently proved an unsatisfactory puppet, and he was attacked in the press and demoted in 1964. In August and September 1969, rumors indicated some sort of serious uprising in Shigatse, followed by reports that the Panchen Lama had been killed while fleeing from Tibet to India.

[6]Wang En-mao, for some years top Han Chinese Communist official in Sinkiang (he had actually replaced Saifuddin) was a target of Red Guard criticism in 1967; and according to recurring reports, he has now been purged. But this information seems even less "definitive" than that concerning Ulanfu in Inner Mongolia. For some information, see June Dreyer, "China's Minority Nationalities in the Cultural Revolution," *China Quarterly*, No. 35 (July-September 1968).

in Tibet (Chang Kuo-hua).[7] Fallout from the Cultural Revolution and from factional fights among the Chinese could conceivably delay the effective integration of the border areas into China proper for many years. Rebuilding a control apparatus as effective as that which existed before the Cultural Revolution will take a long time. Confusion and near anarchy in Peking could lead to greatly enhanced local autonomy in the outlying areas.

TWO DECADES OF CHANGE. The events and policies of the two intervening decades provide the motion picture continuity between the 1949 and 1969 snapshots presented above. Ulanfu's Mao-oriented communism already dominated the Inner Mongolian scene in 1949, and there the continuity is fairly smooth and even. Administratively the Inner Mongolian Autonomous Region under the Communists added the Mongols of Barga[8] and adjoining parts of Western Manchuria to the traditional territories of Inner Mongolia. The Chinese Communists followed the Russian-inspired policy of granting a separate territorial status and the right to use the native language in order to win minority support. They also followed the Russians in imposing Communist ideological dogma and economic planning on the Mongols. In short, the Chinese—like the Russians—followed the slogan, "national in form, Socialist in content."

The major recurrent internal problem has been "Great Han chauvinism," that is, the often unsympathetic and, indeed, arrogant treatment of the Mongols by Han Chinese. The party line called for tolerance and close cooperation, and the Chinese in Inner Mongolia were supposed to learn the Mongolian language. But Mongol complaints continued throughout these twenty years. Moreover, problems certainly accompanied the collectivization of livestock, although there are no reliable statistics to measure the extent of Mongol opposition. Buddhism was apparently never attacked directly, but no lama (or anybody else) was ever excused from fulfilling his work-quota; prayers could be said after work. In some ways, the policy was more to manipulate than to destroy religion. Thus, for example, "official" Buddhists frequently attended international "peace" gatherings and Asian-African solidarity conferences.

One important development, construction of a great steel mill at Paotow, has changed the economic profile of Inner Mongolia considerably, although the labor force at the mill is largely Chinese. But a university at

[7]Chang Kuo-hua had entered Lhasa with the first PLA troops in 1950, and appears to have directed the *de facto* military occupation thereafter. In January 1967, Red Guards reportedly clashed with Chang in Lhasa, but the outcome was clouded by his transfer in May 1967 to Szechuan. See *ibid.*, p. 104.

[8]Barga, the area around Hailar in what used to be Western Manchuria, included an especially activist and nationalistic Mongol population which was separate from Inner Mongolia in traditional Manchu and Chinese administration. The Communists detached the areas west of the Hsingan Mountains, including Barga, from Manchuria and included them with the Inner Mongolian Autonomous Region. See Rupen, *op. cit.*, 71-72.

Kuke Khoto and an Institute of Mongolian Studies do offer new educational opportunities to the Mongols. Indeed, an educational system far superior to anything existing before 1949 has been an important aspect of Communist construction.

Inner Mongolia's main external problem concerns relations with the Mongolian People's Republic and the larger question of Chinese relations with the USSR. During the initial period, arrangements were made for the construction of a Trans-Mongolian Railroad, which would tie the Trans-Siberian Railroad into the main Chinese system and provide a new Moscow-Peking connection. A major entrepot and transshipment complex was envisaged including new highways and other economic and development projects in Inner Mongolia, all of which would have amounted to a basic geopolitical transformation of Inner Mongolia and Central Asia into a bridge between Russia and China. The Trans-Mongolian Railroad was completed in 1956, but the rest of the grandiose plan never came to fruition. In 1965, moreover, the Chinese narrowed the gauge of the Mongolian road on Chinese territory, so that it no longer corresponded to the wide Russian track. And in the same pattern, the policy of adopting the Cyrillic alphabet in the Inner Mongolian Autonomous Region (a step already taken in the neighboring Mongolian People's Republic) was abandoned in 1958, and the Latin alphabet chosen instead. (In practice, the traditional vertical Turkic alphabet continued to be used in Inner Mongolia.)

Soviet troops have reportedly been stationed on the border between Inner Mongolia and the Mongolian People's Republic since early 1966, and Russian missiles were supposedly emplaced there in 1968. Few trains cross the border any more, and incidents occur from time to time; one Chinese-inspired train delay in February 1969 brought an official protest from the Mongolian People's Republic. The border is essentially sealed.

The situation in Sinkiang during the early Communist years, with Russian-controlled joint stock companies, Russian consular and other officials all over the province, and a Russian-trained Uighur Communist as province chief, did not last long. A Trans-Sinkiang Railroad was begun, which was intended ultimately to connect the Chinese system to the Turk-Sib Railroad in Soviet Central Asia. But the Chinese extended that line only as far west as Urumchi. Thus the new railroad now serves to facilitate the development of Sinkiang and its subjection to Chinese control. After Wang En-mao replaced Saifuddin in 1958, Russian influence faded quickly. Serious internal disorders in 1962 resulted in the flight of some fifty thousand Moslem nomads from Sinkiang across the border into Soviet Central Asia, and led the Chinese to close all Russian consulates and expel most Russians living in Sinkiang. Thereafter, large numbers of Han Chinese settlers flowed into the province. Hence, both Inner Mongolia and Sinkiang, which were originally envisaged as bridges of friendship between closely collaborating Communist allies, have instead become closed territories separating two competitive and distrustful empires.

The first object of Chinese Communist policy toward Tibet was to impose the new regime's authority over the territory. Outright military invasion between 1950 and 1951 put an abrupt end to the delicate, centuries-old relationship between Peking and Lhasa.[9] Few Tibetan collaborators were ever found, and the military occupation was hated by the indigenous population. Smoldering resentment broke into open revolt in 1959, when a Chinese move was interpreted as threatening the Dalai Lama himself. The Chinese finally brought the revolt under control, but only after the Dalai Lama and thousands of other Tibetans had fled to India.

A side effect of the Chinese attack on India three years later was to insure that India would not support a Tibetan liberation movement, and to place Tibet ever more tightly under Peking's control. A Chinese Communist attempt to exploit the Panchen Lama as a substitute for the Dalai Lama came to nothing, and the Panchen Lama was openly discarded in 1964. Sporadic Tibetan revolts apparently still break out from time to time.

THE CULTURAL REVOLUTION AND THE MINORITIES QUESTION. The Cultural Revolution, which involved intense factional infighting all over the country, broke the Han "united front" toward the national minorities. In Tibet and Sinkiang, and perhaps in Inner Mongolia as well, the conflicts of Han *versus* Han took precedence over Han relations with the "natives." Economic development, which usually accompanied the influx of Han Chinese, may also have slowed down, and the minorities probably welcomed this. On the other hand, the radicalization of the Chinese revolution also involved a greater Sinification of the minority territories; and the loss of leaders like Ulanfu, for example, certainly weakens the influence of the Mongols in Peking. The new revolutionary committees, which are apparently designed to restore control over the country, assign a key role to the military, that is, to the Han Chinese. The Cultural Revolution and its aftermath may well have as one result a permanent worsening of the position of the national minorities. At present, they seem atomized, divided, and lacking in effective organization or leadership.

Meanwhile, Chinese settlement continues and poses the most serious long term threat, more ominous even than collectivization and communization. Industrialization and urbanization usually favor Han over non-Han. The more economic development in minority areas, the more transportation is improved, the more Han Chinese move in. The minorities can prob-

---

[9]Before 1951, the Chinese government never exerted effective control over Lhasa, but rarely was entirely excluded from a role in its direction. Many of the complications involved in attempting to make a meaningful short statement about the relation of Tibet to China appear in Alfred P. Rubin, "The Position of Tibet in International Law," *China Quarterly*, No. 35 (July-September 1968).

ably survive as identifiable culture units only if they receive special treatment from Peking. A completely consistent "equality" line will lead to their disappearance. But while the natives probably desire meaningful autonomy, they are unlikely to get it. The danger now is not segregation, but rather assimilation and absorption.

Over the long term, the survival of the peoples and cultures geographically situated between Russia and China seems very doubtful. It would be possible for central policy to protect the national minorities against Han chauvinism. Indeed, in the past Peking sometimes did endeavor to help the non-Han against Han incursion and arrogance. But if Peking's policy is otherwise—if, as now seems to be the case, special protection for the national minorities is denounced as "Liu Shao-ch'i—Khrushchevite deviation"—the minorities are in grave danger.

FACTORS AFFECTING THE DEVELOPMENT OF THE MINORITIES. Among the causative factors operating in these areas, a useful distinction may be made between those which are non-Communist, Communist, and specifically Chinese Communist in nature. The non-Communist factors apply over the long term and irrespective of the kind of regime in Peking. An example is the overwhelming numerical superiority of the Han Chinese, and their steady and almost inexorable movement into the outlying minority areas, especially into Inner Mongolia. Where the Han Chinese settle permanently, they acculturate and Sinify the local population. The Sinification of much of Inner Mongolia was already far advanced before 1949. In all of these areas, moreover, the indigenous non-Han population has traditionally feared or at least distrusted the Han, and they almost always have reacted to the Han in accordance with their "national" and cultural identifications rather than according to "class." That is, all native groups tended to coalesce against Chinese incursions; the poorer classes did not collaborate eagerly with Chinese "workers."

The geography of these areas decisively influenced their culture, economy, and population density. It is not necessary to subscribe to an unqualified geographic determinism to suggest that the population was small and scattered because distances were immense and water and plant life scarce. Nomadic livestock herding was often (not always) better suited to the natural conditions than settled agriculture. The fact that national borders shifted only slightly over very long periods of time suggests some fundamental geographical justification for the limits of historical China, the USSR, and the minority areas in between. The Himalayas do affect Tibet's relationship to India; the Tien Shan and other mountains do tend to separate Sinkiang from Soviet Central Asia; and the Gobi Desert does distinguish "Inner" from "Outer" Mongolia.

One should not romanticize the quality of native life, which usually involved illiteracy; health conditions so poor that the size of the population barely held steady if it was not actually declining; a church often more worldly and corrupt than spiritually edifying; a native aristocracy that was often cruel and exacting. Exploitation did exist, and so did "inhuman" torture and punishment. There was much to reform and improve.

Communist factors are those which have been common to both Soviet and Chinese Communist practice, applied in the Mongolian People's Republic as well as in Inner Mongolia, in Soviet Central Asia as well as in Sinkiang. The attack on religion—its manipulation and emasculation, with the ultimate intention of its total elimination—is common to both Communist empires. Russian-style communism manipulated and then eliminated the Jebtsun Damba Khutukhtu[10] in the Mongolian People's Republic much as the Chinese model later dealt with the Dalai Lama—and the Russians had previously attempted unsuccessfully to make use of an equivalent of the Panchen Lama, too.[11] The collectivization of livestock occurred on both sides of the border. Both regimes eliminated the princes and aristocrats, and both confiscated private property. Both attacked "bourgeois nationalism" and any serious attempt at syncretism (that is, the attempt to retain as much as possible of the old while adopting the new) in culture and religion. Both imposed censorship and thought control, and both espoused a dogmatic orthodoxy.

Both Communist China and Soviet Russia also afford a limited type of federalism and a separate territorial identity to their minorities. China's "autonomous regions" are similar in concept and function to the Soviet Union's union republics and autonomous republics. Both encourage the use of native languages, and provide education and publications in it. The education is, however, standardized and "Socialist in content." Both regimes stress the equality of women, and this doctrine has its greatest impact in the formerly Moslem areas of Sinkiang and Soviet Central Asia. Finally, both endeavor to bring industrialization, urbanization, and modernization

---

[10]The eighth Jebtsun Damba Khutukhtu was temporal as well as spiritual ruler of Outer Mongolia when Red Army troops marched into the Mongolian capital in July 1921. They extorted a self-limiting document from him, and gradually transformed his role from one of real power to a decorative function. When he died in 1924, the now-Communist regime forbade the search for and naming of a successor. See detailed discussion in Rupen, op. cit.

[11]Two interesting Russian parallels may be adduced. After 1921, when the Russian Communists wanted to weaken the power of the Jebtsun Damba Khutukhtu, they turned to a Buddhist rival in Mongolia, the Jalkhandza Khutukhtu (roughly an equivalent of the Panchen Lama) as their instrument. But unfortunately for them, the Jalkhandza Khutukhtu died in 1923, while the Jebtsun Damba Khutukhtu lived for another year.

The other case goes back a long way. In 1741, the Tsarist Russian government created a head lama (with the title since 1764 of Pandido Khambo Lama), in order to discourage Buryat Buddhists on Russian territory from identifying with the Jebtsun Damba Khutukhtu in Outer Mongolia or the Dalai Lama in Lhasa. The last Pandido Khambo Lama, Agvan Dorjeev, died in 1938, although there now again exists a Head of Buryat Buddhists in the USSR.

to the minorities; and insofar as they do so, they do increase career alternatives and life options for the native peoples.

A specifically Chinese Communist factor, which is quite different from
Russian practice, is the special role of the army. Tibet was subjected to the
central government by a long continued military occupation. Military settlement also plays a significant role in Sinkiang. The political leaders of the
minority areas are often simultaneously in the military chain of command.
And the new revolutionary committees are also controlled by the military.

The Great Leap Forward and the communes were pressed on the minority
areas. The Cultural Revolution ultimately reached into and changed the
leadership in all three territories. Nevertheless, in some ways and at some
times, the Chinese Communist handling of the minorities—their religion,
history, and tradition—seemed more subtle and sophisticated than the
Russian model. Between 1962 and 1963, China and Inner Mongolia did
public honor to Genghis Khan, while the Soviet Union and the Mongolian
People's Republic attacked him for "feudal" exploitation, and also attacked
China and Inner Mongolia for honoring such an undesirable historical figure. Until the Cultural Revolution, no Chinese equivalent of the Stalinist
purges of the 1930s took place. The Soviet national minorities were especially hard hit by the purges, which also included a crude and aggressive
assault on religion. This whole period of Russian history had, until very recently, no Chinese counterpart.

On balance, however, the minorities in China get more of communism's
disadvantages—its doctrines and ideology, control and censorship—and
less of its advantages—education, modernization, health, and medicine—
than minorities in the USSR. For the peoples of Inner Mongolia and
Sinkiang, no non-Communist alternative exists; and of the Communist
alternatives, the Russian seems to afford greater material advantages. If
given a chance, the Chinese minorities would probably favor "expertness"
over "redness," that is, development and education over ideology.

RELATIONS ACROSS BORDERS. At no time since 1949 have extensive
contacts developed between the Mongols of Inner Mongolia and the Mongolian People's Republic. Even in the friendliest period of Sino-Soviet relations, that between 1953 and 1957, no significant population movement
took place in either direction. It was mostly Russians and Chinese, not
Mongols, who built the Trans-Mongolian Railroad. Formal relations seem
to have been limited to occasional ceremonial visits by Ulanfu to Ulan
Bator, the establishment of a short-lived consulate of the Mongolian People's Republic at Kuke Khoto, and some minor ties of scholarship and
culture. Mongols in the People's Republic are undoubtedly much better off
materially and educationally than those in Inner Mongolia: they enjoy a
de facto Russian subsidy, and Russians do not settle on their land. Yet the
Mongols have never fled across the border in significant numbers, per-

haps because they are so heavily acculturated, because the Gobi Desert separates them from the northern, populated, parts of the People's Republic, and because they can remain less modernized and Westernized if they stay in Inner Mongolia. In any case, they could not escape communism by fleeing to the north; they could only trade the Chinese version for the Soviet.

Although the Chinese officially recognize the Mongolian People's Republic, maintain an embassy in Ulan Bator, and often state that the People's Republic should not be considered part of China, an impression persists that Chinese do view it as *irredenta,* to be restored to Peking's control at some future time. But the presence of Russian troops and missiles at the Chinese border testify to the Soviet Union's determination to maintain the territorial *status quo,* and China is unlikely to challenge it. On the other hand, Ulanfu's removal and the possibility of serious discontent in Inner Mongolia, combined with conditions of near anarchy in China and the consequent weakening of Peking's control, suggest the possibility that Inner Mongolia might cut itself free from China and look to the north for support. But while this is remotely conceivable, it is not very likely. The overwhelming dominance of Han Chinese among the population of Inner Mongolia argues strongly against it.

Turning to the Sinkiang-Soviet Central Asia relationship, some similar and some very dissimilar factors operate. As with the Mongols, no "traditional" alternative exists; and at present, the only available choice is between two brands of communism. The indigenous peoples of Soviet Central Asia are undoubtedly much better off, in terms of education and general standard of living, than those in Sinkiang. And there has always been some contact and movement across the border. When radical collectivization was imposed by the USSR in the 1930s, numbers of natives fled from Soviet Central Asia to Sinkiang. When the Chinese enforced tighter control over Sinkiang, they fled in the opposite direction (in 1962, for example). The Russians are settling in Soviet Central Asia as the Chinese are doing in Sinkiang; but the Russians are more apt to be urban and industrial, and less likely to "rob" pasture land from the natives or to go into farming. Thus far, however, there are fewer Chinese in Sinkiang than in Inner Mongolia, and most of them have not been there nearly so long. Hence, the natives of Sinkiang are less acculturated and Sinified than the Mongols.

China makes no serious claim to Soviet Central Asia, and undoubtedly does not think of it as *irredenta.* The Russians, moreover, probably have no intention of reasserting their former influence in any part of Sinkiang. But prolonged upheaval in China could conceivably lead to some sort of Russian arrangement with the local authorities in Sinkiang, whether Han or native or both.

Tibet is a special case. Historically, the Tibetans had close ties with the various related peoples along the northern border of India. Today, flight from Tibet to these neighboring territories (Nepal, Sikkim, Bhutan) means both escape from communism and refuge in an environment where the traditional culture still flourishes. Moreover, the Dalai Lama himself is alive and functioning. The Tibetans in Tibet still appear to be mounting some effective anti-Chinese resistance. With the limited numbers of Chinese in Tibet fighting among themselves, as they have done during the Cultural Revolution, and with the power of the Peking regime weakening, Tibet may well become the most vulnerable of the outlying minority areas. Many more Tibetans could leave the country if Chinese control relaxed still further, or the Dalai Lama and the refugees could conceivably return someday. But it must be anticipated that a new consolidation of power in China would soon be followed by another invasion of Tibet. Tibet enjoys autonomy almost in direct relation to the effectiveness of the central government in Peking. Moreover, the recent brutal assault on the Buddhist Church in Tibet, the flight of the Dalai Lama, the availability of overwhelming military force, and the enforced settlement of substantial numbers of Chinese immigrants, all make extremely difficult any return to or restoration of traditional Tibet.

The Sino-Indian relationship overlays the local Tibet-northern Indian border connection, just as the Sino-Soviet relationship overlays the connection between Sinkiang and Soviet Central Asia, and between Inner Mongolia and the Mongolian People's Republic. Han Chinese, not Tibetans, invaded India. But Chinese claims on India are undoubtedly limited, and in any case the Himalayas are not yet technologically obsolete. There is no evidence to suggest any significant Chinese intention of or capability for greater adventures to the south.

INNER MONGOLIA, SINKIANG, TIBET: A PROGNOSIS. In the first phase, from 1949 until Stalin's death in 1953, the new regime in Peking appeared to accept the prospect of significant cooperation with the Russians in the border territories between the two Communist giants. Joint stock companies in Sinkiang and Manchuria, and major new railroad connecting links across both Mongolia and Sinkiang, suggested that China was about to make a great geopolitical and economic shift inland, away from the sea. New industrial and hydroelectric projects on or near the Chinese-Russian border also forecast an era of close collaboration. The prospect was that the minority peoples in the areas affected would be swamped by Chinese immigration and Russian-inspired modernization, and that the hitherto remote wastes of Central Asia would become a bridge between Russians and Chinese. Symbolically, at least, the Great Wall was to be torn down.

But in fact, relatively little happened. The joint stock companies were soon dissolved. The Sinkiang rail connection to the Turksib (and thus to the USSR) was never completed. Russian activity in Sinkiang was first discouraged and then prohibited. Russian-oriented cadres among the minorities were curbed or replaced. Chinese soon began to return from the Mongolian People's Republic. China chose to exert an exclusive control over Manchuria, Inner Mongolia, Sinkiang, and Tibet. Even so, Peking's treatment of the national minorities copied Soviet practice; it was "national in form and Socialist in content." Minority languages were encouraged, minority cadres trained, minority customs permitted. A superficial tolerance of religion prevailed. Chinese cadres were ordered to avoid any hint of discrimination against the national minorities, and to learn the native language in the areas where they served. Social change moved fairly slowly and undramatically.

The invasion of Tibet by the People's Liberation Army between 1950 and 1951 showed that Peking meant to claim its own, and that it would be ruthless in doing so. But for some time, fundamental social change moved with deliberate speed. The Great Leap Forward rudely accelerated the pace and deepened the impact. Local nationalists were attacked. Communes and fixed housing were pressed on reluctant nomads. Social revolution went into high gear. And the Chinese poured in. Sinification and communization threatened the minorities. But then the pressure was relieved. A relatively liberal and permissive period allowed for some measure of relaxation and recuperation. Chinese continued to move in, but the communes collapsed and were not re-established. A comparative normalcy reigned. The Han "experts" were apparently dictating to the Han "reds," and the non-Han benefitted thereby. But it did not last.

In 1966, the Cultural Revolution—Red Guards and all—hit the minority areas. The natives apparently tried to avoid involvement in the Cultural Revolution entirely, to stand aloof from it. This led to the accusation that they were "counter-revolutionary." Han Chinese faction fought Han Chinese faction, while the minorities watched, waited, and wondered. The Cultural Revolution waned in 1967-68, with the gradual establishment of revolutionary committees in the minority areas as elsewhere. The revolutionary committees appeared to represent a compromise between the reds and the experts, and an end to wildly doctrinaire Maoist extremism. They also represented a large measure of PLA influence. In the minority areas, native leaders were out; Han army officers (often from other parts of China) were in. An "enlightened" policy toward the national minorities, one which stressed the use of native languages, protected native customs, and shielded the minorities from the overly harsh impact of social revolution, has unfortunately come to be identified with Liu Shao-ch'i and with Russian influence. Even partial Maoist victory demands undifferentiated treatment for all citizens of China, without attention to national differences.

The overall record, between 1949 and 1969, indicates severe blows to the cultures of Inner Mongolia, Sinkiang, and Tibet, and to the leadership of these minorities. What was perhaps the last best hope, namely, that Peking might enforce a relatively generous and protective policy, seems to be fading away. Even the removal of effective central control from Peking does not necessarily help the minority peoples, for the local Han leaders may treat them even worse. Over the long term, they face assimilation and annihilation.

Minorities in the Southwest

China's Southwest includes numerous non-Han minorities closely related to similar groups across the border in Viet-Nam, Laos, Thailand, and Burma. But whereas in the north, China's principal neighbor (the USSR) is a militarily powerful and politically well-organized state, which limits Peking's ability to manipulate the minorities *vis-à-vis* the Soviet Union, in the south her neighbors are for the most part militarily weak, politically "soft," and unsure of the directions which policy should take. The power and (to some extent) the will to oppose China is lacking in the south, where the prevalent ethics and life style are far more ready to "accommodate." Unlike the case in the north, the southern border areas are easily permeable; and the whole territory is relatively vulnerable to aggression and subversion.

SOME GENERAL CONSIDERATIONS. A rough circle from Kunming (China) to Lashio (Burma) to Chiengmai (Thailand) to Phong Saly (Laos) to Dien Bien Phu (North Viet-Nam) to Kunming encompasses substantial non-Han minorities, perhaps twenty million in all, living primarily in mountain areas. Such minorities include the Meo, Yao, Lahu, Lisu, Lolo, Kachin, Karen, Shan, Wan, and many others. They display great ethnic and cultural diversity. Peoples on both sides of the border are often closely related, and many of them move across such boundaries regularly. Their upland world is different from the rest of China, Burma, Thailand, Laos, and North Viet-Nam; and they usually have little in common with the ruling nationalities that dominate them numerically and politically. On the other hand, these peoples rarely have much consciousness of the minority as a whole; their loyalty and self-identification seldom extend beyond their own particular tribe, clan, or local settlement. Neither Peking nor any other government can readily work out from one group of Meo, for example, to find easy access and influence to all other Meo, even within the same country.

These minority groups fear domination by the larger and better-organized nationalities to which they owe a nominal allegiance. Some among them are seething with discontent and already have risen in revolt. Most of them have real grievances and offer dry tinder for the firebrands and arsonists of revolution. On the whole, these mountain tribesmen suspect or hate communism, and supply some of the most effective and dedicated fighters against it. But they also suspect or hate their respective national governments, often with good reason. In some cases, representatives of such minorities do serve as Communist agents and as the bearers of subversion. But more often, those who collaborate with the Communists are simply trying to defend their own way of life and separate identity.

While no generalization will hold everywhere, even for the members of a single minority group, and only careful analysis of each specific case in each particular place can be wholly reliable, nonetheless there are some significant common elements which can be isolated for purposes of analysis. Thus, most of these groups are numerically small, scattered geographically, live in poverty, and are cursed with poor soils and few material resources. To a considerable extent, they rely on the opium trade and other smuggling for their meager livelihood. That is, their major means of economic support are illegal. They live in small tribes or clans or villages, with little identification with a larger world. They are "freedom-loving," some of them aggressively so. They want to be left alone, partly because outside interference has usually meant mistreatment and discrimination and injustice. But their poor health, lack of education, and failure hitherto to obtain any of the central government's investment in economic development also leads them to demand a fair share. Partly they are separatist and anti-government; partly they want the presence and largesse of the central government.

Few, if any, are Communists philosophically or organizationally. There is essentially no indigenous communism of any kind among these mountain minorities. But relationships to communism and the Communists certainly exist, and sometimes to a politically significant extent. The Communists, nearly always Chinese or North Vietnamese, offer autonomy and freedom from the "oppressive" central governments. Some representatives of the minorities are attracted, and a few even go to North Viet-Nam or China for training and indoctrination. Some others are "recruited" through fear, by means of terror and the threat of assassination. But most reject such overtures. They oppose the regimentation of communism; and in addition, they reason that identification with communism will only lead to more suppression and mistreatment by the central government. It seems clear that up till now, at least, there does not exist among the national minorities of this region a Communist organization and infrastructure similar in type and extent to the Viet Cong, for example.

Further complicating their relationship to communism is the mutual distrust and lack of coordination between Peking and Hanoi. There appear to be separate and competing appeals from these capitals to the national minorities in Burma, Thailand, and Laos. Moreover, fallout from the Cultural Revolution, including factional fighting among Chinese Communists operating in Southeast Asia, would appear to weaken both the China-oriented Communist parties (in Burma particularly) and the prestige of China as a model and leader. North Viet-Nam's prestige and organizational efficiency seems likely to have a greater relative power of attraction. The outcome of internal developments in China, and of the Viet-Nam War, will affect both the assessments and conclusions of the national minorities.

The minorities suspect and distrust the central governments in Rangoon, Bangkok, and Vientiane. They fear discrimination, they dislike bureaucracy and control, and they cannot accept suppression of the opium trade without an economic substitute. Their attitude toward an outside power like the United States is a mixture of fear and hope. They fear that anti-communism and the American desire for viable Southeast Asian states will lead to American support for the suppression of the minorities by the central governments. They hope that the United States will provide protection against both suppression by the central governments and exploitation by the Communists from China and North Viet-Nam.[12]

The Meo will serve as an example. They are not necessarily typical; but they are important politically, and they appear in considerable numbers in the high country of Southwest China (2.7 million in Yunnan, Kweichow, and Hunan); North Viet-Nam (219,000); Laos (350,000); and Thailand (50,-000). They illustrate most of the varying political patterns that exist among these minorities. The Meo do not form a cohesive group. They do not react as a group, or think of themselves in that way; and they recognize no single leader or government. Nor are they recruited to communism or anything else because the recruiters happen to be Meo. Hence, the fact that large numbers of Meo are to be found both in China and across the border does not in itself assure a predominant Chinese influence on Meo political attitudes. But there is some Chinese influence. Meo in China unquestionably communicate with those across the border. Peking can find Meo agents and messengers without too much difficulty. Conversely, if Meo in China feel badly treated, they undoubtedly inform their relatives abroad about it. But immediate, local situations probably influence Meo attitudes in any particular area much more than such distant intelligence.

Some of the most effective Communist agents operating in Laos and Thailand are Meo; and some of the most effective anti-Communists are also Meo. The Meo fit into a broad Communist scheme to detach as much as

---

[12]For the national minorities to hope for support from foreign "imperialists" is not new. Great Britain supported the minorities in Burma; and the French did so in Indochina. The British in World War II, the French during the first Indochina War, and now the Americans in Viet-Nam, often seem to count the national minorities as more reliable allies and better fighters than the dominant ethnic group. The pattern of American policy in Thailand today appears to follow similar lines.

possible of northeast Thailand and join it to Communist-controlled northern Laos in a Chinese- or North Vietnamese-dominated "autonomous" Meo
state. Anti-Communist Meo undoubtedly far outnumber the pro-Commu-
nist Meo. But the pro-Communists are effectively backed by the Pathet
Lao (that is, North Viet-Nam) or by China. The United States supports anti-
Communist Meo in Laos and Thailand, but often in the face of strong opposition from Bangkok and Vientiane, especially the former. A concerted
American-Thai-Lao effort to support and win over the Meo could probably
effectively counter the Communists. But in practice, it has tended to be
more of an American effort *versus* the Thai and Lao governments in this
matter, and the Meo know it. So do the Communists.

PROSPECT. Apart from the Meo, there is a range of other ethnic groups
in Southwest China for Peking to play upon. But an emerging impression is
that the non-Han have become less important in the Chinese Communist
scheme of things; that one effect of the Cultural Revolution and its aftermath has been the emergence of a more narrowly "chauvinistic" Han-
dominated orientation. Hereafter, Peking will probably be paying less attention to minority sensibilities than it ever has; and, perhaps consistently
with that, will operate less flexibly and pragmatically among the tribesmen
and "natives." On the other hand, North Viet-Nam will continue to woo
them. And a diminution of the United States position could leave the Thai
and Lao governments free to resume repressive policies toward their
minorities, which is the course they seem to prefer.

Chapter Twelve

China and the Communist World

Richard C. Thornton

Twenty years after the revolution, Communist China stands at the cross-roads. After an initial decade of relative stability and progress, the past ten years have witnessed not only almost continuous domestic travail, culminating in the Great Proletarian Cultural Revolution (which has not yet been brought to a conclusion), but also the entire restructuring of China's foreign relations. Two crucial issues have dominated the preoccupations of the Chinese leadership: China's future role as a world Communist power, and the varying means and time necessary to achieve world power status. These issues have required continuous review of the Sino-Soviet relationship and are, it seems, the root causes of the conflict between them. The growing struggle has, in turn, affected China's policies toward the other Communist powers and the international Communist movement.

In the early years, the Soviet Union's China policy played a key role in crystallizing the alternatives open to the Chinese leadership. The twin strategic objectives of Soviet policy after the Chinese Communist victory in 1949 were to guarantee Chinese inclusion in the "Socialist camp" (the Korean War temporarily accomplished this aim), and to ensure that China would not develop into a threat to the Soviet Union. The Soviets wanted China to be a satisfied member of the Communist bloc, but not so powerful as to cause concern on the Soviet Union's eastern flank. The Chinese, on the other hand, wanted to build state power as quickly as possible. At first, it appeared that the Russians were more than ready to assist them; and as long as they demonstrated a willingness to do so, the Chinese were happy to "lean to one side." The crisis in Sino-Soviet relations came when the Chinese realized that the lengths to which the Russians were prepared to go in assisting them fell short of their expectations. The disparity between Russian intentions and Chinese expectations was the principal reality that governed the course of Sino-Soviet relations, a reality not apparent at the outset because it was clouded by professions of ideological solidarity on both sides.

A common ideological outlook had its advantages and disadvantages. It provided a unified conceptual framework by which each could maximize or minimize differences. In short, ideology has supplied the context of Sino-Soviet relations. But it did not determine the content of the relationship. Ideology may, however, have facilitated the most striking political practice which takes place in the Communist international system—the continuous interference by one state in the internal affairs of another. The Soviet relationship with its East European satellites has long been recognized, but the implications of the practice have yet to be fully appreciated in the Sino-Soviet context.

The Soviet Succession Struggle and De-Stalinization

The succession struggle in the Soviet Union after the death of Stalin in March 1953 provides the perspective for an analysis of Sino-Soviet relations. In the months that followed, first one faction centering around Malenkov, then another around Khrushchev, sought to obtain the support of other Communist parties for their candidacy while maneuvering to establish themselves in direct line of succession as Stalin's heir. In May 1953, the Malenkov faction, which seemed to have the upper hand during the early stages of the struggle, increased Soviet aid to China by agreeing to help construct 91 industrial projects over and above the 65 that had previously been agreed upon.[1] In an article eulogizing Stalin and carried in *Pravda,* Mao Tse-tung expressed his support of Malenkov:[2]

> We profoundly believe that the Central Committee of the Communist Party of the Soviet Union and the Soviet government, headed by Comrade Malenkov, will certainly be able to continue the work of Comrade Stalin.

That issue of *Pravda* contained a picture of Stalin, Mao, and Malenkov ostensibly taken after the conclusion of the Sino-Soviet treaty negotiations in February 1950.[3] The picture had been altered from the original photograph published on February 15, 1950, in which Malenkov was only one of nineteen members of the Chinese and Russian delegations witnessing the signing of the treaty.[4] In the 1953 version, all but Stalin, Mao, and Malenkov were excised!

Over the course of the following year, however, Chinese support shifted from Malenkov to Khrushchev. A key event in this development was Khrushchev's and Bulganin's trip to Peking in September 1954 to sign an-

[1]See David Floyd, *Mao Against Khrushchev* (New York: Praeger, 1964), p. 225. Mao sent a letter of thanks to the Soviet government in September of the same year; see *ibid.,* p. 219.
[2]*Pravda,* March 10, 1953.
[3]See *ibid.,* March 10, 1953.
[4]See *ibid.,* February 15, 1950.

other aid agreement with the Chinese. Khrushchev offered grants and long-term credits amounting to 520 million rubles, agreed to expand the volume of equipment deliveries for industrial projects covered in previous agreements, yielded Soviet holdings in the four Sino-Soviet joint stock companies established by the 1950 treaty, announced plans for the construction of two railroads linking China to the Soviet Union (one through Outer Mongolia and the other through Sinkiang), and agreed to the withdrawal of Soviet forces from Port Arthur by May 1955.[5] The battle lines of the Soviet struggle for power were indicated by the fact that Khrushchev was accompanied to Peking by Bulganin, the Chairman of the Council of Ministers, while the Premier (Malenkov) and the Minister of Foreign Affairs (Molotov) remained in Moscow.

Economic aid undoubtedly helped Khrushchev gain the support of the Chinese; but it was his position on strategic defense policy that decisively turned Peking away from the Malenkov faction toward his own. At the Nineteenth Party Congress in 1952, Malenkov took a relatively mild line toward the West, asserting that "in peaceful competition with capitalism the Socialist economic system will prove its superiority over the capitalistic system more and more vividly year by year."[6] Consistent with this view, Malenkov stated after Stalin's death that he knew of "no objective impediments to the improvement in the relations between the Soviet Union and the United States of America;"[7] and he did, in fact, move toward a settlement of the Korean War.

It was Malenkov's view that another war "with the present means of warfare, means the destruction of world civilization"[8]—a position which implied, among other things, a de-emphasis of the Soviet strategic commitment to China. He said that a "new epoch" had begun, and he saw China as a "mighty stabilizing factor" in Asia.[9] This "new course," as Malenkov termed it, also affected domestic policy. The easing of tensions abroad would permit improvements at home. No longer would heavy industry receive top priority, as it always had in the past. Now light industry and food manufacturing were to develop "at the same rate as heavy industry."[10]

Khrushchev, although later championing "peaceful coexistence," early in 1954 began to take an almost diametrically opposite line from Malenkov.

[5]See Floyd, *op. cit.*, p. 220.

[6]Quoted in Martin Ebon, *Malenkov: Stalin's Successor* (New York: McGraw-Hill, 1953), p. 189.

[7]Quoted in Herbert Dinerstein, *War and the Soviet Union* (New York: Praeger, 1959), p. 72.

[8]Quoted in *ibid.*, p. 71.

[9]Quoted in Alice Hsieh, *Communist China's Strategy in the Nuclear Era* (Englewood Cliffs, N.J.: Prentice-Hall, 1962), p. 24.

[10]Quoted in George Paloczi-Horvath, *Khrushchev, The Making of a Dictator* (Boston: Little-Brown, 1960), p. 155.

A new world war, he countered, would not mean the end of civilization, but rather the destruction of capitalism. The Soviet Union should not merely avoid war, but should actively deter it through a strong military posture, while standing ready to fight the imperialist warmongers if necessary. He saw the Sino-Soviet relationship as a "powerful factor in the struggle for peace in the Far East."[11] Domestically, Khrushchev called for continued stress on heavy industry at the expense of consumer goods production.

It was obvious which of these two positions the Chinese would prefer. The Malenkov emphasis on deterrence implied acceptance of the status quo, while Khrushchev's hard line indicated a far greater willingness to honor the strategic commitment to China. By January 1955, the Chinese Communists publicly endorsed Khrushchev's position, as opposed to Malenkov's, that nuclear war would not mean the destruction of the world, but simply the end of capitalism.[12] By the eve of the Soviet Twentieth Party Congress the following year, the Chinese were clearly supporting Khrushchev as Stalin's successor. In a telegram read to the assembled Congress on February 15, 1956, signed by Mao Tse-tung, the Chinese leader declared that:[13]

> The great successes of the USSR in foreign and domestic policy in recent years are inseparable from the correct leadership of the well-tried Central Committee of the CPSU headed by Comrade Khrushchev.

Khrushchev's secret speech denouncing Stalin, delivered at the Twentieth Party Congress, was a bombshell for the leadership of all the world's Communist parties, and especially for the Chinese. The events surrounding the decision to give the speech, and its significance, are complex matters and open to varying interpretations. It appears that Khrushchev planned to end collective leadership and assume Stalin's mantle himself; but he met with strong eleventh-hour opposition. The previous September, Khrushchev had approved a re-issue of Stalin's *Short Course;* and on the anniversary of Stalin's birthday, December 21, the Soviet press published photographs and editorials lauding the departed *vozhd.* These events suggested a continuation of the "cult of the individual."[14]

The decision to make the turn against the Stalin image, or personality cult, was apparently made sometime in January 1956. In retrospect, a key indicator that an anti-Stalin move was under way came at the conference of historians that took place in Moscow in late January. There an open

[11]Quoted in Hsieh, *op. cit.,* p. 24.
[12]See *Survey of China Mainland Press,* No. 969 (January 15-17, 1955), p. 2.
[13]Quoted in Paloczi-Horvath, *op. cit.,* p. 193.
[14]See *ibid.,* pp. 183-184.

clash occurred between the academic and the *apparatchik* historians when the Deputy Editor-in-Chief of the historical journal *Problems of History,* E. M. Burdzhalov, launched a broadside attack against the falsification of Soviet history. He singled out for special criticism the party histories of the Ukraine and Transcaucasia, and Stalin's *Short Course.*[15] The Ukraine and Transcaucasia had been Khrushchev's responsibility ever since 1937; and criticism of their histories referred principally to the purge of Kossior, the Ukrainian party chief whom Khrushchev had replaced. Reference to the *Short Course* was also meant to implicate Khrushchev, who had released it for republication only a few months before.[16] Both criticisms were repeated by Mikoyan in his public report to the Twentieth Party Congress.[17]

A second move against the cult of the personality was the distribution among the 1,436 delegates to the Congress of a set of documents which contained, among other things, Lenin's "testament" in which he warned against the "immense power" that the "rude" Stalin had arrogated to himself, and also advised enlarging the Central Committee as a means of ensuring collective leadership.[18] If there were anyone for whom these documents constituted a threat, it was Khrushchev. It was he who sought to fill the position left by Stalin's death, and his own "rudeness" was well known. And it was Khrushchev who sought to bring collective leadership to an end.

At the Congress itself, Khrushchev delivered the main report and spoke of Stalin's passing in emotional language ("death tore Joseph Vissarionovich Stalin from our ranks").[19] Ten days later, Khrushchev made a complete turnabout. He declared in the famous secret speech that "Stalin . . . used extreme methods and mass repressions. . . . Stalin showed in a whole series of cases his intolerance, his brutality, and his abuse of power."[20] At the same time, he attempted to exculpate himself from guilt by denying any knowledge of Kossior's arrest and purge until after the fact. He also called for the compilation of a new party history to replace the *Short Course.*[21]

Apparently, Khrushchev had attempted to suppress the speech which, judging from its detailed content, had obviously been in preparation for some time. When he found that he could not suppress it, he decided to read it himself rather than permit someone else to do so. This was necessary to save his own position. Khrushchev faced a dilemma. If he did not read

[15]See Merle Fainsold, "Historiography and Change," in John Keep (ed.), *Contemporary History in the Soviet Mirror,* (New York: Praeger, 1964). Over the next fifteen months, Burdzhalov came under continuous criticism, but it was not until after the ouster of the so-called "anti-party" group in June 1957 that he was fired.

[16]See Paloczi-Horvath, *op. cit.,* p. 187.

[17]See Leo Gruliow, *Current Soviet Policies,* (New York: Praeger, 1957), Vol. 2, pp. 87–88.

[18]See *ibid.,* pp. 211–212.

[19]Quoted in *ibid.,* p. 55.

[20]Quoted in *ibid.,* p. 175.

[21]See *ibid.,* p. 188.

the speech, he would very likely lose his own position, since the attack on Stalin would also be taken as an implied attack on Khrushchev. If Khrushchev did read the speech, he would probably save his own position, but at the cost of incalculable consequences to the total system. Khrushchev chose to read the speech, and thereby saved himself — at least in the short run. But the larger consequences of his attack on Stalin were to set in motion the fragmentation of Stalin's empire, of which the subsequent revolutions in Poland and Hungary were but a part. Whatever the motive, Khrushchev's indictment of Stalin — the "cult of the individual," mass repression, terror, suppression of minority peoples, and so forth — was an implied indictment of every Communist Party leader, of the system that Stalin had built and of the men who operated it.

To Mao Tse-tung, the anti-Stalin speech must have come as a terrific surprise. Being the ranking member of the Communist world, he must have suspected that Khrushchev was attempting to undermine his own position; and his suspicions were undoubtedly strengthened in the months that followed the Congress as Stalin's appointees in the East European satellites were replaced one by one. Moreover, Khrushchev began to sound more and more like Malenkov, placing emphasis on the necessity of avoiding general war, reducing investment in heavy industry, increasing consumer goods, and renewing emphasis on disarmament and peaceful coexistence. Finally, there were indications that a subterranean struggle against the cult of the personality was also taking place in China, and that the target was Mao Tse-tung himself. Mao was able to weather this crisis, and the only visible change that took place at the Eighth Congress of the Chinese Communist Party held later in 1956 was the deletion of the phrase "Thought of Mao Tse-tung" from the party constitution and its substitution by the standard phrase "Marxism-Leninism."

Through it all, Khrushchev hastened to reassure the Chinese that the de-Stalinization campaign was not directed at them; but it is from this point onward that a shift away from Khrushchev is detectable in the Chinese position. There is considerable uncertainty about the extent of the shift, but the Chinese may have moved to the support of Khrushchev's opposition, the Malenkov-Molotov-Kaganovich group, which attempted to unseat Khrushchev in mid-1957 and failed.[22] The month of June 1957 did see the Chinese take a sharp swing to the left domestically. This was reflected not only in the fact that the Hundred Flowers episode was brought to an abrupt halt, but also in a change in economic policy. Po I-po, Chairman of the State Economic Commission, told the National People's Conference in

---

[22]Carl A. Linden, *Khrushchev and the Soviet Leadership, 1957–1964* (Baltimore: Johns Hopkins University Press, 1966), pp. 180–181, cites Khrushchev's radio speech of July 19, 1963, in which he "accused his Chinese foes of 'poking their noses' into CPSU internal affairs and seeking the overthrow of his leadership. . . ." No date is mentioned.

June that China must reduce her "reliance on foreign countries;" and throughout the summer and fall, a break-neck pace of economic development was seen as the "only way out" for China.[23] In this context, the Sino-Soviet defense conference held in Moscow in October 1957 (which Mao himself attended) had all the earmarks of an attempt to reconcile diverging positions. The two partners concluded an "agreement on new technology for national defense" in November, which the Chinese now claim included the supply of a sample atomic bomb;[24] but in the main, the differences between Moscow and Peking were only papered over at the conference.

The Split with Russia: Peking Opts for "Independent Action"

After the Soviet Twentieth Party Congress, the Chinese leaders faced a dilemma of their own. They had supported Khrushchev because he had indicated a willingness to assist them in China's development. But as Khrushchev consolidated his position in the Soviet Union, he seemed less inclined to support the Chinese. Although the agreement on "new technology" was signed in November 1957, no new credits were forthcoming from the Soviet Union after that date (with one exception to be discussed below). It is now apparent that the Chinese and Khrushchev had become estranged. After 1957, Soviet exports to China were on a cash-and-carry basis, a step which placed the Chinese in an increasingly awkward economic position.

If the Chinese permitted this situation to drift, their entire program of rapid industrialization, geared to and dependent upon Soviet aid, would inevitably grind to a slow walk. They would find it harder and harder to maintain current rates of development, let alone increase them. The Chinese were beholden to the Russians for plans, technical assistance, spare parts, and, most of all, for oil. By restricting credits, the Russians were in a position to make China an economic and even a political satellite, effectively controlling its rate of economic growth and freedom of political action.

The debate among the Chinese leadership over the issue of military power most clearly illustrates the alternatives as they developed for the Chinese. In the early 1950s, Soviet aid was essential to China and the Chinese had no choice but to accept Soviet terms. The kinds of materials and know-how required to build a modern industrial and military establishment were impossible to obtain elsewhere. But while helping to build up China's military position, Stalin kept the Chinese dependent upon the Soviet

[23]Donald S. Zagoria, *The Sino-Soviet Conflict, 1956–1961* (Princeton: Princeton University Press, 1962), p. 68.

[24]*The Origin and Development of the Differences Between the Leadership of the CPSU and Ourselves* (Peking: Foreign Languages Press, 1963), p. 26.

Union. He supplied weapons but not all the means to make them. Of course, the Russians could not prevent the Chinese from ultimately building an independent military system, but in this way they could retard its rate of growth.[25]

The Soviet succession struggle after Stalin's death gave the Chinese an opportunity to raise the question of redefining the Sino-Soviet relationship. This was undoubtedly part of the reason for Khrushchev's and Bulganin's trip to China in September 1954. The next few years saw the gradual phasing out of Soviet military aid and training programs. By late 1956, the Chinese were flying their first Chinese-manufactured MiG jets, and the army had become a reasonably well-equipped light infantry force.[26] By then, Chinese military men were already deep in debate over the need for China to acquire her own nuclear weapons. Actually, the debate was never over the issue of whether to acquire nuclear weapons, but only how and when. Some advocated increased resource allocation to heavy industry as a means of establishing an autarkic military establishment and providing the basis for China's own nuclear program. Others argued for continued reliance on the "expedient measure of placing orders with foreign countries" to obtain needed materials.[27] The implied question in both of these positions was, What role would the Soviet Union play? At this stage of the relationship, both positions would continue to depend heavily on the Soviet Union for support, but, depending on the course chosen, for different kinds of support. It was not yet a question of "with or without" the Soviet Union.

The de-Stalinization campaign, the failure of the so-called "anti-party group" to oust Khrushchev, and the growing Sino-Soviet estrangement led to a restructuring of the alternatives open to the Chinese leadership. The choices now facing the Chinese leaders were either to go along with the Russians in the hope of restoring the former relationship at some future date, or to strike out independently—to break the bonds of Soviet economic and political domination. Both choices contained difficulties. To stay with the existing relationship left the Chinese open to the danger of falling further under Soviet domination, even though they gained some Soviet aid in the process. Economic aid was a double-edged sword; it not only served to aid the recipient, it also tended to make the recipient dependent upon the giver. The other choice, to break away from Soviet controls, meant an inevitable period of dislocation and perhaps even chaos until the Chinese could switch over to alternative sources of supply and restructure the economy. In these choices were planted not only the seeds of

[25]See Raymond L. Garthoff, "Sino-Soviet Military Relations, 1945-1966," in Raymond L. Garthoff (ed.), *Sino-Soviet Military Relations* (New York: Praeger, 1966), p. 86.

[26]See *ibid.,* p. 87.

[27]Hsieh, *op. cit.,* pp. 34-62, gives a fascinating analysis of discussions among military men in which the alternatives set forth here are implicit.

the Sino-Soviet split, but the Great Proletarian Cultural Revolution as well.

The issue was, How should China respond to the dilemma posed by the Russians? One wing in the party, headed (as we now know) by Liu Shao-ch'i, apparently favored continued cooperation with the Soviet Union—the choice of staying with the alliance and taking the risk that China would be able to avoid becoming an economic and political satellite. The other wing (the stronger of the two at the time), which was led by Mao Tse-tung, made the decision to strike out on an independent course. The Great Leap Forward symbolized China's determination to break Soviet controls, to disengage the Chinese economy from the Soviet Union, and to reject what the Chinese have since asserted were "unreasonable demands designed to bring China under Soviet military control."[28]

The Great Leap policy also implied a realization on the part of the Chinese that they would have to develop their own nuclear program without Soviet assistance.[29] There is no doubt that they attempted to obtain such assistance; according to the Russians:[30]

> The Chinese leaders have been at great pains to obtain possession of nuclear weapons. They strenuously tried—this is no secret—to get the Soviet Union to give them the atomic bomb. The CPSU and the Soviet government naturally could not consider this, since it might have led to the most serious consequences.

Mao's "paper tiger" speech of 1958, in which he stated that the United States should be feared tactically but not strategically (feared in the short run while China was weak, but despised in the long run when China would be strong), was an implicit recognition of the tactical disadvantage that the Chinese accepted when they embarked upon the Great Leap policy.[31]

Ostensibly, the purposes of the Great Leap were to catch up with Great Britain economically and to move into the stage of full communism ahead of the Soviet Union. The real reason, as suggested above, was to disengage the Chinese economy from Soviet controls. By all conventional economic standards, the Great Leap was an immense failure. Backyard furnaces, the mobilization of millions of people as a substitute for capital, the agricultural communes, the decentralization of industry—all of these became an enormous fiasco. Politically, for Mao Tse-tung, the results were mixed. By the decision of 1958, Mao set China on a new and independent policy

[28]*The Origin and Development of the Differences Between the Leadership of the CPSU and Ourselves*, p. 26.

[29]See Hsieh, *op. cit.,* p. 118.

[30]Radio Moscow, July 10, 1964, as quoted in Garthoff, *op. cit.,* p. 90.

[31]Mao Tse-tung, "Imperialists and All Reactionaries are Paper Tigers," in *Current Background,* No. 534 (November 12, 1958), pp. 2–8.

course that would be extremely difficult to alter, and which in fact continues to this day. For good or ill—and it looked like ill in 1958—China would henceforth develop independently of Soviet economic and, therefore, political controls. But for Mao personally, the results were less than satisfactory. The immediate failure of his policy gave his opponents the necessary political leverage to deprive him of his position as head of state, and to install Liu Shao-ch'i, his principal opponent, in his place. This was a considerable loss of power, which was not entirely offset by the official explanation that Mao wished to devote more time to "theoretical matters." Mao retained his formal party posts, but his rival obtained the important position of Chief of State.

Indicative of the Soviet position was the fact that, as soon as Liu became Chairman of the Chinese People's Republic, the Russians (in an agreement negotiated by Chou En-lai, who had flown to Moscow in January 1959) quickly extended additional economic aid to China by agreeing to build 31 more industrial plants.[32] Liu subsequently, very quietly and without fanfare, attempted to undo Mao's policy of the Great Leap. He began to dismantle the backyard furnaces, recentralize industry, and de-emphasize agricultural communes and the mass mobilization of labor. In summer 1959, the Liu faction—apparently encouraged by Khrushchev—attempted to secure additional positions at the expense of the now politically weakened Mao group.[33] P'eng Teh-huai, who had been in Eastern Europe on a military mission, during which he had had discussions with the Russians, returned to China in time to attend the Eighth Plenum at Lushan, where he denounced Mao Tse-tung's policies as "petit-bourgeois fanaticism."[34] The attempt failed. Instead, P'eng himself was dismissed as Minister of Defense; and Huang K'e-ch'eng, Chief of Staff of the People's Liberation Army, and a number of other supporters, were also relieved of their posts.

In a successful countermove, P'eng's position was assumed by Lin Piao, a supporter of Mao; while the post of Chief of Staff went to Lo Jui-ch'ing, an apparent neutral. In this compromise settlement, Mao made a net gain. Instead of having been ousted completely, he was still in a position of great power, and he had a strong ally in the key post of Minister of Defense.[35] Shortly thereafter, Lo Jui-ch'ing swung toward Mao's opponents, if he had not been one all along. The strength of the Mao-Lin group was more or less neutralized as long as Lo remained as Chief of Staff.

[32]See Franz Michael, "Khrushchev's Disloyal Opposition," *Orbis,* Vol. 7, No. 1 (Spring 1963), p. 64; and Floyd, *op. cit.,* p. 260. The agreement was signed on February 7, 1959.

[33]See David Charles, "The Dismissal of Marshall P'eng Teh-huai," *China Quarterly,* No. 8 (October-December 1961), pp. 64-65.

[34]Quoted in *ibid.,* p. 68. The term is of interest in light of the subsequent Soviet interpretation of Mao as "petit-bourgeois."

[35]Lin returned to an active role in political affairs in May 1958. On May 25th, he was elected as one of the vice-chairmen of the Central Committee and a member of the Standing Committee of the Politburo. See Hsieh, *op. cit.,* p. 114.

Several events seemed to indicate that the Soviets wished to adopt a friendly posture at this time. Shortly after the Eighth Plenum, Khrushchev flew to Peking for the tenth anniversary of the Chinese People's Republic. (He arrived late after returning from talks with President Eisenhower at Camp David.) Suslov, a member of the Soviet delegation, noted in a speech that:[36]

. . . [The Eighth Plenum] criticized the right opportunist mistakes of some party workers who were skeptical of the strength and potentialities of the Chinese people and the realism of the general line of the party. There is no doubt that the decisions of the plenum will rally the Communists of China still more closely around their Central Committee, headed by Comrade Mao Tse-tung.

Then, in mid-October, the Soviet Ambassador Pavel Yudin was relieved of his duties and replaced by Stepan Chervonenko; and the Soviets apparently expanded the terms of the Sino-Soviet Scientific and Technical Agreement of 1955.[37] But all to no avail.

The upshot of the 1959 shifts was that while Mao had become stronger, he was not quite powerful enough to regain his former position. He had recovered sufficiently from the attempt to depose him to frustrate all Soviet maneuvers to re-impose controls, to the extent that the Russians terminated (the Chinese claim "unilaterally tore up")[38] their nuclear assistance program, pulled out all of their technicians in mid-1960, and cut off all further aid. The hardening of positions was further reflected in public commentary. In an article entitled "Long Live Leninism," the Chinese labeled Russian arguments in favor of peaceful coexistence "absurd;" while Khrushchev, during his speech to the conference of Communist parties in Bucharest on June 21, 1960, replied that the Soviets "do not intend to yield to provocations and to deviate from the general line of our foreign policy . . . laid down by the Twentieth CPSU Congress and approved in the Declaration of the Communist and Workers' Parties, adopted in 1957."[39]

Over the next three years, Mao moved to consolidate a political base in the military, using as his instrument the concept of the Thought of Mao Tse-tung. He was ably assisted in this task by the new Minister of Defense,

[36]Foreign Broadcast Information Service, *Daily Report,* Far East, September 29, 1959, p. BBB23.

[37]For Chervonenko's appointment, see Survey of China Mainland Press, No. 2121 (October 22, 1959), p. 44; and for the communique on the agreement, see *ibid.,* No. 2118 (October 16, 1959), p. 45.

[38]*The Origin and Development of the Differences Between the Leadership of the CPSU and Ourselves,* p. 26.

[39]Quoted in Robert H. McNeal (ed.), *International Relations Among Communists* (Englewood Cliffs, N.J.: Prentice-Hall, 1967), pp. 104–106.

Lin Piao. At the same time, Mao heightened the indirect polemics with the Soviet Union. Worsening relations with the Soviet Union were not only consistent with his policy of independent action, but tended also to isolate his internal opposition, who favored closer cooperation with the Soviets. This was the dual significance of the many letters, communiques, and statements that passed between the two as Peking attacked "revisionist" Yugoslavia (but meaning the Soviet Union), while Moscow countered by attacking "doctrinaire" Albania (that is, China).

The issues of the polemic are significant in another respect. The principal areas of disagreement between the Soviets and the Chinese were over the questions of the character of the present epoch, of war, peace, the transition to socialism, the unity of the international Communist movement, and the rules regulating relations among Communist parties.[40] On each question, the Chinese attempted to establish their position as "orthodox" Marxist-Leninists, while labeling the Soviet Union as "revisionist."

One of the most important issues concerned the nature of the decision-making process in the Communist world. While both parties have evinced little disagreement over such broad general concepts as "proletarian internationalism" and "democratic centralism," neither Moscow nor Peking has been able to agree on which party (and country) should determine the content of such terms. The question remains, who will decide on strategy and tactics for the international movement? There was also disagreement over the priority to be given to wars of national liberation. Fearing a Soviet "accommodation" with the West, the Chinese place emphasis on national liberation wars as a means of furthering both the success of the world Communist movement and the growth of their own influence within the movement. Such theoretical questions as the definition of peaceful coexistence, the nature of imperialism, and the inevitability of war bring this issue into sharp focus. Finally, both parties disagreed on the policies to be pursued toward "fraternal" parties and with respect to each other's internal policies. The Chinese urge that high priority be given to the economic development of the bloc. They criticize the Soviets for economic aid to non-Communist countries, and for devoting increased attention to providing consumer goods for their own people, while a great deal of basic capital construction still remains to be accomplished in the Communist world (especially in Communist China).

It was on the basis of such theoretical arguments that the Chinese Communists asserted their leadership of the world Communist movement and justified their attempts to establish "Maoist" parties parallel to or in place of existing Communist parties around the world. At the Soviet 22nd Party Congress in October 1961, however, Khrushchev countered Mao's ideo-

[40]See Zagoria, *op. cit.,* pp. 299-315.

logical ploy by setting forth a new theoretical conception of the "party of the whole people" and the "state of the whole people."[41] One of the Chinese Communists' objectives during the polemic had been to institutionalize the Soviet leadership position, possibly in order to make it vulnerable to attack on doctrinal grounds. The concept of the party and state of the whole people shifted the grounds of the argument from a narrow doctrinal one to a broader plane of societal development. The Soviet claim now was that they were farther ahead on the path to communism.[42] Since all other Communist regimes, including the Chinese, would have to follow the same path, the Soviet position of leadership was historically sanctioned and could no longer be attacked on institutional grounds.[43]

By the time the Tenth Plenum convened in September 1962, Mao Tsetung had forged a strong alliance with the army through Lin Piao, an alliance which was clearly the basis of his political resurgence. The army's role in national affairs continued to increase. Army officers were retired and placed in political and economic positions in the non-military sector where they would be useful in the future as heads of factories, businesses, and other state organizations. Having built a political base in the army, Mao was extending it into other areas under the rubric of "spreading the spirit of the PLA."

At the Tenth Plenum, Mao felt strong enough to strike back at his opponents, both domestic and foreign. The coming internal struggle was intimated in Mao's comment that the conflict in China was between the supporters of capitalism and of socialism. In fact, the so-called "Socialist education" campaign, which was inaugurated at this time, may have been Mao's attempt to achieve his ends without resorting to open conflict.[44] At any rate, there was no admission of a power struggle among the top Chinese leadership; indeed, such an admission was never made while the struggle raged. It was not until some time after the Great Proletarian Cultural Revolution began that Liu was officially revealed as Mao's opponent.

In foreign affairs, too, the Tenth Plenum marked a watershed. Thereafter, Mao began to strike out at Khrushchev, publicly naming him as a wrecker of the Socialist camp and further intensifying the already heated polemics taking place between the two countries.[45] Sino-Soviet relations between the Tenth Plenum in 1962 and the Eleventh Plenum in 1966 cen-

[41]See Franz Michael, "Who is Ahead on the Way to Communism?" *Communist Affairs,* Vol. 4, No. 6 (November-December 1966), p. 9.

[42]See *The Road to Communism: Documents of the 22nd Congress of the CPSU, Oct. 17-31* (Moscow: Foreign Languages Publishing House, 1961).

[43]Michael, "Who is Ahead on the Way to Communism?" *loc. cit.,* p. 9.

[44]See Richard Baum and Frederick C. Teiwes, *Ssu-Ch'ing: The Socialist Education Movement of 1962-1966* (Berkeley: University of California Press, 1968).

[45]*The Polemic on the General Line of the International Communist Movement* (Peking: Foreign Languages Press, 1965).

tered around an interrelated two-front power struggle—the one between Mao and Khrushchev; and the other, which was muted until after Khrushchev's fall, between Mao and Liu.

The Widening Breach

The most widely accepted explanation of Khrushchev's fall is that it was caused by his failures in domestic policy and by differences with colleagues over questions of party power. Khrushchev did suffer several serious policy reverses in agriculture and industry; his virgin lands program failed dismally, and increased emphasis on chemicals and plastics industries at the expense of heavy industry had not met with the expected results.[46] He had also divided the Communist Party into industrial and agricultural hierarchies, and this, too, had not worked well. In the months before his ouster, there were indications that he was preparing new "heresies" in industrial and agricultural organization.[47]

These factors, whether taken separately or together, do not account for the peculiarity of Khrushchev's ouster. It was a sudden move, done secretly and in his absence. Moreover, few substantive changes were made in Khrushchev's policies after his dismissal, except that the party was structurally reunified. According to party statutes adopted in 1961 (and since revised), Khrushchev could not have sat on the Presidium for more than three terms, or twelve years, unless re-elected for a fourth term by a three-fourths majority of the Central Committee voting by secret ballot.[48] Having assumed the position of First Secretary in 1953, this meant that a dissatisfied minority could have ousted Khrushchev in 1965, when the time came to vote on his fourth term. Instead, Khrushchev was ousted one year beforehand. Something happened which made it impossible to wait that one year, something the climax of which would have occurred during the remaining year of his tenure.

That something, it seems, was the threat of a major policy change toward the Chinese People's Republic, combined with an unexpected development in the Viet-Nam War. Since the Great Leap Forward of 1958, Khrushchev had sought to bring about a leadership change in China, replacing Mao Tse-tung with a leader more amenable to cooperation with the Soviet Union. His plan apparently included carefully planned moves on the party, ideological, and state levels, and was to culminate at a conference of the

[46]See Judith Thornton, "The New Soviet Two-Year Plan," *Slavic Review,* Vol. 23, No. 3 (September 1964), pp. 537–562.

[47]See Linden, *op. cit.,* pp. 174ff.

[48]*Program of the CPSU* (Moscow: Foreign Languages Publishing House, 1961), Ch. 3, Section 25.

world's Communist parties in December 1964. The ideological wheels had been set in motion in 1962, when Soviet scholars began to debate the long-buried concept of the "Asiatic mode of production."[49] The discussions implied the argument that the Chinese were not only not Socialist, but were actually heading into a blind alley of societal development. According to the argument, Chinese society under Mao Tse-tung's leadership had regressed into a more primitive stage of development, rather than having achieved progress toward "socialism." Finally, on the state-to-state level, Khrushchev attempted to isolate China. The two most obvious events in this connection were the Taiwan Straits crisis of 1959 and the Sino-Indian border war of 1962. In each case, Khrushchev declined to support the Chinese, and instead adopted an anti-Chinese position.

The world conference of Communist parties was scheduled to open in December 1964, but developments in Viet-Nam upset Khrushchev's timetable. It appears that Tonkin Gulf became Khrushchev's Waterloo, setting in motion a sequence of events that culminated in his ouster. In essence, Khrushchev's China policy interfered with his attempts to aid Hanoi; and, in the face of a mounting international crisis requiring the unity of the Communist world, it led his colleagues to force him from power.

The Tonkin Gulf "incident" occurred on August 2 and 4, at a time when the Viet Cong were on the verge of victory in South Viet-Nam. In less than a week, a massive deployment of American power was initiated. On August 6, Secretary of Defense McNamara reported that reinforcements of various kinds were moving into the area;[50] and two days later, Congress overwhelmingly passed a resolution authorizing President Johnson to employ "all necessary measures . . . to prevent further aggression."[51] Khrushchev also reacted quickly to the incident. On August 5, the Soviet representative at the United Nations presented a resolution inviting North Viet-Nam to send an emissary to discuss the issue.[52] On the 7th, Hanoi appealed to the signatories of the 1954 Geneva Agreements on Indochina to check "U.S. preparations to invade its territory."[53] And on the following day, the Soviet Union assured Hanoi of full support, and demanded that the United States "immediately stop military actions against the Democratic Republic of Viet-Nam."[54] Khrushchev apparently hoped that debate on the Tonkin Gulf incident at the United Nations would freeze the deployment of American power long enough to permit the Viet Cong to win. But Hanoi itself

---

[49]For a survey of these discussions, see the author's "Soviet Historians and China's Past," *Problems of Communism,* Vol. 17, No. 2 (March-April 1968), pp. 71–75.

[50]See *New York Times,* August 7, 1964.

[51]Quoted in *ibid.,* August 9, 1964.

[52]See *ibid.,* August 6, 1964.

[53]Quoted in *ibid.,* August 8, 1964.

[54]Quoted in *ibid.,* August 9, 1964.

rejected the plan to send a representative to the United Nations, maintaining that only the 1954 Geneva Conference signatories could examine the case.[55]

It was at this point that Khrushchev's China policy began to get in the way. When Hanoi rejected the United Nations filibuster plan, Khrushchev's alternative was to neutralize the American deployment with Soviet aid. In order to supply North Viet-Nam, however, Khrushchev needed land access across China. There was no question of aiding Hanoi exclusively by sea. The recent Soviet attempt to aid Cuba by sea had resulted in a dramatic crisis between the Soviet Union and the United States. A transportation route across China was necessary to provide effective assistance to Hanoi. But Khrushchev's refusal to alter his policy toward China (or possibly the Chinese price for land access) persuaded his colleagues to depose him, rather than risk an open break with China at a time when unity was necessary. Thus Khrushchev was ousted, sometime between October 12 and 14, 1964.

After Khrushchev's fall, Sino-Soviet relations remained on about the same level of animosity as before. There was, however, no conference attacking the Chinese; and the Russians imposed a moratorium on their side of the polemical exchanges. After a brief trip to Moscow by Chou En-lai in November to ascertain what changes would be forthcoming (evidently none were actually proposed), the Chinese continued to attack Soviet policy as "Khrushchevism without Khrushchev."

Brezhnev and Kosygin replaced Khrushchev; and in February 1965, Kosygin visited Hanoi and Peking. He failed to negotiate a reconciliation with the Chinese,[56] but he did obtain a vitally important concession—an agreement on a railway route through China to North Viet-Nam.[57] The offer of reconciliation had a galvanizing effect on the Peking leadership, touching off an extremely critical debate over China's role in Viet-Nam and, by implication, on Sino-Soviet relations in general.

Although several leaders were involved in the debate, the principals were the Minister of Defense, Lin Piao, who represented the Mao group, and Chief of Staff Lo Jui-ch'ing, who represented the pro-Soviet group in the Chinese leadership. In early May, Lo gave a speech in which he advanced a strong argument for reconciliation with the Soviet Union in order to afford the most effective aid to a fraternal ally, the Democratic Republic of North Viet-Nam.[58] Lo envisaged the likelihood of a Sino-American

[55]See *ibid.,* August 10, 1964.

[56]"Reputation of the New Leaders of the CPSU on United Action," *Peking Review,* Vol. 8, No. 46 (November 12, 1965), p. 15.

[57]See *New York Times,* April 8, 1965.

[58]"Commemorate the Victory Over German Fascism! Carry the Struggle Against U.S. Imperialism Through to the End," *Hung-ch'i,* May 10, 1965.

conflict; and he urged that to prepare for this, China needed a modern, professional military force-in-being. This implied the need for a closer relationship with the Soviet Union, since it would only be by such means that China could obtain the necessary supplies in a short time. Lin Piao, on the other hand, took the Maoist line of independent action.[59] He argued that there was little probability of a Sino-American conflict; and that should one occur, the Maoist tactic of "people's war" would be the correct response. Therefore, there was no need for a rapprochement with the Soviet Union.

In this debate, which lasted for several months, the Mao group emerged victorious. Their victory and rejection of Soviet offers for a joint effort in Viet-Nam was signalled in November 1965.[60] Lo Jui-ch'ing was removed from his position as Chief of Staff at this time, decisively altering the balance between the contending groups. By Spring 1966, the Mao group had taken the offensive, and was in position to administer the *coup de grace* at the Eleventh Plenum in August 1966. The Eleventh Plenum marked a decisive turning point in the internal struggle, but it was a mixed victory for Mao Tse-tung and his supporters. It was a victory in that Mao obtained sufficient voting strength to carry his policies in the Politburo, to keep China on the course of independent action, and to begin the process of extending his Politburo victory to the country as a whole. It was a setback in the sense that he was unable to achieve his objectives without recourse to violent, even armed, conflict—the so-called Great Proletarian Cultural Revolution.

Apart from its purely internal ramifications, the Cultural Revolution saw an extensive purge of pro-Soviet elements in the Chinese leadership, a fact which has shaped recent Soviet policy toward the Chinese. No longer able to influence the decision-making process from inside China, the Soviets have since the outbreak of the Cultural Revolution attempted to build pressure from without. The Soviet objective remains the same now as it was under Khrushchev: to bring about a leadership change, which will result in a Communist China more responsive to Soviet overtures. The recent skirmishes along the Sino-Soviet border in Manchuria and Sinkiang, rumored Soviet threats to bomb Chinese nuclear emplacements, and the border talks, must be interpreted in light of this larger political objective.

China and the World Communist Movement

While conflicting domestic and foreign policy interests lie at the bottom of the Sino-Soviet conflict, ideological differences not only make rapprochement difficult, but also force an extension of the struggle to the

[59]See his speech, *Long Live the Victory of People's War* (Peking: Foreign Languages Press, 1965).
[60]"Reputation of the New Leaders of the CPSU on United Action," *loc. cit.,* p. 15.

entire movement. Given a continuation of the conflict, there is no long range ideological alternative for the Communist parties of the world but to take a stand beside one or another of the two protagonists, each of which asserts a claim to speak for the entire movement. All parties necessarily have become involved at every level of activity.

During the early 1960s, the Chinese Communists took the initiative in extending the conflict to the world movement, and made initial gains after precipitating factional struggles in virtually every Communist party. Their advances in the international front organizations, which were largely controlled by European Communists, were inconsequential. During 1963, therefore, the Chinese moved to create rival Afro-Asian fronts from which they could exclude the Russians on racial grounds. The action was based on the "strategy of three continents," which focuses on the underdeveloped countries of Asia, Africa, and Latin America as the "storm centers of world revolution."[61] This strategy received its fullest expression in late 1965 in Lin Piao's essay, *Long Live the Victory of People's War.*

A survey of the current state of the world Communist movement permits the general observation that the Great Proletarian Cultural Revolution has erased much of the prestige the Chinese Communists once gained as challengers of the Soviet behemoth. In Western Europe, all Communist parties except the Netherlands and Sweden support the Soviet Union. On the other hand, the Soviet invasion of Czechoslovakia in summer 1968 aroused widespread opposition among the West European parties; only the West German, Luxemburg, and Greek parties supported the Soviet action. The oldest pro-Chinese group in Western Europe, the Belgian Communist Party, has split several times and cannot be considered a significant factor. The Austrian Communist Party is similarly divided. In Italy and France, the Chinese have claimed the establishment of "Marxist-Leninist" parties (in October 1966 and December 1967, respectively). In Italy, the extreme left is sharply divided between Maoist and Trotskyist groups; in France, the Maoists seem more solidly based, although at present they are banned for participating in the student riots and strikes of May and June 1968.

In Eastern Europe, Albania, while firmly committed to the Chinese, has confined its own cultural revolution to the "cultural" field, and has maintained trade relations with all of the East European countries and diplomatic relations with the Czechs, Hungarians, Rumanians, and Bulgarians. At various times, the Chinese have claimed the existence of pro-Chinese groups in Bulgaria, Poland, Yugoslavia, and even a "Stalin faction" in the USSR, but these claims remain to be substantiated.

Chinese influence has deteriorated among the Communist parties of the

[61]See Kevin Devlin, "Boring From Within," *Problems of Communism,* Vol. 13, No. 2 (March-April 1964), p. 27.

Far East, but remains relatively strong among the "militant" Communists of Southeast Asia. The Japan Communist Party's conflict with China dates back to the opening of the Great Proletarian Cultural Revolution in 1966. The Japanese party recalled its remaining two representatives from Peking in August 1967 after they were physically beaten by a gang of Red Guards at Peking airport. The Chinese have since accused the Japanese of betrayal and revisionism.[62] In return, the Central Committee of the Japan Communist Party has denounced Mao's group for its ultra-left opportunism, and for splitting the revolutionary movement in Japan (a reference to the appearance of pro-Chinese groups).

Outer Mongolia, in a "buffer" position between the Soviet Union and China, has been under effective Soviet control since the state was established in 1924, despite Chinese attempts to exert influence through economic aid programs. North Korea is another state initially formed with Soviet "assistance" at the end of World War II, and in which Soviet influence remains paramount, although the Chinese presence is far greater than in Outer Mongolia. The Chinese continue to attack Kim Il-sung as a counter-revolutionary revisionist, but this has not prevented them from maintaining a scrupulously correct posture in formal state relations, and renewing commercial agreements from time to time. Peking has been clearly concerned, however, over the *Pueblo* incident and the growing belligerence of the North Koreans toward the South. This could lead to an increased American presence in Northeast Asia, which would only be to Peking's disadvantage.

Chinese Communist policy toward North Viet-Nam has been to support Hanoi's war effort against the South; and the Chinese have extended substantial, although not lavish, military aid for this purpose. Still, Peking's influence appears to have declined in recent months. Persistent opposition to Chinese efforts to influence military strategy, Red Guard interference with Soviet arms shipments across China, and Hanoi's decision to engage in the Paris talks despite Peking's vocal disapproval, are all indications of this development.

The small, outlawed parties of Burma, Malaya and Thailand are influenced by Peking's concept of "people's war," although the degree of influence varies with each case. In all three areas, guerrilla activity continues on a small scale; although kept in check by the local authorities, it has considerable nuisance value. As a result of the "cultural revolution" launched by the Communist Party of Burma, one of its main factions, the Red Flags, appear to have succumbed, while the victorious faction, the White Flags, seem little better off. For what it is worth, Peking's influence appears quite strong here. The Malayan Communist Party has intensified

[62]See *Jen-min Jih-pao,* August 5, 1967.

guerrilla activity on the Thai-Malaysian border. In its statement of June 1, 1968, issued to commemorate the twentieth anniversary of the Malayan state of emergency declaration, the party's main theme was armed struggle for the overthrow of the Malaysian and Singapore governments. In Thailand, armed clashes between Communist-inspired insurgents and government troops continue to occur along the Laotian and Malaysian borders.

Re-establishment of the Indonesian Communist Party remains a controversial issue between Moscow and Peking. According to documents allegedly issued by pro-Chinese and pro-Soviet groups, there appear to be (1) an Indonesian delegation in residence in Peking, numbering around seven hundred former PKI members; (2) pro-Chinese groups scattered around the archipelago engaging in small-scale guerrilla activity; and (3) a pro-Soviet Marxist-Leninist group, and the so-called Progressive Personalities of the Indonesian Workers Movement, both of which have denounced Chinese "adventurism" and advocate united front tactics. [63]

The Chinese have received varying degrees of support from the splinter groups and parties of India, Ceylon, and the Philippines. In India, the party is fairly evenly balanced between pro-Chinese and pro-Soviet factions, although the trend to increasing factionalism benefits the Chinese. In Ceylon, the pro-Soviet faction remains larger and more influential than the Chinese because of its participation in the opposition coalition. What little is known of the Philippine Communist Party suggests that Peking has had a resurgence of influence there, as the guerrilla movement and urban activism appear to be on the upswing.

In tropical Africa, the Middle East, and Latin America, the established Communist parties are generally pro-Soviet, siding with Moscow on most issues. Africa remains a major area of Sino-Soviet conflict. The Chinese have striven mightily to recapture lost positions, while the Soviets have labored to prevent them from succeeding. [64] Learning from their own setbacks in the area, the Soviets have accepted the strategic necessity of working through existing regimes whether they conform strictly to Marxist "criteria" or not. While the Chinese continue to preach violent revolution, during the past two years they have devoted much energy to improving an image damaged by the excesses of the Cultural Revolution. From time to time, Chinese supporters appear in the Arab countries without, however, succeeding in forming permanent organizations; this indicates the degree of Chinese ineffectiveness in the area. The pro-Chinese splinter parties established between 1960 and 1965 in Brazil, Colombia, Ecuador, Peru,

[63]For the pro-Chinese statement, see "Take the Road of Revolution to Realize the Tasks which should have been Accomplished by the 1945 August Revolution," *New China News Agency,* July 7, 1967; for the pro-Soviet view, see "Appeal of the Marxist-Leninist Group of the PKI," *Information Bulletin* (Prague), No. 10 (1967).

[64]See *Izvestia,* April 28, 1968.

Mexico, and Bolivia have not developed any momentum. Continuing splits characterize these organizations, although the Chinese can claim limited success in Peru, where approximately half the party is pro-Chinese, and in Ecuador, where the student movement exhibits a "Maoist" orientation.

The advent of the Great Proletarian Cultural Revolution led to a change in the style of Chinese foreign relations in the Communist world. For a time, during the height of the Red Guard phase, it was possible to speak of the absence of diplomatic effort by Peking, as most of its top ambassadorial staff were recalled and normal diplomatic activity ceased. After the Ninth Party Congress in April 1969, Peking slowly began to return to some semblance of normality in its diplomatic relations, except, of course, with the Soviet Union. Here only time will tell.

The Search for a Communist Commonwealth

In a larger perspective, what we are witnessing in the form of the Sino-Soviet conflict is the continuing inability of the Communist world to establish a viable system or community. The conflict may be seen as the most serious failure of all those attempts to establish a Communist system since the creation of the Comintern in 1919, when Lenin projected his Bolshevik party onto the Comintern as a "world party." The Comintern was a viable system as long as no other parties were in control of state power. After World War II, the emergence of several "people's republics" required a new organizational form for the movement. This was provided in 1947 by the Communist Information Bureau, or Cominform, which was composed of the Soviet Union and those parties that had gained power in Eastern Europe after World War II. The victory of the Chinese Communists two years later further complicated the organizational structure, but this was compensated for temporarily by the Sino-Soviet Treaty of Friendship, Alliance, and Mutual Assistance of 1950. The Cominform was dissolved in 1956 after the Soviet Twentieth Party Congress. For whatever reason, its dissolution necessitated further attempts to "regulate relations among the fraternal parties," as the Communists put it. Since 1956, such attempts have been made in the form of interparty conferences, of which there have been two, in 1957 and 1960. A third was scheduled to convene in 1964; but it was postponed several times before finally meeting in spring 1969.

The obvious failures of the Communists to work out a viable system should not obscure the fact that they have tried and will try again to establish some sort of "Communist commonwealth"[65] in the future, and with it a common program for the international movement. One important aspect of the Sino-Soviet ideological exchanges was that they reflected an in-

[65]See Kurt London, "The 'Socialist Commonwealth of Nations,'" *Orbis,* Vol. 3, No. 4 (Winter 1960).

ability to define structure and policy both within the Communist world and between the Communist and non-Communist worlds. Whatever the outcome of the Sino-Soviet conflict, further attempts will be made to work out a program for the Communist world. Of course, the leadership which emerges from the present turmoil in China will affect the content of future Sino-Soviet relations and the shape of the "Communist commonwealth." To expect the present state of mutual hostility to continue indefinitely is wishful thinking. A rapprochement will take place on some scale, however small, even if only the resumption of normal diplomatic relations. It may be much less than the one, united Socialist commonwealth the Soviets desire; it may be the creation of two independently functioning blocs for which the Chinese seem to opt;[66] or it may be something in between. But these seem to be the broad parameters of China's future role in the Communist world.

[66]See *Izvestia,* June 4 and 5, 1964.

Chapter Thirteen

Peking's Approach to the Outside World

Richard L. Walker

After twenty years of Communist rule and revolutionary change on the mainland of China, of unremitting hostility to what Peking calls "American imperialism" (and, for the past decade, increasingly strident criticism of "Soviet revisionism"), it is possible to appraise with some confidence the Chinese Communist approach to the outside world. This is an opportune moment to explore the prospects for long-term accommodation with the Peking regime, and the likelihood of moving the highly sophisticated, cultured, and altogether remarkable civilization of mainland China into the mainstream of contemporary world affairs.

New questions are arising concerning the future pattern of China's relations with the world at large. It is increasingly evident that we need to re-examine some of the old clichés. The very word "China," for example, conveys the concept of a single political entity, and it is possible that this is in itself misleading. Perhaps the word can carry only the kind of cultural and civilizational overtones that General de Gaulle imputed to "Europe" in the 1960s. Obviously the world will not deal in the 1970s with the same China that only a few years ago it thought it knew. The divisions and complexities of mainland China today make the unity which we attributed to it in the heyday of Maoist power now seem unrealistic.

At the time the Chinese Communist leaders were completing their surge to power in 1949, they seemed to have at their command a formidable array of international resources. This was an era of extreme anticolonialism, a time when political leaders in the former colonies, particularly in Asia, were building power for themselves by denouncing any form of Western intervention in their affairs, often including even Western cultural influence. As the Chinese Communists exploited national pride and evolved their own anticolonial world view, initially they evoked much sympathy among the newly independent states of Asia—a sympathy which they soon lost through their hard-line foreign policy positions and their support for insurgency in these countries. To most outside observers, theirs seemed to be a wholly indigenous Chinese movement, which in its initial statements promised unity, power, and the fulfilment of legitimate demands for equality in the world. In due course, the new nations, as well as the Communist countries and some Western powers that had been divesting themselves of their colonies, extended recognition to the Chinese People's Republic, which was proclaimed at Peking in October 1949. There was a fascination with the grandiose experiment in human engineering and modernization that the new leader, Mao Tse-tung, promised. Indeed, there was a general enthusiasm throughout the world for the "New China."

China's assets included a friendly Soviet Union willing to help—although at what was later revealed to be a rather high price—with the economic reconstruction of the Chinese mainland. China's "leftover" infrastructure, though damaged by civil war, still offered prospects for adequate initial transportation and communications facilities within the world's third largest country; and far more important, the regime had a certain verve or *élan* which in the initial stages brought the backing of intellectuals, students, businessmen, and many others who reveled in the implications of Mao Tse-tung's proclamation that "China has stood up!"

Looking back from the perspective of twenty years, it can only evoke our astonishment that the Communist leadership squandered so many of the resources that portended a bright and prosperous future for the Chinese people at home and abroad. As the regime reached its twentieth anniversary, it was clear that China was in disarray. For several years, even normal diplomatic relations with the rest of the world were all but severed, while the nation lived in an introspective isolation reinforced by the fantasy, which the Maoist leaders proclaimed, that China was on the side of, and had the support of, ninety percent of the world's people. Yet this came at a time when few people anywhere retained much sympathy for the Maoist regime.

Today the world is confronted by an angry and frustrated giant seeking somehow to break out of the straitjacket of ideological puritanism that Chairman Mao and his "thought" have imposed. Whereas there was an early fascination with the initial experiments of the "New China" at modernization—so that by 1958, Western leaders actually worried about the implications of the so-called "Chinese model" for the rest of the underdeveloped world—by the twentieth year of the Chinese People's Republic, few people outside mainland China had much enthusiasm for, or even interest in, a Chinese or Maoist model of development. The problem of bringing a preponderantly agrarian China into the mainstream of the space-age world has not been solved by Mao's techniques of collectivization and mass mobilization, or by his strategy of "the utility of hostility."

The Maoist Approach to Foreign Policy: Basic Aspects

China's process of adjustment to a rapidly modernizing world—including parts of the traditional Chinese cultural area, such as Japan, Korea, and Viet-Nam—is not likely to be easy for the Chinese people or for others who must bear with them during the process. It is important, therefore, that we understand some background features of the Maoist approach to foreign policy. These are factors that have set the tone of Communist China's foreign policy, and that are likely to have compelling importance into the future. They are, so to speak, *constants*, within the framework of which we can examine some of the specific considerations that have shaped Peking's approach to the outside world.

A first item which deserves immediate attention is the dualism of Chinese Communist foreign policy. From the time of Mao's earliest writings in 1926 down to the present, the Chinese Communist world has been peopled with "good guys" and "bad guys." Since the proclamation of the Chinese People's Republic in 1949, the good guys have obviously been those who have accepted Peking's special interpretations of the world, or at least given them some support, and who seem beguiled by Mao's scenario of the bright future of Communist China. The bad guys have been all those who have opposed the greatness of China as seen by Mao and his colleagues, or who have questioned the infallibility attributed to Mao by his court flatterers. Like Lenin before him, Mao insisted in 1949, in a very important statement that still dictates the foreign policy patterns of the Chinese Communist regime, that "there is no middle ground."[1] His approach was that of Lenin and Stalin: *kto-kogo,* "who-whom," who wins over whom or who destroys whom. Later ridiculous extremes in the statement of Peking's world views, with its outlandish flattery as well as the polemics of violent derogation, have tended to make outsiders skeptical and inclined to underestimate the central importance of this basic, underlying aspect of Chinese Communist policy. Both internally and externally, the Chinese Communists deal with a world in which there is—as Mao promised—no middle ground; those who oppose or disagree are characterized in escalating terms of vituperation as "demons, freaks, and monsters," whereas the praise for those who are willing to bask in the radiance of the new dragon throne in Peking mounts to almost unbelievable heights.

We must understand that this is not simply the dual world of traditional China, which juxtaposed the cultured Chinese with the ignorant "barbarians." There are a number of all too frequently forgotten or overlooked

[1]Wishful thinkers inside and outside mainland China tended to play down Mao's clear statement of intentions in his pamphlet *On the People's Democratic Dictatorship,* written in June 1949 to commemorate the 28th anniversary of the founding of the Chinese Communist Party. See *Selected Works,* Vol. 4.

reasons for viewing it in a different perspective.[2] First, there is in Communist China an entirely different underlying ideology, which has its own language, its own methods of analysis, its own conspiratorial approach to human life. Second, that ideology points outward and speaks in world projections in a far more assertive manner than did traditional Chinese civilization, which expected its natural magnetism to attract the outside world to itself. Third, there is a new emphasis on violence. Long before the Communists came to power, they accepted Mao's dictum that "the seizure of power by armed force, the settlement of the issue by war, is the central task and the highest form of revolution."[3] Fourth, the Marxism-Leninism of Mao, as well as that of the Soviet leadership, calls for world revolution and is, therefore, far more impelled to involve itself in the outside world than was the self-satisfied Confucianism of the Middle Kingdom. Thus, Mao's Marxism-Leninism does more than simply intensify the traditional dual world of the Chinese. It points in a wholly new direction, organizational as well as ideological.

A second constant which persisted through the course of twenty years of Chinese Communist foreign policy has been an emphasis on the so-called Third World. Less than two months after coming to power, the Chinese Communist leaders were proclaiming that their path to power was the path that "should be followed" by other colonial and semicolonial countries. This was Peking's way of announcing its determination to achieve greatness in the world, and of staking out its claim to leadership of the Third World, a claim it has never relaxed and which in due course led to arguments, disagreements, and even conflict with the Soviet Union.

A third constant in Peking's approach to the outside world is the fact that mainland China is a totalitarian state, even though today it is highly fractured and splintered. Totalitarian states cannot be judged on the basis of the societies they rule. They are not amenable to the same forces as other states in the contemporary international system. For totalitarian states, there are no unofficial relations or nonpolitical relations, and to talk about

---

[2]Though there are ample parallels between the approach of dynastic China to the outside world and that of the Chinese Communists, and while I would not argue that the traditions are unimportant, some historians have frequently played down the unique bent which modern totalitarianism has given to traditional attitudes and institutions—a bent which has served to intensify them and throw them out of proportion. See, for example, John K. Fairbank, *The United States and China,* 2nd revised edition (Cambridge: Harvard University Press, 1958); or C. P. FitzGerald, *The Chinese View of Their Place in the World* (London: Oxford University Press, 1964). Others have at times tended to overplay Communist achievements in remaking the traditional culture, and have projected the Communists' new synthesis as a permanent, unified, stable, cohesive unit in world affairs. See, for example, H. Franz Schurmann, *Ideology and Organization in Communist China,* 2nd edition (Berkeley: University of California Press, 1968); and the testimony of A. Doak Barnett and J. M. H. Lindbeck before the Senate Foreign Relations Committee (Fulbright Hearings on China Policy) in March 1966.

[3]*Selected Works,* Vol. 2, p. 219.

"world public opinion" having an impact on such regimes or their policies is to misunderstand the nature of their communications monopoly. Totalitarian governments tend to function in an unreal world, partly because the leadership usually receives only those reports that they want to hear. The consequences of flattery are intensified by the ideological need for infallibility, which then leads to making "unfacts" of very pressing realities; an example is Mao's dictum that the atom bomb is a paper tiger. Further, totalitarian regimes operate in an environment of secrecy. Little wonder after twenty years of totalitarian methods, building one unreal view upon another, that the system has tended to isolate mainland China from the rest of the world. Maurice Ciantar, the French journalist, commented late in 1968, after long experience in mainland China, that ". . . the Chinese are completely cut off from the world and seriously believe themselves the most advanced peoples on earth. Their contempt for the West is limitless and is equalled only by their ignorance of the outside world."[4]

A final constant that helps us to understand the tone of Communist China's approach over the past twenty years has been the tendency to draw on certain vague traditional interpretations of the world, to view relations in cultural and human terms rather than in precise legalistic formulae. Outsiders have frequently misunderstood, for example, the fluid Chinese position on defining boundaries, and they have underestimated the vigor of Peking's efforts to utilize proxies in spreading the Maoist gospel across ill-defined frontiers. The leaders of the Maoist movement have not been especially concerned about the technicalities of proper state behavior in the contemporary international system. They have stressed the transnational values of world struggle. Thus culture and cultural influence, in this case Communist culture and Maoist ideological influence, tend to rank higher in Peking's scheme of things than military forces or regularized positions in international law. This is not to say that the People's Republic of China has not used the canons of international law as a tool of foreign policy when they work in Peking's favor. But the constant emphasis has been on a new outward thrust by means of trained cadres from target countries who are expected to carry the Maoist pattern and the strategy of people's war across intervening national boundaries.

The Maoist Approach to Foreign Policy: Directional Factors

Within the framework of these constants that have set the mode, we turn next to examine other, more specific factors that have given direction to the foreign policies pursued by Peking. First, with respect to the world view of the Chinese Communists, it has been manifestly clear that they have tended to judge the outside world in terms of their own experiences

[4]Maurice Ciantar in *New York Times Magazine,* November 17, 1968.

and beliefs. The result has been to place heavy emphasis on raw power in their attempt to restore the traditional grandeur of China. The Chinese have long regarded themselves as the single most powerful nation in the world; their Communist rulers have insisted that China should be accepted as one of today's superpowers. In the view of the Communist leadership, a superpower is one that must be consulted on any issue of war and peace anywhere in the world. But twenty years of Mao Tse-tung have not yet brought that kind of power position to China. In their efforts to achieve superpower status, the Chinese have accented heavy industry and nuclear military power, but they have also exploited inexpensive methods of power projection such as staffing guerrilla and assassination training centers in Africa;[5] and they have brought numerous foreign leaders to Peking and sought to impress them with their ability to mobilize the masses of the Chinese people.

Peking's attempt to achieve superpower status, and to be accepted as such, is one of the most significant aspects of China's foreign policy. A great deal hinges on this point if we are to understand the pattern of Peking's relations with other foreign capitals. Chinese Communist leaders have displayed a sensitivity over any slight which might seem to derogate from their world position. In large measure, this accounts for their negative attitude toward any negotiations between the Soviet Union and the United States that might lead to decisions of worldwide significance in which Peking was not involved.

The great power aspirations of the Chinese Communists have directed them towards goals of regional hegemony. Here, too, they have run into conflict with the Soviet Union and the United States. For more than twenty years, they have insisted that there can never be peace in the Far East until the American presence has been withdrawn; and they have indicated in numerous actions along the Sino-Soviet border that they are also concerned over the Soviet position in East Asia. The dynamic industrial growth of Japan since World War II constitutes an especially significant roadblock in Peking's path to ultimate hegemony in the Far East. In many respects, the Maoist leadership has been as sensitive about Japan's postwar recovery, its relations with the West, and its growing national power as the Soviet Union has been about West Germany.

Perhaps the single most important obstacle to Peking's ambitions for regional and world status—from its own point of view—has been the unfinished civil war and its inability to "liberate" Taiwan. Obviously a power of the magnitude Peking aspires to be cannot permit this small piece of Chi-

[5]See, for example, the "White Paper" entitled *Nkrumah's Subversion in Africa*, published April 1966 by the Ministry of Information of Ghana; and the article from the African monthly *Drum*, reproduced in *Atlas*, Vol. 12, No. 6 (December 1966).

nese real estate to remain outside its control. Peking has denounced in the past, and can be expected to reject again and again in the future, any attempts at détente that imply the status quo in the Taiwan Straits. It should be noted that such attempts are doubly insulting from the Chinese Communist perspective because they represent intervention by outsiders to impose a solution that at the same time derogates from the great power status Peking so assiduously seeks. The existence of an alternate government on Taiwan has also afforded a different pattern of Chinese world participation and a contrasting approach to the problems of adjustment by Chinese civilization to the process of modernization. This, too, has tended to negate Communist claims that mainland China is a superpower. The Soviets moved with seeming impunity against hapless Czechoslovakia in the summer of 1968, but the Chinese Communist leadership remains unable to resolve the Taiwan problem to its satisfaction.

Related to Peking's world view is an historical factor which has been played up for more than a century by governments attempting to unify China. With real justification, the Chinese—whether Nationalist or Communist—are highly sensitive over the outrages of the past, imposed upon what they regard as their superior culture by technologically and economically more energetic Western powers, and subsequently by Japan. History texts both in Taiwan and the mainland place great emphasis on "lost" Chinese territories and the abuse supposedly heaped upon Chinese civilization by Western powers in the nineteenth century (for example, the "unequal treaties"). The history of the past century or more has reinforced Chinese convictions as to the necessity for building up the nation's military and economic power if China is to occupy a great power position in the revolutionary world of today; and the Communist leadership, given its military background and orientation, has been especially conscious of this need.

If we are to understand Chinese Communist foreign policy and its goals, we must also appreciate the extent to which the Chinese "internalize." Others have noted that the Chinese tend to judge in Chinese terms, but much more than this is involved. China is a country of such vastness, such grandeur, such scope, that it attracts full-time internal attention. Any Chinese leadership is likely to be concerned with foreign policy primarily in relation to internal developments; and Peking's foreign policy has constantly reflected the ebb and flow of the political fortunes of those who lead the nation. To a good Chinese nationalist, there is no subject more worthy of study than China itself—and exclusive study at that. It is not surprising that foreign policy is frequently subordinated to internal considerations. Further, internal problems and attitudes are projected onto the outside world, particularly by a leadership that is attempting to justify its position to its own people and to maintain its grandeur. Thus Peking claims that:[6]

> "Today the attitude toward Chairman Mao Tse-tung and Mao Tse-tung's thought is the touchstone and the dividing line between the revolutionaries and the pseudo-revolutionaries, and the true Marxists-Leninists and the counter-revolutionary revisionists."

That the world could believe such a proposition is obviously absurd to many intellectuals in mainland China today, but not to those who have operated within the Maoist totalitarian mould. China's internalization and her relatively unreal approach to the outside world have intensified over the years of the Mao regime; the process has been largely a result of, and has been accelerated by, the growth of the cult of Mao Tse-tung.[7] Within the framework of this personality cult, it becomes increasingly clear that the outside world can have little impact on Peking. The leadership interprets the whole panorama of international affairs in such a way as to glorify Mao; and in any case, the wide spectrum of domestic activities in China commands overwhelming attention as the items of first importance and magnitude.

Another factor that has proved significant for more than two decades of Chinese Communist foreign policy has been the emphasis on what might be called "the politics of arithmetic." Mainland China's rulers have stressed again and again that, to quote Chairman Mao, "a mighty population is a good thing."[8] The People's Republic has used its vast numbers as a means of projecting the image of great power. They have been able to do so because all too often the outside world has in fact reacted to the seeming power of the "vast hordes of China." But China's almost unbelievable numbers may well be a source of great weakness. The low subsistence level and productivity rates of most of the Chinese population have often been overlooked in estimates that equate numbers with strength. As the emperors of old boasted of their "myriad millions," so Peking too has utilized its ability to mobilize vast numbers in organized parades to demonstrate this component of power before the rest of the world, and especially for visitors from foreign countries, whose populations are minuscule by comparison.

---

[6]*Jen-min Jih-pao,* February 21, 1968.

[7]The writings of James T. Myers have been especially useful in elaborating this thesis. See, for example, his "The Fall of Chairman Mao," *Current Scene* (Hong Kong), Vol. 6, No. 12 (June 15, 1968). His views will be elaborated in his forthcoming volume, *The Glorification of Chairman Mao.*

[8]See S. Chandrasekhar, "Marx, Malthus and Mao," *Current Scene,* Vol. 5, No. 3 (February 28, 1967), pp. 1–14, for a discussion of the Maoist approach to China's great numbers.

Mao's doctrine that masses count, his mass line tactics, and his belief that the mobilized people can accomplish anything, have been part of a standard projection by Communist China in its world relationships.

A related factor, which has been a consistently compelling aspect of the Chinese Communist approach to the outside world, has been the intensity of the leadership's commitment to Marxism-Leninism. In attempts to analyze China in historical perspective, or in the framework of conventional international relations, the factor of Marxism-Leninism and its operational code have sometimes been downgraded. The Chinese Communists have accepted the Leninist theory of imperialism as gospel. They *do* regard themselves as a part of an historically inevitable movement, and they *do* look upon themselves as key leaders of that movement at a stage when "imperialism is heading toward its doom." Their commitment to Marxism-Leninism has given the Chinese Communists a strategic perspective that teaches them how to use alternating periods of tension and relaxation in foreign policy for the attainment of ultimate victory. It has also led them to take their ideology seriously, and they have asserted their ideological interpretations of events vigorously in dealings with the outside world. The Marxist-Leninist commitment also lends a special intensity to the manner in which Peking interprets its involvement in world affairs to the Chinese people—all, it must be noted, within the framework of a dogma made ever more inflexible over the latter years by the Maoist version of the Communist *Weltanschauung*.

This Leninist background has led Peking to adopt the Communist style of conducting diplomatic relations developed in the USSR under Lenin and Stalin, a style which the Chinese accepted at the outset, and at which they have shown themselves increasingly adept over the years. This Communist style has meant not only the use of cultural diplomacy, united front organizations, wide-ranging exchanges of delegations, a monopoly over foreign trade and its utilization for political purposes, and the centralization of all aspects of contact with foreigners; it has also meant considerable ability at vituperation and long-winded polemics.

Political leaders and scholars outside China have urged that we judge the mainland regime by its actions rather than its words. But the words are taken seriously by their authors; they are part of an overall operational code, and an essential ingredient of the guiding rationale for action. It would be a grave mistake not to take at least some of Peking's words, some of the polemics, some of the litany of abuse seriously. In this connection, it is worth pointing out that over the first two decades of Communist rule in China, techniques of analysis which have been successfully employed by the Kremlinologists in studying Soviet foreign policy have also proved useful in relation to Chinese Communist foreign policy. The omission, for example, of a single word of abuse in a list of adjectives preceding the name of the United States can signal the downgrading of a current anti-American campaign.

Another factor, linked to the totalitarian mode of operation and to some of the institutions of Marxism-Leninism, has been the growing intensity of the Maoist cult. This has involved an attempt to tap Chinese national pride with the assertion that China itself has now produced one of the world's greatest Communist leaders. The acceptance of Mao and his thought has become a basis for many of Peking's judgments in the projection of its foreign policy. This feature of its approach to the outside world reached ludicrous proportions in the late 1960s in the claims that were advanced for the scientific relevance of the Thought of Mao Tse-tung for all people everywhere. Despite some doubt as to whether the urbane and sophisticated Chinese people really accepted these assertions of the infallible and all-embracing truth of Maoist teachings, Chairman Mao himself remained in a central position as the guiding spirit behind what his colleagues did and said toward the outside world.

The outside world may have reason for worry about the foreign policy implications of the Maoist cult. The mystical and magical qualities attributed to Mao and his thought are reminiscent of the manner in which the Japanese emperor was treated by the militarists in the years immediately preceding World War II. During the second decade of Communist rule on the mainland, the works of Mao Tse-tung, his picture, and even parades in his honor assumed an almost sacred character; and any defacing of likenesses of the Great Helmsman, whether in India or Italy or Switzerland, could lead to serious diplomatic incidents.

The Pattern of Foreign Policy

A survey of the first twenty years of Chinese Communist foreign policy reveals a striking pattern of tension followed by relaxation, followed by returning tension. These alternating periods of foreign policy are clearly related to changes in Chinese Communist domestic politics. They reflect both a pattern of rule in mainland China and a strategic mode of operation. During periods of rigor, toughness, and tension, the Communist leaders hope to extract concessions at home and abroad from opponents who, in turn, strive to mollify or appease the Communists and persuade them to return to a more reasonable course. In the intervals of relaxation and coexistence that follow, the regime looks for further concessions to forestall a return to the hard line—which comes anyway. For outsiders who have looked for reasonableness from Peking, and have sometimes banked on the continuation of what they interpret as "pragmatism" during a time of relaxation, the return to a climate of tension has been particularly disillusioning—as, for example, in the case of Prime Minister Nehru of India.

A brief review of the foreign policy record offers a useful method for observing and assessing Chinese Communist interaction with the world over the past two decades.

THE "TOUGH" PERIOD, 1949 to 1953. The initial period of Communist rule was devoted to restoring order, reviving the economy, and solidifying control over the vast and disparate Chinese nation. Mao and his colleagues launched their regime with a series of intense campaigns or drives that spread throughout the country, and that allowed no question as to who were the rulers of the country. In foreign affairs, the leaders of the "New China" announced that they intended to learn from Stalin and the Soviet Union, that they would "lean to one side." They expressed a desire to establish diplomatic relations with the other nations of the world, but only on Chinese terms, which included absolute equality as viewed within the Communist framework. Thus, although Great Britain recognized the Chinese Communist government on January 6, 1950, shortly after it was proclaimed, several years elapsed before any significant diplomatic contacts developed.

This was also the period of the Korean War, and it saw the steady intensification of Peking's anti-American campaign.[9] The Korean War offered an opportunity for internal consolidation. It also enabled the Chinese to take a particularly tough line in foreign policy. Statements emanating from Peking against the "imperialist camp" were full of threats, and promised the eventual elimination of "imperialism" in an historically inevitable process that placed the "New China" in the forefront of world affairs.

It has been argued that the interposition of the United States Seventh Fleet between mainland China and Taiwan attendant upon the Korean War was the major cause of Peking's anti-American policy. Certainly in subsequent years it offered a ready-made excuse for Chinese denunciations of American interference in their domestic affairs. But many observers failed to note that the Chinese Communist leadership began its intense anti-American campaign before the end of World War II, and continued it as a major feature of their drive to power from 1945 to 1949. Long before the Americans themselves realized the fact, the Chinese Communist leaders recognized that the United States was *the* major Pacific power standing in their path to regional hegemony. The hate-America campaign was an essential ingredient of this period of toughness. It strengthened the Chinese

[9]A number of commentators have suggested that United States participation in the Korean War, and particularly MacArthur's drive to the north, were responsible for bringing about Chinese Communist intervention by the "Chinese People's Volunteers;" see, for instance, Allen S. Whiting, *China Crosses the Yalu: The Decision to Enter the Korean War* (Stanford: Stanford University Press, 1960). In this connection, it is worth noting that most of Lin Piao's Fourth Field Army had cleared Peking en route north before the North Koreans launched their attack on June 25, 1950.

self-estimation of their world power position; it fit in with the Stalinist two-camp view of global politics; it appealed to national pride that the new Communist rulers seemed able to "take on" the United States; and it offered both excuse and opportunity for purging internal enemies.

Equally important during this "tough" period was Peking's alliance with Moscow, and its support for the "wars of national liberation" that had erupted throughout much of Southeast Asia in 1948. Peking gave asylum, organization, training, and an operational base to guerrillas who functioned in the guise of autonomous revolutionary movements in Malaya, Indonesia, Burma, French Indochina, and the Philippines. This was also the time when Chinese Communists moved in force to "liberate" Tibet. During this period, Peking apparently believed that a policy of forceful support for guerrilla insurgency would bring about the liberation of the remaining areas of Asia (with the possible exception of Japan), and that its own power position would in consequence be enhanced. There was little reason to believe during this first "tough" period that a diplomatic accommodation involving give-and-take on all sides could be made with Mao Tse-tung and his colleagues. In the first flush of victory, they exuded a rugged, belligerent self-confidence, particularly when the war in Korea seemed to give them equal power status with their American enemies.

THE "BANDUNG SPIRIT," 1954 to 1957. After the end of the Korean War, Peking began to realize that support for Communist insurrection against already established governments and their leaders in the newly independent countries of Asia was proving counter-productive. The Chinese Communists found themselves in the untenable position of supporting violence against national heroes. They had misunderstood the full extent to which decolonization had already undercut their foreign policy position in Asia. Since Peking was seeking to enhance its role as a leader of the anti-imperialist forces, a change in tactics was called for. Furthermore, in view of the fact that in 1953 China had embarked on her First Five Year Plan for economic development, there was need for some relaxation at home and détente abroad. Chou En-lai initiated a concerted effort to win support from the leaders of the Third World, notably Nehru, and in 1954 negotiated with the Indian leader a treaty embodying the so-called "five principles of peaceful co-existence." Peking also participated in the Geneva Conference on Indochina that year.

But the high point of the new, soft line came at the Asian-African Conference at Bandung, Indonesia, in 1955. There the Chinese Communist leadership endorsed a world policy of peaceful co-existence, and put on a remarkable display of reasonableness in an effort to win support from the newly independent nations of Asia and those that would soon be attaining statehood in Africa. In the aftermath of Bandung, Peking succeeded in regaining the recognition and sympathy it had enjoyed prior to the Korean

War. The Chinese star seemed to be rising once again, and this period was marked by a new sense of strength throughout the "Socialist camp." When, in October 1957, the Soviets displayed their missile capability by orbiting the world's first satellite, the Chinese leadership decided that the balance of international affairs had changed.

Mao Tse-tung went to Moscow in late 1957 for the fortieth anniversary celebrations of the Bolshevik revolution. There he issued his famous dictum, "The East wind prevails over the West wind," by which he meant that the turning point in world history, long forecast by the Marxist-Leninists, was at hand. Now was the time for the Communist bloc to make an all-out thrust for supremacy. The Russians advised Mao that he was over-optimistic, that the "forces of imperialism are still powerful." Mao argued that they were weak and vacillating, that they would temporize and surrender before the pressure that a united Communist bloc could bring to bear. Failing to win the endorsement of his Russian colleagues, Mao returned to Peking determined to prove his point. In all probability, the Soviet leadership was distressed and even unnerved by Mao's towering ignorance with respect to the power balance in a scientifically sophisticated world that they themselves were only just coming to appreciate.[10]

THE GREAT LEAP FORWARD, 1958 to 1961. Having misread the strategic balance after "Sputnik" and failing to win the support of the Soviet leadership, Mao embarked on a campaign—suited to his own limited scientific knowledge—that aimed at solidifying political control within China, particularly on the countryside, and moving China forward toward a more formidable power position on the world stage. The domestic and foreign policies associated with this campaign constituted Mao's own version of how to go about modernizing a backward country and achieving superpower status. This program, popularly known as the Great Leap Forward, marked the real beginning of China's estrangement from the Soviet Union. The plan for the Great Leap included the establishment of "people's communes." These were criticized by Khrushchev and the Soviet leadership as impractical. "We tried them and they did not work." The Great Leap was accompanied by an intense military confrontation in the Taiwan Straits centering on the offshore islands of Matsu and Quemoy. It was expected that the United States, in its anxiety over Soviet space achievements, would back away from support of the Chinese Nationalists, particularly since the Taiwan Straits crisis was clearly linked to uncompromising, hard-line policies toward Japan and the British in Hong Kong, a combination that seemed to display Peking's supreme self-confidence for the future. In

[10]Much of this argument was to be exposed openly in the polemics between Moscow and Peking in 1963.

all respects, the Maoist assessments proved faulty. Backyard blast furnaces were no substitute for modern industrial equipment. The communes proved a disaster from the point of view of agricultural production. Attempts to force policy changes on Japan and the British in Hong Kong through artfully contrived incidents did not produce the intended results.

The Great Leap was such a traumatic experience, and so disastrous a failure, that for the first time the overall direction being given China by Mao Tse-tung and some of his closest colleagues was called into question. In 1959, a major Communist Party conference at Lushan gave evidence of serious divisions and weaknesses within the top ranks of the Chinese Communist Party that the outside world had not hitherto adequately understood. The facade of monolithic unity in the Chinese Communist leadership was destroyed.

WORLD PARTICIPATION AND STEPPED-UP TRADE, 1961 to 1965. The Great Leap also brought about a steady deterioration in Sino-Soviet relations. In 1960, when the Soviet leaders withdrew their technicians from mainland China and terminated economic assistance, Peking was forced to turn to the non-Communist world. Beginning in 1961, the Chinese resorted once more to the soft line of reasonableness linked to the diplomacy of Chou En-lai. Peking did not, however, abandon important previous commitments in support of wars of national liberation. After the Geneva Conference on Laos in 1962, Chinese Communist leaders fully expected success for the guerrilla movement in Viet-Nam and for the Maoist strategy in other economically underdeveloped areas. Peking continued its support for revolution in various African states, and was especially heavily involved in the Congo. Nevertheless, this period was generally characterized by an effort to woo sundry foreign powers. Chinese Communist diplomats worked diligently to bring about a rapprochement with France, leading to the establishment of formal diplomatic relations with Paris in January 1964. Peking also adopted a new and more conciliatory line toward Japan, although the Japanese were shaken when Communist China became a nuclear power with its first successful detonation in October of that year. In general, Peking's international posture during this period reflected a somewhat relaxed atmosphere on the home front. Indeed, some intellectuals within the party were speaking out and even writing spoofs that poked fun at the stupidities of the Great Leap Forward and at Mao Tse-tung himself. Mao seems to have been pushed into semiretirement.

Toward the end of this period, three events on the world scene hit the Chinese leadership very hard. The first was Peking's inability to bring about a new Asian-African Conference in Algiers, on which the Chinese Communist leadership had staked much of its prestige. Again, the failure of the Communist coup in Indonesia in the fall of 1965 marked a disastrous setback for Peking's policies; the Indonesian Communist Party had been closely linked with China in the dispute with the Soviet Union.[11] Finally, the overthrow of Kwame Nkrumah in February 1966 brought revelations of Peking's involvement in revolutionary training camps in Ghana and lost China much sympathy throughout Africa, as well as a particularly powerful supporter and ally.

Nevertheless, during this period mainland China expanded its foreign relationships more than ever before. By 1965, some 52 foreign governments had recognized the Peking regime, compared with only 32 at the time of the Great Leap. This development was achieved primarily through trade. Purchases of wheat from Canada, Australia, Mexico, France, Argentina, and of full industrial plants from various Western countries and Japan brought more and more outsiders into contact with the Peking leadership, which seemed at the time to be prepared to operate on a reasonable give-and-take basis, at least in the field of foreign trade.

THE FRENZY OF THE FANTASY WORLD, 1966 to 1969. Toward the end of 1965, it began to appear that the real divisions within the top leadership could not be reconciled, or prevented from spilling over into China's foreign relations. A group surrounding Mao Tse-tung was unwilling to see the revolutionary techniques of mass mobilization and organization, and the Maoist approach characterized by the Great Leap, labeled a failure and abandoned. There was still a belief among some of them, particularly Mao's hagiographer Ch'en Po-ta, his wife Chiang Ch'ing, and General Lin Piao, that the grand strategy of the Great Helmsman could prove successful in both domestic and foreign affairs. The power contest that resulted, and the attempt by Mao and his flatterers to reassert Maoist formulas for building power, were expressed in a frenzy even greater than the Great Leap. This was the so-called Great Proletarian Cultural Revolution, which began in 1966.

The impact on foreign relations was more disastrous than the Great Leap Forward. China moved into a stricter self-imposed isolation than ever before. The purges connected with attempts to purify the Communist Party resulted in the recall of most foreign service officers, and their rustication in the villages of mainland China in order to teach them the peasant-proletarian outlook. In early 1969, Peking had only one ambassador stationed abroad (in Cairo), and most of its missions maintained a posture of

[11]It is interesting to note in this connection how Peking used its policies of arithmetic in the contest with the Soviet Union by insisting prior to the Indonesian events that the combined party membership of three million Indonesian Communists, plus approximately seventeen to eighteen million Chinese Communists, gave them a majority vote in the world Communist movement. In this instance, they preferred to vote by individuals rather than by countries.

seclusion or semi-isolation.[12] The hostility of the Maoist leadership succeeded in antagonizing formerly friendly neutrals. Its polemics with the Soviet Union reached new extremes. In the spring of 1969, serious border clashes along the Amur and Ussuri Rivers, and elsewhere along the 4,500-mile Sino-Soviet frontier, underlined the almost complete break with the USSR.

The Great Proletarian Cultural Revolution and its attendant crises in Communist China's foreign relations represented another profligate squandering of the support and sympathy that the Chinese Communist leadership could originally count upon when they took power twenty years before. By the time the regime celebrated two decades in power, the Cultural Revolution had been turned off and the pendulum seemed ready to swing back toward a relaxation. But building contacts with the outside world was proving difficult, and the purge of party ranks meant that foreign policy continued to drift. Even with the return of a few ambassadors to posts abroad, Peking seemed unable to provide them with significant policy guidance.

Perhaps this was a reflection of the extent to which the Cultural Revolution had undermined the unity of mainland China. While various factions were positioning for the power struggle that seemed likely when Mao and other members of the aged elite passed from the scene, foreign relations were simply not considered important enough to warrant attention or the expenditure of energy.

Methodology and Prospects

Within the framework of alternating periods of tension and relaxation over the first two decades of Communist rule in China, it is possible to discern the constant interplay of contradictory forces. The attempt to export a revolutionary ethic has inhibited the conduct of foreign relations in a style acceptable to the rest of the world. It is difficult to build lasting relationships with the new states of Asia and Africa if Maoist doctrine claims that they are "ripe for revolution," and implies a threat to overthrow the present leaders. Again, it is doubtful whether Peking can gain respect for its position as a superpower in world affairs when its representatives insist that the Thought of Mao Tse-tung is the pinnacle of modern scientific achievement. Such aberrations have demonstrated the impossibility of a rational adjustment of Chinese civilization to the twentieth-century world by Maoist methods.

[12]In Spring 1969, Peking again began to assign ambassadors to foreign countries. But the process was slow, and diplomats of rank were present in only a dozen countries by early 1970.

After two decades of Communist rule, despite divisions within the Chinese People's Republic, the split in the leadership of an aging elite, the loss of credibility for Mao himself, the breakdown in lines of authority, problems with national minorities, and growing isolation from the world, mainland China could nevertheless still view itself as a formidable factor on the world scene. Peking still makes its influence felt along its borders. It has achieved nuclear power status, and has been able to convince even its archrivals, the United States and the Soviet Union, that its massive numbers are a source of strength, particularly when imbued with the fire of national pride and the sword of modern organization.

Peking's approach to the outside world has utilized methods peculiarly suited to a large and populous nation that remains essentially a "have-not" power. Following the internal power adjustments attending the Ninth Party Congress in April 1969, China may now turn away from the tough line of the Great Proletarian Cultural Revolution and move back to a period of relaxation and peaceful coexistence with the outside world—especially if Mao dies or is pushed aside. But so long as the leadership maintains its Marxist-Leninist ideology and totalitarian mode of operation, Communist China will continue to emphasize those foreign policy techniques for achieving great power status that have seemed efficacious during the first two decades. They may be summarized as follows.

DISPLAYS AND UTILIZATION OF MILITARY POWER. Communist China's participation in the Korean War (1950 to 1953), the military "liberation" of Tibet, the Taiwan Straits crisis (1954 to 1955 and 1958), the border war with India (1962), and skirmishes with Soviet forces (1969), all have helped to build the image of Communist China as a major world power—indeed, a nuclear power—militarily able and, if necessary, willing to "take on" all comers.

SUPPORT FOR NATIONAL LIBERATION MOVEMENTS. Here Peking can gain status with nothing more than vocal support for insurgent forces in faraway places. For example, Communist China gave full moral support to the Palestine Liberation Organization even when the United Arab Republic and the Soviet Union were holding back. Peking's support for the Thailand People's Liberation Army, for the Burmese White Flag Communists, and other such groups has proved a relatively inexpensive method for gaining respect for its power position even if as an adversary. In many areas of Southeast Asia, Peking has been able to use the Overseas Chinese as channels of communication, intelligence, and financial support, as well as a source of cadres for the "liberation" movements; although in some cases, particularly in Indonesia and Malaysia, this has proved counterproductive because of the strong anti-Chinese bias among the local population.

CULTURAL DIPLOMACY. During its first two decades, the Chinese Communists displayed a remarkable capacity for utilizing cultural contacts and cultural missions abroad to build an image of Chinese strength and standing in the world. Although cultural diplomacy suffered during the course of the Great Proletarian Cultural Revolution and the attempt to build up the Thought of Mao Tse-tung as the epitome of modern thought and science, the Chinese Communist leadership has demonstrated a formidable ability to employ cultural communications effectively in order to maximize its influence abroad; and this has included the use of techniques learned from the Soviet Union.

LINKING OF ECONOMICS AND POLITICS. As a centrally controlled state monopolizing all aspects of its economy, Communist China showed an early ability to utilize foreign trade and other international economic dealings—including limited amounts of foreign assistance beginning in the latter half of the 1950s—for the purposes of power projection.

TRAINING CADRES FOR REVOLUTIONARY WARFARE. From the beginning, selected nationals from Third World countries have been trained in mainland China as guerrilla leaders for wars of national liberation in their homeland. The training given to Burmese, Indonesians, Thais, Laos, Nagas, and other cadres from Southeast Asia has proved a remarkably cheap and effective method for projecting Chinese power and influence abroad. During the course of its first two decades in power, the Communist leadership expanded this technique of power projection by setting up cadre training centers in Africa and by helping to staff guerrilla, ideological, and military schools in the Middle East and Latin America.[13]

Such are some of the methods which have been part of the Chinese Communist approach to building a leadership position in a revolutionary world in which China has not yet gained acceptance as a superpower. These methods can pose a serious challenge to the peace and harmony of the international community, especially since they are backed by the ever-present possibility of irrational action by the Maoist leadership, now armed with nuclear weapons, and since they are predicated on Mao's thesis of the need for and desirability of revolutionary violence to solve political problems.

As Communist China entered its third decade, it seemed that the Great Helmsman had connived in the destruction of much of his own totalitarian creation. Despite the proclaimed success of the Ninth Congress in April

[13]On Peking's approach to Latin America, see Daniel Tretiak, "China and Latin America," *Current Scene,* Vol. 4, No. 5 (March 1, 1966). Mainland China's involvement in the Middle East is discussed in Harold Hinton, *Communist China in World Politics* (Boston: Houghton Mifflin, 1966). By early 1970, Peking was appealing increasingly to the Arab world in propaganda that pictured Israel as the tool of American imperialism bent on the destruction of Arab independence.

1969, the party was a shambles and the country was being run by the military. When the regime celebrated its twentieth anniversary on October 1, 1969, the leaders boasted that China was more unified and stronger than ever. But this was clearly not so. In fact, it is unlikely that the Maoist regime can ever be restored to its former vigor. In both internal and foreign affairs Chinese civilization, with its values of harmony and accommodation, was proving the major opponent of Maoist policies of struggle and violence. In the 1970s, it is now entirely possible that the energetic and talented Chinese people will turn toward other approaches to the problem of modernization and to dealing with the outside world. When this eventuates, the doors must be open and opportunities available for assisting mainland China to reenter the family of nations.

CHAPTER FOURTEEN

The United States and Communist China

Frank N. Trager and William Henderson

The issue of United States relations with Communist China has been hotly debated in this country ever since the formal establishment of the Peking regime in October 1949. After two decades of Communist power on the mainland, it remains in the forefront of public discussion as one of the great unresolved dilemmas of American foreign policy. The Nixon Administration has made clear its determination to move toward "improved practical relations" with Communist China.[1] Some initiatives have already been taken in this respect, notably the resumption of ambassadorial talks in Warsaw; removal of the ban on travel to the mainland for Members of Congress, scholars, physicians, journalists, and Red Cross representatives; and permission for American subsidiaries abroad to trade in non-strategic goods with Communist China. But the long term prospects of these acts and statements are still obscure.

How are we to deal with the People's Republic of China? Obviously, we cannot ignore the largest political construct of human history, at once so impressive in its millenial accomplishment and apparently so menacing in its contemporary configuration. For the past two decades, the relationship has been informed by almost total hostility on both sides, at least at the official level. A persistent school of policy criticism insists, however, that we have misunderstood the nature and significance of Communist China for the United States; that the Peking regime has been preeminently concerned with the manifold problems of domestic reform and reconstruction; that the main thrust of foreign policy has been simply to reclaim for China a principal role (but no more) in the politics of Asia, and a respected voice in the counsels of the nations; and, finally, that the undoubted bellicosity of its foreign policy pronouncements reflects primarily the defensive reaction of a still weakened and historically much abused nation to the manifest hostility of others. This general analysis

[1] *U.S. Foreign Policy for the 1970's, A New Strategy for Peace. A Report to the Congress by Richard Nixon, President of the United States, February 18, 1970* (Washington: Government Printing Office, 1970), p. 141.

leads inevitably to the prescription that the United States should speedily normalize relations with Communist China all across the board. While it applauds the measures already taken by President Nixon to ameliorate the most stringent rigidities of containment-through-isolation, it is not content with an approach limited to the cautious exploration of practical possibilities through *ad hoc* negotiations of one kind or another spread out over a long period of time.

It is the purpose of this brief, concluding essay to examine the place of Communist China in United States foreign policy. Our intention is not to deal prescriptively with the particular issues that properly clamor for contemporary attention: recognition, non-strategic trade, exchanges of personnel, and the like; but rather to place Communist China against the perspective of United States policy in Asia as that policy has evolved during the twentieth century. There is nothing foreordained about the international process. Despite Peking's emerging place as a leading actor in the Asian power balance, the mechanics of the balance of power do not require either an inescapable hostility or its obverse. Here the choice lies in the main with Peking, with the long-term objectives of its grand policy, and perhaps most of all with the ultimate imperatives of its Communist faith.

The Evolution of Asian Policy

Opponents of the American involvement in Viet-Nam, who with remarkable frequency are also critics of United States containment policy toward Communist China, often argue that our military intervention in Southeast Asia represents a tragic deviation from the "traditional" Far Eastern policy of this country. Our intervention in South Korea against Communist aggression from the North two decades ago was criticized in much the same way. This is the point of view that is occasionally expressed in such seductive simplicities as the maxims, "The United States must never become involved in a land war in Asia," or "Asian affairs should properly be settled by Asians." It is reflected, too, in the estimate that the possible reassertion of China's "traditional" hegemony over some of the smaller countries of mainland Asia is not a proper concern of United States policy, or is a concern that may be bartered away for something else.

Leaving aside the political wisdom, the *realpolitik,* of such aphorisms, the thing that can be said with certainty is that they do not reflect the traditional American approach to East Asia—at least, as that policy has evolved in the twentieth century. At the outset, therefore, it may be worthwhile to sketch in outline the authentic tradition of United States policy in East Asia as we understand it. To be sure, traditional policy may have been wise or unwise, and today may still be apposite or else outmoded. But surely the accumulated experience of many decades of policy is entitled to respectful consideration before it is summarily junked by those who seek to change it.

East Asia has always exerted a special fascination on American policy makers. A thesis of the *Federalist Papers* held that a strong central government was necessary to defend and support American trade with East Asia, which was bound to become a major factor in our overseas commerce. The nineteenth century was punctuated by a series of American initiatives throughout the region. Our sailing ships in pursuit of trade and missionaries in pursuit of souls made Canton a familiar place to many Americans, even including support for such charitable ventures as an eye hospital in that city. We concluded our first treaty with an Asian country, Siam, as early as 1833. Eleven years later we entered into treaty relations with imperial China. We played a leading part in the opening of Japan in 1854, and were heavily involved in the foreign politics of Korea, the erstwhile Hermit Kingdom, in the 1870s and 1880s. Nor should it be forgotten that in 1845, an American naval captain attempted clumsily and unsuccessfully to interfere in the internal affairs of Annam (as Viet-Nam was then known)—more than a century before our present military involvement in that unhappy country.[2]

But the significance of these episodes should not be overstated. They did not add up to a policy. They reflected the hopes, ambitions, and enthusiasms—however much these three may properly be questioned—of a growing nation still preoccupied with subduing the American continent. The politics of East Asia were then made by the Asian countries themselves, especially China and Japan, and by the European powers most intimately concerned: Great Britain, Russia, and to a lesser extent, France and Germany. Our vital interests in the area—as they later came to be defined—were not yet involved, nor even clearly understood; and in any case, we did not have the power to play a major role. We were, indeed, the beneficiary, not the instigator, of the so-called "unequal treaty" system reluctantly accepted by the declining governmental power of the Ch'ing dynasty.

The great turning point came with the end of the nineteenth century. In 1895, China suffered a crushing defeat at the hands of Japan, and thereafter faced the imminent danger of complete collapse and partition. Ten years later, it was Russia's turn to feel the weight of Japanese power, and thereafter Russian expansion in East Asia was curtailed for several decades. Meanwhile, the European powers were increasingly preoccupied by the threatened collapse of the European balance, which in 1914 led

[2]The attempt made by Captain John Percival, commanding the U.S.S. *Constitution,* to obtain the release of an imprisoned French missionary, Bishop Dominique Lefébvre, was subsequently disavowed by the Washington government, which also offered a formal apology to the Court of Hue. On this interesting episode, see Joseph Buttinger, *The Smaller Dragon, A Political History of Vietnam* (New York: Praeger, 1958), pp. 332, 391-392.

to the outbreak of World War I. By the first decade of the twentieth century, Japan was already emerging as the dominant power of East Asia.

By this time, too, the United States had grown up as a nation. We had conquered a continent, and had become a major industrial power. We had also become a Pacific power, with the longest Pacific coastline of any nation except Russia's, and with a mid-ocean outpost in the Hawaiian Islands. Then in 1898, almost by inadvertence, the United States acquired a major territorial stake in East Asia as an unforeseen consequence of the Spanish-American War with the annexation of the Philippines and Guam; in 1899, a part of Samoa was added to this budding empire. Overnight we became a player in the game of Asian politics, no longer able to ignore the rivalries and ambitions of the other great powers, and no longer largely ignored by them.

The next four decades, down to Pearl Harbor in 1941, are the history of a steadily deepening American involvement in the affairs of East Asia. It imposes too great a pattern on history to suggest that American policy makers formulated from the beginning a coherent concept of our vital interests in East Asia, or that they thereafter pursued a wholly consistent pattern of policies in the area. In any event, foreign policy rarely develops in this way. It is rather the sum total of the frequently conflicting assessments and responses of successive Presidents and Secretaries of State, and of leading personalities in the Congress, to the evolving circumstances —in this case—of East Asian politics; and it is only in retrospect that we can discern a symmetry to our growing involvement. Despite the inconstancy of statesmen and the inevitable contradictions of particular policy initiatives, there did emerge in the first four decades of the twentieth century a distinctive pattern of involvement, a set of particular policies that became traditional, and that added up to a consistent interpretation of the American interest in East Asia.

It may be worthwhile to summarize briefly what came to be the main traditions of Far Eastern policy. The first, and most easily understood, was that the United States had a territorial stake in East Asia—the Philippines and Guam, and that like any self-respecting nation we would fight to protect it. The second, which was initially less manifest, was the American interest in the preservation of an independent China, an interest first articulated in the Second Open Door Notes in 1900. To be sure, this interest was initially conceived as a utilitarian principle: equality of commercial opportunity in China could be effectively safeguarded only if the administrative integrity of China itself was preserved. But in time the principle took on a life of its own quite apart from its presumed relationship to commercial opportunity, although it was some time before we understood clearly why this should be so.

A third tradition cast the United States as being, in some special way, the friend and protector of China against its enemies. This special relationship finds expression as early as the First and Second Open Door Notes, in the policies of Theodore Roosevelt at the time of the Russo-Japanese War, and in President Wilson's efforts to mitigate the consequences of Japan's Twenty-One Demands on China in 1915 and at the Versailles Conference. It formed the basis of Secretary Hughes' diplomacy at the Washington Conference in 1922, and of Secretary Stimson's proclamation of the Doctrine of Nonrecognition following Japan's conquest of Manchuria in 1931. Such episodes as these also serve to explain a fourth tradition, namely, that the main threat to the East Asian interests of the United States came from imperialist, expansionist Japan. This appreciation began to take form with Japan's annexation of Chinese territory (Taiwan) following the Sino-Japanese War, gained momentum with Japan's victory over Russia in 1905 and its subsequent annexation of Korea, and became a national preoccupation with Japan's expansionist moves during and after World War I. By the time of Pearl Harbor, Japan had already become an almost hereditary enemy.

For a long time, publicists and statesmen found it difficult to articulate clearly the profound national interests that this complex of policies reflected. This could only be done in terms of a sophisticated power analysis, and until World War II the concept of power politics and all that it connoted had little currency in American political discussion. This is somewhat surprising in view of the fact that the United States had entered World War I to prevent German domination of the European continent, and that this fact had come to be clearly understood by most students of foreign policy. Not until Nicholas J. Spykman published his seminal volume on *America's Strategy in World Politics* in 1942 did a ranking commentator point out the importance for the United States of maintaining a balance of power in *both* Europe *and* Asia.[3] To put it another way, the American interest required that no one power become dominant on either continent.

There can be no doubt that the United States became involved in World War II precisely to prevent the domination of East Asia by a hostile power, Japan, and of Europe by Nazi Germany. The record is wholly clear that President Franklin D. Roosevelt's policy for the containment of Japanese expansion, culminating in the freezing of Japanese assets in July 1941, confronted the Tokyo government with the critical choice of abandoning its aggressive aims in East Asia or defeating the United States in war as the necessary preliminary to completing its program of conquest. While it is absurd to accuse Roosevelt of deliberately provoking the

[3]Nicholas J. Spykman, *America's Strategy in World Politics* (New York: Harcourt, Brace & World, 1942). For an earlier and suggestive formulation of United States interests in East Asia in balance-of-power terms, see Tyler Dennett, *Americans in Eastern Asia* (New York: Macmillan, 1922).

conflict, he was well aware that the vindication of the main traditions of our Far Eastern policy involved the danger of war with Japan. But the choice had to be made. The United States could not tolerate the establishment of a hostile hegemony in East Asia.

In recent years, a growing literature has analyzed the evolution of our Far Eastern policy in explicitly balance-of-power terms. In 1951, for example, Hans J. Morgenthau defined the "permanent interest of the United States in Asia" as "the maintenance of the balance of power."[4] More recently, Charles Wolf, Jr. has stated that our fundamental interest in Asia was "to prevent the domination of the area by a single power, or by a group of powers acting in concert."[5] Fred Greene has offered a similar formulation.[6] And in his excellent new study, *Towards Disengagement in Asia,* Bernard K. Gordon states:[7]

> The U.S. opposed Japan *because that policy served the more basic objective of trying to achieve a balance of power in Asia.* That objective in turn was sought *because it would best serve the U.S. national interest of preventing one-nation hegemony.*

And he concludes his thoughtful analysis of the evolution of American policy in Asia with the observation that traditionally:[8]

> ... the United States (has) sought as its objective an over-all Asian balance because, by definition, such a balance would be the manifestation and reflection of the United States national interest: that no one nation achieved general dominance in East Asia.

Traditional Policy and the New Asia

Against the background of this historical perspective, there are ironic elements of *deja vu* in the development of Asian politics since World War II. To be sure, there have been fundamental changes in the *dramatis personae,* and a number of new players have emerged onto the stage of Asian politics. To use the terminology of a bygone era, a "diplomatic revolution" has taken place. It is perhaps less apparent that, beneath this striking transformation of roles, the basic problem of Asian politics has paradoxically not changed very much. The overriding national interest of the United States in the area remains much the same: to prevent the

[4]Hans J. Morgenthau, *In Defense of the National Interest* (New York: Knopf, 1951), p. 6.

[5]Charles Wolf Jr., *United States Interests in Asia* (Santa Monica: RAND, 1966), quoted in Bernard K. Gordon, *Toward Disengagement in Asia* (Englewood Cliffs, N.J.: Prentice-Hall, 1969), p. 28.

[6]Fred Greene, *U.S. Policy and the Security of Asia* (New York: McGraw-Hill, 1968).

[7]Gordon, *op. cit.,* p. 41. Emphasis in original.

[8]*Ibid.,* p. 58.

emergence of a hostile hegemony capable of marshaling the power of East Asia against us.

On one level, the face of Asian politics has been transformed by two parallel and sometimes overlapping developments. The first is the consequence of the rise of revolutionary nationalist movements in the former Asian colonies that shook and ultimately destroyed the old colonial empires. These movements have resulted in the appearance of a host of newly independent countries that are, however, weak and for the most part unable to defend themselves, prey to Communist insurrectionary movements aided and abetted from abroad. The second of these profoundly disturbing developments has been the emergence of a bloc of Communist states on the mainland of East Asia, expanding enormously the vast Asian territory already under Communist control (that is, the Soviet Far East and Outer Mongolia). So far, this bloc includes North Korea, the creation of Soviet conquest in 1945; Communist China, whose victory on the mainland was sealed with the proclamation of the People's Republic in October 1949; and North Viet-Nam, where an indigenous (although externally supported) Communist movement established paramountcy over the northern half of the country by 1954, and achieved international recognition of its victory at the Geneva Conference in July of that year.

Since World War II, the judgments of five successive Presidents and their Secretaries of State with respect to these two revolutionary developments has shown a remarkable consistency. They have viewed the emergence of the new states of Asia as an historically inevitable development, congenial to the frequently articulated anticolonial traditions of our own country and to our abiding belief in the right of all peoples to self-determination, and also consistent with a profound American interest in a plural world environment characterized by a multiplicity of sovereign, independent states. On the other hand, it has been their consistent appraisal that the second development (that is, the emergence of a bloc of Communist countries in East Asia) poses a direct and portentous challenge to fundamental American interests as well as to the continued independence of the new states. This was not so much because the imposition of a Communist tyranny, anywhere or at any time, was judged to be a moral disaster. Despite the more vocal critics of American policy in Asia, such moral judgments have had relatively little to do with informing that policy since World War II. Rather it was primarily because of an evaluation that the Communist countries, and especially Communist China, might succeed in organizing the power of mainland and island Asia as a hostile hegemony, and that the actual—and still more the potential—power of this complex could ultimately threaten the vital security and other interests of the United States.

The balance of this essay is not directly concerned with North Korea as an element in this Communist challenge to American interests in Asia. The total hostility of the Pyongyang regime to the United States since 1945 is, however, a matter of historical record, as is North Korea's aggression against the South during the years 1950–53. To this day, moreover, Pyongyang continues to proclaim openly its ultimate intention to conquer South Korea by force if necessary, and thereby to extinguish a non-Communist polity and to expand the world sphere of Communist power. Nor are we immediately concerned here with North Viet-Nam as a continuing challenge to American interests in Southeast Asia, although its inspiration and leadership of the Communist-led insurrection against the Saigon regime—now largely prosecuted by North Vietnamese regulars—are, again, a matter of historical record. Moreover, Hanoi's outright invasions of Laos and Cambodia, and its manipulation of dissident guerrilla movements in both countries, also constitute a serious threat to American interests in Southeast Asia, however much these events may be related primarily to the Viet-Nam War.

Rather, the balance of this essay is devoted to an appraisal of Communist China's foreign policy, and seeks to answer the question whether Peking is attempting to establish a Communist Chinese hegemony in mainland and island Asia that would threaten the vital interests of the United States.

Communist China: The Goals of Policy

Does the foreign policy of Communist China constitute such a threat? Does the thrust of Peking's policy carry with it the challenge of a new imperialism in Asia? This is the great riddle that specialists on Asian affairs have debated for the past twenty years. In the sweep of history, of course, the record of two decades is perhaps insufficient to permit definitive judgment. But we believe that an analysis of the long-term objectives of Peking's foreign policy, together with the style of policy implementation since 1949, do reveal acts and tendencies that cannot be gainsaid.

In analyzing the long-term objectives of Peking's policy, a distinction has often been drawn—validly, we think—between the *national* goals of policy, on the one hand, and the regime's peculiarly *Communist* ambitions, on the other. What we call national goals are those derived by the Chinese from their conceptions of history and geopolitical circumstance. They are the objectives that any Chinese regime, whether Communist, non-Communist, or even anti-Communist, would in general be likely to pursue, although the nature of the regime would undoubtedly affect the strategy and tactics employed to achieve them. Thus it is no accident that Taiwan and Peking, for all their implacable hostility toward each other, share substantially identical views on a number of foreign policy questions (such as Tibet) affecting, as it were, the historical Chinese state as a political entity. This is not to imply, of course, that distinctly national goals are necessarily "just" in historical terms, or that their accomplishment serves any material interest of the Chinese people, or that Peking's strategy and tactics in the pursuit of these objectives can be squared with the requirements of orderly international process. It is simply to suggest that such goals can be understood primarily in Chinese terms rather than as an aspect of Communist dogma.

The specific content of many of these goals is discussed elsewhere in the present volume, notably in Professor Walker's contribution.[9] Perhaps the most important in this whole category, as he points out, is Peking's determination to eliminate the rival Nationalist regime still entrenched on the island of Taiwan. While this has been a continuously destabilizing element in Asian politics ever since 1949, we must recognize that throughout Chinese history a regime that had lately succeeded to the Mandate of Heaven invariably pursued the remnant of its predecessor with implacable ferocity. From this conflict, too, Peking has derived its intransigent policies on state recognition and on participation in the United Nations. Here again both Peking and Taipei oppose a "Two Chinas" policy.

It need hardly be argued that this explanation is entirely insufficient to justify acquiescence — as some commentators suggest — in the extinction of the Republic of China on Taiwan. At the very least, the population of that island has an undeniable right to determine its own political future without compulsion from the mainland. Furthermore, the Nationalist regime is a staunch and loyal ally of the United States, one to which we are bound by treaty obligations that have not yet been amended or abrogated. Additionally, it is precisely because we view the long-term objectives of Communist China's foreign policy as posing a fundamental threat to American interests that we support the continued independent existence of the Republic of China on Taiwan as a guardian against the further expansion of Communist power.

A second category of Chinese national objectives relates to the recovery of territories that are presumed to have been "lost" through the weakness and ineptitude of predecessor regimes. Taiwan and the offshore islands of Matsu and Quemoy are obviously in this category. So, tragically, is Tibet. We believe that a powerful case — analogous to that of Poland after the Third Partition — can be made for an independent Tibet, in terms both of history and of the unique ethnic characteristics of its people and culture. Nevertheless, it is equally true that the Chinese leadership, whether Communist or Nationalist, view Tibet as an inalienable part of the national domain, and any resurgent Chinese regime would strive to

[9]See pp. 281-299, above.

reassert authority over the region. On the other hand, no possible justification can be found to extenuate the cruelty that has characterized Peking's policy toward Tibet since 1949; in brief, it has amounted to genocide. The Chinese also lay undefined claim to various territories allegedly lost through "unequal treaties" with the European imperial powers. Pre-eminently at issue here are China's contemporary borders with India, and as has become increasingly apparent in recent years, with the Soviet Union. We cannot doubt that different Chinese regimes would handle the problems involved in different ways; and most of the civilized world deplored Peking's use of massive force against India in 1962, which was, by any standard, a flagrant violation of accepted principles of international order and the peaceful settlement of disputes. It is interesting, however, that Chinese Communist and Chinese Nationalist maps dealing with China's "rightful" boundary with India show a remarkable similarity. They are both of pre-1914 vintage, and ignore—as do Indian maps—the rival claims of empire pursued by both the Indians and the Chinese in their respective days of advancing imperial acquisitions.

Chinese territorial ambitions in South and Southeast Asia are less easy to define with assurance and clarity, partly because they have even less historical justification. The relentless movement of the Han people to the *Nan Yang,* the South Seas, since before the beginning of the Christian era is a matter of historical record. China's march to the tropics has been a compound of peaceful penetration and deliberate conquest; especially in periods of national rejuvenation and strength, China has consciously looked and moved to the South. But such moves—relatively successful through the Mongol period, less so during the Ming dynasty, and defeated by Southeast Asians even in the great eighteenth century days of the Manchu dynasty—have lost whatever validity such claims to territory and people may once have had long, long ago. However, we are dealing here with an historical perspective, a traditional Chinese point of view, that successive regimes necessarily inform with distinctive content. As for the Chinese Communists, Mao himself proclaimed in 1937 that they would restore China's historical relationship (that is, of dominance) to such territories as Korea, Mongolia, the Soviet Maritime Provinces, Tibet, and Annam (as Viet-Nam was then known). Three years later, he referred to the "blows . . . dealt to China's far-flung feudal empire," with the implication that a Communist regime would strive to reclaim Chinese suzerainty to territories lost to the European imperial powers, including (in the south) Bhutan, Nepal, Burma, and Viet-Nam.[10] These themes have been reiterated frequently in Chinese Communist documents and maps ever since.

[10]Mao, in this regard, seems to be echoing Sun Yat-sen's fourth lecture on the *Three Principles of the People* (translated by Frank W. Price) (Chungking: Ministry of Information, 1943), pp. 91-93. See also Frank N. Trager, *Burma From Kingdom to Republic* (New York: Praeger, 1966), Ch. 11, "Burma and China."

Finally, any Chinese regime would aspire to a position of prominence and political leadership in East Asia. A nation of seven hundred to eight hundred million people, with the oldest continuous political tradition on earth, could not be expected to accept supinely a status of inferiority, particularly in its own region. A resurgent China necessarily means a China whose voice carries weight and respect in Asian affairs, and—equally necessarily—a comparative diminution of the presently dominant influence of the two superpowers, and prospectively of Japan as well. What this national objective means in practice is something else. If it implies the requirement of subservience on the part of China's neighbors to its whim and will, and correspondingly the elimination of American power and influence from the region, then it obviously reflects an objective contrary to America's interest, as well as to the interests of China's neighbors. In this connection, it is interesting that even those specialists on Asia most inclined to view Communist China's foreign policy with equanimity, tend to agree that Peking aims at this kind of regional dominance.

The complex of national objectives briefly summarized here, if pursued with sufficient power and determination, suggests that a resurgent China—whether Communist or not—would constitute a serious problem for American policy in East Asia. Much would depend, of course, on how China itself interpreted these objectives, and the strength and tenacity of its efforts to achieve them. But if we accept the premise that it is contrary to the vital interests of the United States to permit a hostile hegemony in East Asia, because of the threat that this implies to the power balance in the region, then this country must necessarily view with caution the emergence of any strong and potentially expansionist regime on the mainland. To be sure, the United States and China are not "natural" enemies. But the possibilities demand awareness.

The analysis is complicated by the fact that in addition to national Chinese aims (however defined in practice), the Peking regime also strives for the accomplishment of another range of policy objectives. These are the ambitions that derive from the avowedly Marxist-Leninist character of the regime. We agree with Professor Walker[11] and others in this symposium on the "commitment" of the Chinese leadership to Marxist-Leninist doctrine, as reinterpreted by Chinese ideologues including Mao himself. We believe that this imparts a special set of purposes and a revolutionary dynamic to Peking's policy that simply cannot be explained in terms of history or of political and economic circumstance. The fact that such objectives are sometimes identical with, or parallel to, more traditional policy goals in no way detracts from the validity of this perspective. In fact, the combination increases the danger to all states and peoples affected by that confluence.

[11]See especially pp. 283-284, 289-290, above.

Some commentators challenge the hypothesis of specifically Communist goals in mainland China's foreign policy. The Communist leaders, we are told, are "after all" profoundly "Chinese," and this is supposed to prove that their commitment to Communist doctrine is somehow superficial or unimportant, or at least that it is not determinative in the formulation of policy. One hears in this the echoes of an earlier and, in our view, equally erroneous appraisal that the Chinese Communists were preeminently "agrarian reformers" who used the slogans of Marxism-Leninism without being imprisoned by its spirit. While we do not deny that the strength of commitment to an ideology may attenuate with time, we can find no evidence to support the view that the Chinese Communist leadership does not take its doctrine seriously.

On the contrary, both the literature and the practice of communism in mainland China have shown an intense preoccupation with ideology from the beginning, and carrying forward to the traumatic excesses of the Great Proletarian Cultural Revolution in the latter 1960s. In the foreign policy field, there can be no denial of the fact that Chinese Communist theoreticians have given special attention to the Leninist two-camp theory of world politics, which divides the world into a Communist camp destined by history to triumph everywhere, and an enemy camp doomed to violent destruction. In this world view, which has been articulated most notably by Mao Tse-tung, Liu Shao-ch'i, and others, there is no room for any third grouping, such as the neutralist countries of Asia have aspired to be. In short, the Chinese Communists have embraced Lenin's dictum that "there is not, nor can there be, any third path, nor can there be any sentimentality" in dealing with those who oppose, or do not wholeheartedly cooperate with, the Communist juggernaut.

Chinese Communist doctrinal writings have also dealt extensively with problems of revolutionary warfare. Here the works of Mao and his "closest comrade-in-arms," Lin Piao, are presumed to provide an infallible guide for Communist seizures of power. While Chinese Communist claims as to the originality of their contributions to the theory and practice of revolutionary war are grossly overstated — much of it is cribbed from, or is a logical development of, Leninist theories of war and the "liberation" of semi-colonial and colonial peoples — there is no reason whatever to believe that they do not take all this seriously. One recalls how often we were told during the 1930s that we need not give credence to the preachments and polemics of Nazi Germany. "After all," the Nazi leaders were profoundly "German." But the terrifying historical reality was that the Nazis meant precisely what they said. Prudence demands, in turn, that we heed the Chinese Communists as Communists, however much we may hope for the best.

In the present context, operationally the most significant Communist objective espoused by the Peking regime is its support for Communist revolution in other countries. In his report to the Ninth Party Congress in April 1969, Lin Piao publicly pledged China to "firmly support" revolutionary struggle in the countries of South and Southeast Asia, although he omitted specific mention of such expedient "friends" as Pakistan and Sihanouk's Cambodia in his table of current targets.[12]

The record of Communist China's policy in Southeast Asia since 1949 supports the point. While a detailed account of that record would be out of place here, it may nevertheless be worthwhile to recall some of the more important episodes. Almost the first policy initiative of the new regime was to lend all-out logistical support to the Viet Minh insurrectionaries in Indochina; this intervention was probably decisive in the Communist victory over the French by 1954. (That the French should have been defeated is not here relevant.) Since that time, Peking has continued to support the Hanoi regime on a lavish scale. While greater publicity has been given to the sophisticated weapons and other equipment supplied by the Soviet Union, the bulk of the external assistance continuously flowing to Hanoi for the prosecution of revolutionary warfare against South Viet-Nam has always come from Communist China. Meanwhile, the Chinese have now penetrated at many points south of the conventional border with India, Bhutan, Nepal, Burma, Thailand, and Laos. An impressive if little known road construction program to the south (for example, into Laos) facilitates the exertion of Chinese power against its mainland Southeast Asian neighbors. Communist China's spectacularly successful attack on India in 1962 served not only to secure vital border areas claimed by both countries, but also to impede India's economic development program and to demolish its claims to leadership of the Third World. Finally, in fulfilment of Lin Piao's pledge the Peking regime has actively and publicly espoused guerrilla movements in almost every country of mainland and island Southeast Asia, and affords significant leadership and material support to most of them. Such support has included the training of cadres at special schools on the mainland, and the harboring of Burman, Kachin, Thai, and other ethnic guerrillas who are also provided bases from which to operate against their respective homelands.

This is not to assert that such Communist-led guerrilla movements are necessarily and always the puppets or tools of Peking policy. It would be uncritical not to recognize the indigenous roots of revolutionary movements in South and Southeast Asia. While subservience is undoubtedly a desideratum of Chinese Communist policy—and the training and support that they afford to ethnic revolutionaries obviously conduces to this objective—presumably Peking would be sufficiently rewarded if such move-

[12]See Frank N. Trager, with Robert F. Bordonaro, "The Ninth CCP Congress and the World Communist Conference: Their Meaning in Asia," *Orbis*, Vol. 13, No. 3 (Fall 1969).

ments acted in general concert with the larger aims of that policy. On the other hand, we do not doubt that it is also a major objective of Chinese policy to achieve leadership over the world Communist movement. The violence of Peking's polemic against Moscow's "modern revisionists," and the ferocity of the factional struggles that have rent asunder almost every non-governing Communist party in the world, and especially in Asia, provides sufficient evidence of the seriousness of this purpose. The fact that the Chinese Communists have been largely unsuccessful in asserting leadership over the worldwide movement thus far should not mislead us into minimizing the importance of this objective for the Chinese, and their determination to force upon it their own interpretation of Marxism-Leninist doctrine and the appropriate strategy to be followed by Communist movements everywhere in the present historial epoch.

Peking: Aspects of the Policy Record

There is no need to review here the details of Peking's record in the conduct of foreign policy since 1949. The subject has been sufficiently dealt with by other contributors to the present volume. It may be worthwhile, however, to summarize at this point several observations relating to Peking's overall performance in this field.

The first of these generalizations is that, in practice, the pursuit of foreign policy objectives has consistently been subordinated to domestic policy considerations. One gains an inescapable impression that the main preoccupations of the Chinese Communists themselves have revolved around such monumental issues as the consolidation and preservation of Communist power on the mainland, the economic development and industrialization of the country at forced draft, and latterly the dispute over the succession to leadership. Even China's conflict with the Soviet Union has taken a subordinate place, in Chinese Communist eyes, to more pressing problems relating to domestic ideological directions. However, this is not to say that Mao and his followers have adopted the policy—with all its implications—of Stalin's temporary device embedded in the slogan, Build socialism in one country, the USSR. In fact, the Maoist thrust for "world revolution," and the policy implications flowing from this, place Chinese Communist foreign policy in the forefront of Communist theory and practice, and only slightly behind the emphasis on domestic revolutionary fulfilment. In this version of the classic Stalin-Trotsky conflict over theory and practice, the weight of Mao's leadership and followership in Communist China is on the side of Trotsky.

It also seems clear to us that, in the implementation of foreign policy, Peking has been generally careful to minimize the current risks of all-out confrontation (that is, likely to involve the use of nuclear weapons) with either the United States or the Soviet Union. Genocide against Tibet in the 1950s and aggression against India in 1962 were essentially limited liability enterprises. If prudently managed, there was almost no risk of superpower intervention. Meanwhile, Peking has not pursued its vendetta against the Nationalist government on Taiwan to its logical conclusion, and has refrained from attempting an all-out assault on the offshore islands, obviously in order to avoid direct military conflict with the United States. This is still the case even after the United States has in the main discontinued the use of elements of the Seventh Fleet to patrol the Taiwan Straits. In similar vein, the scope of Peking's support for the North Vietnamese and, even more, for revolutionary movements elsewhere in South and Southeast Asia, has been kept within the balance of manageable risk.

The Korean case is more ambiguous. There is little doubt that Peking supported the North Korean aggression from the beginning. At a crucial moment in the conflict, moreover, the Communist Chinese intervened massively, in open defiance of the United Nations and in face of the certainty of large scale involvement against the United States. Nor could they have known beyond a reasonable doubt that this commitment would not escalate into all-out war and a nuclear attack upon the mainland. On the other hand, there is much evidence that Chinese intervention in the Korean War was the counsel of desperation, undertaken as the only means of preventing the extinction of a "fraternal Socialist state," and perhaps also out of fear that the American offensive would carry over into Manchuria. This does not, of course, condone the Chinese action in any way. It does illustrate that while Communist weakness has forced prudence on Chinese policymakers, there are limits beyond which they would choose to fight rather than yield.

But in our view, the correct explanation for this appearance of restraint in the actual conduct of foreign policy during the past twenty years is that it is primarily a consequence of China's present weakness in relation to the superpowers. To be sure, genuine—if still limited—success has been achieved in the development of nuclear weapons and delivery systems, and the purely *defensive* military capabilities of the regime are undoubtedly substantial. But in terms of superpower capabilities, the evidence is that Communist China has not yet built a military machine able to sustain large scale foreign adventures; in particular, the development of a sophisticated logistical capacity has been neglected.

However, the case for the present utility of Chinese nuclear strength against Asian powers, including Japan, is another matter. In any evaluation of Peking's foreign policy record, some estimate of its present nuclear capability and future potential is required. Since 1964 and through September 1969, Peking has conducted a series of nine nuclear tests. The fourth (October 1966) effort was a nuclear warhead carried by a guided missile for some four hundred miles before detonation. The fifth (December 1966) was Peking's first thermonuclear device. The series as a whole, and the successful launching of an earth satellite, lead inescapably to the conclusion that Peking now has, or soon will have, a deliverable medium and intermediate range ballistic missile with a powerful nuclear warhead. The consequences of such capabilities obviously do not, as indicated above, directly challenge the superpowers in the short run. In this sense, even after Communist China acquires an ICBM, its military effectiveness at best is defensive with respect to Moscow and Washington. But its offensive potential with respect to its Asian neighbors is something else again. Indeed, it necessarily promotes nuclear considerations in both Japan and India. (In the spring of 1969, some 45 percent of the respondents in a Japanese opinion poll believed that Japan should now—or in time—arm itself with nuclear weapons; and India, at this writing, has still refrained from adherence to the non-proliferation treaty.) Further, Peking's MRBM and IRBM capacity, whether used strategically, or tactically as part of its modernizing, already large conventional forces, adds to the perceived and actual threat of its third military prong: that is, support for "people's wars" throughout Asia.

On the other hand, if the United States maintains an active interest and presence on the mainland of Asia, the Chinese Communists will probably proceed with caution so as not to provoke general or nuclear war. The analysis suggests, in short, that the Peking regime has foresworn the all-out pursuit of its foreign policy objectives, whether national or Communist, not because it is not dedicated to them, but rather because the time—that is to say, the Chinese Communist estimate of what Marxist-Leninists call "objective conditions"—in relation to the superpowers is not yet ripe.

There are other aspects of the record, however, that give more immediate cause for continuing concern. It has already been pointed out, for example, that the Chinese Communists embrace a strict and implacable interpretation of Lenin's two-camp theory of world politics. The unremitting ferocity of Peking's polemics against the United States and the whole non-Communist world, and latterly against the "modern revisionists" of the present Soviet leadership must give one pause. After twenty years, this aspect of Communist China's propaganda is, if possible, more violent and more intransigent than ever. The fanaticism of Communist hatred affords little prospect for anything more than the expedient normalization of relations in the time-frame of the Mao-Lin Piao leadership. And the succeeding leadership after Mao's death is not likely in the short run to mitigate his posture of external hostility to the West in general and to the United States in particular. For the military-political succession will require an external "enemy" in order to consolidate its own internal position.

Another aspect of the foreign policy record is even more worrisome.

This is Peking's penchant to resort to military force and violence for the accomplishment of policy objectives whenever this can be done without serious risk. This is the meaning of its policy of the offense in connection with people's wars. The ideological glorification of force epitomized in Mao's celebrated maxim that "political power grows out of the barrel of a gun" has found repeated application in Chinese foreign policy—in Korea, Tibet, the offshore islands, India, Viet-Nam, and in its support for revolutionary movements throughout South and Southeast Asia. The place of naked force and violence in Chinese domestic politics should also be commented upon. This tendency to resort to the sword, in defiance of the settled consensus of the international community, is already disturbing and will become progressively more so as Communist China inevitably waxes in strength and military power.

Finally, the Peking regime has shown an occasional capacity for irrational action on a truly terrifying scale. While the two principal examples of such irrationality—the monumental stupidities of the Great Leap Forward and the astonishing excesses of the Cultural Revolution—have occurred in China's domestic political life, they reflect a capacity to risk national suicide in the pursuit of doctrinal and policy objectives. There is no *a priori* reason to assume that the Chinese Communists might not attempt such adventures in the field of foreign policy. Indeed, the current border conflict with the Soviet Union, at the risk of massive Soviet retaliation including a preemptive nuclear strike, suggests the possibilities. The dangers are immeasurably enhanced if we are to take at face value Mao's stated indifference to the appalling human price that would be exacted by a thermonuclear holocaust.

The Meaning

The foregoing analysis leads us inescapably to the conclusion that the foreign policy of Communist China poses an unlimited threat to American interests in Asia. We have defined those interests in traditional terms, that is, to prevent the organization of East Asia under the leadership of a power, or concert of powers, hostile to the United States. The power potential of such a coalition would obviously jeopardize the American position in East Asia, and our abiding interest in the continued independence of the non-Communist Asian countries. Further, such a coalition might, in time, attain sufficient military potential to threaten the security of the Western Hemisphere itself.

Even if the foreign policy objectives of the Peking regime were limited to what we have termed national goals, Communist China's future role in Asia would require the most serious concern. Peking's determination to stamp out its rival on the island of Taiwan; its ambition to recover the

so-called "lost territories," and most of all, its pursuit of regional dominance; all bespeak a China-on-the-move, a nation determined to alter in
fundamental ways the existing balance of power on the continent. On this
reading, much would depend on how the Peking regime interpreted the
pursuit of regional dominance. There is little in the record so far that
would afford the comfortable conclusion that Chinese Communist ambitions in this respect are essentially modest or cautious.

But when one adds to the pursuit of these national goals the assessment
that Communist China has also dedicated itself to the unlimited expansion
of Communist power elsewhere in Asia (and, indeed, everywhere in the
world), the implications for policy become especially serious. Nor is this
appraisal merely a cold warrior's nightmare. This is what the Chinese
Communists themselves boast that they are striving for, and what—on
the record—they are actively engaged in.

It may be argued that for the Chinese Communists, this statement of
policy is simply a reformulation in Communist ideological dressing of
China's traditional aspirations for regional hegemony. Here everything
depends on what value is given to the Communist dynamic of the Peking
regime. We would argue, for example, that there has been a qualitative
difference in the traditional imperialism of Czarist Russia and the aggressive expansionism of the Soviet Union; and we believe that it is ideology
that has made the difference. The analogy to contemporary China is
obvious. At the very least, the possibilities suggest prudence.

It may also be argued that, even if Communist movements were to
achieve power in a number of other Asian countries, especially in Southeast Asia, Peking would have enormous difficulty in organizing them into
a coherent bloc responsive to its leadership. This is the so-called "Titoist"
argument, which in the case of North Viet-Nam states, for example, that
Hanoi and Peking are inevitable enemies over the long term, for two or
three thousand years of historical and other reasons. Maybe so. But the
East European countries including East Germany have a comparable
legacy of hostility to Czarist Russia and its successor, the Soviet Union;
and yet Moscow has succeeded in organizing them into some kind of
coherent political and military bloc, and of enforcing its will upon them
when necessary, as Hungary 1956 and Czechoslovakia 1968 demonstrated.
No one can be conclusive on this point. But again, the possibilities demand
concern. On balance, we believe that, in light of the realities of power
and proximity, there is a lively prospect that Communist China could
organize the present and future Communist countries along its eastern
and southern peripheries into a coherent bloc, with at least a congruence
or parallelism of grand policy even if Peking did not wholly control the
bloc; and that the actual and potential power of this coalition would constitute an overwhelming threat to the Asian interests of the United States.

It is true—we readily concede the point—that thus far in its twenty-year history, Communist China has been cautious to avoid an all-out military confrontation with either of the superpowers. Hopefully its military inferiority will dictate a similar caution in the years ahead. But we would also call attention again to Peking's penchant for violence, to its occasional capacity for monumental irrationality, and to its enormous drive to "catch up" in purely military terms. Communist China today is not yet strong enough to challenge the world. But Peking does have the capacity to endanger the world with ruin. This, and the potential menace of an Asia united under Peking's leadership, are the measure of the threat that Communist China poses for the United States—now and in the years ahead.

Brief Chronology: 1949–1969

1949   **Oct. 1** The People's Republic of China inaugurated, with Mao Tse-tung as Chairman.

1950   **Feb. 12** Chinese Communist regime and Soviet Union sign treaty of "friendship, mutual assistance, and alliance" in Moscow.

June 25 Korean War begins.

June 30 Peking promulgates a drastic "land reform" law.

Oct. 14 Chinese Communist forces under the command of Marshal P'eng Teh-huai enter North Korea as "volunteers," and engage U.N. forces on Oct. 25.

1951   **Feb. 21** Mao promulgates "Regulations for the Punishment of Counter-revolutionaries," demanding imprisonment, life imprisonment, or death for those guilty of "counter-revolutionary activities."

May 23 Chinese Communist troops enter Tibet. "Measures for the Peaceful Liberation of Tibet" announced in Peking.

1952   **Jan. 10** "Three-Anti" campaign initiated against corruption, decay, and bureaucracy.

Mar. 1 "Five-Anti" struggle against bribery, tax evasion, theft of state assets, and theft of state economic secrets.

1953   **Jan. 1** First Five Year Plan inaugurated.

Mar. 4 The death of Joseph Stalin.

July 26 Korean truce agreement signed at Panmunjom.

Oct. 23 The "General Line for Transition to Communism" announced. It was to become the overall guideline for the rapid communization of industry, business, and agriculture.

1954   **Jan. 8** Establishment of "agricultural production cooperatives" ordered by the Chinese Communist Party, creating Soviet-style collective farms.

Feb. 6 First major power struggle within the Chinese Communist regime. Kao Kang, Chairman of the State Planning Commission, and Jao Shu-shih, Director of the Central Committee's Organization Department, purged for anti-party activities.

June 25 Chou En-lai and Prime Minister Jawaharlal Nehru of India issue a joint statement on the so-called "five principles of peaceful co-existence."

Aug. 26 "Regulations for Reform Through Labor" promulgated to deal with intellectual opposition to the regime.

Sept. 2 "Regulations Governing Establishment of Industries and Enterprises Under Public-Private Joint Ownership" promulgated, marking the beginning of the confiscation of private enterprises.

1954 **Sept. 28** Promulgation of 1954 constitution.

1955 **April** The Bandung Conference in Indonesia, attended by Communist China, gives rise to an "era of good feelings" in relations between Peking and other Asian countries. The so-called "Bandung Spirit" was soon marred by bitter disputes, particularly between Communist China and India.

May 13 *Jen-min Jih-pao* publishes article attacking Hu Feng, marking first major purge of literary and artistic personalities.

1956 **Feb. 14** Khrushchev's famous "de-Stalinization" speech.

May 2 Mao's first use of the phrase, "Let the hundred flowers bloom! Let the hundred schools of thought contend!" The movement was launched as a party campaign by Propaganda Minister Lu Ting-yi on May 26 in an attempt to enlist the cooperation of the intellectuals.

1957 **Feb. 27** Mao discloses in his speech, "On the Correct Handling of Contradictions Among the People," that eight hundred thousand persons were liquidated between October 1949 and 1954.

Apr. 27 The CCP Central Committee issues "Directive on the Rectification Movement," beginning another purge within the party.

June 26 The CCP warning that the right to "bloom and contend" does not permit criticism damaging to Socialist construction is intensified at the opening of fourth conference of the First National People's Congress.

Dec. 11 The State Council adopts draft plan for phonetizing the Chinese language. The plan was eventually abandoned.

1958 **Jan. 31** Communications Minister Chang Po-chun, Timber Industry Minister Lo Lung-chi, and Food Minister Chang Nai-ch'i, along with 38 delegates to the National People's Congress dismissed for criticism of the regime during the Hundred Flowers campaign.

Feb. 1 NPC conference formally launches the Great Leap Forward campaign, with the slogan, "Twenty Years in a Day."

Mar. 10 Armed rebellion breaks out in Tibet. It is quickly put down.

June 13 Communist China completes its first atomic reactor.

July First communes formed.

Aug. 29 CCP Central Committee announces resolution to establish "people's communes." Before the end of the year, the entire mainland had been organized into 26,500 communes.

Sept. People's Militia established.

Oct. 27 *Jen-min Jih-pao* publishes Mao's article, "All Imperialists and Reactionaries are Paper Tigers," an important document in the developing quarrel between Moscow and Peking.

Dec. 17 CCP Central Committee announces that Mao will "step down" as Chairman of the Peking regime.

1959   **Spring and Summer** Communist China accuses India of supporting Tibetan revolt; lays claim to nearly forty thousand square miles of territory inside Indian borders.

Mar. 10 Tibetan revolt begins. Dalai Lama flees Lhasa on March 17, and arrives in India by end of month. Peking appoints the Panchen Lama as acting head of the "Tibetan Autonomous Region Committee."

Apr. 27 Liu Shao-ch'i is elected by NPC as Chairman of the Chinese People's Republic. Mao remains as Chairman of the Chinese Communist Party.

June Soviets reportedly abrogate nuclear-sharing agreement guaranteeing protection to China.

Aug. 26 CCP Central Committee, at Kuling conference, admits grave statistical errors in announced agricultural production figures. Since then, no really meaningful economic statistics have ever been released by Peking.

Sept. 17 Marshal Lin Piao is named Defense Minister, replacing Marshal P'eng Teh-huai. P'eng and Huang K'e-ch'eng, Chief of the General Staff, are purged for anti-party activities in the second major intramural struggle in the history of the regime.

Oct. 26 The Ministry of Foreign Affairs asserts that considerable territory inside India's northern frontier "has always been Chinese territory."

1960   Mao Tse-tung begins a series of public statements denouncing the "imperialists" and assuring Chinese support for the peoples of Asia, Africa, and Latin America.

April 16 In an editorial entitled, "Long Live Leninism," the Chinese Communist leadership launches a detailed and bitter attack against "revisionists" who "whitewash the war preparations of the imperialists."

July 16 Moscow secretly notifies Peking of its decision to terminate economic and technical aid.

Nov. Moscow meeting of 81 Communist parties attended by Liu Shao-ch'i; Sino-Soviet dispute worsens.

Dec. 29 Radio Peking reports "worst natural calamities" in a century.

1961   **Jan. 20** CCP Central Committee admits serious food shortages, and blames them on natural disasters as well as "landlords, bourgeois, and other bad elements."

1962   **Sept. 24** The "Socialist education" campaign launched to rectify revisionist tendencies, foreshadowing the Great Proletarian Cultural Revolution.

Oct.–Nov. The Sino-Indian border war. Soviet failure to support Communist China diplomatically exacerbates the Sino-Soviet split. Peking orders a cease-fire on Nov. 21.

1963   **April** Directive on political work circulated in PLA, pointing up problem of party control of the army.

   May The Soviet Union and China agree to meet and discuss their ideological differences.

   July 25 Nuclear test ban treaty signed. On July 31, a Peking statement terms it "a big fraud to fool the people of the world," and China refuses to join it.

   Sept. 6 *Jen-min Jih-pao* and *Hung-ch'i* print the first of a series of articles attacking Soviet revisionism.

1964   **June** National Congress of Chinese Communist Youth League inaugurates campaign to train "revolutionary successor generation."

   Aug. 2 Gulf of Tonkin crisis. Peking warns that "U.S. aggression against Viet-Nam" is tantamount to "aggression against China."

   Oct. 16 Peking conducts first atomic test at Lop Nor, Sinkiang, with a crude device equivalent to twenty kilotons.

1965   **Jan. 14** CCP issues a directive. "Some Problems Confronting Us in the Rural Socialist Education Movement," proclaiming that "revisionism has penetrated the Chinese Communist Party" and that "persons in authority following the capitalist road are operating at all levels of the party." Mao appoints P'eng Chen, Peking party boss, as head of a five-man "Cultural Revolution Group" charged with working out a rectification drive to eliminate the revisionist danger, especially among the intellectuals.

   May 14 Peking's second atomic test, in which a seventy-kiloton bomb is dropped from the air.

   May 24 Mao abolishes all ranks in the PLA, and changes insignias and uniforms to combat "professionalism" in the armed forces.

   Sept. 3 Lin Piao issues famous article, "Long Live the Victory of the People's War," calling on the world's "countryside," meaning Asia, Africa, and Latin America, to encircle the "cities," meaning Europe and North America.

   Nov. 6 Shanghai *Wen-hui Pao* publishes an article by Yao Wen-yuan entitled, "Comments on the Historical Play 'The Dismissal of Hai Jui,'" ostensibly aimed at the playwright Wu Han, Deputy Mayor of Peking. It was later revealed that the article was prepared under the personal direction of Mao Tse-tung, who was in Shanghai to plot for his return to power. The article was later hailed as "sounding the first bugle call of the Great Proletarian Cultural Revolution."

1966   **Jan.** Third Five Year Plan officially launched.

   Apr. 16 Cultural Revolution comes to Peking. An article attacking Wu Han, Deputy Mayor, Teng T'o, Editor of *Jen-min Jih-pao,* and Liao Mo-sha, Propaganda Director of CCP Peking

1966   Committee, marks the spread of the purge to journalists, literary and art workers.

Apr. 18 *Liberation Army Daily* publishes editorial entitled, "Hold High the Great Red Banner of Mao Tse-tung's Thought, and Actively Participate in the Great Proletarian Cultural Revolution." By now, it is clear that the army is largely calling the tune, and that Lin Piao has emerged as Mao's heir apparent.

May 9 Third nuclear test in Sinkiang is reported to contain "thermonuclear material."

May 16 CCP sets up a new Cultural Revolution Group, replacing one headed by P'eng Chen. Mao's personal secretary, Ch'en Po-ta, is appointed as Chief, and Mao's wife, Chiang Ch'ing, as First Deputy Chief, of this all-powerful group to direct the purge. The Cultural Revolution spreads to the universities. Prominent among those removed are Lu P'ing, President of Peking University, and Li Ta, President of Wuhan University.

May 25 The Cultural Revolution reaches the topmost party level. The CCP orders the relief of Mayor P'eng Chen of Peking, who formerly ranked eighth in the hierarchy. The move was not announced until June 3. Mao and Lin consolidate their hold on the party and government. Lo Jui-ch'ing, Chief of the General Staff, Lu Ting-yi, Minister of Propaganda, and Yang Shang-k'un, Director of the CCP General Office, also purged in June and July.

June 13 The CCP, in a joint directive with the State Council, orders a sweeping reorganization of higher education, and a six-month suspension in the admission of new students. In fact, all universities, colleges, high schools, and elementary schools were closed for the next two years in order to let students "make revolution."

Aug. 1 CCP plenum called in Peking to confirm Mao's policies. A CCP "Decision Concerning the Great Proletarian Cultural Revolution," the now-famous sixteen-point declaration, adopted several days later.

Aug. 18 Liu Shao-ch'i, who could not be dismissed from his post as Chief of State except by the National People's Congress, is demoted from second to eighth place in the listing of important party officials attending a Peking rally, attended by over a million people, celebrating the Cultural Revolution and launching the Red Guards. Liu had already been put under house arrest along with Teng Hsiao-p'ing.

Aug. 31 Mao and Lin appear at the first giant rally of the Red Guards, held under the chairmanship of Chiang Ch'ing. Eight such rallies were eventually held in Tienanmen Square, with a total attendance of eleven million.

1966   **Oct. 27** Fourth atomic test held in Sinkiang. The thirty-kiloton warhead was carried by a guided missile.

Nov. 30 *Jen-min Jih-pao,* in front-page article, makes clear that Lin Piao was now the only Vice Chairman of the CCP, and therefore the heir-apparent to Mao.

Dec. 3 CCP orders the Red Guards remaining in major cities to return home.

Dec. 15 Red Guard rally in Peking publicly tries and humiliates P'eng Chen, Lu Ting-yi, Lo Jui-ch'ing, and Yang Shang-k'un.

Dec. 26 Mao's 73rd birthday. A *Jen-min Jih-pao* editorial entitled, "Welcome the High Tide of the Cultural Revolution in the Industrial and Mining Enterprises," gives the formal go-ahead for a full-scale extension of the Cultural Revolution to factories and farms.

Dec. 28 Peking explodes fifth atomic bomb.

1967   **Jan. 4** Maoist "revolutionary rebels" in Shanghai seize the *Wen-hui Pao,* and on January 5 issue a "Manifesto to the Citizens of Shanghai." The action, praised by Mao himself as the "January revolutionary storm," signaled the beginning of the Maoist campaign against entrenched party and government officials.

Jan. 8 A giant rally of a hundred thousand Maoist workers and Red Guards in Peking denounces Liu, Teng, and T'ao Chu, who took over only six months previously as CCP Propaganda Minister.

Jan. 12 First reorganization of the People's Liberation Army's Cultural Revolution Group. Hsu Hsiang-ch'ien replaced Liu Chih-chien, who had been in charge since September 1966.

Jan. 23 A joint directive calls on the People's Liberation Army to intervene in fighting between different factions in order "to support the left revolutionary masses," thus beginning an army takeover in many areas.

Jan 26 Ulanfu, First Secretary of the Inner Mongolian section of the CCP, is branded an anti-Maoist. Wang En-mao, Military Commander for Sinkiang, was also charged with resisting Maoist takeover attempts.

Jan. 31 Establishment of Heilungkiang Revolutionary Committee, headed by P'an Fu-sheng, former Commissar for the military district, marks the beginning of this new type of Maoist organ, which eventually replaces both party and government structures in the provinces.

Feb. 5 Maoists claim a successful seizure of power in Shanghai, and announce the establishment of a so-called "people's commune," patterned after the Paris Commune. The term was quietly dropped five days later.

Mar. 1 CCP orders the opening of high schools, closed since June 1966.

Mar. 7 Mao issues secret directive on "the great strategic plan for cultural revolution in the schools," in an attempt to restore

1967 order and curb Red Guard activities. The directive was not made public for a year.

Mar. 29 *Hung-ch'i* prints first article attacking Liu and Teng in CCP official press, although the two had been targets of Red Guard posters for months. A new wave of mass rallies and propaganda articles all over the mainland denounces Liu as the "top person in the party taking the capitalist road."

Apr. 13 Second reorganization of PLA Cultural Revolution Group. Hsiao Hua, General Political Commissar, replaces Hsu Hsiang-ch'ien, who held the job for only three months.

Apr. 17 Ch'en Yi, Vice Premier and Foreign Minister, becomes a target of Red Guard criticism for his "revisionist foreign policy." By this time, all but one of Peking's ambassadors abroad had been recalled to attend "Mao-Thought" classes, resulting in a nearly complete breakdown in the normal conduct of China's foreign relations.

June 17 Detonation of first hydrogen bomb at Lop Nor, Sinkiang, two years and eight months after China's first atomic test, and the sixth in the series.

July 22 The month-long Wuhan Incident comes to an end as the local military commander, at Chou En-lai's personal mediation, finally releases Hsieh Fu-chih and Wang Li, emissaries representing the CCP, after a week's detention.

Aug. 16 Third reorganization of PLA Cultural Revolution Group. Wu Fa-hsien, Air Force Commissar, replaces Hsiao Hua (who lasted four months).

Sept. 5 Chiang Ch'ing makes a speech repudiating armed struggle and the widespread attacks on the PLA that followed the Wuhan Incident. On the same day, the CCP ordered the confiscation of all weapons seized from the armed forces and authorized the army to hit back in self-defense.

Oct. 1 Lin Piao, speaking at Communist China's National Day celebration, called on all CCP cadres to "combat self-interest and criticize and repudiate revisionism." The slogan became a guideline for the Cultural Revolution.

Nov. Evidence that Chiang Ch'ing is losing her influence is seen as *Hung-ch'i*, the CCP theoretical journal usually published twice each month, ceased publication and did not reappear for almost nine months. Its chief editor, Ch'i Pen-yu, was last seen in public on December 31, 1967. Two other members of the Cultural Revolution Group. Wang Li and Kuan Feng, were also purged about this time. All three had been considered as working closely with Chiang Ch'ing.

Dec. 24 Peking conducts seventh nuclear test, but makes no announcement of the fact, leading to speculation that something might have gone wrong.

1968   **Jan. 1** A joint editorial entitled, "Ushering in the All Round Victory of the Great Proletarian Cultural Revolution," urges further struggle against the anti-Maoists.

Mar. 26 Lin Piao announces a dramatic purge in PLA. Yang Ch'eng-wu, Acting Chief of the General Staff, Fu Chung-pi, Peking Garrison Commander, and Yu Li-chin, Air Force Commissar, were purged for anti-Maoist activities. Huang Yung-sheng, Canton Military Commander, took over as Chief of Staff.

Sept. 6 Peking celebrates the establishment of revolutionary committees in Tibet and Sinkiang, completing the formation of such organs in 29 provinces, autonomous regions and municipalities. All but eight were headed by military men.

Sept. 13 *Hung-ch'i,* in its third issue for 1968, called for revolution in medical education and the development of more "barefoot doctors"—health workers who divide their time between farming and medical work.

Nov. 2 Liu Shao-ch'i is attacked by name for the first time as "a renegade, traitor, and scab hiding in the party," and as "a lackey of imperialism, modern revisionism, and the Kuomintang reactionaries." Liu was stripped of "all posts both inside and outside the party," including his job as Chairman of the People's Republic.

1969   **Jan. 1** A joint editorial entitled, "Place Mao Tse-tung's Thought in Command of Everything," sets Communist China's goals for 1969, including the Ninth Congress of the CCP.

Mar. 3 Chinese Communist and Soviet border guards clash on Damansky Island in the Ussuri River. Both sides report heavy casualties.

Apr. 1 The Ninth Congress of the CCP, delayed for several years, finally opens at Peking.

Apr. 14 The Ninth Congress "unanimously" adopts Lin Piao's political report and a new party constitution.

June 5 An International Meeting of Communist and Workers' Parties opens in Moscow and becomes a forum for denouncing the Peking regime.

July 10 Soviet Foreign Minister Gromyko charges that Peking has done "everything" to break relations between the two countries, and reveals that Sino-Soviet trade has dwindled to almost nothing.

Selected Bibliography

I. General

Ruth *Adams* (editor). *Contemporary China.* New York: Pantheon Books, 1966. Contributions by American scholars and others who have visited mainland China. Two chapters on education.

Theodore Hsi-en *Chen. The Chinese Communist Regime: Documents and Commentary.* New York: Praeger, 1967. An invaluable presentation of official sources. Topically arranged in three sections: a general survey of events since 1949; the organization of the government and Communist Party; and the general direction of economic and social change.

Ralph C. *Croizier* (editor). *China's Cultural Legacy and Communism.* New York: Praeger, 1970. An anthology of Western commentators, together with selections from Chinese Communist writers on history, philosophy, the arts, and science: with particular attention to Communist attempts to blend traditional Chinese culture with modern theories.

John K. *Fairbank* (editor). *The Chinese World Order.* Cambridge: Harvard University Press, 1968. Focuses on the Ch'ing dynasty and its relations with the inner and outer barbarians. Two background articles are especially rewarding: Yang Lien-sheng's historical notes, and Wang Gungwu's essay on Ming relations with Southeast Asia.

Albert *Feuerwerker* (editor). *History in Communist China.* Cambridge: M.I.T. Press, 1968. A collection of essays dealing with Communist attitudes towards various periods and issues of Chinese history.

Ping-ti *Ho* and Tsou *Tang* (editors). *China in Crisis,* 2 vols. Chicago: University of Chicago Press, 1968. These essays are the product of a high-powered conference held at the University of Chicago a few years ago. The leadoff piece by Ping-ti Ho lucidly establishes a theoretical framework for thinking about modern China in the light of Chinese history. The rejoinders are interesting, too.

G. F. *Hudson. Fifty Years of Communism.* New York: Basic Books, 1968. A literate and perceptive summary of the Communist record and of ongoing problems. The focus is not on China primarily, though there is a chapter on "Maoism;" but the broad sweep presented here is essential for thinking about contemporary China.

Donald W. *Treadgold* (editor). *Soviet and Chinese Communism: Similarities and Differences.* Seattle and London: University of Washington Press, 1967. Comparative analyses of Chinese and Russian political and economic developments, including a useful chapter on Communist law and social change.

329

Y. C. *Wang. Chinese Intellectuals and the West, 1872-1949.* Durham: University of North Carolina Press, 1966. An important study of a subject that had previously received little attention. Describes the evolution of a Western-educated elite (numbering over a hundred thousand) and their subsequent role in Chinese affairs.

II. Government and Politics

A. Doak *Barnett,* with a contribution by Ezra Vogel. *Cadres, Bureaucracy, and Political Power in Communist China.* New York: Columbia University Press, 1967. A seminal work describing the organization and operation of the CCP at three bureaucratic levels: the ministry, the county, and the commune. Based largely upon extensive interviews with ex-cadres.

Theodore Hsi-en *Chen. Thought Reform of the Chinese Intellectuals.* Hong Kong: Hong Kong University Press, 1960. A study of Communist policy toward intellectuals during the first decade of the regime.

Arthur A. *Cohen. The Communism of Mao Tse-tung.* Chicago: University of Chicago Press, 1964. A short but well-conceived study dealing with the question of Mao's contribution to Communist theory. Mao is found to be not a profound theorist who has made original contributions to Communist doctrine, but rather a practitioner executing revolutionary strategems.

Boyd *Compton. Mao's China: Party Reform Documents 1942-44.* Seattle: University of Washington Press, 1952. A documentary study (with commentary) of the period in which Mao established himself as doctrinal leader of the Communist Party.

Congressional Quarterly Service. *China and U.S. Far East Policy, 1945-1966.* Washington: Congressional Quarterly Service, 1967. A useful compendium of information on China, including a chronology, documents, and major speeches and testimony by American China-watchers.

Edward *Hunter. Brain-Washing in Red China.* New York: Vanguard, 1951. An early journalistic work dealing with the regime's attempt to alter the values of its citizens. Concludes that it (brain-washing) is "perverted evangelism and quack psychiatry." One of the first uses of the concept of "brain-washing."

E. Stuart *Kirby* (editor). *Youth in China.* Hong Kong: Dragonfly Books, 1965. Articles on the political role of youth, their frustrations and problems.

John W. *Lewis. Leadership in Communist China.* Ithaca: Cornell University Press, 1963. Describes the ideal functioning of the CCP apparatus. Stresses leadership doctrine and the role of cadres. The material is drawn from official Chinese documents and interviews conducted in Hong Kong.

Robert Jay *Lifton. Thought Reform and the Psychology of Totalism.* New York: Norton, 1961.

K. H. *Fan* (editor). *The Chinese Cultural Revolution: Selected Documents.* New York and London: Monthly Review Press, 1968. An anthology of important documents relating to the Cultural Revolution, accompanied by brief explanatory notes.

Hans *Granqvist. The Red Guard: A Report on Mao's Revolution.* New York: Praeger, 1967. A general account by a Swedish newspaper reporter. Mao is pictured as a revolutionary romantic who is determined to force equality and utopia through a "cultural revolution."

Keesing's Research Report. *The Cultural Revolution in China: Its Origins and Course.* New York: Scribner, 1967. Brief report on the events of and participants in the Cultural Revolution.

IV. The Role of the Military

Lionel Max *Chassin. The Communist Conquest of China.* Cambridge: Harvard University Press, 1965. A moving, well organized, but frequently inaccurate portrayal of the civil war.

Jürgen *Domes.* "The Cultural Revolution and the Army," *Asian Survey,* Vol. 8, No. 5 (May 1968). An excellent summary of the pre-March 1968 role of the PLA in the Cultural Revolution.

Michael *Elliot-Bateman. Defeat in the East.* London: Oxford University Press, 1967. A stimulating analysis of Maoist political-military strategy and tactics applied to Asian countries in "wars of national liberation."

Harrison *Forman. Report from Red China.* New York: Holt, 1945. A sympathetic treatment of the Communist struggle in North China by an eye-witness.

Alexander *George. The Chinese Communist Army in Action.* New York: Columbia University Press, 1967. An account of Chinese Communist military operations in the first stages of the Korean War.

John *Gittings. The Role of the Chinese Army.* London, New York, Toronto: Oxford University Press, 1967. A valuable study of the army in Communist China, with particular attention to its political and social roles.

Samuel B. *Griffith,* II. *The Chinese People's Liberation Army.* New York: McGraw-Hill, 1967. An historical analysis of the PLA, with special attention to its structure and its role within the Chinese revolution. Several very useful organizational charts are included.

Alice L. *Hsieh. Communist China's Strategy in the Nuclear Era.* Englewood Cliffs: Prentice-Hall, 1962.

Ellis *Joffe. Party and Army: Professionalism and Political Control in the Chinese Officer Corps, 1949–64.* Cambridge: Harvard University Press, 1965. One of the best analyses of the historic struggle between commissars and commanders.

Chalmers A. *Johnson. Peasant Nationalism and Communist Power.* Stanford: Stanford University Press, 1962. A stimulating discussion of Communist operations against the Japanese in North China.

Mao Tse-tung. *Selected Military Writings.* Peking: Foreign Languages Press, 1963. The military thoughts of the Great Helmsman.

Ralph L. *Powell.* "Maoist Military Doctrines," *Asian Survey,* Vol. 8, No. 4 (April 1968). The author identifies several themes of controversy between the professionals and Mao.

Robert B. *Rigg. Red China's Fighting Hordes.* Harrisburg: The Military Service Publishing Company, 1951. A popular, readable description of the PLA in 1950.

Agnes *Smedley. The Great Road.* New York: Monthly Review Press, 1956. A stimulating if somewhat inaccurate account of Chu Teh's life in the Red Army before the outbreak of the Sino-Japanese War.

William W. *Whitson.* "The Concept of Military Generation: The Chinese Communist Case," *Asian Survery,* Vol. 8, No. 11 (November 1968). A discussion of the significance of different generations in the PLA.

V. Economics

Kuo-chun *Chao. Agrarian Policy of the Chinese Communist Party, 1921–1959.* New Delhi: Indian School of International Studies, 1960.

Audrey G. *Donnithorne. China's Economic System.* New York: Praeger, 1967. A comprehensive study on economic organization and institutional change up to 1966.

Alexander *Eckstein. Communist China's Economic Growth and Foreign Trade.* New York: McGraw-Hill, 1966. A general analysis of economic growth with special reference to its interrelationship with external economic relations, including both trade and aid.

Humphrey *Evans. The Adventures of Li Chi, A Modern Chinese Legend.* New York: Dutton, 1967. Immensely valuable for the insight it gives on Chinese peasant psychology.

Joint Economic Committee, 90th Congress, 1st Session. *An Economic Profile of Mainland China,* 2 vols. Washington: Government Printing Office, 1967. A compilation of papers on specialized topics, including a large collection of statistical data (official and other estimates) culled from many open sources. A very comprehensive reference book.

Werner *Klatt* (editor). *The Chinese Model: A Political, Economic and Social Survey.* Hong Kong: Hong Kong University Press, 1965.

Choh-ming *Li. Economic Development of Communist China.* Berkeley: University of California Press, 1959. One of the best accounts of Chinese economic development through the First Five Year Plan.

Sven *Lindquist. China in Crisis.* London: Faber and Faber, 1965. Based in part on the author's personal experiences in mainland China.

T. C. *Liu* and K. C. *Yeh. The Economy of the Chinese Mainland: National Income and Economic Development, 1933-59.* Princeton: Princeton University Press, 1965. The most comprehensive set of national income and output estimates, as well as other related statistical information, on China up to the period of the Great Leap Forward.

Jan *Myrdal. Report from a Chinese Village.* New York: Pantheon, 1965.

T. H. *Shen. Agricultural Resources of China.* Ithaca: Cornell University Press, 1951.

Dick *Wilson. A Quarter of Mankind: An Anatomy of China Today.* London: Weidenfeld and Nicolson, 1966.

Yuan-li *Wu. An Economic Survey of Communist China.* New York: Bookman Associates, 1956. An analysis of economic policies and problems during the period of the "takeover," providing the necessary historical link to the pre-Communist period.

Yuan-li *Wu. The Economy of Communist China: An Introduction.* New York: Praeger, 1965. A descriptive account of Chinese economic development through the Great Leap period and its aftermath, together with an interpretation of the mechanism of decision-making and the perceptions of Chinese decision-makers whose policies have resulted in the pattern and path of development actually observed.

VI. Education

Richard *Baum* and Frederick C. *Teiwes. Ssu-Ch'ing: The Socialist Education Movement of 1962–1966.* Berkeley: University of California Press, 1968. An account of educational developments on the eve of the Cultural Revolution.

Chu-yuan *Cheng. Scientific and Engineering Manpower in Communist China, 1949–1963.* Washington: National Science Foundation, 1965. The training and employment of scientists and engineers in Communist China. Contains useful statistical data.

Stewart *Fraser. Chinese Communist Education: Records of the First Decade.* Nashville: Vanderbilt University Press, 1965. A collection of Chinese Communist writings on education, with an introduction by the editor.

Chang-tu *Hu. Chinese Education Under Communism.* New York: Teachers College, Columbia University, 1962.

Mo-jo *Kuo, et. al. Culture and Education in New China.* Peking: Foreign Languages Press, 1951. A compilation of brief articles describing facilities and resources inherited from republican China.

Leo *Orleans. Professional Manpower and Education in Communist China.* Washington: National Science Foundation, 1968. A survey of education and professional manpower, with many statistical tables.

K. E. *Priestley. Education in China.* Hong Kong: Dragonfly Books, 1961. Has brief but useful sections on the main characteristics of Communist education, and on the various levels of education.

VII. Literature

Wu *Ai. Steeled and Tempered.* Peking: Foreign Languages Press. 1961. The widely acclaimed novel about factory workers.

Cyril *Birch* (editor). *Chinese Communist Literature.* New York: Praeger, 1963. Papers commissioned by the *China Quarterly* for its special number on Chinese Communist literature (No. 13, January–March 1963). Most of these were originally presented at a conference sponsored by the journal.

Ching-mai *Chin.* "The Song of Ou-yang Hai," *Chinese Literature,* Nos. 7–11 (1966). An abridged translation by Sidney Shapiro. A famous example of a biographical novel which measures the hero's every thought and action against the Thought of Mao Tse-tung.

Li-po *Chou. Great Changes in A Mountain Village.* Translation by Derek Bryan. Peking: Foreign Languages Press, 1961. The work of a conscientious Communist novelist with a high regard for objective truth.

D. W. *Fokkema. Literary Doctrine in China and Soviet Influence, 1956–1960.* The Hague: Mouton, 1965. This scholarly work provides background information on the literary debates of 1956–60. Remarkable for its trenchant criticism of Maoist literary doctrine, and for its utilization of Soviet Russian sources.

Merle *Goldman.* "The Fall of Chou Yang," *China Quarterly,* No. 27 (July–September 1966). Discusses the fall from power of the man who had been Mao's chief literary spokesman.

Merle *Goldman. Literary Dissent in Communist China.* Cambridge: Harvard University Press, 1967. A succinct survey of literary debates and persecutions in China from the middle 1930s to 1959.

C. T. *Hsia. A History of Modern Chinese Fiction, 1917–1957.* New Haven: Yale University Press, 1961. The standard work on the subject. Traces the modern Chinese writer's tragic involvement with the Communist Party from the early 1920's to the Great Leap Forward.

C. T. *Hsia.* "Obsession with China: The Moral Burden of Modern Chinese Literature," in *China in Perspective.* Wellesley, Mass.: Wellesley College, 1967. An attempt to define the moral essence of modern Chinese literature as distinguished from traditional and post-1949 literature.

Tsi-an *Hsia. The Gate of Darkness: Studies on the Leftist Literary Movement in China.* Seattle and London: University of Washington Press, 1968. An illuminating study of several representative modern writers burdened with tradition and confronted with the lure and menace of the Communist Party.

Kai-yu *Hsu. Twentieth Century Chinese Poetry.* New York: Doubleday, 1963. Excellent translations of a large number of modern Chinese poets.

Chan *Lien. Hu Shih's Thought in Communist China.* Doctoral Dissertation. Chicago: University of Chicago, 1965.

Walter J. and Ruth I. *Meserve* (editors). *Modern Drama from Communist China.* New York: New York University Press, 1970. An anthology of Communist Chinese plays which utilizes Communist translations.

Shan *Ou-yang.* "Three Families Lane," *Chinese Literature,* Nos. 5–6 (1961). A prominent novel of the late 1950s, cited in the text as *The Three-Family Lane;* remarkable for its nostalgic romanticism.

A. C. *Scott. Literature and the Arts in Twentieth Century China.* New

York: Doubleday, 1963. A brief survey useful for its coverage of modern developments in the theater, cinema, and the fine arts.

Vincent Y. C. *Shih.* "Satire in Chinese Communist Literature," *The Tsing Hua Journal of Chinese Studies.* New Series, Vol. 7, No. 1 (August 1968).

VIII. International Relations

A. Doak *Barnett. Communist China and Asia.* New York: Harper, 1960. A summary of Chinese Communist policies toward Asian nations over the first decade of Mao's rule. Useful analysis and specifics on policies toward individual countries.

R. G. *Boyd. Communist China's Foreign Policy.* New York: Praeger, 1962. A short volume by an Australian scholar who summarizes various aspects of Peking's foreign policy. He lays stress on Chinese chauvinism.

V. P. *Dutt. China and the World: An Analysis of Communist China's Foreign Policy.* New York: Praeger, 1966. An Indian scholar takes a look at some of the major features of Chinese Communist policies toward the world and the failure of the outside world to understand them.

David *Floyd. Mao Against Khrushchev.* New York: Praeger, 1964. A straightforward exposition of the history of Sino-Soviet relations, with a chronologically arranged listing of important documents.

Raymond L. *Garthoff* (editor). *Sino-Soviet Military Relations.* New York: Praeger, 1966. A collection of articles by Soviet and Chinese specialists, who focus on the military aspect of the Sino-Soviet conflict.

Fred *Greene. U.S. Policy and the Security of Asia.* New York: McGraw-Hill, 1968. A thoughtful analysis of American involvement, commitments, and options in the Far East, with a major focus on the challenge of Peking and Hanoi to stability in the area.

William E. *Griffith. Albania and the Sino-Soviet Rift.* Cambridge: M.I.T. Press, 1963. The function of Albania in the struggle between Moscow and Peking.

Emmanuel John *Hevi. The Dragon's Embrace: The Chinese Communists and Africa.* London: Pall Mall Press, 1967.

Harold *Hinton. Communist China in World Politics.* Boston: Houghton Mifflin, 1966. A detailed and comprehensive treatment of Chinese Communist foreign policy, with much insight and documentation.

Akira *Iriye, Across the Pacific, An Inner History of American-East Asian Relations.* New York: Harcourt, Brace and World, 1967. This is a pioneering work that analyzes and compares the wildly incompatible views of one another that the United States, China, and Japan held throughout the Second World War, and still hold today.

Arthur *Lall. How Communist China Negotiates.* New York: Columbia University Press, 1968. An Indian diplomat discusses the problems of negotiating with the Chinese Communists at the time of the Laotian crisis.

Klaus *Mehnert. Peking and Moscow.* New York: Mentor, 1964. A broadly based discussion of Sino-Soviet relations from the point of view of elemental societal differences.

Franz *Michael.* "Communist China and the Non-Committed Countries: Motivations and Purposes of Communist China's Foreign Policy," in Kurt L. *London* (editor), *New Nations in a Divided World.* New York: Praeger, 1963. A lucid account of the ways in which the Sino-Soviet conflict has been felt in the Third World.

Ishwer C. *Ohja. Chinese Foreign Policy in an Age of Transition: The Diplomacy of Cultural Despair.* Boston: Beacon Press, 1969. An analysis of Chinese foreign policy in terms of China's self-image, especially as interpreted by Mao Tse-tung. Ohja's attention to the concept of people's war and the effects of the Cultural Revolution lend an interesting, current perspective to the subject.

Richard C. *Thornton.* "The Emergence of a New Comintern Strategy for China: 1928," in Milorad *Drachkovitch* (editor), *The Comintern: Historical Highlights.* New York: Praeger, 1968. A new analysis of Moscow's role as a factor in the shift in Chinese Communist policy to agrarian revolution.

Frank N. *Trager.* "The Communist Challenge in Southeast Asia," in William *Henderson* (editor), *Southeast Asia: Problems of United States Policy.* Cambridge: M.I.T. Press, 1963.

Frank N. *Trager.* "American Foreign Policy in Southeast Asia," in Robert K. *Sakai* (editor), *Studies on Asia.* Lincoln: University of Nebraska Press, 1965.

Frank N. *Trager.* "Pax Asiatica?" *Orbis,* Vol. 10, No. 3 (Fall 1966).

Frank N. *Trager.* "The United States and Communist China: War or Peace in Asia," in Chonghan *Kim* (editor), *Communist China.* Williamsburg: College of William and Mary, 1967.

Frank N. *Trager,* with Robert F. *Bordonaro.* "The Ninth CCP Congress and the World Communist Conference: Their Meaning for Asia," *Orbis,* Vol. 13, No. 3 (Fall 1969).

Richard L. *Walker. The Continuing Struggle: Communist China and the Free World.* New York: Athene Press, 1958. A discussion of how mainland China conducted foreign policy during the Taiwan Straits crisis of 1958.

Allen S. *Whiting. China Crosses the Yalu: The Decision to Enter the Korean War.* Stanford: Stanford University Press, 1960. A scholarly analysis of an important decision in Chinese foreign policy.

Kenneth T. *Young. Negotiating with the Chinese Communists.* New York: McGraw-Hill, 1968. A former American ambassador surveys the record of Sino-American negotiations at the ambassadorial level since 1955 and finds that the two countries have been out of phase in their approaches to each other.

Clement J. *Zablocki* (editor). *Sino-Soviet Rivalry: Implications for U.S. Policy.* New York: Praeger, 1966. A collection of various points of view culled from the testimony of leading scholars before the House Foreign Affairs Subcommittee on the Far East and Pacific in March 1965.

Donald S. *Zagoria. The Sino-Soviet Conflict, 1956–1961.* Princeton: Princeton University Press, 1962. An example of the application of Kremlinological techniques to the analysis of Sino-Soviet relations.

IX. Minorities

Area Handbooks. U.S. Government Printing Office. *Burma* (DA Pam. No. 550–61, June 1968); *Communist China* (DA Pam. No. 550–60, October 1967); *North Vietnam* (DA Pam. No. 550–57, June 1967); *Thailand* (DA Pam. No. 550–53, September 1968). Useful and inexpensive studies of each country, with chapters on ethnic minorities including the Overseas Chinese in Southeast Asia. Other chapters deal with the geography, culture, history, politics, and economics of the country concerned.

Chih-i *Chang. The Party and the National Question in China.* Edited and translated by George Moseley. Cambridge: M.I.T. Press, 1966. A high party functionary, Chih-i Chang, who specialized in minority affairs, was responsible for this frank and cogent expression of CCP policy. Moseley has added a brief bibliography relating to minorities in Communist China.

June *Dreyer.* "China's Minority Nationalities in the Cultural Revolution," *China Quarterly.* No. 35 (July–September 1968). An interesting study of the development of Chinese policies towards the minority nationalities, culminating in the events of the Cultural Revolution.

June *Dreyer.* "Inner Mongolia: The Purge of Ulanfu," *Current Scene,* No. 6–20 (November 15, 1968).

"Figures and Tables on Non-Chinese Races". *China News Analysis,* No. 569 (June 18, 1965). A compilation of population statistics regarding minorities based upon the *1952 People's Handbook* (Shanghai), the 1953 census, and the *1961 Nationalities of China Report.*

Paul *Hyer* and William *Heaton.* "The Cultural Revolution in Mongolia," *China Quarterly,* No. 36 (October–December 1968). A study of the Cultural Revolution in Inner Mongolia, which reveals another aspect in Chinese-minority group relations.

Peter *Kunstadter* (editor). *Southeast Asian Tribes, Minorities, and Nations,* 2 vols. Princeton: Princeton University Press, 1967.

George *Moseley. A Sino-Soviet Cultural Frontier: The Ili Kazakh Autonomous Chou.* Cambridge: Harvard University Press, 1966. A case study of Chinese Communist policy toward a sensitive and proud minority.

Robert A. *Rupen. Mongols of the Twentieth Century,* 2 vols. Bloomington: Indiana University Press, 1964. A massive accumulation of data focusing on the "key Mongols of this century, relating their lives and actions to the forces flowing from the north and the south." Volume 2 supplements the first with the most thorough bibliography available in English on Mongolia; over 2,600 items are listed.

"Symposium on Northeastern Thailand," *Asian Survey,* Vol. 6, No. 7 (July 1966). Papers and comments by members of the panel on Northeast Thailand at the Association for Asian Studies Annual Conference, April 4, 1966, dealing with politics, economic developments, and ethnic identity.

Index

A

Academy of Sciences, 11, 234
Administrators, 95, 97, 98, 99, 104, 105, 112, 115, 116, 117, 118, 120, 121
Advanced War College, 118-119
Africa, 276, 278, 292, 295, 296, 298, 323, 324
Afro-Asian World, 132, 276
Agrarian Reformers, 312
Agricultural Production Cooperatives, 162, 209, 321
Ai Wu, 207, 207n, 208, 209, 210
Albania, 21, 119, 190, 219, 270, 276
"All Imperialists and Reactionaries are Paper Tigers," 322
Alma Ata, 119
America's Strategy in World Politics, 305
Amur River, 296
An Tzu-wen, 91n
Anhwei, 81n, 83, 85n, 99
Annam, 303, 310
"Anti-Party Anti-Socialist Scientific Program," 233, 240
Anti-Party Group, 266
Anti-Rightist Campaign, 238
Argentina, 295
Asia, 276, 292, 296, 302, 303, 304, 306, 307, 310, 312, 313, 314, 315, 316, 317, 318, 323, 324
Asian-African Conference,
  at Algiers, 294
  at Bandung, 292, 322
Asiatic Mode of Production, 273
Atomic Energy Institute, 234
Auschwitz, 232
Australia, 154, 169, 295

B

Baku Congress, 30, 32n
Ballistic Missiles, 315, 316, 326

Balzac, Honoré de, 201
Bandung Conference, *see* Asian-African Conference
Bandung Principles, *see* Five Principles of Peaceful Co-Existence
Bandung Spirit, 21, 292, 322
Bangkok, 257, 258
Barefoot Doctors, 195, 328
Barga, 246n
Bhutan, 253, 310, 313
Bitter Struggle, 213
Black Line, 206n
Black Sea, 118
Bogunovic, Branko, 75, 75n, 76n
Bolivia, 279
Bolshevik Revolution, 29, 46, 52, 293
Book of Odes, 237
Borodin, Michael, 173
Brain-Washing, 49, 225, 226
Brazil, 278
Brecht, Bertold, 220
Brezhnev, Leonid, 274
Bright Cloud, 213
Bucharest Conference of Communist Parties, 269
Buddhism, 7, 10, 246
Bulganin, N.A., 260, 261, 266
Bulgaria, 276
Burdzhalov, E. M., 263, 263n
Burma, 20, 95, 255, 256, 257, 277, 292, 310, 313
Buryat Buddhists, 250n

C

Cairo, 295
California Institute of Technology, 234
Cambodia, 308
Camp David, 269
Canada, 169, 219n, 295
Canton, 80, 84, 90n, 98, 101, 113, 162, 213, 303

Capitalism, 29, 38, 119, 156, 167, 261, 262, 271

Central Committee of CCP, 36, 39, 40, 44n, 56, 65, 66, 67, 68, 70, 71, 75, 76, 77, 77n, 79, 82, 83, 85, 86, 91, 180, 192, 193, 194, 203, 269, 322, 323
  General Office, 75n
  Military Affairs Committee, 37, 82, 101, 107n, 108, 112, 113
  Organization Department, 63, 64
  Politburo, 39, 57n, 64, 68, 70, 73, 75, 77, 86, 91, 218n, 275
  Propaganda Department, 66, 75, 81, 111, 203
  Seventh Central Committee, 64
  Eighth Central Committee, 69, 70, 76, 78, 85, 91, 106, 268, 269, 271, 275, 325
  Ninth Central Committee, 91

Central Kingdom, 2

Central Labor Union, 78

Central People's Government of PRC, 64, 123, 291
  Ministry of Foreign Affairs, 323
  National People's Conference, 265
  State Supreme Conference, 67

Central States, 10

Central Soviet Republic, 109

Ceylon, 278

Ch'a-kuan, 237

Chan, Wing-tsit, 226n

Chang Chi-ch'un, 91n

Chang Ching-wu, 91n

Chang Hsueh-liang ("Young Marshal"), 16

Chang Kuo-hua, 246, 246n

Chang Kuo-t'ao, 64

Chang Nai-chi, 322

Chang Po-chun, 322

Chang Ta-chih, 91n

Chang Ting-ch'eng, 91n

Chang Tso-lin ("Old Marshal"), 16n

Chang Wen-t'ien, 77, 91n

Chang Yun-yi, 91n

Changsha, 77

Chao Erh-lu, 91n

Chekhov, Anton Pavlovich, 201n

Chekiang, 81n, 82n, 83n, 84n, 98

Ch'en Hsi-lien, 90n, 92

Ch'en Po-ta, 35, 36, 37, 69, 77, 91n, 92, 295, 325

Ch'en Shao-min, 91n

Ch'en Shao-yu, 91n

Ch'en Tsai-tao, 81

Ch'en Wen-t'ing, 213

Ch'en Yi, 91n, 96, 98, 100, 327

Ch'en Yu, 91n

Ch'en Yun, 69, 91n

Chenery, H. B., 147

Ch'eng Tzu-hua, 91n

Cheng Wei-san, 91n

Cheng Wei-shan, 90n

Ch'eng-fen, 49

Cheng-feng Campaigns, 49

Chengtu, 90n, 97
  Chengtu Military Region, 116

Chervonenko, Stepan, 269

Ch'i State, 11, 12

Ch'i Pai-shih, 202, 202n

Ch'i Pen-yu, 82n, 327

Chi Teng-k'uei, 93

Chia Pao-yu, 213, 214

Chia T'o-fu, 91n

Chiang Ch'ing, 77, 78, 81, 82, 83, 92, 205n, 217, 218, 241, 295, 325, 327

Chiang Kai-shek, 16n, 200n

Chieh-fang Chun-pao, 75n

Ch'ien Hsueh-shen, 234

Chien Po-tsan, 21n, 240

Chien San-ch'iang, 234

Ch'ien Ying, 91n

Chiengmai, 255

Ch'in Dynasty, 5n, 12, 13, 14, 17

Ch'in Chao-yang, 204, 204n

Ch'in Chi-wei, 90n

Chin Ching-mai, 219

Ch'in Shih Huang-ti, 59, 232

Ch'in Te-kuei, 208

Chin Yueh-lin, 227, 227n

China News Analysis, 55n, 64n, 65n, 67n, 82n, 191n, 197n, 198n

China People's University, 231

Chin-Cha-Chi Border Region, 101

Chinese Buddhist Association, 245n
Chinese Communist Party, 27, 28, 30, 32, 37, 39, 43, 47, 50, 51, 52, 53, 54, 55, 57, 59, 63, 64, 67, 83, 86, 88, 96, 99, 106, 116, 123, 125, 132, 134, 135, 142, 146, 162, 180, 182, 183, 200, 200n, 201, 202, 206n, 211, 227, 230, 231, 233, 234, 241, 276, 294, 295, 322, 324, 326, 327
   Central Committee of, see Central Committee of CCP
   Congresses of,
      Eighth, 34, 66, 68, 86, 122, 264
      Ninth, 21, 43, 58, 83, 85, 86, 122, 218n, 279, 297, 298, 313, 328
   National Delegates Conference, 64
Chinese Communist Youth League, 73, 76, 324
Chinese Language, 14, 15, 19, 20, 187
Chinese People's Volunteers, 104, 291n
Ch'ing Dynasty, 10, 14, 212, 213, 214, 303
Chingkangshan, 108
Ch'iu Hui-tso, 92
Chou En-lai, 42, 65, 66, 67, 68, 69, 70, 77, 78, 81, 82, 91n, 92, 93, 108, 109, 115, 121, 268, 274, 292, 294, 321, 327
Chou Hsin-fang, 202, 202n
Chou Ku-ch'eng, 240
Chou Li-po, 209, 210
Chou Ping, 213, 214
Chou Tso-jen, 204, 204n
Chou Yang, 74, 75, 202, 203, 204, 204n, 206n, 212, 214, 215, 217, 218, 219, 220, 229
Ch'u T'ao, 213
Chu Teh, 91n, 92
Chungking, 97, 98, 201, 207, 214, 219
Chungshan University, 49
Ciantar, Maurice, 285
Class Struggle, 135n, 170, 182, 190, 193, 198, 240
Colombia, 278
Cominform, 35, 279
Comintern, 32, 33, 35, 174, 279
Commanders, 95, 96, 97, 98, 99, 100, 103, 109, 110, 112, 113, 114, 115, 116, 117, 118, 119, 120, 121, 122, 142, 179
"Comments on the Historical Play 'Hai Jui's Dismissal,'" 324
Commissars, 76, 95, 96, 103, 105, 106, 107, 108, 109, 110, 111, 112, 113, 114, 115, 116, 120, 122, 326
Common Program (1949), 132, 135n, 159, 180n
Commune System, 56, 57, 69, 78, 79, 90, 119, 135, 156, 164, 165, 168, 170, 177, 181, 240, 254, 293, 294, 322
Communism (see also Marxism-Leninism), 15, 16, 29, 30, 31, 34, 141, 159, 167, 168, 172, 173, 174, 200, 211, 212, 216, 228, 237, 252, 255, 257, 271, 312
Communist Commonwealth, 279, 280
Communist Man, 131, 134, 140
Communist Manifesto, 182
Communist Party of Austria, 276
   of Belgium, 276
   of Burma, 277
   of Indonesia, 278, 295
   of Japan, 276, 277
   of Malaya, 277
   of Philippines, 278
Concentrate a Superior Force to Destroy the Enemy Forces One by One, 31n
Confucianism, 9, 10, 12, 13, 48, 60, 284
   Confucianist system, 45, 47
   Neo-Confucianism, 217, 226
Congo, 294
Congress of Literary and Art Workers, 201, 202
U.S.S. Constitution, 303n
Consumerism, 156
Critical Realism, 201n, 206n
Criticizing My Bourgeois Pedagogical Ideology, 227
Cuba, 190, 274
Cult of the Individual, 262, 264
Cultural Revolution Group, 77, 80, 82, 83, 85, 93, 114, 218n, 324, 325
   People's Liberation Army Cultural Revolution Group, 326, 327

Current Background, 37n
Czechoslovakia, 119, 276, 287, 318

D

Dalai Lama, 244, 245, 245n, 248, 250, 252, 323
Damansky Island, 119, 328
"Decision Concerning the Great Proletarian Cultural Revolution, 77, 325
Declaration of the Communist and Workers' Parties (1957), 269
DeGaulle, Charles, 57, 281
Democratic Centralism, 270
Democratic Dictatorship, 176
Denmark, 156
De-Stalinization, 33, 266, 322
Dien Bien Phu, 255
"Directive on the Rectification Movement," 322
Dismissal of Hai Jui, 214n, 240, 324
Divide the Family Campaign, 161
Dostoevsky, Feodor Mikhailovich, 201n
Dream of the Red Chamber, 203, 213

E

"East Is Red," 28, 238n
"East Wind Prevails Over the West Wind," 293
Eastern School of Socialist Thought, 29
Ecuador, 278
Einstein, Albert, 234
Eisenhower, Dwight D., 269
Engels, Friedrich, 29, 182
Evening Talks at Yen-shan, 240

F

Fa-Chih, 55
Fan Hsiang, 39n
"Father and Mother are Dear but Mao Tse-tung is Dearer," 28
Federalist Papers, 303
Federation of All-China Literary and Art Circles, 203
Feng Hsueh-feng, 203, 204
Feudalism, 11, 12, 200n, 211, 212

Field Army,
    First, 97, 100, 101, 102
    Second, 97, 98, 100, 101, 103, 105, 118
    Third, 98, 100, 101, 103, 105
    Fourth, 98, 100, 101, 291n
    North China ("Fifth"), 100, 101
Fifth Extermination Campaign, 117
First-Class Struggled-Againsts, 161
Five-Anti Campaign, 321
Five-Good Movement, 107, 107n
Five Principles of Peaceful Co-Existence, 119, 119n, 292, 321
Five Relationships, 8, 13
Five Year Plans, 24
    First, 64, 65, 124, 126, 137, 140, 141, 146, 148, 161, 163, 167, 292, 321
    Second, 68, 137n, 163
    Third, 127, 324
Foochow, 80, 90n, 101, 113
Foochow Military Region, 101
Foreign Devils, 171
Four-Fixes System, 168
Four-Good Movement, 107, 107n
Fourth Encirclement Campaign, 108
Fourth Extermination Campaign, 117
France, 57n, 96, 147, 219n, 276, 294, 295, 303
Frunze Military Institute, 112
Fu Chung-pi, 84, 328
Fukien, 81n, 85n, 90n, 98
Fundamentals of Marxism-Leninism, 30
Fung Yu-lan, 226

G

"General Line of Socialist Construction," 69
"General Line for Transition to Communism," 321
Generation of Heroes, 213
Geneva Agreements on Indochina (1954), 273, 274, 292, 294
Geneva Conference (1954), 307
Genghis Khan, 251
Germany, 303
    East Germany, 318
    Nazi Germany, 27, 305, 312
    West Germany, 147, 276, 286

Ghana, 295
Gobi Desert, 249, 252
Gogol, Nicolai Vasilevich, 201n
Golden Line, 105
Gordon, Bernard K., 306
Gorky, Maxim, 201
Grand Canal, 14, 19
Great Britain, 69, 147, 156, 185, 257, 267, 291, 303
Great Changes in A Mountain Village, 209
Great Han Chauvinism, 246, 248
Great Leap Forward, 18n, 21, 35, 36, 37, 57, 63, 69, 89, 106, 107, 109, 111, 118, 137, 140, 145, 163, 164, 165, 166, 167, 168, 211, 244, 251, 254, 267, 268, 272, 293, 294, 295, 317, 322
Great Proletarian Cultural Revolution, 19, 21, 23, 24, 27, 32, 33, 37, 38, 39, 40, 41, 43, 44n, 46, 49, 51, 53, 54, 56, 57, 58, 63, 71, 76, 78, 80, 82, 91, 93, 97, 101, 107, 109, 113, 115, 116, 117, 118, 121, 123, 127, 132, 134, 137, 142, 143, 144, 145, 146, 161, 166, 167, 170, 177, 178, 190, 191, 192, 193, 194, 195, 196, 199, 201, 202n, 203, 207n, 208, 214n, 216, 217, 219, 219n, 229, 234, 236, 241, 244n, 245, 246, 248, 251, 253, 254, 257, 258, 259, 267, 271, 275, 276, 277, 278, 279, 295, 296, 297, 298, 312, 317, 323, 324, 326, 327
Great Revolution, 200n
Great Socialist Cultural Revolution, 75
"Great Strategic Plan for Cultural Revolution in the Schools," 326
Great Wall, 10, 14, 19, 59, 253
Greene, Fred, 306
Gromyko, Andrei, 328
Guam, 304
Guillain, Robert, 228
Gulf of Tonkin Crisis (1964), 324

H

Hai Jui, 202n
Hailar, 246n

Han Dynasty, 4, 9, 13, 237
Han Hsien-ch'u, 90n
Hangchow University, 197
Hanoi, 256, 273, 274, 276, 308, 313, 318
Hawaiian Islands, 304
Hegel, Georg Wilhelm Friedrich, 22
Heilungkiang, 80n
   Heilungkiang Revolutionary Committee, 326
Hermit Kingdom, 303
Himalayas, 249
Ho Ch'i-fang, 204, 204n
Ho Lung, 78n, 91n, 97, 100
Hohsi, 97
"Hold High the Great Red Banner of Mao Tse-tung's Thought, and Actively Participate in the Great Proletarian Cultural Revolution," 325
Homeward Journey, 208
Honan, 81n, 83n, 84n, 85
Hong Kong, 156, 169, 195, 202, 203, 224, 292, 294
Hopei, 81n, 84n
Hou Wai-lu, 21n
How the Foolish Old Man Removed the Mountains, 198
How To Be A Good Communist, 58, 58n
Hsi Chung-hsun, 91n
Hsi wang Ch'ang-an, 237
Hsia-fang Movement, 240, 240n
Hsia Yen, 215, 215n
Hsiao Ching-kuang, 91n
Hsiao Chun, 201
Hsiao Hua, 91n, 327
Hsiao K'e, 91n
Hsiao Kung-ch'uan, 5n
Hsieh Chueh-ts'ai, 91n
Hsieh Fu-chih, 77n, 81, 83, 91n, 92, 327
Hsieh Yao-huan, 239
Hsingan Mountains, 246n
Hsu Hai-tung, 91n
Hsu Hsiang-ch'ien, 77n, 91n, 326, 327
Hsu Kuang-ta, 91n
Hsu Pei-hung, 202, 202n
Hsu Shih-yu, 90n, 92
Hsu T'e-li, 91n
Hsun Tzu, 9, 13
Hu Ch'iao-mu, 91n

Hu Feng, 203, 204, 207, 227, 228, 228n, 229, 322
Hu Shih, 219, 234
Hu Yao-pang, 91n
Hua Lo-keng, 234, 240
Huai-Hai, Battle of, 103
Huan, Duke, 11, 12
Huang K'e-ch'eng, 70, 73, 91n, 268, 323
Huang Yung-sheng, 84, 90n, 92, 328
Huang-ming Jih-pao, 67n
Hudson, Geoffrey, 22
Hue, 303
Hughes, Charles Evans, 305
Hunan, 77, 81n, 85n, 98, 159, 209, 239, 257
Hundred Flowers Campaign, 34, 63, 66, 67, 68, 213, 229, 232, 233, 235, 264, 322
Hundred Regiment Campaign, 101, 109, 117
Hundred Schools, 9
Hungary, 264, 318
Hung-ch'i (Red Flag), 35, 69, 70n, 73n, 80, 82, 87n, 168, 324, 327, 328
Hupei, 81n, 82n, 84n, 90n, 98
Hurricane, 209
Hydraulic Society, 3

I

Ibsen, Henrik, 220
Ideologues, 95, 97
In Memory of Norman Bethune, 198
India, 20, 32, 147, 245n, 248, 249, 253, 278, 290, 310, 313, 317, 322, 323
Indochina, 257n, 292, 313
  Indochina War, 257n
Indonesia, 95, 292, 294, 296, 297, 322
Institute of Advanced Study (Princeton), 234
Institute of Mathematics, 234
Institute of Mongolian Studies, 247
Institute for Railway Science, 234
International Congress of Orientalists (1961), 2

International Meeting of Communist and Workers' Parties (1969), 328
Italy, 27, 147, 276, 290

J

Jalkhandza Khutukhtu, 250n
Jao Shu-shih, 23, 63, 64, 65, 66, 321
Japan, 45, 123, 136, 144, 147, 148, 200, 283, 286, 287, 292, 293, 294, 295, 303, 304, 305, 311, 315
Jebtsun Damba Khutukhtu, 250, 250n
Jen-min Jih-pao (People's Daily), 40n, 55n, 59n, 64n, 65n, 69n, 74, 74n, 78, 87n, 162, 180n, 193, 194, 194n, 196, 197n, 234n, 241, 288, 322, 324, 326
Johnson, Lyndon Baines, 273
Jones, Edwin F., 130
Juichin, 105

K

Kachin, 255
Kaganovich, Lazar, 264
K'ang Sheng, 74, 77, 91n, 92
K'ang Yu-wei, 52
Kansu, 81n, 82n, 84n
Kao Kang, 23, 55, 56, 57, 63, 64, 65, 66, 321
Karen, 255
Karol, K. S., 220
Keep the Red Flag Flying, 212
Ke-ming ch'uan-lien, 70n
Khrushchev, Nikita S., 33, 35, 53, 87n, 249, 260, 261, 262, 263, 264, 265, 266, 268, 269, 270, 271, 272, 273, 274, 275, 293, 322
Kiangsi, 81n, 83n, 84n, 96, 98, 100, 108, 117
  Kiangsi Industrial College, 198
Kiangsu, 82n, 84n, 90n
Kim Il-sung, 277
Kirin, 81n, 84n, 85

Ko P'ei-ch'i, 231
Komsomol, 49
Korea, 105, 109, 126, 147, 283, 292, 305, 310, 317
  North Korea, 20, 277, 307, 308, 321
  South Korea, 95, 104
  Korean War, 18n, 102, 103, 104, 105, 106, 112, 207n, 211, 261, 291, 291n, 292, 293, 297, 302, 308, 315, 321
Kossior, 263
Kosygin, Alexei, 274
Kuan Chung, 11, 12
Kuan Han-ch'ing, 239
Kuang Feng, 82n, 327
Kuang-ming Jih-pao, 191n, 193n, 233
Kuke Khoto, 247, 251
Kuling Conference (1959), 323
Kung-jen Jih-pao, 87n
Kunming, 80, 90n, 255
  Kunming Military Region, 101
Kuo Mo-jo, 11, 202, 202n, 203, 207
Kuomintang, 16, 31, 64, 82, 159, 206n, 207, 208, 211, 213, 217, 227, 228
Kuo-yu (National Language), 15, 187
Kutien Conference (1929), 107, 108
Kwangsi, 81n, 82n, 85, 85n, 117, 239
Kwangtung, 81n, 82n, 83n, 84n, 85, 90n, 213, 214
Kweichow, 80n, 82n, 198, 257

L

Lahu, 255
Lanchow, 90n, 97, 101, 119
  Lanchow Military Region, 101
Lao She, 203, 234, 237, 238, 240
Laos, 20, 255, 256, 257, 258, 294, 308, 313
Lashio, 255
Latin America, 276, 278, 298, 323, 324
Latinization, 187, 188
Lean to One Side Policy, 24, 159, 291
Learn from the PLA Movement, 108
Lefèbvre, Bishop Dominique, 303n
Leftism, 200n, 201, 202

Legalism, 9, 10, 13
Lei Feng, 217
Lenin, 13, 28, 29, 30, 32, 36, 166, 181, 182, 201, 206n, 283, 289, 312, 316
  Testament, 263
"Let the Hundred Flowers Bloom, Let the Hundred Schools of Thought Contend," 322
Lhasa, 245n, 246n, 248, 248n, 250n, 323
Li Ch'ing-ch'uan, 91n
Li Fu-ch'un, 65, 77, 91n
Li Hsien-nien, 91n, 92
Li Hsueh-feng, 91n, 93
Li Li-san, 57, 91n
Li Pao-hua, 91n
Li Po, 237, 238
Li Shao-ch'un, 219n
Li Ssu, 12, 13, 227
Li Ta, 241, 325
Li Teh-sheng, 93
Li Tso-p'eng, 92
Li Wei-han, 91n
Liang Ch'i-ch'ao, 52, 219
Liang Hsing-ch'u, 90n
Liang Pin, 212
Liao Ch'eng-chih, 91n
Liao Mo-sha, 324
Liaoning, 81n, 85n, 90n
Liberation Army Daily, 325
Life of Wu Hsun, 203
Lin Chieh, 82n
Lin Feng, 91n
Lin Mo-han, 75
Lin Piao, 22, 23, 37, 38, 42, 43, 44, 58, 74, 75, 77, 78, 79, 80, 82, 84, 86, 89, 91n, 92, 98, 100, 105, 106, 110, 114, 120, 205, 215, 268, 270, 274, 275, 276, 291, 295, 312, 313, 323, 324, 325, 326, 327, 328
Lin T'ieh, 91n
Lisu, 255
Literati, 6, 12, 13, 232
Liu Ch'ang-sheng, 91n
Liu Chih-chien, 326
Liu Hsiao, 91n
Liu Ke-p'ing, 91n

Liu Lan-t'ao, 91n

Liu Ning-i, 91n

Liu Po-ch'eng, 91n, 92, 97, 100, 112, 118

Liu Shao-ch'i, 32, 33, 36, 54, 56, 58, 58n,
    59, 65, 66, 67, 68, 69, 70, 71, 73, 77,
    78, 79, 85, 86, 91, 91n, 120, 214,
    227, 244n, 249, 254, 267, 268, 271,
    272, 312, 323, 325, 326, 327, 328

Liu, T. C., 130

Liu Ta-nien, 21n

Liu Yu-sheng, 210

Lo Jui-ch'ing, 74, 91n, 110, 117, 117n,
    268, 274, 275, 325, 326

Lo Keng-mo, 87n

Lo Kuei-po, 91n

Lo Lung-chi, 322

Lolo, 255

London, 117

Long Live the Victory of People's War,
    276, 324

Long March, 28, 65, 66, 96, 100, 108,
    116, 117

Lop Nor, 324, 327

Lu Cheng-ts'ao, 91n

Lu Hsiang-shan, 226, 226n

Lu Hsun, 201n, 204, 204n, 205

Lu Ling, 207, 207n

Lu P'ing, 325

Lu Ting-yi, 59, 66, 74, 75, 77, 91n, 207,
    322, 325, 326

Lung Shu-chin, 244n

Lushan Conference (1959), 70, 106, 113,
    268, 294

Luxemburg, 276

M

Ma Ming-fang, 91n

Ma Nan-tsung, 39n

Ma Sitson (Ma Ssu-ts'ung), 202, 202n

Macao, 169

MacArthur, Douglas, 291n

Make the PLA a Great School of Revo-
    lution Movement, 108

Malaya, 277, 278, 292

Malaysia, 278, 297

Malenkov, Georgi M., 260, 261, 262, 264

Manchu Dynasty, 246n, 310

Manchuria, 42, 55, 57, 64, 65, 98, 101,
    105, 113, 119, 144, 222, 246, 246n,
    253, 254, 275, 305, 315

Mandate of Heaven, 169, 309

"Manifesto to the Citizens of Shanghai,"
    326

Mao I-sheng, 234

Mao Tse-tung,
    Thought of Mao, 27, 28, 30, 31, 36,
        37, 38, 39, 40, 43, 44n, 60, 87, 118,
        120, 132, 171, 182, 184, 198, 215,
        216, 217, 218, 241, 264, 269, 282,
        288, 290, 296, 298, 327
    and revolutionary concepts, 41, 97,
        198, 201n, 298, 326
    and utopian concepts, 42, 43, 167
    Theories on education, art, and litera-
        ture, 191, 192, 193, 194, 195, 197,
        200n, 201, 201n, 202, 205, 206, 207,
        214, 215, 218, 220, 235
    Theories of democratic dictatorship,
        176
    and Lenin's writings, 29
    Writings quoted, 36, 153, 159, 179,
        184, 260, 262, 288, 322
    Writings popularized, 28, 29, 32, 58,
        197, 283
    Reputation of Mao, 23, 28, 30, 31, 36,
        37, 38, 39, 40, 41, 49, 57, 58, 59, 61,
        66, 70, 106, 109, 121, 175, 273, 282,
        286, 297, 310, 321
    Cult of Mao, 27, 38, 39, 43, 44, 44n,
        288, 290
    Dicta of Mao, 154, 284, 285, 293
    Directives of Mao, 31, 31n, 42, 56,
        195, 197, 241
    Criticism of Mao, 34, 41, 67, 109, 323
    "Heresy" of Mao, 33
    and the masses, 22, 30, 37, 43, 79, 282
    and the peasants, 140, 159, 206n, 209,
        212
    and the intellectuals, 223, 224, 231
    and youth, 76, 113, 236; *see also* Red
        Guards
    and his supporters, 89, 275

and his opponents, 71, 73, 74, 91, 271

and Chinese Communist Party, 27, 28, 37, 52, 67, 68, 91n, 92, 122, 142, 203, 268, 325

and People's Liberation Army, 79, 80, 84, 85, 271

and military role, 103, 104, 107, 108, 111, 115, 269

and development policy, 68, 69, 70, 71, 107, 134, 137, 142, 148

and agricultural collectivization, 52, 64, 133, 135, 162, 282

and the Great Leap Forward, 63, 293, 294, 295

and the Hundred Flowers campaign, 229

and the Cultural Revolution, 21, 24, 33, 37, 39, 40, 43, 44n, 77, 80, 93, 191, 192, 193, 194, 201, 295, 323

and the question of succession, 37, 43, 44, 86, 119, 167, 170, 173, 316

and foreign policy, 286, 288, 290, 291, 292, 297, 310, 314, 317

and "lean to one side" policy, 24, 47, 60, 159, 291

and the Soviet Union, 136, 264, 267, 272, 293

and the Communist world, 277, 279

and "paper tiger" speech, 267

Mao Tse-tung Thought Propaganda Teams, 196

Mao Tun, 202, 202n, 203, 207

Marx, Karl, 11, 13, 22, 28, 29, 59, 182, 206

Marxism-Leninism (see also Communism), 15, 28, 30n, 31, 32, 33, 36, 37, 40, 44, 47, 48, 60, 67, 87, 164, 178, 184, 205, 215, 227, 230, 234, 241, 264, 276, 284, 288, 290, 297, 311, 312, 314, 316

Marxist-Leninist Institute, 71

Massachusetts Institute of Technology, 234

Masses, 36, 37, 41, 43, 85, 87, 120, 161, 167, 169, 175, 177, 182, 188, 189, 191, 192, 194, 286

Matsu, 293, 309

May Fourth Movement, 1919, 199, 200n, 202, 214

May Thirtieth Movement, 1925, 200n

McNamara, Robert, 273

"Measures for the Peaceful Liberation of Tibet," 321

Mediterranean Sea, 118

Mei Lan-fang, 202, 202n

Mencius, 9, 21, 221, 226, 226n, 236
  Mencian philosophy, 12, 13

Meng Ch'ao, 214

Meo, 255, 257, 258

Mexico, 279, 295

Middle East, 278, 298

Middle Kingdom, 17, 284

Mikoyan, Anastas, 263

Military and Administrative Committees, 64, 64n, 65, 99

Ming Dynasty, 19, 21n, 240, 310

Ming Pao, 75n

Molotov, Vyacheslav M., 264

Mongolia, 101, 253, 310
  Inner Mongolia, 20, 81n, 82n, 83n, 101, 119, 243, 244, 244n, 245, 245n, 246, 247, 248, 249, 250, 251, 252, 254, 255
  Outer Mongolia (Mongolian People's Republic), 20, 245, 245n, 247, 249, 250, 250n, 251, 252, 253, 254, 261, 277, 307

Moravia, Alberto, 220

Morgenthau, Hans J., 306

Moscow, 31, 33, 35, 65, 233, 244, 261, 262, 265, 270, 274, 278, 292, 293, 314, 318, 322, 323, 328

Mountaintopism, 100

Mu Hsin, 82n

Mutual Aid Teams, 161, 162, 210

N

Nan Yang, 310

Nanchang, 108
  Nanchang Uprising, 100

Nanking, 46, 80, 90n, 112
  Nanking Military Region, 101, 105

National Defense Scientific and Tech-
    nology Commission, 96
National People's Congress,
    First, 50, 104, 322
    Second, 70
    Third, 75
Nationalist Government, 46, 59, 174,
    187, 214, 309
Nehru, Jawaharlal, 291, 292, 321
Nepal, 253, 310, 313
Netherlands, 276
New China News Agency, 77n, 78n
New Economic Policy,
    in Communist China, 167, 170, 173
    in USSR, 135n, 169
New Right, 69, 73
New Trend (ssu ch'ao), 60
Nieh Jung-chen, 77n, 91n, 96, 98, 100,
    234
Ninghsia, 83n, 85n
Ningtu Conference (1932), 108
Nixon, Richard M., 301, 302
Nkrumah, Kwame, 295
Nuclear Weapons, 315, 316, 324, 325,
    326, 327
    Nuclear Reactor Completed, 322
    Sino-Soviet Nuclear-Sharing Agree-
        ment, 323
    Nuclear Test Ban Treaty (1963), 324

                        O

On Contradiction, 28, 29
On the Correct Handling of Contradic-
    tions Among the People, 34, 175,
    322
On Correcting Mistaken Ideas in the
    Party, 31n
On New Democracy, 29, 31n, 153, 159
On People's Democratic Dictatorship,
    31, 31n, 48, 180n, 283n
On Practice, 28
On Protracted War, 31n
Open Door Notes, 304, 305
Oppose Stereotyped Party Writing, 179
Oriental Despotism, 13

Ou-yang Ch'in, 91n
Ou-yang Shan, 209, 213, 215

                        P

Pa Chin, 207, 207n, 213, 236
Pa Jen, 204, 204n
Pakistan, 20, 95, 147, 313
Palestine Liberation Organization, 297
Pan Fu-sheng, 326
Panchen Lama, 245, 248, 250, 250n, 323
Pandido Khambo Lama, 250n
Panmunjom, 321
Pao-chia System, 5
Paris, 32, 118, 294
    Paris Commune (1871), 42, 89, 326
Participatory Communism, 132
Party Central, 76, 78
Party is Completely Capable Of Offer-
    ing Leadership to Science, 234
Pearl Harbor, 304, 305
Pei Li-sheng, 234
Peitaiho, 69
Peking, 21, 32, 35, 42, 46, 47, 50, 53, 57,
    59, 60, 61, 64, 65, 73, 74, 76, 78, 79,
    80, 80n, 81, 82, 83, 84, 85, 86, 90n,
    91, 98, 101, 112, 119, 120, 122, 126,
    135, 136, 148, 156, 162, 165, 166,
    169, 201, 204, 214, 219, 219n, 237n,
    240, 244, 244n, 245n, 246, 248, 249,
    252, 254, 255, 256, 257, 258, 260,
    261, 265, 269, 270, 274, 277, 278,
    279, 281, 282, 283, 284, 285, 286,
    287, 288, 289, 290, 291, 291n, 292,
    293, 294, 295, 296, 296n, 297, 302,
    308, 309, 310, 311, 313, 314, 315,
    316, 317, 318, 319, 321, 323, 324,
    325, 326, 327, 328
Peking Military Region, 101, 105
Peking Municipal Party Committee,
    39, 73, 75, 111
Peking University, 240, 325
Peking Review, 40n, 43n, 68n, 86, 87n,
    117n, 181n, 194n, 195n, 196, 196n,
    197n, 215

P'eng Chen, 39, 66, 67, 69, 73, 74, 75, 76, 77, 78, 91n, 111, 240, 325, 326

P'eng Teh-huai, 18, 37, 39, 56, 57, 58, 69, 70, 73, 77, 91n, 97, 98, 100, 105, 106, 107, 108, 109, 268, 321, 323

People's China, 176

People's Liberation Army, 18n, 23, 24, 31, 37, 38, 40, 43, 47, 52, 58, 74, 75, 76, 78, 79, 80, 81, 82, 83, 84, 85, 86, 88, 89, 90, 93, 96, 102, 103, 105, 106, 107, 108, 109, 111, 113, 114, 116, 118, 121, 123, 206n, 215, 216, 217, 219, 246n, 250, 254, 268, 323, 324, 326, 328

General Political Department, 96, 102, 114

General Rear Services Department, 103

General Staff, 102, 103, 112, 119

High Command, 114, 117, 119

People's Militia, 322

People's Publishing House of the New China Bookstore, 28n

People's Republic of China, 33, 45, 48, 49, 52, 70, 93, 97, 132, 201, 252, 268, 269, 272, 282, 283, 288, 297, 301, 302, 307, 311, 313, 317, 318, 319, 321, 322, 323, 328

Central People's Government of, *see* Central People's Government of PRC

Foreign Policy of, 283-290, 308-317

People's War, 275, 277, 316, 317

Percival, Captain John, 303n

Peru, 278

Pervading Fragrance, 213

Philippines, 278, 292, 304

Phong Saly, 255

Pin-yin, 19

Ping Hsin, 239, 240

PLA Literature, 199

"Place Mao Tse-tung's Thought in Command of Everything," 328

Plekhanov, 13

Po I-po, 91, 264

Poland, 264, 276, 309

Port Arthur, 261

Pravda, 260, 260n

Precious Clasp, 213

Present Situation and Our Tasks, 31n

Problems of History, 263

Production and Construction Army, 102

Progressive Personalities of the Indonesian Workers Movement, 278

Proletarian Intelligentsia, 188, 189, 196

Proletarian Internationalism, 270

Proletarian Literature, 200n

Proletarian Politics, 183, 192

Proletarian Revolution, 30, 41, 182, 183, 189

Problems of Strategy in China's Revolutionary War, 31n

Problems of War and Strategy, 31n, 37

Pueblo Incident, 277

P'u-t'ung-hua ("ordinary speech"), 19

Pyongyang, 308

Q

Quemoy, 293, 309

Question of Agricultural Cooperation, 163n

Quotations from Chairman Mao Tsetung, 28, 38, 107, 331

R

Rangoon, 257

Realism, 201, 201n

Rectify the Party's Style of Work, 184

Red Army Academy, 105

Red Cross, 301

Red Experts, 164, 182, 191

Redness, 232, 233, 251

Red Flag Communists (Burma), 277

Red Guards, 22, 41, 42, 76, 77, 78, 79, 80, 81, 82, 83, 85, 88, 89, 111, 112, 113, 115, 116, 117, 118, 121, 123, 178, 193, 197, 202n, 203, 234, 236, 240, 245n, 246n, 254, 277, 279, 325, 326, 327

"Regulations for the Punishment of Counter-Revolutionaries," 321

Regulations Governing Establishment of Industries and Enterprises Under Public-Private Joint Ownership," 321

"Regulations for Reform Through Labor," 321

Rent Collection Compound, 217

Revolutionary Cadres, 41, 85, 90, 91

Revolutionary Committees, 43, 80, 90, 97, 115, 116, 118, 170, 241, 328

Revolutionary Literature, 200n

Revolutionary Rebels, 42, 43, 89, 111, 326

Revolutionary Romanticism, 211, 212

Robespierre, 218n

Role of the Chinese Communist Army in National War, 31n

Romance of the Three Kingdoms, 114

Romantic Movement, 201, 201n

Roosevelt, Franklin D., 305

Roosevelt, Theodore, 305

Russo-Japanese War, 305

S

Saifuddin, 244, 244n, 245n, 247

Saigon, 308

"Sailing the Seas Depends on the Helmsman," 28

Samoa, 304

Sartre, Jean-Paul, 220

Schwartz, Benjamin, 218n

Scientific and Technological Commission for Defense, 234

Second United Front, 28

Selected Works of Mao Tse-tung, 28, 28n, 31, 33, 48n, 153n, 198n, 215n, 283n, 284n

Selections from China Mainland Magazines, 39n

Serve the People, 198

Seventh Fleet, 315

Sha T'ing, 207, 207n

Shahidi, Burkhan, 244n

Shan, 255

Shang Dynasty, 19

Shanghai, 42, 70, 74, 79, 81, 82n, 83, 89, 90, 98, 105, 162, 197, 201, 202, 203, 205n, 207, 213, 214, 215n, 219, 324, 326

Shanghai Forum on Work in Literature and Art in the Armed Forces, 205n

Shanghai Machine Tool Plant, 196

Shanghai People's Commune, 89, 326

Shansi, 3, 73

Shantung, 80n, 82n, 83n, 90n, 101

Shantung Medical Center, 195

Shao Ch'uan-lin, 204, 204n, 215

Shaw, George Bernard, 220

Shen Yueh-(Yu-)ting, 227

Shensi, 3, 80n, 81n, 85n

Shenyang, 90n

Shigatse, 245n

Shih T'o, 207

Shu T'ung, 91n

Shun-ming, 18, 21, 226, 226n

Sian Incident, 16

Sihanouk, 313

Sikkim, 253

Singapore, 278

Sinkiang, 20, 80, 81n, 85, 85n, 90n, 97, 101, 102, 113, 119, 243, 244, 245, 245n, 247, 248, 249, 250, 251, 252, 253, 254, 255, 261, 275, 324, 325, 326, 327, 328

Sinkiang Military Region, 98, 244n

Sinkiang Revolutionary Committee, 98, 244n

Sino-Indian Border War, 323

Sino-Japanese War, 46, 99, 100, 101, 117, 159, 305

Sino-Soviet Relationship, 14, 119, 121, 141, 251, 253, 259, 260, 261, 262, 265, 266, 267, 271, 273, 274, 275, 278, 279, 280, 286, 294, 296, 323, 328

Scientific and Technical Agreement, 269

Treaty of Friendship, Alliance, and Mutual Assistance, 279

Sixteen-Point Declaration, 40, 41, 42, 325

Socialism, 30, 31, 38, 141, 163, 164, 178, 180, 241, 271, 273, 314

Socialist Construction, 182, 190

Socialist Education, 38, 109, 134, 177, 196, 271, 323

Socialist Realism, 200n, 201n, 211, 215, 228

"Some Problems Confronting Us in the Rural Socialist Education Movement," 324

Son of Heaven, 13

Song of Ou-yang Hai, 206n, 216, 217, 219

Song of Youth, 212

South China Morning Post, 119n

Southeast Asia, 257, 277, 292, 297, 298, 302, 308, 310, 313, 315, 317, 318

Soviet-American Conspiracy, 110, 118, 120

Soviet Union (Russia), 17, 31, 34, 46, 48, 49, 54, 64n, 65, 118, 156, 167, 185, 201, 201n, 247, 250n, 260, 261, 262, 264, 266, 272, 273, 274, 276, 281, 284, 293, 303, 305

Soviet Asia, 20, 247, 249, 250, 252, 253, 307, 310

Missiles, 119, 247

Foreign policy of, 246, 259, 275, 289

and Communist China, 35, 47, 51, 57, 60, 105, 106, 109, 110, 112, 117, 117n, 119, 120, 121, 122, 123, 126, 132, 136, 137, 141, 147, 159, 166, 243, 244, 244n, 245, 246, 247, 249, 250, 252, 254, 255, 265, 266, 267, 268, 269, 270, 272, 275, 276, 277, 279, 282, 291, 295, 295n, 296, 298, 310, 317, 323, 324

and North Viet-Nam, 313

and the United States, 261, 274, 286, 297, 315

Communist Party Central Committee, 260, 262, 263, 267, 272

Communist Party Congress, 33, 261, 262, 263, 265, 269, 270, 279

Spanish-American War, 304

Spare-Time School, 180, 186, 190

Sputnik, 293

Spykman, Nicholas J., 305

Ssu-ma T'an, 8

Stalin, Joseph, 17, 28, 29, 30, 31, 32, 33, 36, 49, 57, 167, 173, 182, 206n, 232, 260, 262, 263, 264, 266, 283, 289, 291, 314, 321

Short Course, 262, 263

Stalin prize, 209

Stalinist constitution, 50

State Council, 76, 78, 82, 101, 322, 325

State Economic Commission, 264

State Planning Commission, 63, 64

State Statistical Bureau, 185

Steeled and Tempered, 208

Stimson, Henry L., 305

Strong, Anna Louise, 32

Strout, A. M., 147

Struggle in the Chingkang Mountains, 31n

Su Yu, 91n, 100

Su-fan ("Purge of the Opposition") Campaign, 55

Sui Dynasty, 14, 17, 59

Sun Shines Over the Sangkan River, 209

Sun Yat-sen, 23, 46, 52, 60, 160, 310n

Sung Dynasty, 19

Sung Jen-ch'iung, 77n, 91n

Survey of China Mainland Press, 35n, 195n

Suslov, Mikhail, 269

Sweden, 276

Switzerland, 290

Symbolism, 201n

Szechuan, 73, 81n, 83n, 85, 85n, 90n, 97, 98, 101, 102, 162, 246n

T

T'ai, 20

Taipeh, 309

T'ai-p'ing Rebellion, 46

Taiwan, 20, 118, 147, 148, 173, 188, 202, 241, 286, 287, 291, 305, 308, 309, 315, 317

Taiwan Straits Crisis, 273, 287, 293, 297, 315

Taiyuan, 98

Talks at the Yenan Forum on Literature and Art, 205, 211, 214, 215
T'an Chen-lin, 91n
T'an Cheng, 91n
T'ang Dynasty, 14, 59, 237, 238n, 239
Tanyug, 75
T'ao Chu, 77, 78, 91n, 326
Taoism, 7, 8
Technology Commission, 96
Teng Hsiao-p'ing, 67, 69, 78, 91n, 97, 325, 326, 327
Teng Hua, 91n
T'eng Tai-yuan, 91n
Teng T'o, 21n, 75, 240, 324
Teng Tzu-hui, 91n
Teng Ying-ch'ao, 91n
Thailand (Siam), 20, 255, 256, 257, 258, 277, 278, 303, 313
  Thailand People's Liberation Army, 297
There is a Need to Show an Earnest Concern Regarding the Livelihood of Artists and a Desire to Improve It, 239
Third-Class Objects of Struggle, 161
Third World, 284, 292, 298, 313
Three-Anti Campaign, 321
Three-Family Lane, 213
Three-Family Village, 39n
Three-Fixes System, 167
Three Kingdoms, 118
Three Principles of the People, 310n
Three Red Banners, 69, 70, 71
Tibet, 20, 81n, 85n, 90n, 113, 243, 244, 245, 246, 248, 249, 251, 252, 254, 255, 292, 297, 309, 310, 315, 317, 321, 322, 323, 328
  Tibetan Autonomous Region Committee, 323
  Tibetan Liberation Movement, 248
  Tibetan Military Region, 101
T'ien Han, 207, 207n, 214, 239
Tien Shan, 249
Tienanmen Square, 325
Tientsin, 81n, 83, 83n, 98
Ting Ling, 203, 204, 209, 229
Toilers of the East, 30

Tokyo, 305
Tolstoy, Leo, 201n
Tonkin Gulf Incident, 273
Torrent Trilogy, 213
Towards Disengagement in Asia, 306
Transcaucasia, 263
Trans-Mongolian Railroad, 247, 251
Trans-Siberian Railroad, 247
Trans-Sinkiang Railroad, 247
Trotsky, Leon, 314
  Trotskyist, 33, 276
Ts'ai Ch'ang, 91n
Tseng Hsi-sheng, 91n
Tseng Shan, 91n
Tseng Ssu-yu, 90n
Tseng Yung-ya, 90n
Tsinan, 76, 80, 90n
  Tsinan Military Region, 101
Tsinghai, 81n, 82n, 83n, 195
Tsinghua University, 76, 227, 233
Tsingtao, 77, 83
Tu Chin-fang, 219, 219n
Tu Fu, 238, 238n
Tu Jun-sheng, 235
Tuan-mu Hung-liang, 207, 207n
Tung Pi-wu, 91n, 92
Tung-fang Hung, 79n
Turgenev, Ivan, 201n
Turk-Sib Railroad, 247, 253
Twelve-Year Agricultural Program, 162, 163
"Twenty Years in a Day," 322
Twenty-One Demands, 305, 306
Two Chinas Policy, 309
Tz'u-hsi ("Empress Dowager"), 24

U

Ukraine, 263
Ulan Bator, 251, 252
Ulanfu, 91n, 244, 244n, 245, 245n, 246, 248, 252, 326
Uncle Kao, 209
"Under the Banner of Comrade Mao Tse-tung," 35
Unequal Treaties, 303, 310
United Arab Republic, 297

United Nations, 20, 103, 104, 106, 273, 274, 309, 315, 321
United States, 110, 114, 119, 120, 147, 155, 156, 157, 257, 258, 261, 267, 274, 281, 286, 290, 291, 291n, 292, 293, 297, 324
   Policy Toward Communist China, 301–319, *passim*
   Seventh Fleet, 291
Urumchi, 247
"Ushering in the All Round Victory of the Great Proletarian Cultural Revolution," 328
Ussuri River, 119, 121, 296, 328

V

Versailles Conference, 305
Vientiane, 257, 258
Viet Cong (Viet Minh), 256, 273, 313
Viet-Nam, 190, 255, 257n, 273, 275, 283, 294, 310, 317
   North Viet-Nam, 20, 109, 110, 118, 255, 256, 257, 258, 273, 274, 277, 307, 308, 318
   South Viet-Nam, 273, 313
   Viet-Nam War, 207n, 257, 272, 302, 308
Visiting Ch'ing-lung ch'iao for the Second Time, 239–240
Voluntarism, 164

W

Walker, Richard L., 309, 311
Wan, 255
Wang Chang-ling, 224n
Wang Chen, 91n, 98
Wang Chia-hsiang, 91n
Wang En-mao, 90n, 91n, 98, 244n, 245, 245n, 247, 326
Wang Hao, 227
Wang Kan-ch'ang, 234
Wang Li, 81, 82, 114, 327
Wang Shih-wei, 201
Wang Shou-tao, 91n

Wang Shu-sheng, 91n
Wang Ts'ung-wu, 91n
Wang Tung-hsing, 93
Wang Yang-ming, 226n
War Communism, 167
Warring States, 14
Warsaw, 119, 120, 122
   Warsaw Talks, 301
Washington, 316
   Washington Conference (1922), 305
Wei Kuo-ch'ing, 91n
"Welcome the High Tide of the Cultural Revolution in the Industrial and Mining Enterprises," 326
Wen Yu-ch'eng, 84
Wen-hui Pao, 21n, 74n, 192n, 193n, 324, 326
Whampoa, 105
White Experts, 177, 191
White Flag Communists (Burma), 277, 297
White-haired Girl, 216
Why Is It That Red Political Power Can Exist In China? 31n
Wilson, Woodrow, 305
Wittfogel, Karl August, 3, 4, 5, 13
Wolf, Charles Jr., 306
Work-Study School, 180
Workers Provost Corps, 118
World War,
   World War I, 52n, 304, 305
   World War II, 16, 17, 37, 95, 114, 117n, 155, 257, 277, 279, 286, 290, 291, 305, 306, 307
Writers' Union, 213
Wu, Emperor, 13
Wu, Empress, 239
Wu Chih-p'u, 91n
Wu Fa-hsien, 92, 327
Wu Han, 21, 39n, 74, 75, 214, 214n, 239, 240, 324
Wu Hsiu-ch'uan, 91n
Wu Leng-hsi, 74
Wu Nan-hsiang, 39n
Wu Tsu-kuang, 234, 238, 239
Wu Wen-tsao, 240
Wu Yu-chang, 91n

Wuhan, 70, 80, 81, 90n, 98, 114, 117
  Wuhan Incident, 82, 327
  Wuhan Military Region, 113, 116
  Wuhan Plenum, 70, 73n
  Wuhan University, 241, 325
Wuta, 241

XYZ

Yang Ch'eng-wu, 84, 114, 328
Yang Hsien-chen, 71, 91n
Yang Hsiu-feng, 91n
Yang Mo, 212
Yang Shang-k'un, 91n, 325, 326
Yang Shih-chan, 231
Yang Te-chih, 90n, 91n
Yangtze River, 27, 76, 98, 144
Yao, 255
Yao Wen-yuan, 21n, 92, 218, 218n, 226,
  226n, 324

Yeh Chi-chuang, 91n
Yeh Chien-ying, 77n, 91n, 92
Yeh Ch'un, 93
Yeh Fei, 91n
Yeh Sheng-lan, 219n
Yellow River, 3
Yenan, 28, 29, 57, 159, 201, 202, 203,
  204, 205, 209, 216, 235, 237
  Yenan Forum on Literature and Art
    (1942), 200n, 201, 205, 205n, 206n,
    211, 235
  Yenan Spirit, 106, 111
Yin Fu-sheng, 227
Young China Communist Party, 57n
Yu Li-chin, 84, 328
Yu P'ing-po, 203
Yuan Dynasty, 10
Yuan Shih-hai, 219n
Yudin, Pavel, 269
Yugoslavia, 270, 276
Yunnan, 81n, 82n, 83n, 85n, 257